Houghton Mifflin
English

Shirley Haley-James John Warren Stewig

Marcus T. Ballenger   Jacqueline L. Chaparro   Nancy C. Millett

June Grant Shane   C. Ann Terry

HOUGHTON MIFFLIN COMPANY   BOSTON

Atlanta   Dallas   Geneva, Illinois   Palo Alto   Princeton   Toronto

Acknowledgments

"Before Misty," adapted and condensed from *Misty of Chincoteague* by Marguerite Henry. © 1947 by Rand McNally & Co. Copyright renewed 1975 by Marguerite Henry. By permission of Rand McNally & Company.

"Comma in the Sky," from *In the Woods, in the Meadow, in the Sky* by Aileen Fisher. Copyright © 1965 by Aileen Fisher. Reprinted by permission of the author.

"Deer at Dusk" by Elizabeth Coatsworth. Reprinted by permission of Grosset & Dunlap from *The Sparrow Bush* by Elizabeth Coatsworth, copyright © 1966 by Grosset & Dunlap.

"Far, far will I go" from *Beyond the High Hills, A Book of Eskimo Poems*, translated by Knud Rasmussen.

Haiku: "Ah leafless willow . . ." by Buson. Reprinted from *Cherry Blossoms*, © 1960 Peter Pauper Press. Reprinted with permission.

Haiku: "Blinding wild snow" by Chora, from *The Four Seasons*, edited by Peter Beilenson, copyright © 1958. Reprinted by permission.

Haiku: "Weeping . . . willows" by Kyorai. Reprinted from *Cherry Blossoms*, © 1960 Peter Pauper Press. Reprinted with permission.

"A Horse's Body," from *A Horse's Body* by Joanna Cole. Copyright © 1981 by Joanna Cole. Abridged by permission of William Morrow & Company, Inc.

"I Go Forth to Move About the Earth" by Alonzo Lopez from *The Whispering Wind*, edited by Terry Allen. Copyright © 1972 by The Institute of American Indian Arts. Reprinted by permission of the publisher.

"I Hole Up in a Snowstorm," from *My Side of the Mountain* by Jean George. Copyright © 1959 by Jean George. Reprinted by permission of the publisher, E.P. Dutton, a division of New American Library, and The Bodley Head.

"I'm Nobody! Who are you?," excerpt reprinted by permission of the publishers and the Trustees of Amherst College from *The Poems of Emily Dickinson*, edited by Thomas H. Johnson, Cambridge, Mass.: The Belknap Press, Copyright 1951, © 1955, 1979, 1983 by the President and Fellows of Harvard College.

"Interviewing: Doing Your Homework," adapted with permission from Melvin Mencher, *News Reporting and Writing*. Copyright © 1977 Wm. C. Brown Publishers, Dubuque, Iowa. All rights reserved.

"The Needle in the Haystack" by John Hamma. Copyright © 1982 by John Hamma. Reprinted by permission of Doris Hamma.

"Problems" by Calvin O'John from *The Whispering Wind*, edited by Terry Allen. Copyright © 1972 by The Institute of American Indian Arts. Reprinted by permission of Doubleday & Company, Inc.

"Runs all day and never walks" from *The American Mother Goose* by Ray Wood. Copyright 1940 by Ray Wood. Copyright © renewed 1968 by Willis J. Wood. Used by permission.

"Sarah, Plain and Tall," abridged from *Sarah, Plain and Tall* by Patricia MacLachlan (Newbery Award Winner). Copyright © 1985 by Patricia MacLachlan. Reprinted by permission of Harper & Row, Publishers, Inc., and Julia MacRae Books.

(Acknowledgments continued on page 575.)

Table of Contents

UNIT 4

Literature and Writing: Instructions

UNIT 5

Language and Usage: Verbs

Getting Ready to Write

Sometimes if we are not listening we might miss some of the best stories of all, the ones about ourselves and the people around us.

Lucille Clifton
from "Meet Your Author"

Do the words you say make a difference?

Word Power

By Jean Little

I was eating my porridge when Hugh, hurrying too fast, fell down the back stairs. Before Mother could get up, he limped in, sniffling slightly, and displayed a bumped elbow for her inspection. Mother examined it gravely.

"A slight haematoma," she said in a serious voice. "And an abrasion almost invisible to the naked eye. You'll live."

Hugh, who always recovered with the speed of light and who won Mother's admiration with his bravery, chuckled at the impressive words.

"What does that mean?" he asked.

"A little bruise and a scrape I can hardly see."

That night I asked Mother, "What are the long words for what's wrong with my eyes?"

I was standing beside her chair. She looked up at me. "Why?" she asked.

"I want to know, that's all. They call me cross-eyed. I want to know the long words, the ones doctors use."

She rhymed off a whole list.

"Say it again. Slowly."

"Strabismus, nystagmus, corneal opacities and eccentric pupils."

2

I practised.

The next day I was late coming out of school. The same grade-seven boy was waiting for me. He had his first snowball ready.

"Cross-eyed, cross-eyed," he chanted and waited for me to start running so that he could chase me, pelting me with hard-packed snowballs.

I turned on him instead.

"I am not cross-eyed," I said in a strong, clear voice. "I have corneal opacities and eccentric pupils."

I glared at him as I spoke, and my eyes were as crossed as ever. But he was so surprised that he stood there, his mouth gaping open like a fish's.

Then I turned my back and walked away. Perhaps his aim was off because he was so used to firing his missiles at a running target. But the first snowball flew past me harmlessly. The second exploded with a smack against a nearby tree.

I kept walking, chin in the air.

In the last two days, I had learned a lot about the power of words.

This story comes from the book *Little by Little* by Jean Little. The book is full of entertaining stories about growing up.

Think and Discuss
1. What words did Jean's mother use to describe her eyes? What kind of words are they?
2. Why do you think Jean stopped being afraid of the bully who called her cross-eyed?
3. What do you think happened the next time Jean saw the bully?

The Writing Process

STEP 1: PREWRITING

How to Get Ideas: Journal Writing

A journal is your own private book. The pages are yours for writing thoughts, telling stories, describing feelings. The more you write, the easier it becomes, and the more ideas you get on paper. When you have a writing assignment, open up your journal. Something you wrote weeks ago may give you just the idea you need.

Tim needed a topic for a comparison and contrast paper. Looking through his journal, he found this entry.

> *Joey's amazing! Sat with him on the bus today. He told me how he finally stopped those kids from teasing him. What a great idea!*

GUIDELINES FOR JOURNAL WRITING

- Let your mind wander through your day.
- Write whatever you want—a thought, a feeling, a memory, an event, or just a list of your activities.
- Relax, and let the words come easily.
- Understand that some days you will jot down only a phrase; other days you will write pages.
- Write in your journal often.

Tim realized that Joey was a lot like Jean in the story "Word Power." He would compare Jean and Joey!

Writing Your Own Journal

Let your mind wander through the day. Then write in your journal. Now read what you have written. What ideas can you get for writing a comparison and contrast paper?

How to Explore Your Topic: Brainstorming

How do you discover all you have to say about your topic? Brainstorming is a quick way to get ideas on paper, and working with a partner is a good way to brainstorm.

Tim told Becky some ways that Jean and Joey were alike and different. Becky listed them. When Tim couldn't think of any more ideas, Becky asked him questions. Tim had more ideas. Becky listed them too.

ALIKE: *Both Joey and Jean*

handicapped	*clever and creative*
teased because of handicaps	*stopped kids from teasing them*

DIFFERENT

Joey	*Jean*
likes math	*hates math*
likes to learn facts	*likes learning new words*
figures out how things work	*makes up stories*

GUIDELINES FOR BRAINSTORMING

- Work with a writing partner.
- Think about your topic. What idea quickly comes to mind?
- Have your partner jot down your idea. Think of another. Keep going, and don't judge your ideas.
- When you get stuck, have your partner ask you questions.

Brainstorming with a Partner

Take turns brainstorming to explore the topic that each of you chose after writing in your journal.

How to Write a First Draft

One of the amazing things about writing is that it helps you think. Sometimes ideas that you didn't know you had will fly out of your pen. You probably came up with many interesting ideas about your topic when you brainstormed. You will discover even more when you write your first draft.

Here is the beginning of Tim's first draft.

Think and Discuss

- Is Tim's beginning good? Why or why not?
- Is anything unclear?
- What details might Tim add?

> Joey and Jean are alike in a lot of ways. Both Joey and Jean have a handicap. They both figured out ~~that~~ how to stop some people from teasing them. Jean learned words for her problem. Joey invited kids to ride his new bike.

GUIDELINES FOR DRAFTING

- Keep in mind your purpose and who your audience will be.
- Write your ideas down quickly.
- Skip every other line so you can add ideas later.
- Don't worry if your paper looks messy.
- Try experimenting. You might write three or four beginning sentences and pick the best.
- Don't be concerned about spelling and other mistakes. You will correct them later.

Drafting on Your Own

Write your first draft. Use your list of ideas from brainstorming, and be open to new ideas as well.

How to Have a Writing Conference

Are your beginning sentences strong? Does the ending sound right? Sometimes these questions are difficult to answer by yourself. Having a writing conference can help.

Here is how Tim had a writing conference with Carlos.

Think and Discuss

- What questions did Carlos ask Tim?
- How could these questions help Tim improve his writing?

When you are listening to someone else's writing, try to listen carefully. Make suggestions, but don't tell the writer what to do. Encourage the writer by telling what you like about the writing. Always be polite.

Questions for a Writing Conference

- Tell me more about . . .
- Can you explain why . . . ?
- What happened when . . . ?
- How did that happen?
- What do you like best about what you have written?
- This seems out of order. Where else could it go?
- What parts of your writing do you think need more work?
- I liked the part where you showed . . .
- Is this important . . . ?
- How did you feel when . . . ?
- What was special about . . . ?

Having a Writing Conference

Have a writing conference with a partner, and take turns sharing your writing. As the listener, use the conference questions and make suggestions. As the writer, listen to your partner's questions and suggestions.

How to Revise Your Draft

Revising your work is as important as writing the first draft. When you revise, take a fresh look at your writing. What needs to be clearer? Where do you need to add details? What should be changed or taken out? Make every word count.

Here is how Tim revised the beginning of his draft.

> When I read about Jean in "Word Power,"
> I thought of my friend Joey.
> Joey and Jean are alike in a lot
> of ways. Both Joey and Jean have
> *Joey is deaf, and Jean has an eye problem.*
> a handicap. They both figured out
> that how to stop some people from
> *the medical*
> teasing them. Jean learned words
> *(and surprised the boy who was teasing her)*
> for her problem. Joey invited
> *the boys who were teasing him*
> kids to ride his new bike.

Think and Discuss

- What sentence did Tim add to his beginning? Why?
- What details did he add? Why?

GUIDELINES FOR REVISING

- Write new words in the lines you skipped or in the margins.
- Cross out unnecessary words. Do not erase them.
- Do not worry if your draft is messy.
- If you want to move a sentence, circle it. Then draw an arrow showing where it should go.

Revising on Your Own

Think about your partner's suggestions. Do you have any other ideas for improving your writing? Make your revisions.

How to Proofread Your Writing

When you proofread your writing, you have a clear purpose in mind—to make your writing error free. Carefully check it for mistakes in spelling, punctuation, and grammar.

Here is how Tim proofread the ending of his draft.

Think and Discuss

- Which words did Tim correct for spelling?
- Which punctuation marks did he add? Why?
- Which words did he capitalize?

> In some ways, Joey and Jean are very different. Joey ~~has~~ is also different from Jean. Joey *really* ~~sealy~~ likes math, but jean hates it. Also, Joey likes to learn things *facts* from *science* books, and he *enjoys* likes to figure *ing* out how things work. jean likes learning new words. she also is imagenative *imaginative* and makes up stories.

GUIDELINES FOR PROOFREADING

- Proofread for one kind of error at a time.
- Make sure that you indented where necessary.
- Check that you used capital letters and punctuation marks correctly.
- Use a dictionary to check your spelling.
- Use proofreading marks.

Proofreading Marks

- ¶ Indent
- ∧ Add something
- ℓ Take out something
- ≡ Capitalize
- / Make a small letter

Proofreading on Your Own

Proofread your writing. Use the guidelines.

How to Publish Your Writing

Congratulations. You are now ready to publish your writing. These guidelines will help you.

GUIDELINES FOR PUBLISHING

- Copy your writing neatly, and add a title.
- Think of someone special who would enjoy your work.
- Think of a creative way to share your writing.

Here is the way Tim presented his writing. He wrote up newspaper headlines about what had happened to Jean and Joey. Next, he copied his writing into four parts and pasted them on a large piece of paper. Then he attached each headline near the matching part.

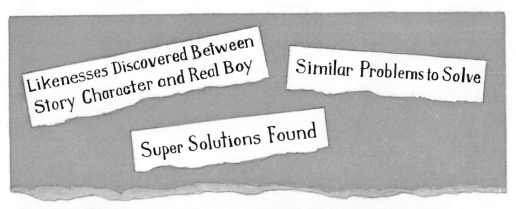

Ideas for Publishing

- Design a poster about the two things you compared and contrasted. Illustrate it with drawings or photographs. Tape your writing to the poster.
- Read what you have written to a partner. Ask your partner to illustrate your writing.

Publishing on Your Own

Use the guidelines to publish your writing.

Language and Usage

WHAT IS PAST
IS PROLOGUE

Memorable sentences are memorable on account of some single word.

Alexander Smith

The Sentence

Getting Ready We speak in sentences as soon as we learn to speak. We write sentences as soon as we learn to write. We can go on creating new and more interesting sentences all our lives! In this unit, you will learn more about writing clear, interesting sentences that hold a reader's attention.

ACTIVITIES

Listening

Listen as the sentence on the facing page is read. *Memorable* means "worth remembering." Memorable words might be hard words or easy words. They could be beautiful names of people or places. List several hard, easy, and beautiful words that you like. Use them in sentences.

Speaking

Look at the picture. Read the sentence that is carved in stone. There is a memorable word, *prologue,* in this sentence. A *prologue* is an introduction, usually to a book or a play. What does *prologue* mean in this sentence?

Writing

How can the past tell us about the future? Write your ideas in your journal.

1 | What Is a Sentence?

A **sentence** is a group of words that expresses a complete thought. A sentence begins with a capital letter.

SENTENCES
Lightning flashed in the sky.
The alert ranger spotted fire.

A group of words that does not express a complete thought is called a **sentence fragment**. A fragment is not a sentence.

SENTENCE FRAGMENTS
Flashed in the sky.
The alert ranger.
During the storm.
When the tree fell.
Soaked by rain.
Thunder in the distance.

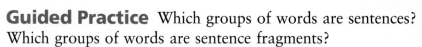

Guided Practice Which groups of words are sentences? Which groups of words are sentence fragments?

Example: The dark, cloudy sky.   *sentence fragment*

1. A storm was coming.
2. Behind the pine tree.
3. After the lightning.
4. The wind broke several branches.
5. Surprised by a loud noise.
6. Luckily, the storm ended quickly.

Summing up

▶ A **sentence** is a group of words that expresses a complete thought.
▶ A **sentence fragment** is a group of words that does not express a complete thought.

Independent Practice For each pair, write the group of words that is a sentence.

Example: Heard the weather report.
A tornado was predicted.
A tornado was predicted.

7. Tornadoes are dangerous.
Winds of high speed.
8. They sound like a freight train.
After the hottest part of the day.
9. Often in the Midwest.
They spin like tops.
10. Suddenly, whirling clouds.
We saw a cloud shaped like a funnel.
11. Scooped up trees and houses.
Many buildings were leveled.
12. The downpour lasted all afternoon.
Stayed indoors for several hours.
13. Rescue workers arrived.
Shelter in the surrounding towns.
14. Food and clothing were sent right away.
Began rebuilding their homes and schools.
15. Speeds of up to three hundred miles per hour.
It was the worst storm in ten years.
16. Reporters have written articles.
From different parts of the country.
17. All the radio stations.
Many people have been interviewed.
18. People are returning to their homes.
In the weeks after the storm.

Writing Application: A Description
Imagine that you are watching a big storm from your window. What unusual things do you see? What noises do you hear? What words describe the sights and sounds of a storm? How does the storm make you feel? Write a paragraph about it. Check to see that your sentences are complete.

For Extra Practice, see p. 41.   **What Is a Sentence?** 15

2 | Four Kinds of Sentences

There are four kinds of sentences. Each kind does a different job. All four kinds begin with a capital letter. The end mark varies, however.

Declarative: A **declarative sentence** tells something. It ends with a period.	Deserts are dry.
Interrogative: An **interrogative sentence** asks something. It ends with a question mark.	Do you like deserts?
Imperative: An **imperative sentence** gives an order. It ends with a period.	Always carry water.
Exclamatory: An **exclamatory sentence** expresses strong feeling. It ends with an exclamation point.	How hot it was! It was so hot!

Guided Practice Identify each sentence as *declarative, interrogative, imperative,* or *exclamatory.* Which end punctuation would you use?

Example: Desert winds blow the sand into mounds
  declarative   period

1. Are these mounds called sand dunes
2. This is a terrible sandstorm
3. Do sand dunes always stay in the same place
4. Try to protect your eyes from the dust
5. How thick the dust is

▶ A **declarative** sentence tells something and ends with a period.

▶ An **interrogative** sentence asks something and ends with a question mark.

▶ An **imperative** sentence gives an order and ends with a period.

▶ An **exclamatory** sentence expresses strong feeling and ends with an exclamation point.

Independent Practice Copy each sentence and add correct end punctuation. Then label each sentence *declarative, interrogative, exclamatory,* or *imperative.*

Example: Rosa visited the Painted Desert

　　　　Rosa visited the Painted Desert. **declarative**

6. Is the Painted Desert in Arizona
7. Look at this photograph of the desert
8. What beautiful colors the sand dunes are
9. The colors change as the sun sets
10. What an amazing sight that is
11. The sand looks like choppy pink waves
12. Did you see the movie about the Sahara Desert
13. It is the world's largest desert
14. How strong the camels looked
15. Sometimes people think they see water in the desert
16. Are their eyes playing tricks on them
17. What a strange sight it is
18. Did you see an oasis in the desert
19. Please tell us exactly how the oasis looked
20. It looked like a green island

Writing Application: A Dialogue

Pretend that you and a friend are crossing the desert on camels. Write a conversation with your friend. Use two declarative sentences, two interrogative sentences, two imperative sentences, and two exclamatory sentences.

For Extra Practice, see p. 42.

Four Kinds of Sentences　**17**

3 | Complete Subjects and Complete Predicates

Every sentence has two parts—a subject and a predicate. The **subject** tells whom or what the sentence is about. The **predicate** tells what the subject is or does.

SUBJECT	PREDICATE
Captain Ortega	is a good pilot.
The large jet	carries many people.

All the words in the subject make up the **complete subject**. All the words in the predicate make up the **complete predicate**.

The complete subject may be either one word or more than one word.

Pilots waved.

The pilots of the plane waved.

The pilot and the copilot waved.

The complete predicate may also be one word or more than one word.

Several helicopters landed .

Several helicopters landed in the field .

Guided Practice
Find the complete subject and the complete predicate in each sentence.

Example: The capital of Brazil is Brasilia.
  complete subj.: The capital of Brazil
  complete pred.: is Brasilia

1. Brazil is a country in South America.
2. This country has mountains and jungles.
3. The jungles are hot and rainy.
4. Many trees and bushes grow.
5. The Amazon River flows through Brazil.

▶ A sentence has two parts, a subject and a predicate.
▶ The **subject** tells whom or what the sentence is about.
▶ The **predicate** tells what the subject is or does.
▶ The **complete subject** contains all the words in the subject.
▶ The **complete predicate** contains all the words in the predicate.

Independent Practice
Write each sentence. Draw a line between the complete subject and the complete predicate.

Example: Mr. Santos traveled on the Amazon River.
Mr. Santos│traveled on the Amazon River.

6. His friend pointed out turtles and alligators.
7. Other passengers spotted colorful birds.
8. One of the birds screeched.
9. Another boat passed by.
10. Mr. Santos and the other passengers waved.
11. A man next to Mr. Santos caught a huge fish.
12. A group of children sang fishing songs.
13. Mr. Santos ate some Brazil nuts.
14. Brazil nuts come from forests near the Amazon.
15. Some of the trees are 150 feet tall.
16. People use oil from the nuts on their salads.
17. The captain anchored the boat in the afternoon.
18. A tour guide led the passengers on a walk.
19. He taught them about the animals of the jungle.
20. Very few people live near the Amazon River.
21. All of the passengers returned to the boat.
22. Mr. Santos enjoyed his interesting trip.

Writing Application: Creative Writing
Pretend that you are a parrot in the jungle. Some tourists are exploring the area around your favorite tree. What do the tourists look like? What are they doing in your area? Write a paragraph about these tourists. Make sure that each sentence has a subject and a predicate.

For Extra Practice, see p. 43.　　　**Complete Subjects and Predicates**

4 | Simple Subjects

You have learned that the complete subject contains all the words in the subject. In every complete subject, there is a main word that tells whom or what the sentence is about. It is called the **simple subject**.

Many bats live in caves.

They sleep during the day.

The body of the bat is small.

The bat's wings are very large.

The simple subject can sometimes be exactly the same as the complete subject.

Bats look like mice with wings.

Sometimes the simple subject may be several words that name a person or a place.

Linda Lee Carver showed us a picture of a bat.

South America is the home of many bats.

Guided Practice The complete subject is underlined in each sentence below. What is the simple subject?

Example: Some fish live in strange places. *fish*

1. Cavefish live in dark underwater caves.
2. Kim Lee told us about cavefish.
3. These fish lack ordinary eyesight.
4. Their other senses take the place of sight.
5. Everyone in my class liked meeting an interesting visitor named Kim Lee.
6. Kim's talk made all of us want to read about many other kinds of fish.
7. Rosa Perez decided to learn about salmon.
8. Another student is studying shellfish.

▶ The **simple subject** is the main word or words in the complete subject.

Independent Practice The complete subject is underlined in each sentence. Write the complete subject of each sentence. Then underline the simple subject.

Example: The Robinson family moved to New Mexico.
The Robinson *family*

9. Susan Robinson liked her new home.
10. Her family visited Carlsbad Caverns.
11. Carlsbad Caverns is a series of caves.
12. Several caves are open to the public.
13. Most tourists wear sweaters in the caves.
14. The temperature in the caves is always 56°F.
15. Susan's family took the three-mile tour.
16. The tour guide showed them the different kinds of underground rocks.
17. The rocks looked like icicles.
18. Some of the rocks were hanging from the ceiling.
19. Others rose from the floor.
20. The rocks in the caves were tan, red, and yellow.
21. The dark caves contained very few living things.
22. Susan's brother enjoyed Carlsbad Caverns.
23. His favorite part was the Bat Cave.
24. Everyone on the tour ate a meal in the underground lunchroom.
25. An elevator brought everyone above ground.
26. The sun seemed very bright.

Writing Application: A Description
Imagine that you discover a waterfall in the woods. Write a description of the waterfall. Underline the simple subject in each sentence.

For Extra Practice, see p. 44.

5 | Simple Predicates

You know that the complete predicate contains all the words in the predicate. In the complete predicate, one main word tells what the subject is or does. It is called the **simple predicate,** or the verb.

Abigail runs to her singing class.

Singing is her favorite activity.

The simple predicate may be more than one word. There may be a main verb and a helping verb.

Abigail has sung in many musicals.

She will be performing again tonight.

My favorite musical was performed last month.

Guided Practice The complete predicate is underlined in each sentence below. What is the simple predicate?

Example: Louis Armstrong had a rough and unusual voice.   *had*

1. He sang with many jazz bands.
2. He has been called a great singer.
3. He became very famous.
4. People have been copying his music for years.
5. Armstrong was hired by many concert halls.
6. Armstrong also played the trumpet.
7. His hit records will be played for a long time.

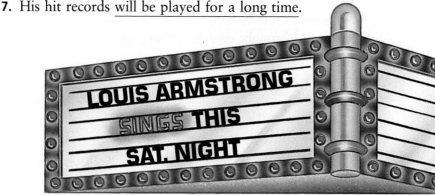

> ▶ The **simple predicate,** or verb, is the main word or words in the complete predicate.
> ▶ The simple predicate may be more than one word. There may be a main verb and a helping verb.

Independent Practice The complete predicate is underlined in each sentence. Write the complete predicate of each sentence. Then underline the simple predicate.

Example: Bessie Smith <u>sang sad songs</u>. *sang sad songs*

8. The songs <u>were called "the blues."</u>
9. Bessie <u>made many records of her songs.</u>
10. Thousands of people <u>bought these records.</u>
11. Bessie <u>performed in many theaters.</u>
12. She <u>traveled in a special railroad car.</u>
13. "Queen of the Blues" <u>was written on the car.</u>
14. Bessie <u>starred in a short movie in 1929.</u>
15. Many people <u>have loved her songs.</u>
16. Country and western music <u>is also popular.</u>
17. Many famous singers <u>have recorded it.</u>
18. Loretta Lynn <u>has been singing country music for years.</u>
19. Her songs <u>are being played all over the country.</u>
20. Many loyal fans <u>have been enjoying her music.</u>
21. People <u>are buying her records today.</u>
22. Many singers <u>have listened to her records.</u>
23. I <u>am collecting country and western records.</u>
24. My family <u>listens to them on Saturday afternoons.</u>
25. My collection <u>has been growing quickly.</u>
26. The record cabinet <u>has very little room now.</u>

Writing Application: An Interview
Imagine that you have just interviewed your favorite singer. Write a report about the interview. The information may be true or made up. Underline the simple predicate in each of your sentences.

For Extra Practice, see p. 45.   **Simple Predicates   23**

6 | Subjects in Imperative Sentences

You have learned that the subject of a sentence tells whom or what the sentence is about.

Dan is in the play.

We are going tonight.

Plays can be fun.

In an imperative sentence, *you* is always the subject. It is usually not stated in the sentence. We say that *you* is the "understood" subject.

IMPERATIVE: (You) Please bring your camera.

(You) Take lots of pictures.

Guided Practice
What is the simple subject of each sentence below? Which sentences are imperative?

Example: Find three seats.
(You) *imperative*

1. Susan will sit beside me.
2. Watch the red curtain.
3. Look at that fancy costume.
4. My brother is the king.
5. The audience loves this play.
6. Everyone is sitting very quietly.
7. Please read this name to me.
8. Clap as hard as you can.
9. I really enjoyed that play.

Summing up

► The subject of an imperative sentence is *you*.
► Usually the word *you* is understood, not stated.

Independent Practice

A. Write the simple subject of each sentence.

Example: Look in the newspaper. *(You)*

10. I want to go to the movies.
11. Find a good film.
12. I like movies about real people.
13. Please buy me two tickets.
14. Listen to the exciting music.
15. The hero really climbed that mountain.
16. Tell my sister about this movie.
17. She is interested in mountain climbing.
18. Remember the name of that mountain.

B. Label each sentence *declarative* or *imperative*. Then write the simple subject of each sentence.

Example: We are visiting a theater in Los Angeles.
         declarative   *We*

19. Tell me the name of the theater.
20. Look carefully at the unusual sidewalk.
21. People made footprints in the cement.
22. Find Mickey Mouse's footprints.
23. I found some handprints.
24. Famous people also signed their names.
25. Stand at this end of the street.
26. Count all the names of the movie stars.
27. A horse made these marks.
28. Trigger belonged to Roy Rogers.
29. Roy Rogers had his own television show.
30. Look for his footprints too.

Writing Application: Persuasive Letter

Imagine that you have just seen a movie, a TV show, or a play that you liked. Write a letter with three declarative sentences and two imperative sentences telling your best friend to see it. Explain why you think your friend might like the show. Then list the simple subject of each sentence.

For Extra Practice, see p. 46.   **Subjects in Imperative Sentences**   25

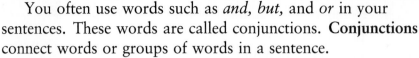

7 | Conjunctions

You often use words such as *and, but,* and *or* in your sentences. These words are called conjunctions. **Conjunctions** connect words or groups of words in a sentence.

Conjunctions can connect two subjects, two predicates, or two sentences.

Gulls and puffins are sea birds.

They swim and dive well.

Gulls soar, and puffins swim gracefully.

Conjunctions can also connect other words in a sentence.

Sam looked on the cliff and near the shore.

He walked quickly but quietly.

He did not see any puffins or gulls.

Each conjunction has a different meaning. When you write, use the conjunction that best expresses your meaning.

Conjunction	Use	Example
and	joins together	Swans and penguins swim.
but	shows contrast	Swans live on ponds, but penguins live on land.
or	shows choice	Penguins slide or waddle.

Guided Practice
What is the conjunction in each of these sentences?

Example: Parrots have bright feathers and large beaks. *and*

1. Their beaks and feet are good for climbing.
2. Parrots live in wild places or in zoos.
3. Tame parrots are friendly and loyal to their owners.
4. Most parrots live in jungles, but some live in grasslands.
5. They eat seeds and drink at water holes.

▸ A **conjunction** is a word that connects words or groups of words.

▸ *And, but,* and *or* are conjunctions.

Independent Practice

A. Complete each sentence, using the conjunction that best expresses the meaning shown in parentheses.

Example: Bats and insects fly, ____ only birds have feathers. (shows contrast) *Bats and insects fly, but only birds have feathers.*

6. Their feathers keep them warm ____ dry.   (joins together)

7. They shed old feathers ____ grow new ones.   (joins together)

8. Many birds fly south in winter, ____ others do not.   (shows contrast)

9. Eagles build nests on cliffs ____ in tall trees.   (shows choice)

10. Swallows ____ sparrows often build nests in buildings. (joins together)

B. Complete each sentence, choosing the conjunction in parentheses that fits the sentence better.

Example: Hummingbirds are tiny (but, or) very brave.
Hummingbirds are tiny but very brave.

11. They are colorful, (and, or) bright flowers interest them.

12. Their beaks are long, (but, or) their bodies are short.

13. Their legs are weak, (and, but) their wings are strong.

14. Their tiny wings beat (and, but) make a humming sound.

15. They can fly fast (but, or) hang in the air.

16. They can fly forward (but, or) backward.

17. The bird's beak (and, but) tongue are useful tools.

18. Its beak may be narrow (and, or) wide.

Writing Application: Creative Writing

If you could be any bird, which would you choose? Why? Write a paragraph describing yourself. Use a conjunction in each sentence.

For Extra Practice, see p. 47.   Conjunctions   **27**

8 | Combining Sentences: Compound Subjects

Sometimes you can combine two similar sentences into one longer, more interesting sentence. One way to do this is to join the subjects of two sentences that have the same predicate. When you combine two or more simple subjects, you form a **compound subject**. Use a conjunction, such as *and* or *or,* to join the simple subjects.

Sue will bring the wood.
Nick will bring the wood.

Sue or Nick will bring the wood.

Nails will be needed.
Hammers will be needed.
A saw will be needed.

Nails , hammers , and a saw will be needed.

Guided Practice

A. What is the compound subject in each sentence? What conjunction joins the simple subjects?

Example: Yoko and Lena watch the adventure movie.
Yoko   Lena   **conjunction:** *and*

1. Men and women are traveling to Mars.
2. The robots and computers are working well.
3. Captain Kroll or Dr. Vek will check the controls.
4. Rockets, meteors, and comets streak past the spaceship.

B. Combine each pair of sentences by forming a compound subject. Use the conjunction *and*.

Example: Hans had read about robots.
His dad had read about robots.
Hans and his dad had read about robots.

5. Sundar boarded the ship.
   Starla boarded the ship.

6. Discoveries were ahead.
   Dangers were ahead.

> ▶ A **compound subject** is two or more simple subjects that have the same predicate.
> ▶ Use a conjunction, such as *and* or *or*, when you join the simple subjects.

Independent Practice

A. Write the compound subject in each sentence. Then write the conjunction that joins the simple subjects.

Example: The moon and stars were shining brightly.
moon   stars   **conjunction:** *and*

7. The boys and girls saw a shooting star.
8. Mr. Ling and his class discussed it.
9. Filmstrips and books were ordered.
10. Nadia or Ann will give a report on outer space.
11. Jupiter, Venus, and Mars are three of the planets.

B. Combine each pair or group of sentences into one sentence with a compound subject. Use the conjunction shown in parentheses.

Example: Engineers inspected the spaceship.   (and)
Scientists inspected the spaceship.
Engineers and scientists inspected the spaceship.

12. Experts were checking the computers.   (or)
Crew members were checking the computers.
13. Captain Novak entered the space capsule.   (and)
Her copilot entered the space capsule.
14. Mr. Levine watched the rocket launching.   (and)
His son watched the rocket launching.
His daughter watched the rocket launching.

Writing Application: A Story
Imagine that you are traveling in a spaceship with several robots. Write a story telling about your adventure. Use compound subjects in some sentences.

For Extra Practice, see p. 48.   **Compound Subjects   29**

9 | Combining Sentences: Compound Predicates

You have learned how to join the subjects of two sentences to form a new sentence. You can also combine the predicates of sentences that have the same subject. When you join two or more simple predicates, you form a **compound predicate**. Use a conjunction, such as *and* or *or,* to join the simple predicates.

The crowd stood .
The crowd waited . > The crowd stood and waited .

Reporters observed the crew.   Reporters observed ,
Reporters interviewed the crew. >   interviewed , and
Reporters photographed the crew.   photographed the crew.

Guided Practice

A. What is the compound predicate in each sentence? What conjunction joins the simple predicates?

Example: The computers flashed and buzzed.
        flashed   buzzed   conjunction: and

1. The astronauts checked and used their controls.
2. The captain double-checked and confirmed their position.
3. He sent, received, and answered messages.
4. The co-captain helped the captain or listened.

B. Combine each pair of sentences by forming a compound predicate. Use the conjunction *and.*

Example: The spacecraft re-entered.
        The spacecraft landed.
        The spacecraft re-entered and landed.

5. The astronauts reported.
    The astronauts rested.
6. Doctors examined them.
    Doctors treated them.

▶ A **compound predicate** is two or more simple predicates that have the same subject.

▶ Use a conjunction, such as *and* or *or,* when you join the simple predicates.

Independent Practice

A. Write the compound predicate in each sentence. Then write the conjunction that joins the simple predicates.

Example: Scientists build and launch satellites.
build   launch   ***conjunction:** and*

7. Satellites orbit Earth and track weather.
8. They photograph and send information.
9. Engineers collect, record, and examine the data.
10. Weather experts check or report weather conditions.

B. Rewrite each pair or group of sentences as one sentence with a compound predicate. Use the conjunction shown in parentheses.

Example: A strange, bright star appeared.   (and)
A strange, bright star fell.
A strange, bright star appeared and fell.

11. Harriet pointed.   (and)
Harriet shouted.
12. Her friend followed her.   (and)
Her friend looked up.
13. The star surprised them.   (and)
The star frightened them.
14. The scientists spotted the meteor.   (and)
The scientists tracked the meteor.
The scientists photographed the meteor.

Writing Application: A Description
Write a paragraph describing the sky at night. Include some compound predicates in your sentences.

For Extra Practice, see p. 49.   **Compound Predicates   31**

10 | Combining Sentences: Compound Sentences

You have learned how to combine two sentences by using compound subjects and compound predicates. You can also combine complete sentences that have similar or related ideas. When you combine two complete sentences, you form a **compound sentence**.

Most bears sleep all winter.　Most bears sleep all winter,
　　Nothing disturbs them.　　and nothing disturbs them.

Use a conjunction, such as *and, but,* or *or,* to connect the sentences. Use a comma before the conjunction.

　　Cubs can climb trees.　　Cubs can climb trees, but
　　Big bears are too heavy.　big bears are too heavy.

A mother bear must catch fish.　　A mother bear must catch fish,
　　Her cubs will be hungry.　　or her cubs will be hungry.

Guided Practice

A. Which sentences are compound sentences?

> Example: Zebras look like horses, but their colors are different.
> ***compound sentence***

1. Zebras have black and white stripes.
2. They eat coarse grass, and most are fat and healthy.
3. Male zebras will bark fiercely or fight.

B. What is the conjunction in each sentence? What are the two sentences that the conjunction joins?

> Example: Male zebras fight, but females do not.
> > ***conjunction:*** *but*
> > *Male zebras fight　females do not*

4. Zebras live in small groups, and the herds travel together.
5. Males fight attackers, or the herd runs away.
6. Zebras are peaceful, but lions are their enemies.

> ▶ A **compound sentence** contains two sentences with related ideas.
> ▶ Use a conjunction to connect these sentences. Use a comma before the conjunction.

Independent Practice

A. If the sentence is a compound sentence, copy it and underline the conjunction. If the sentence is not a compound sentence, write *not compound* and copy the conjunction.

Example: You must pay a dollar, or you can't enter the zoo.
You must pay a dollar, or you can't enter the zoo.

7. A woman showed slides and gave a tour.
8. The dolphins and sea lions were my favorite animals.
9. John liked the zebra, and his dad took pictures of it.
10. Is that big cat a leopard, or is the leopard hiding?
11. The baby turtles swim and walk.
12. Adam wanted to see the big turtle, but it didn't appear.
13. The tiger may be fierce, but her cubs are playful.

B. Combine each pair of sentences into a compound sentence. Use the conjunction shown in parentheses. Remember to use a comma before the conjunction.

Example: Pandas are rare. People must protect them. (and)
Pandas are rare, and people must protect them.

14. They are good climbers. Leafy trees hide them from their enemies. (and)
15. Pandas eat meat. Bamboo is their favorite food. (but)
16. Tigers are very big. Adult tigers are the world's biggest cats. (and)
17. Monkeys are very strong. Gorillas are stronger. (but)
18. Gorillas are shy. Most of them never fight. (and)

Writing Application: A Description
Write a paragraph about an animal that you have seen. Can you combine any of your sentences to form a compound sentence? Combine sentences only if the ideas are related.

For Extra Practice, see p. 50.   **Compound Sentences   33**

11 | Run-on Sentences

The pail tipped. paint spilled on the floor.

A **run-on sentence** is two or more sentences that are run together incorrectly. One way that you can correct a run-on sentence is to make it into a compound sentence.

RUN-ON: Some jobs require special clothing these clothes provide protection.

CORRECTED: Some jobs require special clothing, and these clothes provide protection.

To correct a run-on that has three parts, try dividing it into one compound sentence and one short sentence.

RUN-ON: Some firefighters wear flameproof suits the suits are coated with metal they totally cover the firefighter.

CORRECTED: Some firefighters wear flameproof suits. *(short)* The suits are coated with metal, and they totally cover the firefighter. *(compound)*

Another way to correct a run-on sentence is to divide it into separate sentences.

RUN-ON: Electricians often wear rubber gloves electricity cannot go through rubber.

CORRECTED: Electricians often wear rubber gloves. Electricity cannot go through rubber.

Guided Practice
Which sentences are correct? Which are run-ons? What is one way that you could correct each run-on sentence?

Example: Ms. Ling is a judge her robe is long and black.
   Ms. Ling is a judge. Her robe is long and black.

1. Some dancers wear special shoes the toes are stiff.
2. Rita is a police officer her badge tells her rank.
3. Clowns paint their faces, and they wear funny costumes and colorful wigs.
4. Pete works on a dairy farm he often walks in mud his boots keep his feet dry.

> ▶ A **run-on sentence** is two or more sentences that run together.
> ▶ Correct a run-on sentence by making separate sentences or by making a compound sentence.

Independent Practice

Rewrite each of these run-on sentences correctly. Remember to use commas before conjunctions.

Example: Climbers should wear spiked shoes they might fall.
Climbers should wear spiked shoes, or they might fall.

5. Scuba divers often dive into very cold water special rubber suits keep them warm.
6. Lifeguards wear brightly colored bathing suits these suits are easily spotted on the beach.
7. People fish for trout in deep water, high boots keep their legs very dry.
8. Astronauts wear space suits these suits allow them to move freely in space.
9. Carol has a special cast on her foot she wears the cast during the day she removes it at night.
10. Jockeys wear suits called silks their trousers are white their jackets are colorful.
11. Scott is a figure skater he wears lightweight clothes he moves like the wind.
12. Baseballs are hard balls pitchers throw them very fast catchers must wear face masks.
13. People wash dishes in hot water the soap can be very harsh rubber gloves protect their hands.
14. Carpenters must keep their tools with them they wear overalls with many pockets a special belt holds their nails.

Writing Application: A Description

Imagine that you are at a costume party. Write a paragraph about your costume. Use both short sentences and compound sentences. Check your writing to make sure that you did not write any run-ons.

For Extra Practice, see p. 51.

Grammar-Writing Connection

Varying Sentence Length

To make your writing more interesting, you should vary the lengths of your sentences. The paragraph below contains only short sentences. Notice how choppy and dull the writing sounds.

ORIGINAL: Some streams are wide and deep. These streams are called rivers. Clean rivers usually contain many healthy fish. Dirty rivers often do not contain fish. It is sad to see a river without fish.

In the paragraph below, the writing sounds smoother. The first four sentences have been combined to form two longer sentences, and the last sentence has been left short.

REVISED: Wide, deep streams are called rivers. Clean rivers usually contain many healthy fish, but dirty rivers do not. It is sad to see a river without fish.

Revising Sentences

Revise the sentences below by varying their lengths. Write one short sentence and one longer one.

1. Some streams are narrow and shallow. These streams are called brooks or creeks. People like to fish in these streams.
2. People can be careless. People have ruined some streams. Industry and road construction have destroyed others.
3. Sometimes people clean up dirty streams. They rebuild the banks. They treat the water.
4. Sick plants become healthy again. The fish also become healthy. New fish and plants thrive in the clean water.
5. Streams provide drinking water. They also produce electricity. Streams are an important natural resource.
6. People today worry about streams and wildlife. Governments try to protect these resources. Several private groups also try to protect them.

Creative Writing

What could possibly equal the majesty of the blazing sun? For this painter the answer would surely be the majestic power of the lion, king of all beasts.

- Why do you think this picture was painted with a simple setting?
- How does this picture make you feel? Why?

The Two Majesties, Jean-Léon Gérôme,
Milwaukee Art Museum

Activities

1. **Write a dialogue.** Imagine that the sun and the lion are talking together. Are they praising each other or discussing the day's events? Are their voices loud or quiet? gentle or fierce? Write their conversation as a dialogue.

2. **Write a poem.** Have you ever seen a sunset that you remember well? What did it look like? Write a poem that describes either the sunset you remember or the sunset in the painting.

Check-up: Unit 1

What Is a Sentence? *(p. 14)* Write *sentence* or *fragment* for each group of words below.

1. A tornado hit the barn.
2. In the middle of the day.
3. It happened very fast.
4. Did you see the twister?
5. How still!

Kinds of Sentences *(p. 16)* Copy each sentence and add the correct end punctuation. Then write *declarative, interrogative, imperative,* or *exclamatory* to identify each of the sentences.

6. What an exciting movie we saw
7. It was about the adventures of a brave knight
8. What happened in the movie
9. Listen to what the knight did
10. He rescued the king's son from many dangers
11. How the crowd cheered

Complete Subjects and Complete Predicates *(p. 18)* Copy each sentence. Draw a line between the complete subject and the complete predicate.

12. A helicopter flies over the city.
13. A reporter observes the traffic.
14. Many cars move slowly.
15. The drivers turn on their radios.
16. They hear news about the traffic.

Simple Subjects and Simple Predicates *(pp. 20, 22)* Copy each sentence. Underline the simple subject once. Underline the simple predicate twice.

17. The parade has started late.
18. Our school band is marching.
19. The musicians play a lively tune.
20. Their instruments are gleaming.
21. A huge float will appear next.
22. Bright flowers cover the float.
23. Jen James is waving at us.

Subjects in Imperative Sentences *(p. 24)* For each sentence, write *declarative* or *imperative*. Then write the simple subject of the sentence.

24. Buy two tickets for the concert.
25. Ask for seats in the front row.
26. I love banjo music.
27. Jay is my favorite musician.
28. Don't forget your money.
29. We will get the tickets today.

Conjunctions *(p. 26)* Choose the conjunction in parentheses that best fits each sentence.

30. Sue (and, but) I were lost.
31. We needed a map (or, but) a good compass.
32. Should we go east (but, or) west?
33. We had water (but, or) no food.
34. Sue was nervous, (but, or) I stayed calm.
35. A ranger came (and, or) helped us.

Combining Sentences: Compound Subjects *(p. 28)* Rewrite each group of sentences shown below as one sentence with a compound subject. Use the conjunction that is shown in parentheses.

36. Ms. Lee may teach pottery.   (or)
Ms. Art may teach pottery.
Mr. Cole may teach pottery.

37. Chunks of clay are needed.   (and)
Buckets of water are needed.
Special tools are needed.

38. Flat pieces can be joined.   (and)
Coils can be joined.

39. A bowl can be built by hand.   (or)
A pitcher can be built by hand.
A vase can be built by hand.

Combining Sentences: Compound Predicates *(p. 30)* Rewrite each group of sentences shown below as one sentence with a compound predicate. Use the conjunction that is shown in parentheses.

40. A river crossed a high plain.   (and)
A river formed the Grand Canyon.

41. The canyon is in Arizona.   (and)
The canyon has become a park.

42. Visitors hike in the canyon.   (or)
Visitors ride mules on the trails.
Visitors use rafts on the river.

43. The canyon delights artists.   (and)
The canyon amazes travelers.
The canyon interests scientists.

44. Some people take snapshots.   (or)
Some people make movies.
Some people paint pictures.

Combining Sentences: Compound Sentences *(p. 32)* Rewrite each group of sentences shown below as one compound sentence. Use the conjunction that is shown in parentheses.

45. The book sold well.   (and)
The movie is very popular.

46. The plot is simple. (but)
The movie is exciting.

47. A family is lost at sea.   (but)
The parents do not give up hope.

48. The family can stay together.   (or)
One member can swim as far as possible for help.

49. A plane might spot them.   (or)
The swimmer might reach land.

50. They decide that they should wait together.   (and)
Finally, a ship finds them.

51. The ship takes them home.   (and)
Everyone celebrates.

Run-on Sentences *(p. 34)* Correct each of these run-on sentences.

52. Japan is a chain of islands the islands are covered by hills there are a few flat plains.

53. Japan has very little farm land some farmers carve out flat areas on hillsides.

54. Some of the fields are flooded with water every year rice is usually grown in them.

55. Rice is planted in the spring the crop must be tended all summer the harvest is in the fall.

Enrichment

Using Sentences

ANIMAL LOVERS

You are the director of a zoo. You need to hire a new zoo keeper. You decide to advertise in the newspaper. What will you say in the ad? What should a zoo keeper be like? Write an ad, using declarative, interrogative, imperative, and exclamatory sentences. Make the job sound like fun!

Haiku

Pick something that you like in nature and write a one-sentence haiku on that topic. A haiku is a short Japanese poem. Most haiku have three lines and seventeen syllables. The first line has five syllables, the second line has seven, and the third line has five. Draw a picture to illustrate your haiku.

> One lacy snowflake
> Falls and adds its delicate
> Beauty to a branch.

Scrambled Messages

Solve this scrambled message. Match each subject with the right predicate. (Subjects are in order.) *Hint:* The message is from the American Revolution.

> The British must be protected! Our families and homes should bring a weapon and food to the village green tonight. Every man are coming!

Extra! Create your own scrambled message from history. Exchange with a friend.

1 What Is a Sentence? (p. 14)

● Copy the complete sentence in each pair.

Example: The rain ruined our picnic.
Ate sandwiches in the car. *The rain ruined our picnic.*

1. A very bad storm.
   The sun came out.
2. A soft breeze across the lake.
   The breeze made little waves.
3. Yesterday at the game.
   The rain started to fall.
4. Many rainy days in June.
   July may bring better weather.
5. Are you afraid of thunder?
   The end of the storm.

▲ Copy each group of words that is a sentence. Write *sentence fragment* for each group of words that is not a sentence.

Example: The bright sun. *sentence fragment*

6. We practiced yesterday. S
7. During the soccer game. F
8. Did Sandy drop the ball? S
9. The fog on the highway. F
10. We could not see the road. S

■ If the group of words is a sentence, write *sentence*. If it is a sentence fragment, add words to make it a complete sentence.

Example: On a windy morning. *I flew a kite on a windy morning.*

11. Last winter in Vermont. I went skiing
12. I wore boots and a heavy coat. S
13. Covered with soft snow. The roads were
14. Clouds hung over the mountain. S
15. Coldest winter in fifteen years. It was
16. Have you ever been to Vermont? S

2 | Four Kinds of Sentences (p. 16)

● Copy each sentence and add the correct end punctuation. The kind of sentence is shown in parentheses.

Example: Camels are useful in deserts   (declarative)
Camels are useful in deserts.

1. Study a picture of a camel (imperative)
2. How many humps does a camel have (interrogative)
3. Camels may have one or two humps (declarative)
4. What good travelers camels are (exclamatory)
5. They need very little water (declarative)
6. Can they carry heavy loads (interrogative)
7. How strong and rugged they are (exclamatory)

▲ Copy each sentence and add the correct end punctuation. Then label each sentence *declarative, interrogative, imperative,* or *exclamatory.*

Example: Do you know where the Gobi Desert is
Do you know where the Gobi Desert is?   **(interrogative)**

8. The Gobi Desert is in northeastern Asia
9. Find it on this map of the world
10. It is twice the size of Montana
11. What a huge desert it is
12. Is the Gobi Desert hot and dry
13. There are very few grassy areas
14. Tell me about the people who live there

■ Answer each of the following questions by writing a complete sentence. Write the kind of sentence shown in parentheses.

Example: Do you want to visit a desert?   (declarative)
I would love to visit a desert.

15. What should I wear in a desert?   (imperative)
16. What will the weather be like?   (declarative)
17. Should I take a jug of water?   (imperative)
18. Should I ride a camel or a horse?   (imperative)
19. How will I find my way?   (declarative)
20. Will I see any sand dunes in the Gobi Desert?   (declarative)

3 | Subjects and Predicates (p. 18)

● In each of these sentences, a line separates the complete subject from the complete predicate. Copy each sentence. Underline the part named in parentheses.

Example: Peru | is a South American country.   (predicate)
Peru | is a South American country.

1. A large part of Peru | is in the Andes Mountains.   (subject)
2. The people in the mountains | live in small villages.   (predicate)
3. Their houses | are made from sun-dried brick.   (predicate)
4. Most people | are farmers and shepherds.   (subject)
5. They | grow crops on the sides of mountains.   (subject)
6. The narrow fields | look like steps.   (predicate)
7. Potatoes | grow well in these fields.   (subject)

▲ Copy the sentences below. Underline the complete subject once and the complete predicate twice.

Example: Brazil covers nearly half of South America.
Brazil covers nearly half of South America.

8. Spanish explorers discovered Brazil in 1500.
9. This country was a Spanish colony until 1822.
10. Dom Pedro ruled Brazil from 1822 to 1831.
11. The major language of Brazil is Portuguese.
12. Huge numbers of cattle are raised in Brazil.
13. Two thirds of the people live in cities.

■ Write complete sentences by adding words to the following subjects and predicates. Use correct capitalization and end punctuation.

Example: the small boats   *The small boats sailed on the river.*

14. the tourists
15. surprised us
16. the noisy birds
17. waited on the crowded dock
18. my uncle's cattle ranch
19. is hiding behind that tree
20. paddled a canoe

4 | Simple Subjects (p. 20)

● Choose a simple subject from the words in the box to complete each sentence. Then write each sentence.

Example: _____ hiked in the Grand Canyon.
Uncle Larry hiked in the Grand Canyon.

| sounds |
| photograph |
| Grand Canyon |
| camera |
| trip |
| eagle |
| rocks |
| Uncle Larry |

1. His two-day _____ was exciting. *trip*
2. An _____ flew above him. *eagle*
3. Noisy _____ of wildlife filled the night. *sounds*
4. The _____ was carved out by the Colorado River. *Grand Canyon*
5. The _____ of the Grand Canyon are very colorful. *rocks*
6. Uncle Larry's _____ showed a plant fossil. *photograph*
7. His _____ takes excellent pictures. *camera*

▲ The complete subject is underlined in each sentence. Copy each complete subject. Then underline the simple subject.

Example: <u>My family</u> went camping in Acadia National Park.
My family

8. <u>Acadia National Park</u> is on Mount Desert Island.
9. <u>The island</u> has seventeen peaks.
10. <u>The highest point</u> is Cadillac Mountain.
11. <u>A long, winding road</u> goes to the top.
12. <u>The ocean view at sunrise</u> is beautiful.
13. <u>Everyone in my family</u> got up early to see it.
14. <u>The temperature on top of the mountain</u> was chilly.

■ Write the complete subject of each sentence. Then underline the simple subject.

Example: Hoover Dam is considered a tall dam.
Hoover Dam

15. The walls of the dam are steep and very white.
16. The clear water is bright blue against the white walls.
17. Aunt Alice sent us a picture of the dam.
18. This huge dam controls the Colorado River.
19. Towns in a wide area are provided with electric power.
20. Aunt Alice's trip to the Hoover Dam last summer was very interesting.

5 | Simple Predicates (p. 22)

● Choose a simple predicate from the words in the box to complete each sentence. Then write the sentences.

Example: Jeff ＿＿ onto the stage.
Jeff walks onto the stage.

is bringing	has invited
are clapping	will be
play	are enjoying
sings	walks

1. The musicians ＿＿ *play* their instruments.
2. Jeff ＿＿ his song. *sings*
3. People ＿＿ their hands to the music. *clap*
4. They ＿＿ the concert tonight. *are enjoying*
5. There ＿＿ a party after the concert. *will be*
6. Jeff ＿＿ his friends and his family. *has invited*
7. Tanya ＿＿ her guitar. *is bringing*

▲ The complete predicate is underlined in each sentence. Copy each complete predicate. Then underline the simple predicate.

Example: Our class <u>saw an opera last week.</u>
<u>saw</u> an opera last week

8. Everyone <u>knew the story already.</u>
9. The opera <u>is *Hansel and Gretel*.</u>
10. Many children <u>have heard the story.</u>
11. The story <u>has been enjoyed for years.</u>
12. Two children <u>are wandering in the woods.</u>
13. A mean woman <u>keeps them in her house.</u>
14. The children <u>finally escape.</u>
15. The Opera Company <u>will perform this opera many times.</u>

■ Write the complete predicate of each sentence. Then underline the simple predicate.

Example: An opera is a musical drama. *<u>is</u> a musical drama*

16. The performers sing the words.
17. That woman is singing an aria.
18. An aria is sung by one person.
19. Those people were singing together.
20. Many operas contain dances and fancy costumes.
21. Amy and Bill will enjoy the opera *Carmen*.
22. Janet will be going to the last performance.

6 | Subjects in Imperatives (p. 24)

● Four of the sentences below are imperative. Copy each imperative sentence and put the subject in parentheses.

Example: Come into the theater.   *Come into the theater.   (You)*

1. He sits in the middle row.
2. Read the program quietly.
3. Now watch the stage.
4. The Smiths enjoy the dancing.
5. Sit here next to my brother.
6. Remember the first three songs.
7. Jenny will buy the album of all the songs.
8. We will listen to the album at her house.

▲ Label each sentence *declarative* or *imperative*. Then write the subject of each sentence.

Example: Peter is an actor.   **declarative**   *Peter*

9. Go to one of his films.
10. Listen to his musical voice.
11. One film was a great success.
12. Peter was a clever scientist.
13. Please tell me the name of that film.
14. You can rent it at that new film store.
15. Watch the small dog at the beginning of the film.
16. I have seen that dog in several other films.

■ If the sentence is imperative, rewrite it as declarative. If it is declarative, rewrite it as imperative.

Example: Look at this list.   *Marilyn looks at this list.*

17. She is reading it aloud.
18. Count the plays in this contest.
19. Eric will play the part of the robot.
20. He moves his arms stiffly.
21. Listen for the last line.
22. The robot guides the rocket ship.
23. Close the curtain after the last scene.
24. Discuss the play with the audience.

7 | Conjunctions (p. 26)

● Write the conjunction in each sentence.

Example: All penguins can swim fast, but none can fly.   *but*

1. Penguins live at the South Pole or in warmer areas.
2. Wild storms and high waves hardly bother penguins.
3. They swim as well as seals or fish.
4. Penguins eat all summer, and their fat protects them.
5. One parent or the other sits on the eggs.
6. The newborn chicks are protected and fed.
7. The chicks lose their down and grow feathers.

▲ Write the conjunction that fits each sentence better.

Example: A puffin's wings are short (and, or) stubby.   *and*

8. Puffins swim well, (or, but) penguins swim faster.
9. The puffin can dive deep (or, but) swim a long distance.
10. Puffins eat small fish (but, and) shrimp.
11. Some puffins feed on the surface, (or, but) others dive for food.
12. Puffins dig burrows with their beaks (and, but) claws.
13. Most birds fly well, (but, or) puffins fly poorly.
14. The puffin's beak (and, but) webbed feet are bright red.
15. Explorers (and, but) sailors have hunted these birds.

■ Complete each sentence, using the conjunction that expresses the meaning in parentheses.

Example: Owls hunt at night ____ rest during the day.   (joins together)
Owls hunt at night and rest during the day.

16. Barn owls are good hunters, ____ field mice must watch out for them.   (joins together)
17. The tiny elf owl is the size of a sparrow, ____ the great gray owl is three feet long.   (shows contrast)
18. All owls have large eyes ____ excellent vision.   (joins together)
19. Owls cannot move their eyes, ____ their heads can turn in almost any direction.   (shows contrast)
20. Their feathers have soft edges, ____ their flight is silent.   (joins together)

● ▲ ■ **Three levels of practice   47**

8 | Compound Subjects (p. 28)

● Each sentence contains a compound subject. One simple subject is underlined. Write the other simple subject.

Example: Music and unusual <u>settings</u> were often used to create an imaginary world in movies. *Music*

1. <u>Harburg</u> and Arlen wrote the music for *The Wizard of Oz*.
2. <u>Sets</u> and props were designed by Edwin Willis.
3. Men and <u>women</u> at the MGM Studios built new cities.
4. <u>Masks</u> and special costumes were worn by many actors.
5. Lively <u>tunes</u> and dances helped create the imaginary world.

▲ If the sentence has a compound subject, list each simple subject. If the sentence does not have a compound subject, write *no compound subject*.

Example: Cowardly Lion and Scarecrow were characters in *The Wizard of Oz*. *Cowardly Lion Scarecrow*

6. Bert Lahr played the Cowardly Lion.
7. A long tail and a furry mask made him look like a lion.
8. Scarecrow helped the Cowardly Lion in his search for courage.
9. Alice, Tanya, and Pedro have seen *The Wizard of Oz*.
10. Tanya or Pedro will describe the other characters.

■ Combine each pair of sentences into one sentence with a compound subject. Use the conjunction shown in parentheses.

Example: Props were created by Gillespie.   (and)
Special effects were created by Gillespie.
Props and special effects were created by Gillespie.

11. The house could not really fly.   (and)
Glinda could not really fly.
12. Model makers fooled us.   (and)
Photographers fooled us.
Lighting experts fooled us.
13. Horses might turn green in the Emerald City.   (or)
People might turn green in the Emerald City.
14. Trees could talk in the movie.   (and)
A scarecrow could talk in the movie.

9 | Compound Predicates (p. 30)

● Each of the following sentences contains a compound predicate. One of the simple predicates in each sentence is underlined. Write the other simple predicate.

Example: Astronauts <u>train</u> and prepare for trips into space. *prepare*

1. They exercise and <u>practice</u> for many months.
2. They <u>study</u> and examine their ships before the flight.
3. In space they often orbit and <u>photograph</u> Earth.
4. They eat and <u>sleep</u> in their space capsules.
5. They first <u>landed</u> and walked on the moon in 1969.

▲ Read each sentence below. If it has a compound predicate, write the simple predicates. If it does not have a compound predicate, write *simple predicate*.

Example: In 1961 Yuri Gagarin flew and returned in minutes.
  flew   returned

6. In 1963 Valery Bykovsky flew and orbited for days.
7. Russia and America have sent many people into space.
8. Two American astronauts walked on the moon in 1969.
9. The astronauts explored and photographed the moon.
10. I watched or listened to reports.
11. In school we study, design, and build models of rockets.

■ Rewrite each pair of sentences as one sentence with a compound predicate. Use the conjunction shown in parentheses.

Example: The space shuttle orbits planets.   (and)
        The space shuttle observes planets.
        The space shuttle orbits and observes planets.

12. Astronauts send radio messages.   (and)
    Astronauts receive radio messages.
13. Neil Armstrong found samples of moon dust.   (and)
    Neil Armstrong collected samples of moon dust.
14. Sally Ride flew in the space shuttle.   (and)
    Sally Ride worked in the space shuttle.
15. Alexei Lenov walked in space.   (or)
    Alexei Lenov floated in space.

10 | Compound Sentences (p. 32)

● Copy each compound sentence below. For each sentence that is not a compound, write *not a compound*.

Example: Many animals belong to a group called mammals.
        not a compound

1. A whale is a mammal, but a fish is not a mammal.
2. Mammals have hair on their bodies, and fish do not.
3. Dogs, people, and whales are examples of mammals.
4. Dogs have thick coats of hair, but whales do not.
5. Whales have only a few hairs on their bodies.
6. Birds are not mammals, but cats are.
7. Did a cat just run by, or was it a dog?

▲ Combine each pair of sentences to form a compound sentence. Use a comma and the conjunction shown in parentheses.

Example: Most fish live in clear water. Catfish live in muddy water.   (but)
        Most fish live in clear water, but catfish live in muddy water.

8. Fish live in fresh water. They live in salt water.   (or)
9. Sunfish live in lakes. Sharks live in oceans.   (and)
10. Most fish have many bones. Sharks have no bones.   (but)
11. Fish lay eggs. The eggs hatch into tiny fish.   (and)
12. We use our lungs to breathe. Fish use gills.   (but)
13. Some fish are toothless. Others have sharp teeth.   (but)

■ Combine each pair of sentences to form a compound sentence, using the best conjunction.

Example: Some animals sleep all winter. Others do not.
        Some animals sleep all winter, but others do not.

14. A frog sleeps in mud. A bear may sleep in a cave.
15. Most chipmunks sleep all winter. Squirrels do not.
16. Ponies grow thick coats. Their coats keep them warm.
17. Many birds travel to warm areas. Some birds stay in cold places.
18. Robins fly south. Sparrows stay in the chilly north.
19. Some animals rest in the summer. Insects like the heat.
20. Turtles dig into cool mud. Fish seek deep pools.

11 | Run-on Sentences (p. 34)

● Correct each of these run-on sentences. Separate each one into two sentences.

Example: Football is dangerous players wear helmets and pads.
Football is dangerous. Players wear helmets and pads.

1. In the past, they wore shorts their legs were not protected.
2. In 1878 heavier uniforms were made pads were required.
3. Most players wore leather helmets some wore canvas ones.
4. Modern helmets are hard they also have chin straps.
5. Players today also wear heavy pads these pads protect their arms, legs, and shoulders.

▲ If the sentence is correct, write *correct*. If it is a run-on sentence, rewrite it correctly.

Example: *Peter Pan* is a great play I have seen it many times.
Peter Pan *is a great play. I have seen it many times.*

6. The character Peter Pan is not really flying we are fooled by special effects.
7. The actor hangs from wires, and a fan creates wind.
8. Set designers create an imaginary world flight is only a part of this world.
9. Designers build a pirate ship they construct huge rocks.
10. The rocks are made of paper they weigh only a pound each.

■ If the sentence is correct, write *correct*. If it is a run-on sentence, rewrite it correctly.

Example: Beth owns a horse named Rusty he is a great jumper.
Beth owns a horse named Rusty. He is a great jumper.

11. Rusty went to the Olympics he competed against other horses.
12. A man rode Rusty in the Olympics he wore a red jacket.
13. Rusty won two medals one was a silver medal the other was a gold medal.
14. We could not go to the Olympics we watched Rusty on television we cheered him
15. I saw Rusty's picture on a magazine cover I sent it to Beth she was delighted.

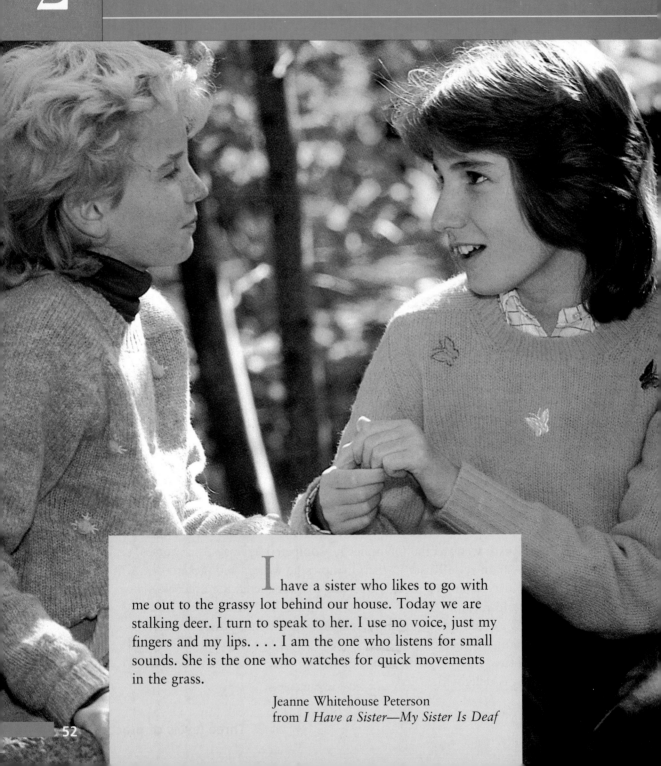

UNIT
2
Literature and Writing

I have a sister who likes to go with me out to the grassy lot behind our house. Today we are stalking deer. I turn to speak to her. I use no voice, just my fingers and my lips. . . . I am the one who listens for small sounds. She is the one who watches for quick movements in the grass.

Jeanne Whitehouse Peterson
from *I Have a Sister—My Sister Is Deaf*

Personal Narrative

Getting Ready A personal narrative tells the *story* of something you have experienced. It is a much more interesting way to write about yourself than if you began, "I am eleven years old and I live in Minnesota." When you write a personal narrative, your reader can get to know you by finding out how you act when you are being yourself. In this unit, you will read a personal narrative and write one of your own.

ACTIVITIES

Listening
Listen as your teacher reads the paragraph on the facing page. What did you find out about the writer? What did you learn about her sister? What is the title of the writer's book?

Speaking
Look at the picture. The girls in this picture are not the two sisters described in the quotation. Who do you think they are? What has just happened? What will happen next?

Writing
Think about someone who is special to you. Could you write a story about you and this person? Write your ideas in your journal.

LITERATURE

Do animals have embarrassing moments? What happens when Wol has a new experience with water?

Wol Walks on Water

By Farley Mowat

We used to go to our cave a couple of times a week during the summer holidays, and usually we took the owls along. Wol had learned how to ride on the handle bars of my bicycle; but Weeps couldn't keep his balance there, so we built a kind of box for him and tied it to the carrier behind the seat. Mutt and Rex used to come too, chasing cows whenever they got a chance, or racing away across the prairie after jack rabbits.

We would bike out to the end of Third Avenue and then along an old Indian trail that ran along the top of the river-

54

bank. When we got close to the cave we would hide our bikes in the willows and then climb down the bank and follow a secret path. There were some pretty tough kids in Saskatoon, and we didn't want them to find our cave if we could help it.

Wol loved those trips. All the way out he would bounce up and down on the handle bars, hooting to himself with excitement, or hooting out insults at any passing dog. When we came to the place where we hid the bikes, he would fly up into the poplars and follow us through the tops of the trees. He usually stayed pretty close, though; because, if he didn't, some crows would be sure to spot him and then they would call up all the other crows for miles around and try to mob him. When that happened he would come zooming down to the cave and bang on the door with his beak until we let him in. He wasn't afraid of the crows; it was just that he couldn't fight back when they tormented him. As for Weeps, he usually stayed right in the cave, where he felt safe.

One summer afternoon, when we were at the cave, we decided to go for a swim. The three of us shucked off our clothes and raced for the sand bar, hollering at each other: "Last one in's a Dutchman!"

In half a minute we were in the water splashing around, and rolling in the slippery black mud along the edge of the sand bar. It was great stuff to fight with. Nice and soft and slithery, it packed into mushy mud-balls that made a wonderful splash when they hit something.

Whenever we went swimming, Wol would come along and find a perch in the Hanging Tree where he could watch the fun. He would get out on the big limb that hung over the water and the more fuss and noise we made the more excited he became. He would walk back and forth along the limb, *hoo-hooing* and ruffling his feathers, and you could tell he felt he was missing out on the fun.

This particular day he couldn't stand it any longer, so he came down out of the tree and waddled right to the river's edge.

We were skylarking on the sand bar when I saw him, so I gave him a yell: "Hey Wol! C'mon there, Wol old owl! C'mon out here!"

Of course I thought he would fly across the strip of open water and light on the dry sand where we were playing. But I forgot Wol had never had any experience with water before, except in his drinking bowl at home.

He got his experience in a hurry. Instead of spreading his wings, he lifted up one foot very deliberately and started to walk across the water toward us.

It didn't take him long to find out he couldn't do it. There was an almighty splash and spray flew every which way. By the time we raced across and fished him out, he was half-drowned, and about the sickest-looking bird you ever saw. His feathers were plastered down until he looked as skinny as a plucked chicken. The slimy black mud hadn't improved his looks much either.

I carried him ashore, but he didn't thank me for it. His feelings were hurt worse than he was, and after he had shaken most of the water out of his feathers he went gallumphing off through the woods, toward home on foot (he was too wet to fly), without a backward glance.

This story comes from the book *Owls in the Family* by Farley Mowat. The book is the story of Wol and Weeps from the time they were found to the time their owner was forced to give them up.

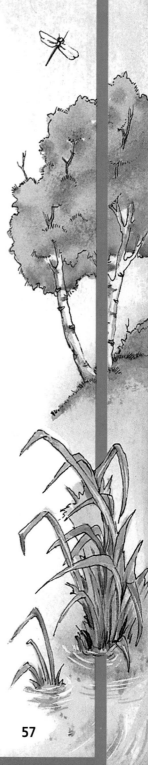

Think and Discuss

1. What embarrassed Wol? Why didn't Wol fly to the sand bar?

2. The position from which a story is told is called the **point of view**. "Wol Walks on Water" is told from the first-person point of view. That is, the storyteller speaks as "I" and is a character in the story. Events are seen through his eyes. How do you think Wol would describe his adventure with water if he were the storyteller? How would his description be different from the one in the original story?

3. What kind of person do you think the storyteller is? Give some reasons for your opinion.

I Go Forth to Move About the Earth

By Alonzo Lopez

I go forth to move about the earth.
I go forth as the owl, wise and knowing.
I go forth as the eagle, powerful and bold.
I go forth as the dove, peaceful and gentle.
I go forth to move about the earth,
*   in wisdom, courage, and peace.*

Think and Discuss

1. What does the poet mean when he says "I go forth to move about the earth"? What qualities will he bring with him?

2. **Repetition** is simply repeating words or phrases over and over. In this poem, repetition is used to emphasize the main idea and help you remember it. It also makes you notice the parts that are *not* repeated. In addition, repetition helps move the poem forward. What main idea does the repetition emphasize? What parts of the poem do you notice more as a result of the repetition?

3. The owl was chosen to show wisdom and knowledge, the eagle to show power and boldness, and the dove to show peace and gentleness. What animals would you choose to represent these qualities?

RESPONDING TO LITERATURE

The Reading and Writing Connection

Personal Response Wol's first experience with water was an unexpected adventure for him. Have you ever had an experience that was embarrassing for you? Write a paragraph telling what happened and how you felt. Tell what you learned.

Creative Writing In the poem "I Go Forth," the poet uses animals to represent qualities. What qualities are important to you? What animals could represent them? Write a poem in the form of "I Go Forth," using those animals.

Creative Activities

Draw What mental pictures did you form as you read "I Go Forth to Move About the Earth"? Draw or paint a picture to illustrate this poem.

Act out Wol the owl perched in the Hanging Tree to watch the children having fun. Choose a partner. Imagine that you and your partner are Wol and another owl. Make up a conversation that you might have as you perch on the branch, watching the children. As you speak, use pantomime to show the actions of owls.

Vocabulary

After Wol's rescue, he is described as "gallumphing off." Write a meaning for the verb *gallumph*. Share your definition with a classmate.

Looking Ahead

Personal Narrative In the following composition lessons, you will be writing a story about yourself. "Wol Walks on Water" is about the writer's own experiences. Start keeping a journal of your experiences. Include your thoughts and feelings.

VOCABULARY CONNECTION

Synonyms

One way to vary your writing is to use synonyms. **Synonyms** are words that have almost the same meaning. Look at how the author used two different words for *slick.*

In half a minute we were in the water splashing around, and rolling in the **slippery** black mud along the edge of the sand bar. It was great stuff to fight with. Nice and soft and **slithery**, it packed into mushy mud-balls. . . .
from "Wol Walks on Water" by Farley Mowat

Notice how the synonyms *slippery* and *slithery* help vary the writing. They have almost the same meaning as *slick,* but they look and sound different.

Here are some other synonyms for *slick.*

oily   greasy   smooth   waxy   soapy

When you write, use a thesaurus to look up synonyms.

Vocabulary Practice

A. Rewrite each sentence. Replace each underlined word with one of these words from "Wol Walks on Water."

shucked   waddled   tormented   skylarking

1. Hot, tired, and <u>bothered</u> by mosquitos, the hikers came upon a clear mountain stream.
2. They <u>threw</u> off their boots and ran into the icy water.
3. Soon everyone was laughing and <u>playing</u> in the stream.
4. No one noticed the skunk that <u>walked</u> across the clearing.

B. Use the Thesaurus Plus in this book to find two synonyms for each of these words from "Wol Walks on Water."

5. hollering   **6.** skinny   **7.** wonderful   **8.** glance

Prewriting
Personal Narrative

Listening and Speaking: Sequence

Events in a story follow a certain order, or **sequence**. To help you follow a sequence, listen for words such as *after, when, by the time,* and *while*. These words help you figure out which things happen before or after others and which things happen at the same time.

Notice the sequence in this passage.

> After school I would jump on my bike and pedal like forty over the bridge and down our street. When I got close to home I would give a couple of owl-whoops to let Wol and Weeps know I was coming. By the time I skidded into the yard and parked my bike, they would be tramping impatiently up and down the cage.
>
> *from* Owls in the Family *by Farley Mowat*

- Did the storyteller call to the owls before he entered the yard?
- When did the owls tramp up and down the cage?
- What order words do you find in the paragraph?

You will find that writers do not always use order words in their writing. The sequence of events can sometimes be shown by the flow of sentences. Read the next passage. Is the sequence of events clear?

> Whenever we went swimming, Wol would come along and find a perch in the Hanging Tree where he could watch the fun. He would get out on the big limb that hung over the water and the more fuss and noise we made the more excited he became. He would walk back and forth along the limb, *hoo-hooing* and ruffling his feathers, and you could tell he felt he was missing out on the fun.
>
> *from "Wol Walks on Water" by Farley Mowat*

- Where was Wol while the boys were in the water?
- When did Wol become excited?
- What was the sequence of events?

Guidelines for Listening for Sequence

1. Picture each event as you hear it described.
2. Notice how one event leads to another.
3. Listen for order words that help make the sequence clear.

When you tell a story, it is easy to get events out of order. Have you ever found yourself saying, "Oh, I forgot; that didn't happen next. It was . . ." Hearing events told out of order can confuse your listeners.

Guidelines for Telling Events in Order

1. Review the sequence before you begin.
2. Picture the events in your mind as you tell them in order.
3. Use order words if they will help make the sequence clear.

Prewriting Practice

A. Listen as your teacher reads a passage. Write the sequence.
B. Does the story "Wol Walks on Water" remind you of something that happened to you? Tell a partner about your experience. Could your partner follow the sequence?

Thinking: Recalling

When you tell a story, it is important that you **recall,** or remember, as many details as you can. It is the details that make the events come alive. Notice all the details as you read this passage about Wol's adventure.

> There was an almighty splash and spray flew every which way. By the time we raced across and fished him out, he was half-drowned, and about the sickest-looking bird you ever saw. His feathers were plastered down until he looked as skinny as a plucked chicken. The slimy black mud hadn't improved his looks much either.
>
> *from "Wol Walks on Water" by Farley Mowat*

- What did the storyteller do? What did he hear?
- What details help you picture what Wol looked like?

Before you write about an experience of your own, follow these guidelines to help you recall the details.

Guidelines for Recalling

1. Imagine you are looking at a movie of your life that is running backward. Slow it down when you find an experience that interests you.
2. Focus on the time and place of the experience. How do things look? sound? feel? smell? taste? Take notes.
3. Focus on the experience, event by event. How do you feel about what is happening? Who else is involved? What details do you notice?
4. Use brainstorming to recall more details. Jot down everything that comes to mind about the experience. Write as quickly as you can.

Prewriting Practice

Recall an experience you have had. Use the guidelines above to recall the details. Take notes.

Writing a Good Beginning ☑

A good beginning catches the reader's interest right away. It makes the reader curious about what is going to happen.

Read this story beginning. The writer hints at what is going to happen but doesn't give it away.

> Wol was usually good-natured but he *could* get mad. One morning Mother sent me to the store to get some groceries. My bike had a flat tire, so I had to walk, and Wol walked beside me. We were only a little away from our house when we met the postman coming toward us.
>
> *from* Owls in the Family *by Farley Mowat*

- How does the writer catch your interest?
- What else would you like to know?

Some story beginnings, like the one above, give hints about the action. Others tell about character or setting.

> When the owls first came to live with us, Mutt [the writer's dog] didn't think much of them. He was jealous of all my pets, and he was particularly jealous of the owls because they took up so much of my time.
>
> *from* Owls in the Family *by Farley Mowat*

- Does this beginning tell about character or setting?
- What questions do you have after reading this?

Prewriting Practice

Work with a partner to write a good beginning for each topic.

a strange new sound   the bus that never came

Supplying Details ☑️

Once you have captured your reader's attention, try to keep it. To do this, you need to give enough details. Show your reader what happens rather than just tell about it. Let your reader feel what you felt. Help your reader picture the action. Include enough details to make the events seem real, but do not tell too much.

What happens if you do not use enough details? Compare these paragraphs.

1. We went into the water near the sand bar. There was mud all along the edge of the sand bar. It was messy stuff. We played in it and had a really good time.

2. In half a minute we were in the water splashing around and rolling in the slippery black mud along the edge of the sand bar. It was great stuff to fight with. Nice and soft and slithery, it packed into mushy mud-balls that made a wonderful splash when they hit some-thing.   *from "Wol Walks on Water" by Farley Mowat*

- Which paragraph tells enough to hold your interest?
- Which details were added to the second paragraph to give you a clearer picture of what happened?
- Which words were added to let you know how the writer felt?

Prewriting Practice

Imagine that the following paragraph is your own. Rewrite it by using details that describe the people, places, and events. Let the reader feel what it was like to be there.

```
We went on a picnic. We decided to go
exploring. We found a cave. It was wet inside. I
could not see, but I could hear something. There
was a funny smell too. Then something moved
toward us in the darkness, and we ran.
```

The Grammar Connection

Stringy Sentences

Long, stringy sentences are difficult to read. They go on and on without a break. Long, stringy sentences can be broken up into shorter sentences that are easier to understand. Read the paragraph below. Is it easy to follow?

> The only thing different about that Sunday was that my cousin Larry was late. He was always the first to come to our big, old house at the beach and then all the cousins would arrive with their parents and the street would be loaded with cars and we always had a great time! Larry lived only a few blocks away and his bike was brand new and beautiful and he usually rode it to our house on Sundays. We were in the middle of our usual game when Larry finally arrived. He had quite a funny story to tell!

Practice The paragraph above contains two stringy sentences. Decide where to break them into shorter sentences. Rewrite the paragraph so that it is easier to read.

Writing Dialogue ☑

Conversation in a story is called **dialogue**. Using dialogue in your own writing will bring your characters to life by having them tell what they think and feel. Dialogue can also show what a person is like—funny, silly, kind, angry, or happy, for example.

When you write dialogue, begin a new paragraph each time a new person is speaking. Make your dialogue sound realistic. Listen to the way people really talk!

Read the dialogue on the next page. The storyteller and his two friends have just found the owl who will be named Wol. Does the dialogue between the storyteller and Bruce help you to know what each of them is like? Is the dialogue realistic? Do these characters sound like people that you know?

> "Guess he's your owl, all right," Bruce said, and I could see he was a little jealous.
>
> "No sir, Bruce," I replied. "He can live at my place, but he's going to be our owl—all three of us."
>
> *from* Owls in the Family *by Farley Mowat*

- What kind of person do you think each character is?
- Why is dialogue a good way to tell this part of the story?

Prewriting Practice

Work with a partner to write a short dialogue about an upcoming event. Look at page 292 to make sure that you are punctuating the direct quotations correctly. Then take the parts of the speakers in your dialogue. Read only their exact words.

Writing a Good Title ☑

Give your story a title that will attract your reader's interest. A good title gives your reader an idea of what the story is about without giving it away.

Look at this list of story titles.

1. The Day the Rain Spoiled Our Swimming Trip
2. The Case of the Missing Bicycle
3. Finding My Lost Owl in a Cave
4. The Owl and the Bicycle

- Which two story titles tell too much?
- Which story might be a mystery?
- Which story might be humorous?

Prewriting Practice

Make up another title for Wol's adventure with water. Remember to capitalize the first and last words as well as each important word. Share your title with a partner. Does your title tell something about the story without giving it away?

The Writing Process
How to Write a Personal Narrative

Step 1: Prewriting—Choose a Topic

Robin made a list of some of the things she had done. Then she thought about her list.

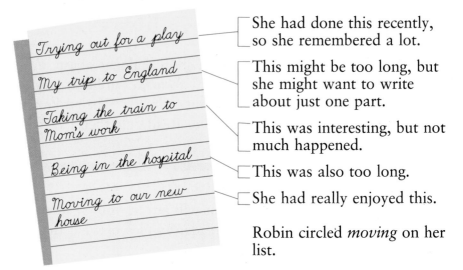

Trying out for a play — She had done this recently, so she remembered a lot.

My trip to England — This might be too long, but she might want to write about just one part.

Taking the train to Mom's work — This was interesting, but not much happened.

Being in the hospital — This was also too long.

Moving to our new house — She had really enjoyed this.

Robin circled *moving* on her list.

On Your Own

---

1. **Think and discuss** Make a list of some things that you have done. Use the Ideas page to help you. Discuss your ideas with a partner.
2. **Choose** Ask yourself these questions about each of your topics.
   Would this make an interesting story to write and read?
   Do I remember enough details to hold a reader's interest?
   Would this story be too long? too short?
   Circle the topic you want to write about.
3. **Explore** What will you write? Do one of the activities under "Exploring Your Topic" on the Ideas page.

Ideas for Getting Started

Choosing Your Topic

Topic Ideas

My first try at ——
My favorite mud story
A race to remember
The art contest
The shopping trip
The camping trip
My best birthday
Spring cleaning day
The new baby

Brainstorm and Cluster

Brainstorm ideas for a story. Think of experiences you've had. Jot them down in any order. Let your mind roam freely. Do not screen out ideas.

Use **clustering** to think of ideas. In the middle of your paper, write a word, like *water,* and circle it. What word comes to mind when you think of experiences you've had with water? Write the word, circle it, and join it to the previous word, using an arrow. Keep going.

Exploring Your Topic

Beginnings

How will you grab your reader's interest? Don't write one beginning —write three! Pick your favorite for your first draft. Here are Robin's:

We moved into our house in winter.
Moving to our house was a disaster.
Nothing went well on moving day.

Talk About It

Have a friend interview you about your story. What parts did your friend like best? What would your friend like to know more about?

Step 2: Write a First Draft

Robin decided to write her story for her grandmother. She wanted her to know how funny their moving day had been.

Robin wrote her first draft. She did not worry about making mistakes. She would have a chance to correct them later.

Robin's first draft

Think and Discuss

- How does Robin catch your interest?
- What details help you share her feelings?
- What parts would you like to know more about?

> Moving to our new house was a disaster. ~~We~~ On the coldest day of the whol year, we moved in. It was really dirty and in bad shape the kitchen was really awful. Then my mother thought of a cleanup party. Her briliant idea saved the day. All our friends came to help, and it didn't even feel like work.

On Your Own

1. **Think about purpose and audience** Ask yourself these questions.

   For whom shall I write this story?
   What is my purpose?
   What feelings do I want to share?
   Which part of the story should I tell first?

2. **Write** Try to put your reader in your shoes. Write on every other line so that you will have room to add or make changes later. Do not worry about mistakes. Just write your story.

Step 3: Revise

Robin read her first draft. She saw where she could add some more details about the house. She wanted her readers to know what a mess it really was. She made some changes in her first draft.

Robin wanted to find out if she had told her story well. She read it to Amy.

Reading and responding

Robin added some details about the kitchen. Then she added some dialogue to give her readers more of a feeling of being there with her on moving day.

Part of Robin's revised draft

> Moving to our new house was a
> disaster. ~~We~~ On the coldest day of the
> whol year, we moved in. *The house* ~~It~~ was really
> *and paint was peeling off the walls,*
> dirty and in bad shape the kitchen was
> *sticky and greasy*
> ~~really awful.~~ Then my mother *said. Let's* ~~thought~~
> *have*
> of a cleanup party. Her briliant idea

Think and Discuss ☑

- What phrases did Robin leave out? Why?
- What details did she add? Why?
- Where did she add dialogue?

On Your Own

Revising Checklist

☑ Does it begin in an interesting way?

☑ What details could I add to make my story clearer?

☑ Where could I use more dialogue to add interest?

1. **Revise** Make changes in your first draft. Add details. If you need to find exact words, use the thesaurus below or the one in the back of the book. Replace words by crossing them out and adding new words above them.

2. **Have a conference** Read your story to someone else—a friend or your teacher. Make notes about their remarks.

Ask your listener:	**As you listen:**
"Can you imagine what this was like?" "Which parts help you know how I felt?" "Where isn't it clear?" "Where could I add details or dialogue?"	Is it clear? Can I picture this in my mind? Can I tell how the writer felt? What would I like to know more about?

3. **Revise** Think about your listener's suggestions. Can you think of any other changes you might like to make? Make those changes on your paper.

Thesaurus

also in addition, besides
asked inquired, questioned
big huge, gigantic
foolish silly, crazy
funny amusing, comical, humorous, laughable
great terrific, fantastic
happy cheerful, glad
important significant

new fresh, original
scary frightening, terrifying, alarming
shouted yelled, cried
some a few, several
strange odd, unusual
upset worried, nervous, troubled, disturbed

Step 4: Proofread

Robin proofread her story for mistakes in spelling, capitalization, and punctuation. She used a dictionary to check spelling. She used proofreading marks to make her changes.

Part of Robin's proofread narrative

Moving to our new house was a
disaster. ~~We~~ On the coldest day of the
~~whol~~ whole year, we moved in. ~~It was really~~ The house
~~dirty~~ and paint was peeling off the walls,
and in bad shape the kitchen was
sticky and greasy said, "Let's
really awful. Then my mother, thought
have ~~brilliant~~
of a cleanup party!" ~~Her briliant~~ idea

Think and Discuss

- Which words did Robin correct for spelling?
- Where did she add quotation marks? Why?
- What other punctuation marks did she change or add?

On Your Own

1. **Proofreading Practice** Proofread this paragraph. Correct the mistakes in grammar and spelling. Find one mistake in a compound sentence and one run-on sentence. Find one incorrect end mark and five spelling mistakes. Write the paragraph correctly.

   Last summur I went on a trip with my grandmother. We started early in the morning and drove for several hours? At noon we reched Stone Mountain. First, we had a reelly good lunch. Then we went to a ranch there we saw diffrent animals. Finally, we climed the mountain and a cable car brought us back down.

Proofreading Marks

⌐ Indent
∧ Add some-
  thing
ℓ Take out
  something
≡ Capitalize
/ Make a small
  letter

2. Proofreading Application Now proofread your paper. Use the Proofreading Checklist and the Grammar and Spelling Hints below. You may want to use a colored pencil to make your corrections. Use a dictionary to check spellings.

Proofreading Checklist

Did I

☑ **1.** indent?

☑ **2.** make each sentence a complete thought?

☑ **3.** use capital letters correctly?

☑ **4.** use punctuation marks correctly?

☑ **5.** spell all words correctly?

The Grammar/Spelling Connection

Grammar Hints

Remember these rules from Unit 1 to write sentences.

- Use a comma to separate the parts of a compound sentence. *(A kite had blown away, and a girl was running after it.)*
- Be careful not to write run-on sentences. *(The park was far we biked there. — The park was far. We biked there.)*

Spelling Hints

- The (ē) sound is often spelled *ee* or *ea*. *(greet, heat)*
- The final (ər) sound in a two-syllable word is spelled *ar, or,* or *er*. *(dollar, actor, powder)*

Step 5: Publish

Robin titled her story "Moving Day Disaster." She shared her story by reading it aloud to her classmates and showing "Before" and "After" photographs of her new house. Then she sent her story to her grandmother.

On Your Own

1. **Copy** Write or type your story as neatly as possible.
2. **Add a title** Think of a title to catch your reader's interest. Remember to capitalize the first, last, and all important words.
3. **Check** Read over your story to make sure that you have not left out anything or made any mistakes in copying.
4. **Share** Think of a special way to share your story.

Ideas for Sharing

- Write your story in the form of a comic strip.
- Present your story as a short play or skit.
- Write your story on a poster. Show the main events with drawings or with pictures cut from magazines.

Applying Personal Narrative

Literature and Creative Writing

In "Wol Walks on Water," on pages 54–57, the writer's pet owl has an embarrassing experience with water—he tries to walk on it!

Have fun using what you have learned about writing a personal story to complete one or more of these activities.

Remember these things ☑

Write a good beginning to interest your reader.

Include enough details to help your reader picture the action.

Use dialogue.

Write a good title that does not tell too much.

---

1. **Pet pranks!** Have you ever had a funny experience with a pet? Write a story about your experience. What did the pet do? How did it act? What did you imagine the pet was thinking?

2. **Come to the hide-out.** Wol's owner had a cave that he and his friends had found. Write a story about a place that is special to you. Where is it? Why do you like it?

3. **What's in a name?** The author named his owl Wol, after the owl in A. A. Milne's Pooh stories. Have you ever chosen a name for a pet or helped someone else do this? Write a story about how you chose that name. Why was the choice of name a good one?

Writing Across the Curriculum
Economics

Do you want more things than you are able to buy? This is true for most people. Economists study how people spend money and when they spend it. They also study how goods are transported to stores and markets. Economics is a subject you can read about in newspapers and magazines.

Try doing one or more of these activities.

1. Decide what to buy. Write a story about a time when you made your own decision on what to buy. What did you buy? Did you make a good choice? On what did you base your decision?

Writing Steps

1. Choose a topic
2. Write a first draft
3. Revise
4. Proofread
5. Publish

Word Bank

bargain
sale
discount
quality
brand name
comparison

2. Be a salesperson. What have you done to earn money? Have you sold goods (newspapers, books) or services (lawn mowing, babysitting)? Write a story about one of your attempts to earn money. What did you sell? How did you sell it? What were the results? Share your story.

3. Take a survey. Ask several people about the best place in town to shop for a certain product. Write a story about your experience. Did you enjoy talking to the people? Did they agree or disagree on the best place? Include some of your conversation in your story.

Extending Literature
Writing a Book Report

When Manuel read *Owls in the Family*, he liked the way the author told a lot about himself while writing about his pet owl. At the library, he found another book about a real person and animals. He wrote this book report to share with his class.

Title: Little Rascal
Author: Sterling North

Introduction: When the author was eleven, he found Rascal the raccoon. Little did he know what was ahead of him! Later he wrote this nonfiction book about their experiences.

About the Book: Sterling lived with his father in a big house in a small town in Wisconsin. He had a pet crow, orphan skunks, cats, and a dog, but his favorite pet was Rascal. Rascal was a great pet, but he was always getting into trouble. Once, when Sterling's oldest sister was visiting, her diamond ring disappeared. Rascal and the crow both liked shiny things. That night Sterling heard them fussing at each other. Which one had the ring?

My Opinion: I enjoyed reading about Rascal. He was so cute and such a good pet! I also liked learning about Sterling's life. He had so many unusual pets and hobbies. I've never known anyone who built a canoe in a living room!

Think and Discuss

• What did you learn about Sterling?
• What did you learn about his home and family?
• How did Manuel feel about the book?

Share Your Book

Write a Book Report

1. **Title and Author:** Capitalize every important word in the title. Write the author's full name.
2. **Introduction:** Tell whether the book is fiction or nonfiction. Say something to get your reader interested.
3. **About the Book:** Choose part of the story to share. Mention the setting and the main characters.
4. **My Opinion:** Tell what you think of the book. Would your classmates enjoy it? Explain why or why not.

Other Activities

- Think about the setting of your story. Does the action take place in the present or in the past? Draw or collect pictures that illustrate this setting. Show them with your report.
- Make a puppet to represent a character in your book. Play another part yourself and act out a scene from the story.
- Create a future for a character in your book. Imagine what happens to that character on the day after the book ends. What might that character be doing five years later?
- Find out all you can about the author of your book. Has the author written other books that you might like to read? Share this information with your class.

 # The Book Nook

The Dog Who Wouldn't Be *by Farley Mowat* The author of *Owls in the Family* writes about life with his dog Mutt, a dog with real character and personality.	**The Enormous Egg** *by Oliver Butterworth* A boy's hen has been sitting on an enormous egg. When the egg hatches into a dinosaur, there is a lot of excitement.

Language and Usage

W hat will you find at the edge of the world?
A footprint,
a feather,
desert sand swirled?

Eve Merriam, from "Landscape"

Nouns

Getting Ready Every day you probably use thousands of nouns. Because nouns name the objects and people and places around you, it would be very difficult to talk about anything at all without them. In this unit, you will learn about using nouns correctly in writing.

ACTIVITIES

Listening   Listen as the poem on the opposite page is read. Listen for the nouns. What are they?

Speaking   Look at the picture. With your class, think of as many nouns as you can to name the things in the picture. Choose a class "secretary" to make a list of the nouns on the board.

Writing   What other nouns name things you might find "at the edge of the world"? Make a list and use it to write a poem of your own in your journal.

A word that names a person, a place, or a thing is called a **noun**.

> Pablo lives in a house on my street .

> His grandparents came from Puerto Rico .

Notice that the noun *Puerto Rico* is two words that name one place. Nouns can be two or more words.

Nouns		
Persons	boy student	writer Tammy Robbins
Places	lake country	field New York
Things	boat calendar	sweater basketball

Nouns can also name feelings, thoughts, and ideas.

excitement   fear   freedom   anger   happiness

Guided Practice What words in each sentence are nouns?

Example: The students planned a party. *students   party*

1. Three girls performed songs.
2. The band played happy, loud music.
3. Excitement filled the air!
4. Pedro Casals won a prize.
5. The bandstand was covered with ribbons and streamers.

Summing up

> ▶ A **noun** is a word that names a person, a place, a thing, or an idea. A noun can be more than one word.

Independent Practice

A. Copy each noun. Then write whether it names a person, a place, a thing, or an idea.

Example: river   *river   place*

6. candle
7. juggler
8. joy
9. Statue of Liberty

10. trumpet
11. South America
12. friendliness
13. Luisa Perez

B. Write each noun in these sentences.

Example: Mexico is a beautiful country.
           Mexico   country

14. Maria Rodrigo enjoyed her trip.
15. Her family stayed in a village.
16. The harbor was filled with small boats.
17. Many colorful flowers grew on the hillside.
18. A festival was held in Veracruz.
19. People in costumes filled the streets.
20. Boys in white robes were leading a parade.
21. One woman was wearing a bright red hat.
22. Gaily colored flags hung from the windows.
23. Musicians played drums and flutes.
24. Men, women, and children danced.
25. The sound of laughter was heard in the town.
26. Maria and her parents also went to a sandy beach.
27. Her mother swam in the warm water.
28. Maria built a huge castle in the wet sand.
29. The vacation was a great thrill!
30. The Rodrigos will have many happy memories.
31. A taxi brought the family to the airport.
32. A huge jet flew to the airport near their home.

Writing Application: Writing About Yourself

Think about a time when you went to a new place with a friend or a relative. What did you see there? What did you do? Write a paragraph about the trip. Underline each noun.

For Extra Practice, see p. 102.   **What Is a Noun?**

2 | Singular and Plural Nouns

You have learned that nouns are naming words. A **singular noun** names one person, place, thing, or idea. A **plural noun** names more than one person, place, thing, or idea.

SINGULAR: The farmer drove to the market with the box .

PLURAL: The farmers drove to the markets with the boxes .

Rules for Forming Plurals	
1. Most singular nouns: Add *s*.	street – street**s** house – house**s**
2. Nouns ending in *s, x, ch,* or *sh*: Add *es*.	dress – dress**es** ax – ax**es** bench – bench**es** dish – dish**es**
3. Nouns ending with a vowel and *y*: Add *s*.	valley – valley**s** joy – joy**s**
4. Nouns ending with a consonant and *y*: Change the *y* to *i* and add *es*.	city – cit**ies** cranberry – cranberr**ies**

Guided Practice   What is the plural form of each noun?

Example: class   *classes*

1. cherry
2. chore
3. fox
4. monkey
5. letter
6. bird
7. alley
8. boss

9. bush
10. panda
11. porch
12. bunch
13. pocket
14. family
15. holiday
16. ostrich

ONE PEACH . . . . . 25¢

FIVE PEACHES $1.00

> ▶ A **singular noun** names one person, place, thing, or idea.
> ▶ A **plural noun** names more than one person, place, thing, or idea.
> ▶ Form the plural of most nouns by adding *s* or *es*. Look at the ending of a singular noun to decide how to form the plural.

Independent Practice

A. Write the plural forms of these nouns.

Example: hobby *hobbies*

17. glass	**23.** flute	**29.** picture
18. idea	**24.** marsh	**30.** ranch
19. month	**25.** basket	**31.** library
20. wrench	**26.** doctor	**32.** business
21. ocean	**27.** body	**33.** birthday
22. party	**28.** paper	**34.** notebook

B. Write the plural form of each underlined noun.

Example: At dawn the <u>harbor</u> of the <u>city</u> became busy.
harbors cities

35. The ocean <u>liner</u> arrived in the <u>bay</u>.
36. Everyone watched the <u>tugboat</u> tow the big <u>ship</u>.
37. The <u>lobster</u> crawled in the <u>trap</u>.
38. The <u>ferry</u> went back and forth to the <u>island</u>.
39. The crew unloaded the <u>net</u> on the fishing <u>boat</u>.
40. The <u>boss</u> showed the <u>worker</u> where to put the <u>anchor</u>.
41. Fish were packed in the <u>crate</u> and sent to the <u>market</u>.
42. At night the bright <u>flash</u> beamed from the <u>lighthouse</u>.
43. A <u>wave</u> softly lapped the <u>side</u> of the <u>dock</u>.
44. A <u>seagull</u> looked for food on the <u>beach</u>.

Writing Application: A Paragraph

Imagine that you have an exciting job. Write a paragraph about the tasks that you do in your job. Use singular and plural nouns in your sentences. Draw one line under each singular noun and two lines under each plural noun.

For Extra Practice, see p. 103.   **Singular and Plural Nouns 85**

3 | More Plural Nouns

Some nouns do not become plural according to the regular rules. There are, however, patterns that will help you remember how to form the plurals of these nouns. The chart below groups some of these nouns according to their patterns. You can also use your dictionary to find the plural spellings of nouns.

More Rules for Forming Plurals	
1. Nouns ending in *f* or *fe*: Change the *f* to *v* and add *es* to some nouns. Add *s* to other nouns.	life – lives calf – calves leaf – leaves cliff – cliffs
2. Nouns ending with a vowel and o: Add *s*.	rodeo – rodeos radio – radios studio – studios
3. Nouns ending with a consonant and o: Add *s* to some nouns. Add *es* to other nouns.	solo – solos piano – pianos hero – heroes echo – echoes tomato – tomatoes
4. Nouns that have special plural spellings.	foot – feet woman – women
5. Nouns that remain the same in the singular and the plural.	trout – trout deer – deer sheep – sheep

Guided Practice

Guided Practice What is the plural form of each noun? You may use your dictionary to help you.

Example: wolf *wolves*

1. echo
2. cliff
3. radio
4. tooth
5. half
6. hero
7. deer
8. wife
9. giraffe

> ▸ To form the plural of some nouns ending in *f* or *fe,* change the *f* to *v* and add *es.* For others, simply add *s.*
> ▸ To form the plural of nouns ending in *o,* add *s* or *es.*
> ▸ Some nouns have special plural forms.
> ▸ Some nouns have the same singular and plural forms.

Independent Practice

A. Write the plural form of each noun. Use your dictionary to check your spelling.

Example: scarf *scarves*

10. moose	**15.** man	**20.** auto
11. rodeo	**16.** roof	**21.** mouse
12. sheep	**17.** tooth	**22.** child
13. belief	**18.** soprano	**23.** studio
14. potato	**19.** thief	**24.** cuff

B. Write the plural form of each noun in parentheses to complete each sentence correctly. You may use your dictionary.

Example: I took two ____ from the oven. (loaf) *loaves*

25. I used two different ____ to cut the bread.   (knife)
26. Jill cut a few ____ for the salad.   (tomato)
27. I scrubbed the ____ with a stiff brush.   (potato)
28. My sisters caught two ____ in the lake.   (trout)
29. I will rake the ____ until dinner.   (leaf)
30. The ____ are repairing the wooden fence.   (woman)
31. The ____ of the house and shed must be fixed.   (roof)
32. The ____ will fix them tomorrow.   (man)
33. The tools are on those ____.   (shelf)
34. The ____ are playing in the yard.   (child)
35. They will soon feed the noisy ____.   (goose)
36. Some ____ hid in the corner of the barn.   (mouse)

Writing Application: A Story
Write about an adventure on a ranch or a farm. Use the plural forms of at least five nouns from the chart.

For Extra Practice, see p. 104.   **More Plural Nouns**

4 | Common and Proper Nouns

When you talk or write about persons, places, or things in general, you use a **common noun**.

Scientists work hard. They come from many countries .

When you talk or write about a particular person, place, or thing, you use a **proper noun**.

Marie Curie was a scientist. She came from Poland .

Study the chart below. Notice that every proper noun begins with a capital letter. When a proper noun is made up of more than one word, only the important words in the noun begin with a capital letter. Do not capitalize words such as *the, of,* or *for.*

Common and Proper Nouns

Common nouns	Proper nouns	Common nouns	Proper nouns
street	North Drive	river	Hudson River
city	Vancouver	building	White House
state	Maryland	law	Bill of Rights
continent	Asia	author	Emily Dickinson
ocean	Arctic Ocean	holiday	Fourth of July
mountain	Mt. McKinley	month	November
lake	Great Salt Lake	day	Monday

Guided Practice Which words are proper nouns and should be capitalized? Which words are common nouns?

Example: europe *proper (cap.): Europe*

1. august
2. creek
3. book
4. face
5. italy
6. student
7. san diego
8. game
9. north carolina
10. john adams
11. gulf of mexico
12. program
13. francis scott key
14. calendar
15. sears tower

▶ A **common noun** names any person, place, or thing.

▶ A **proper noun** names a particular person, place, or thing.

▶ Begin each important word in a proper noun with a capital letter.

Independent Practice

A. Write each pair of nouns. Capitalize the proper nouns.

Example: stanley – brother   *Stanley   brother*

16. united states – country
17. president – thomas jefferson
18. statue of liberty – monument
19. author – louisa may alcott
20. avenue of the americas – avenue
21. building – empire state building

B. List the common nouns and the proper nouns in each of the following sentences.

Example: Naomi read about some important women.
            common: *women*   ***proper:*** *Naomi*

22. Maria Tallchief is a famous ballerina.
23. This dancer has performed in New York and Paris.
24. Tallchief has received the Indian Achievement Award.
25. Marian Anderson is best known for singing opera.
26. Anderson was the first black singer to perform with the Metropolitan Opera.
27. This singer received honors from several countries.
28. Amelia Earhart flew across the Atlantic Ocean.
29. This pilot was the first woman to cross that ocean alone.
30. Her last flight was over the Pacific Ocean.

Writing Application: A Paragraph

Write a paragraph about a person who travels. This person may be someone you know or someone you have never met. Use common nouns and proper nouns in your paragraph. Be sure that you have capitalized proper nouns correctly.

For Extra Practice, see p. 105.   **Common and Proper Nouns**

5 | Singular Possessive Nouns

You have learned that a singular noun names one person, place, or thing. A **singular possessive noun** shows that one person, place, or thing has or owns something. To make a singular noun show possession, add an apostrophe and *s* (**'s**).

the fur of the dog   the dog's fur

the collar that the pet has   the pet's collar

Using possessive nouns is shorter and better than other ways of showing possession.

LONGER: The dog belonging to Joel is barking.

BETTER: Joel's dog is barking.

Singular noun	Singular possessive noun
child	child's toy
Tess	Tess's bike
pony	pony's tail
fish	fish's fins

Guided Practice Each phrase can be changed to show possession in a shorter way. What is the possessive form of each underlined singular noun?

Example: the paw of the <u>lion</u>
          the _____ paw   *lion's*

1. the tail of the <u>fox</u>
   the _____ tail

2. the pet that the <u>child</u> has
   the _____ pet

3. the name of the <u>poodle</u>
   the _____ name

4. the dog that <u>Alex</u> has
   _____ dog

5. the hat of my <u>sister</u>
   my _____ hat

6. the book that <u>Lee</u> owns
   _____ book

▶ A **singular possessive noun** shows that one person, place, or thing has or owns something.

▶ Form a singular possessive noun by adding an apostrophe and *s* (**'s**) to the singular noun.

Independent Practice

A. Write each phrase to show possession.

Example: hamster___ nest   *hamster's nest*

7. Alice___ job   **10.** hen___ chicks
8. fox___ teeth   **11.** Toby___ shoes
9. friend___ rabbit   **12.** Liz___ prize

B. Rewrite each sentence. Change the underlined words to include a singular possessive noun.

Example: I visited the pet store that belongs to Bess.
            I visited Bess's pet store.

13. The gerbil that Jason has came from this store.
14. Have you ever heard the hiss of a snake?
15. The tail of a puppy swished back and forth.
16. The nose that a bulldog has is short and wrinkled.
17. One cat looked just like the cat belonging to Mia.
18. The teeth that a rabbit has are sharp and pointed.
19. The feathers of the parakeet are bright blue.
20. I jumped at the cry of the parrot.
21. The tail of the white mouse is very long.
22. The food for the fish floated on the water.
23. Bart is the name of my goldfish.
24. The cage that the hamster lives in has a water bottle.

Writing Application: Comparison and Contrast
Pretend that you are an animal in a pet store. Write a paragraph comparing two animals you see. Use at least three singular possessive nouns.

For Extra Practice, see p. 106.

6 | Plural Possessive Nouns

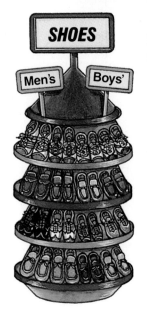

You have learned that a plural noun names more than one person, place, or thing. A plural noun that shows ownership, or possession, is called a **plural possessive noun**.

The cars that belong to the teachers are parked here.

The teachers' cars are parked here.

When a plural noun ends in *s*, add only an apostrophe after the *s* to make the noun show possession.

boys' books   wolves' pups   babies' mothers

Not all plural nouns end in *s*. When a plural noun does not end in *s*, add *'s* to form the plural possessive noun.

the shoes of the men	the men's shoes
the food of the mice	the mice's food
the scales of the trout	the trout's scales

Singular	Singular possessive	Plural	Plural possessive
girl	girl's	girls	girls'
calf	calf's	calves	calves'
pony	pony's	ponies	ponies'
child	child's	children	children's
mouse	mouse's	mice	mice's
deer	deer's	deer	deer's

Guided Practice How would you change each phrase to show possession?

Example: brothers__ cars   *brothers' cars*

1. swimmers__ medals
2. runners__ speeds
3. musicians__ skills
4. women__ sports
5. carpenters__ nails
6. sailors__ uniforms

> ▸ A **plural possessive noun** shows that more than one person, place, or thing has or owns something.
> ▸ If a plural noun ends in *s*, add only an apostrophe to form the plural possessive. If a plural noun does not end in *s*, add *'s* to form the plural possessive.

Independent Practice

A. Write each phrase to show possession.

Example: catchers__ mitts   *catchers' mitts*

7. teachers__ pens
8. cooks__ aprons
9. men__ boots
10. countries__ flags
11. joggers__ sneakers
12. neighbors__ yards
13. guests__ coats

B. Rewrite each sentence. Change the underlined words to include a plural possessive noun.

Example: <u>The players on the teams</u> practiced after school.
The teams' players practiced after school.

14. Each day <u>the scores of the groups</u> improved.
15. There was <u>a team of boys</u> and <u>a team of girls</u>.
16. The kneepads <u>that the players wore</u> were new.
17. Numbers were sewn on <u>the shirts of the athletes</u>.
18. <u>Points made by the teammates</u> were put on the scoreboard.
19. The players enjoyed <u>the cheers of their friends</u>.
20. <u>The whistles of the coaches</u> stopped the game.
21. <u>The helmets belonging to the children</u> were in the gym.
22. <u>The calls of the umpires</u> helped the games run smoothly.

Writing Application: A Description

Write a paragraph about a championship game. Use at least three plural possessive nouns.

For Extra Practice, see p. 107.   **Plural Possessive Nouns   93**

Grammar-Writing Connection

Telling More About Nouns

One way to add interesting or important details to a sentence is to tell more about the nouns. The first sentence below tells only one thing about the subject. The second sentence adds words that tell more.

> Henry Ford was born in 1863.
> Henry Ford, a pioneer in making cars, was born in 1863.

You can also combine sentences to tell more about the nouns. In the combined sentence, notice how commas set off the words that tell more.

Ford made his first car in 1896. It was a "horseless carriage." > Ford made his first car, a "horseless carriage," in 1896.

Revising Sentences

Rewrite each group of sentences as a single sentence. Use commas to set off words that tell more about the nouns.

1. The famous Model T appeared in 1908. It was the first car produced on an assembly line.
2. The Model T brought in very large profits. The Model T was Ford's most famous car.
3. Henry Ford's goal was the production of good, cheap cars. This goal was reached by 1932.
4. His other aims were shorter hours and higher wages for workers in his company. These aims were also achieved.
5. Henry Ford bought many small companies. He was a very smart businessman.
6. Ford also established Greenfield Village. Greenfield Village was a group of American historical buildings and landmarks.
7. Edsel was Henry's only son. He became president of the company.
8. Edsel introduced the Ford Model A. The Ford Model A was a more expensive and fancier car than the Model T.

Creative Writing

Except for his strange costume, the boy in this painting could be a modern-day boy. He could even be a student in your class! However, the real-life boy that Judith Leyster painted lived over 350 years ago. Like many old portraits, this one shows that clothing may have changed over time, but people's faces have not.

- Does this portrait seem stiff and posed? Why or why not?
- What details make the painting seem real?

A Boy Playing a Flute, Judith Leyster, National Museum, Stockholm

Activities

1. **Write the song.** The boy is playing a happy tune on his flute. It could be a song he has heard or a song he is making up. Write the words for the tune.
2. **Write a journal entry.** What is the boy thinking? Is he wishing he were somewhere else—like outside playing? Write down his thoughts as a journal entry.
3. **Describe the boy's visit.** Imagine that this boy steps out of the picture and visits you for a day. Where would you take him? What would he think of modern inventions, such as cars and television? What would people think of him and his clothing? Write a letter to a friend describing the boy's imaginary visit.

What Is a Noun? *(p. 82)* Write each noun in these sentences.

1. Ann visited London in July.
2. London is the capital of England.
3. London was once a small village.
4. This city is now very large.
5. A trip to London is great fun.
6. Go during the summer.
7. Many buses have two decks.
8. The police are called bobbies.
9. People rest in the afternoon.
10. Refreshments are often served.
11. Go to Buckingham Palace to see the royal family.
12. See if the royal flag is flying.
13. That means the Queen is at home.
14. Look for the Prince of Wales.
15. Watch the guards.
16. Sit by the Thames River.
17. This river flows through the city.
18. Look for London Bridge.
19. The Tower of London was a prison.
20. Now a museum is in the tower.
21. Go and see the beautiful jewels.
22. Try to visit Kew Gardens.
23. The plants are unusual.
24. The buildings and lawns are lovely.
25. The British Museum has treasures.
26. Ann saw many ancient objects.
27. London has many historical sights.
28. Its shops are also interesting.
29. A map of the city is helpful.
30. Look through this book of colorful pictures.

Singular and Plural Nouns *(p. 84)* Write the plural form of each underlined noun.

31. Wendell rode the small gray don-key down the trail.
32. He took the path into the forest.
33. The bridge crossed the stream.
34. The moss covered the rock.
35. Soon the boy reached the valley.
36. He knew the mystery of the place.
37. The magical butterfly lives there.
38. Wendell sat quietly on the bench.
39. The small basket held his lunch.
40. The bread and cheese tasted good.
41. His hungry donkey ate the apple.
42. Then Wendell made the wish.
43. The butterfly flew onto his hand.

More Plural Nouns *(p. 86)* Write the plural of each underlined noun.

44. Megan performed at the rodeo.
45. She roped the calf in record time.
46. It was the happiest day of her life.
47. She wore a bright blue scarf.
48. There were stripes on her cuff.
49. Later a man rode the wild horses.
50. He became the hero of the day.
51. Did you listen to the radio?
52. The studio had sent reporters.
53. They sat in the row under the roof.
54. A happy child was loudly singing.
55. I liked the sound of his solo.
56. I still hear the echo in my ears.

Common and Proper Nouns

(p. 88) Write a list of all the common nouns. Then list all the proper nouns. List each noun only once.

57. Benjamin Franklin led a useful life.
58. His family lived in Boston.
59. His parents had seventeen children.
60. Ben could read many languages.
61. His education came from books.
62. Ben worked as a printer for his older brother.
63. Later Ben moved to Philadelphia.
64. Deborah Read became his wife.
65. Ben started a newspaper that was called *The Pennsylvania Gazette*.
66. Ben wrote and published *Poor Richard's Almanac*.
67. Science interested Ben.
68. Ben performed many experiments and also invented a stove.
69. His stove worked better than a fireplace.
70. Ben Franklin started many important services.
71. Ben organized a library that lent books to people.
72. A hospital for the poor was built.
73. A fire department was set up.
74. Ben started a school that became the University of Pennsylvania.
75. Ben was appointed the postmaster of Philadelphia.
76. Later Franklin became a statesman and lived in England and France.
77. People in America and Europe admired this man.
78. Benjamin Franklin is remembered for his many achievements.

Singular Possessive Nouns *(p. 90)*

Rewrite each phrase, using a singular possessive noun.

79. the hat of the ringmaster
80. the pranks of the monkey
81. the roar of the lion
82. the costume of the acrobat
83. the trunk of the elephant
84. the stunts of the clown
85. the bicycle of Carlos
86. the tricks of the dog
87. the dance of the bear
88. the trainer of the horse
89. the excitement of a child
90. the stripes of the tiger
91. the skill of the juggler
92. the cheers of the crowd

Plural Possessive Nouns *(p. 92)*

Rewrite each phrase, using a plural possessive noun.

93. the hoses of the gardeners
94. the tunes of the musicians
95. the laughter of my friends
96. the joy of the dancers
97. the jackets of my cousins
98. the songs of the birds
99. the umbrellas of the uncles
100. the gloves of the aunts
101. the scarves of the women
102. the talents of the singers
103. the bonnets of the babies
104. the smiles of the parents
105. the feathers of the geese
106. the balloons of the children
107. the notebooks of the students
108. the flowers of the girls

Cumulative Review

Unit 1: The Sentence

What Is a Sentence? *(p. 14)* Write whether each of the following groups of words is a *sentence* or a *fragment.*

1. The Gulf Stream has warm water.
2. The clear, bright blue stream.
3. Boats travel fast in this water.
4. Flows northeast in the Atlantic.
5. Many kinds of fish are found in this stream.

Four Kinds of Sentences *(p. 16)* Copy each sentence and add correct end punctuation. Then write *declarative, interrogative, imperative,* or *exclamatory.*

6. These caves are interesting
7. Have you seen them
8. Bring a good flashlight
9. How strange the rocks are
10. Be careful down there

Complete Subjects and Complete Predicates *(p. 18)* Write each sentence. Draw a line between the complete subject and the complete predicate.

11. Beautiful Kenya is in East Africa.
12. Wild animals roam the plains.
13. Eight national parks protect them.
14. Many travelers visit the parks.
15. A camera trip can be great fun.

Simple Subjects and Simple Predicates *(p. 20)* Write each sentence. Underline simple subjects once and simple predicates twice.

16. The small dog ran rapidly.
17. A big, black cow watched the dog.
18. The owner of the dog appeared.
19. He ran into the pasture.
20. The frisky dog rushed to him.

Subjects in Imperative Sentences *(p. 24)* For each sentence, write *declarative* or *imperative.* Then write the simple subject of the sentence.

21. We would enjoy going on a harbor boat trip.
22. Please buy two tickets for me.
23. Don't forget your lunch.
24. Sometimes the harbor is windy.
25. Bring a warm sweater.

Conjunctions *(p. 26)* Choose the conjunction in parentheses that better fits each sentence.

26. Wild hamsters are found in Central (and, but) Northern Asia.
27. Some hamsters are pets, (but, or) most live in the wilderness.
28. Bea (and, but) Eva have a hamster.
29. The hamster rests all day (and, or) stays up all night.
30. Bea is bothered by the noise, (but, or) Eva sleeps through it.

Combining Sentences *(pp. 28, 30, 32)* Combine each group of sentences by forming a compound subject, a compound predicate, or a compound sentence. Use the conjunction shown. Write each of the sentences.

31. My sister planned a party.   (and)
My sister invited her friends.
32. Grace chose the games.   (but)
Burt bought the prizes.
33. Joe could not come.   (and)
Sandy could not come.
Lisa could not come.
34. Mother prepared the salad.   (and)
Grace prepared the salad.
35. The guests made puppets.   (or)
The guests listened to music.
The guests played volleyball.
36. Friends were invited.   (but)
Neighbors stopped by.

Run-on Sentences *(p. 34)* Write each of the following run-on sentences correctly.

37. Ms. Trill worked in her garden she weeded the flowers.
38. She had waited too long the garden was overgrown.
39. Ms. Trill finished her work the garden looked very nice she was proud of it.
40. Some tomatoes were ripe she chose them for dinner they would taste delicious.
41. Ms. Trill picked roses she put them in a vase they smelled lovely.

Unit 3: Nouns

Common and Proper Nouns *(pp. 82, 88)* Write the common nouns in a list. Then list all the proper nouns. List each noun only once.

42. Wanda Landowska played piano.
43. Wanda was born in Warsaw.
44. This performer soon left Poland.
45. Paris was her new city.
46. Landowska started a school.
47. Landowska composed music.
48. This composer also wrote books.

Plural Nouns *(pp. 84, 86)* Write the plural of each underlined noun.

49. We rode away from the city.
50. I heard the piano on the radio.
51. We saw the deer and the goose.
52. I carried our lunch in a box.
53. Jill cut the loaf in half.
54. We ate the trout and the tomato.
55. We traveled toward the valley.
56. The roof of a house appeared.

Possessive Nouns *(pp. 90, 92)* Rewrite each phrase, using a possessive noun.

57. the speeches of the mayors
58. the question of the lawyer
59. the answer of the witness
60. the thoughts of the officers
61. the comments of the boys
62. the decision of the judge
63. the opinions of the players
64. the story of the reporter

Enrichment

Using Nouns

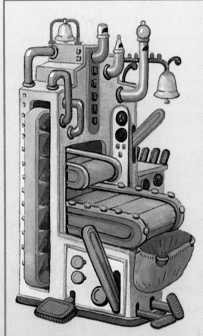

Inventive Interviews

A famous scientist, Mrs. Ursala Becker, has just invented a new gadget called a *gamfel*. Pretend that you are interviewing her for the school newspaper. Write your questions and Mrs. Becker's imaginary answers. Find out details about the *gamfel*. What exactly does this new noun mean? Ask about Mrs. Becker's other inventions. Make up new nouns for each one. Use complete sentences for all interview questions and answers. Underline each noun.

Seeing What's There

Scientists use their powers of observation to examine and compare the sizes, the shapes, the colors, and the textures of things. Be scientific. Compare two objects in your class. Use at least two different possessive nouns in your comparison of these objects. Underline each possessive noun.

On top of my desk is a stack of books. Mrs. Miller's desk top also holds a stack of books. Both of our desks are rectangular. However, my desk is smaller than my teacher's.

◳ Classifying Nouns

Players—2. **You need**—paper and a three-minute timer. **How to play**—Pick a scientific topic, such as the sky, the sea, or the planets. Start the timer. Write down as many nouns as you can think of that have to do with your topic.

SEA—jellyfish, octopus, seaweed, and oyster

Scoring—1 point for each correct noun. The player with the most points wins the game.

F O O D   F I T N E S S

Pretend that you are asked to explain the rules of good nutrition to a younger student. You decide to make a booklet about the four food groups. First, staple together four sheets of paper. Next, label each page with one of the four food groups, such as fruits and vegetables. Then list examples of each group. Use plural nouns, such as *tomatoes*. Find pictures from old magazines to illustrate some of your examples.

A Grocery List

Use the newspaper to make a grocery list. Cut out the names and prices of at least five products. These products should include possessive nouns in their names, such as *Johnson's Tomato Sauce—5 / $1.00*. Paste the names and prices to make a list. Add up the prices to show your total grocery bill.

Extra Practice: Unit 3

1 | What Is a Noun? (p. 82)

● Each sentence contains two nouns. One noun is underlined. Write the other noun.

Example: Christopher Columbus was born in Italy.
Christopher Columbus

1. His father was a weaver.
2. Columbus decided to be a sailor.
3. His ships came from the Spanish queen.
4. This explorer traveled to the New World.
5. Central America and South America were reached.
6. A short route to the Far East was never found.

▲ Write each noun in these sentences.

Example: Columbus discovered the island of Puerto Rico.
Columbus   island   Puerto Rico

7. Another explorer set up a Spanish colony.
8. The people planted sugar.
9. This crop is still grown on many farms.
10. Furniture and textiles are other important products.
11. Puerto Ricans are now citizens of the United States.
12. Freedom from Spain came after a war.

■ Make four columns labeled *Person, Place, Thing,* and *Idea.* Write each noun in the correct column.

Example: Pat traveled by jet to Jamaica.

Person	Place	Thing	Idea
Pat	*Jamaica*	*jet*	

13. Her pen pal lived on that island.
14. Their friendship had grown through their letters.
15. The two friends met at the airport.
16. Ana was wearing a blue hat and a green dress.
17. Ana showed Pat many beautiful cities and beaches.
18. The girls climbed Blue Mountain.

2 | Singular and Plural Nouns (p. 84)

● Write the plural form of each noun.

Example: horse *horses*

1. storm	**8.** dress	**15.** picture
2. book	**9.** tray	**16.** donkey
3. folder	**10.** jelly	**17.** patch
4. tax	**11.** window	**18.** calendar
5. lunch	**12.** grass	**19.** strawberry
6. paper	**13.** branch	**20.** winner
7. wish	**14.** clown	**21.** baseball

▲ Write the plural form of each underlined noun.

Example: Nantucket is an island far out at sea.
          islands   seas

22. I live there with my family in the summer.
23. We drive our car onto a ferry.
24. The bay has calm water.
25. The beach is five miles from the town.
26. Sometimes I ride my pony to the ocean.
27. I take a sandwich, juice, and a bag of crackers.
28. I sit on a bench and gaze at the sea's beauty.
29. I once saw a play at the outdoor theater.
30. It was about a boy and a hawk in a faraway country.

■ Copy each underlined noun. If it is singular, write the plural
form. If it is plural, write the singular form.

Example: The museum guide showed me old boxes.
          guide   guides   boxes   box

31. The ivory piece in a box came from a whale.
32. Oil and wax also come from the body of a whale.
33. I saw an interesting dish at the exhibit.
34. A sailor had made it at sea.
35. He had used shells and branches.
36. He had written a message with paint from berries.
37. The dish was a gift for his sons.
38. The message told of his love for his family.

3 | More Plural Nouns (p. 86)

● Write the plural form of each of these singular nouns.

Example: cliff   *cliffs*

1. piano	**8.** stereo	**15.** solo
2. elk	**9.** wife	**16.** fowl
3. man	**10.** moose	**17.** radio
4. trout	**11.** roof	**18.** deer
5. safe	**12.** tomato	**19.** child
6. auto	**13.** tooth	**20.** hero
7. thief	**14.** shelf	**21.** leaf

▲ Look at each underlined plural noun. If the noun is spelled correctly, write *correct*. If it is not correct, write it correctly.

Example: We picked <u>tomatos</u> and corn.   *tomatoes*

22. We fed bread crumbs to the <u>geese</u>.

23. We also fed the chickens and the <u>calfs</u>.

24. The <u>cuffs</u> of my pants were filled with straw.

25. We caught five large <u>trouts</u> for dinner.

26. My uncle made three <u>loafs</u> of brown bread.

27. His two <u>childrens</u> helped him.

28. My sister and I made <u>shelfs</u> for the kitchen.

29. The boards were five <u>feet</u> long.

30. Men and <u>woman</u> work hard on farms.

■ Write an answer. Use the plural of a noun in the box.

Example: How do we usually buy bread?   *loaves*

31. Where do banks keep money?

32. What do people use for chewing food?

33. Where could you put books?

34. What vegetables can you eat baked or boiled?

35. What do we call brave people?

36. What sounds might you hear in a cave?

37. What are red and juicy and good in salads?

38. What do we wear around our necks?

39. What parts of houses can you see from a plane?

40. What musical instruments have keys?

hero
scarf
echo
roof
piano
loaf
tomato
shelf
safe
potato
tooth

4 | Common and Proper Nouns (p. 88)

● Write each pair of nouns. Capitalize the proper nouns.

Example: author – mark twain   *author – Mark Twain*

1. columbus day – holiday
2. state – west virginia
3. spain – country
4. robert redford – actor
5. war – battle of bunker hill
6. colorado river – river
7. day – saturday
8. john hancock building – building
9. month – november

▲ Make two columns labeled *Proper* and *Common*. Find each noun, and list it in the correct column.

Example: Joan of Arc was a French woman.

Proper	*Common*
Joan of Arc	*woman*

10. This heroine helped French soldiers defeat England.
11. Betsy Ross lived in Philadelphia.
12. George Washington met this excellent seamstress.
13. Washington talked about the Declaration of Independence.
14. The general asked Ross to make the first flag.
15. Mary Hays became famous in the Revolutionary War.
16. Hays carried water at the Battle of Monmouth.
17. Her name became Molly Pitcher.

■ Write each noun, capitalizing proper nouns correctly. Label each noun *common* or *proper*. Then write a proper noun for each common noun and a common noun for each proper noun.

Example: country   *country* **common**   *Norway*

18. pacific ocean
19. movie star
20. king george
21. city
22. bill cosby
23. utah
24. book
25. july
26. car
27. singer
28. missouri river
29. holiday
30. gwendolyn brooks
31. mountain
32. fernwood drive

5 | Singular Possessive Nouns (p. 90)

● Write each phrase to show possession.

Example: the woman— coat   *the woman's coat*

1. the cat— tail
2. the puppet— hand
3. a baby— smile
4. Trish— plan
5. Ernesto— pen
6. the doctor— bag
7. Magda— book

8. the giraffe— neck
9. my aunt— apartment
10. Mr. Swartz— shoes
11. a child— bicycle
12. Tomas— idea
13. the prince— name
14. Umeko— calendar

▲ Rewrite each phrase. Use a singular possessive noun.

Example: the costume that Celie wore   *Celie's costume*

15. the newspaper of the lawyer
16. the car belonging to my grandfather
17. the camera of that photographer
18. the notebook that Alfie has
19. the guitar of Carlotta
20. the lawn mower that my brother owns
21. the typewriter that Gregory has
22. the magazine that belongs to Roberta
23. the office of the dentist
24. the journal of the student

■ Rewrite each sentence, using a singular possessive noun.

Example: The cat that belongs to my sister is yellow.
          My sister's cat is yellow.

25. The father of Russ is a great golfer.
26. The house that my uncle lives in is gray.
27. The legs of that moose are long.
28. The song that Jill wrote was funny.
29. Did you find the book that belongs to Amy?
30. Have you seen the scarf that Jade owns?
31. The pictures that Shani made are beautiful.
32. The jacket that Josie has is bright green.
33. The desk of Nita is always piled with papers.
34. The sewing machine that belongs to my cousin is excellent.

6 | Plural Possessive Nouns (p. 92)

● Write each phrase to show possession.

Example: the children__ pencils   *the children's pencils*

1. the dancers__ legs
2. the goats__ pens
3. the boys__ sneakers
4. the men__ meeting
5. the robins__ nest
6. the turtles__ bowl
7. the horses__ tails
8. the Solanos__ porch

9. the officers__ badges
10. the women__ cars
11. the dentists__ bills
12. the Clarks__ garage
13. the sheep__ pasture
14. the musicians__ drums
15. the actors__ roles
16. the geese__ nests

▲ Rewrite each phrase, using a plural possessive noun.

Example: the rugs that the weavers made   *the weavers' rugs*

17. the flowers that my aunts grow
18. the house of the Rileys
19. the suitcases that belong to the women
20. the raincoats of the children
21. the boots that the climbers wear
22. the coins that belong to the collectors
23. the playroom that my cousins have
24. the excellence of the players
25. the reports of the planners

■ Write a sentence for each noun, using the form shown.

Example: artist   (plural possessive)
         Have you seen the sketches in the artists' notebooks?

26. writer   (singular possessive)
27. Samuelson   (plural possessive)
28. Gus   (singular possessive)
29. speaker   (singular possessive)
30. woman   (plural possessive)
31. voter   (singular possessive)
32. Garcia   (plural possessive)
33. secretary   (plural possessive)
34. Thea   (singular possessive)

Literature and Writing

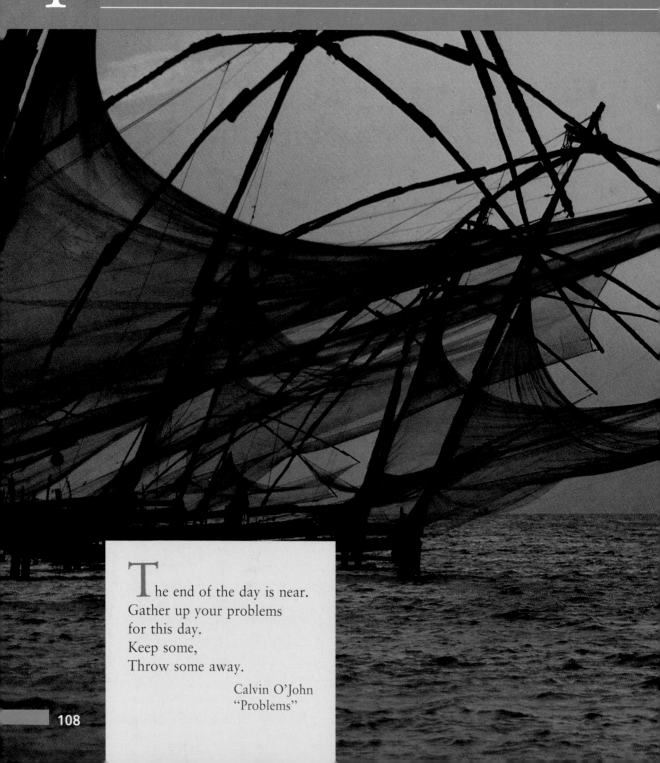

The end of the day is near.
Gather up your problems
for this day.
Keep some,
Throw some away.

Calvin O'John
"Problems"

Instructions

Getting Ready Suppose you want to put together a new model sailboat. Can you understand the instructions on the box? Can you explain clearly to someone else how to put the model together? Perhaps you know the way to a pond where you can sail your ship. Can you give clear directions to a friend who wants to meet you there? Giving and following instructions are like two sides of a coin. We use both sides! In this unit, you will read some instructions and write some of your own.

ACTIVITIES

Listening

Listen as the poem on the facing page is read. You have just been given some instructions. Did you listen carefully enough to remember what you were told to do? State the instructions in your own words.

Speaking

Look at the picture. Why is the end of the day a good time to "gather up your problems"? What advice would you add for the end of the day?

Writing

What advice would you give yourself? Write a set of instructions to yourself in your journal.

Have you ever been surprised by the price of something that you wanted to buy? How did Rufus react when he saw the price of toothpaste?

The Toothpaste Millionaire

By Jean Merrill

Rufus Mayflower did not start out to make a million dollars. He just wanted to make an inexpensive toothpaste. Rufus was twelve years old at the time. His friend Kate Mackinstrey tells the story in the book *The Toothpaste Millionaire*. Here is how it all began.

I remember the morning Rufus got the idea for toothpaste. He had to do some shopping for his mother, and I went along with him. We were in the Cut-Rate Drugstore, because toothpaste was one of the things on Rufus's list.

I was looking at some name-brand eye shadow that was on sale, when I heard Rufus say, "79¢! 79¢ for a six-inch tube of toothpaste. That's crazy!"

"It's better than 89¢," I said. I pointed to some 89¢ tubes farther down the shelf.

"That's even crazier," Rufus said. "What can be in those tubes anyway? Just some peppermint flavoring and some paste."

"Maybe the paste is expensive to make," I said.

"Paste!" Rufus said. "You don't need powdered gold to make paste. Paste is made out of everyday ordinary stuff. Didn't you ever make paste?"

"Toothpaste?" I said.

"I mean just plain paste for pasting things together," Rufus said. "My Grandma Mayflower showed me how to make paste when I was four years old."

"How do you do it?" I asked.

"Simple," Rufus said. "You just take a little flour and starch and cook them with a little water till the mixture has a nice pasty feel. Then you can use it to paste pictures in a scrapbook. Or paste up wallpaper."

"But you couldn't brush your teeth with *that*," I said.

"Well, I don't know," Rufus said. "I never tried. But I bet toothpaste isn't any harder to make. Anyway, I'm not paying any 79¢ for a tube of toothpaste."

Rufus crossed toothpaste off his mother's shopping list.

"But your mother said to get toothpaste," I said. "You can't help it if it's expensive."

"I'll make her some," Rufus said. "I bet I can make a gallon of it for 79¢."

Well, that's how Rufus's toothpaste business started. With Rufus figuring out that if he sold the toothpaste for only a penny more than it cost him to make—it cost him about 2¢ a tube—that he'd soon have millions of customers.

He had to start in a small way, of course. When he started his business, Rufus packed the toothpaste in baby food jars. A baby food jar holds about as much as a big tube, and the jars didn't cost him anything.

People with babies were glad to save jars for Rufus, as nobody had thought of a way of instantly recycling baby food jars before. When Rufus put a sign on the bulletin board at

school saying he could use the jars, kids brought us hundreds of them.

We sterilized and filled the jars. When we had about five hundred jars, Rufus and I stuffed our saddlebags with as many as they would hold and rode our bikes around the neighborhood selling the toothpaste.

We sold quite a few jars. At only 3¢ a jar, most people felt they could afford to give it a try, and most of the customers said it was good toothpaste.

Still, I could not see how Rufus was going to get rich on 3¢ toothpaste unless millions of people knew about it. Then I had this idea about how he could get some free advertising.

Everybody in Cleveland watches a program called "The Joe Smiley Show." On the show, Joe interviews people who have interesting hobbies.

I wrote Joe Smiley a letter telling him I had this friend who had a hobby of making toothpaste and could make about two years' supply for the price of one tube. And Joe Smiley called up Rufus to ask if he would be on the show.

Rufus was very good on the show, though I was afraid that he never would get around to talking about the toothpaste. I was worried because when Joe Smiley asked Rufus how he had learned to make toothpaste, Rufus started telling about his Grandmother Mayflower.

He not only told about the scrapbook paste, but about how his Grandma Mayflower had made her own furnace out of two 100-gallon oil barrels. Joe Smiley was so interested in that furnace that it was hard to get him off the subject of Rufus's grandmother.

Rufus told about his grandmother taming raccoons, woodchucks, mice, chipmunks, and catbirds. And, of course, about her brushing her teeth with plain baking soda. You wouldn't think all that stuff about Rufus's grandmother would sell toothpaste. But then, as my father pointed out, you wouldn't

112

think Rufus's way of advertising the toothpaste would sell toothpaste, either.

Joe Smiley is the kind of guy who is always saying things are the "greatest" thing he ever heard of. Or the most "fantastic." What I mean is, he exaggerates. And everybody Joe has on his show is one of the greatest people he ever met or has done the most fantastic thing.

So when Joe does get to Rufus's toothpaste, he naturally gives it this big build-up. Which is what I was counting on. And what does Rufus do?

The conversation went something like this:

JOE: Now, Rufus, this fantastic toothpaste you make—I suppose it has a special, secret formula.

RUFUS: No. It's made out of stuff anybody can buy for a few cents and mix up at home in a few minutes.

JOE: Fantastic! And, of course, it's much better than the kind you buy at the store.

RUFUS: I don't know about that. But it tastes pretty good. And for about 2¢ you can make as much as you get in a 79¢ tube.

JOE: Fantastic! And where can people get some of this great toothpaste?

RUFUS: If they live in East Cleveland, I'll deliver it to them on my bike. Three ounces costs 3¢—it costs me 2¢ to make and I make 1¢ profit. If anyone outside East Cleveland wants some, I'll have to charge 3¢ plus postage.

JOE: Fantastic! And what do you call this marvelous new product?

RUFUS: TOOTHPASTE.

JOE: Just toothpaste? It doesn't have a name like SPARKLE or SHINE or SENSATION or WHITE LIGHTNING or PERSONALITY PLUS?

RUFUS: No, it's just plain TOOTHPASTE. It doesn't do anything sensational such as improve your smile or your personality. It just keeps your teeth clean.

Who would have thought that telling people toothpaste wouldn't do one thing for their personality would sell toothpaste?

But three days after Rufus was on "The Joe Smiley Show," he got 689 orders for TOOTHPASTE. One came all the way from Venice, California, from a man who happened to be telephoning his daughter while she was watching the show in Cleveland. The daughter said, "There's a kid here who's selling toothpaste for 3¢ a jar." And her father ordered three dozen jars.

Fantastic!

Think and Discuss

1. Why did Rufus decide to make toothpaste?
2. **Tone** in a written work is very much like tone of voice in speaking. Stories may vary greatly in tone. For example, some stories have a happy tone, some a sad or angry tone. Some stories have an informal tone; others are formal.

   The words that writers choose and the kinds of sentences they write help set the tone of a story. What tone of voice do you hear in these sentences from this story?

   > Joe Smiley is the kind of guy who is always saying things are the "greatest" thing he ever heard of. Or the most "fantastic." What I mean is, he exaggerates.

   Is the tone mysterious? sad? friendly? formal? informal?
3. What makes someone buy a product? List four things that you think would make a new product successful.

114

Have you ever wished for a second chance to do something? What second chance might this reporter want?

Interviewing: Doing Your Homework

By Melvin Mencher

In the locker room, the athlete was putting his warm-up suit and track shoes into a battered black bag. Standing near the door was a nervous young man holding a pencil and notepad.

"I'm from the high school paper," the young man said. "You looked sharp out there. Mind if I ask you some questions?"

The athlete nodded and went on packing.

"Is this the first time you've been to this part of the West?" the reporter asked. There was another nod. This was not going to be easy, the reporter thought. He tried again.

"What do you think of our town?"

The athlete looked at the reporter for the first time.

"I don't know anything about this town," he said. "I'm here to run. They give me a plane ticket at school to go east or west and I go. My business is to run." He stopped talking.

The reporter struggled on, but in the twenty-minute interview, the athlete never really opened up.

Back at the school newspaper office, the reporter told his editor how things had gone.

"I wish you had talked to me before the interview," she said. "If you want to do a good interview, you have

to do some homework. First, learn all you can about the person you are interviewing. Call somebody—like your athlete's coach—who can give you information. Check the newspaper files at the library. While you are getting information, try to guess what your readers would find most interesting. Next, use your information to think of questions that will get the person talking. Try to avoid questions that can be answered 'yes' or 'no.'

"Then when you start the interview, use your questions to help the person feel at ease. People like to talk about themselves if they think you are really interested. While the person is talking, be sure to listen carefully. You might think of some other good questions to ask. Finally, listen for a good quote or two. Some of the most interesting things are said when the interview is officially over."

"Not doing my homework was a big mistake," said the reporter. "Now what can I do?"

"Well, you did get one good quote. Remember what your athlete said about the business of running? You can still write something fairly interesting if you find out where he's been in the last few months. It's too late for another interview with him, but you can try the coach at the college. And you can still get to the library."

Think and Discuss

1. If given a second chance, what might the reporter want to do differently?
2. What was the editor's suggestion for making the person being interviewed feel at ease?
3. **Dialogue** is conversation quoted exactly as it was spoken. It can make the people in a story come alive for you. It can also liven up information that may be dull to read. What is taught in the conversation between the editor and the reporter? Why is this information presented in dialogue?

RESPONDING TO LITERATURE

The Reading and Writing Connection

Personal Response Think of a time when you would have liked a second chance. If you were given a second chance, what would you change? Write about the situation and what you would do differently.

Creative Writing Pretend that you have a television show and you are about to interview anyone you wish. Write a list of questions to ask that person. Then write an interview between you and that person, using your questions.

Creative Activities

Draw Rufus sold his toothpaste in used baby food jars. Design a label for Rufus's toothpaste. Include the name of the product. Use at least two colors in your design.

Read Aloud On page 113, Rufus is interviewed by Joe Smiley for his television show. Choose a partner and decide who will be Joe and who will be Rufus. Then read aloud the interview with your partner. Remember, read only the words that Joe and Rufus actually say.

Vocabulary

According to the author, Joe Smiley tends to exaggerate. The author points out that Joe often uses words like *greatest* and *fantastic*. Find synonyms for *greatest* and *fantastic*.

Looking Ahead

Instructions Later in this unit, you will be writing a paragraph of instructions. Read the first two paragraphs on page 116. What words does the editor use to show the order of steps for preparing an interview?

VOCABULARY CONNECTION

Compound Words

Some words are made up of two or more words that are used as one word. These words are called **compound words**.

> "...**Anyway**, I'm not paying any 79¢ for a tube of **toothpaste**."
>
> *from "The Toothpaste Millionaire" by Jean Merrill*

Anyway and *toothpaste* are compound words made from two words joined together. Compound words can also be written with a hyphen or as separate words. Look at these compound words from "The Toothpaste Millionaire."

One Word	Hyphenated Word	Separate Words
peppermint	six-inch	baking soda

Most of the time you can figure out the meanings of compound words by adding together the meanings of the words from which they are made. Check your dictionary for spellings.

Vocabulary Practice

A. Find the compound word from "The Toothpaste Millionaire" in each sentence. Write the word and the words from which it is made.

1. My grandmother interviews athletes on television.
2. She gives the viewing audience a big build-up of the athlete.
3. One athlete brought a family scrapbook to the show.
4. Everybody she interviews has a good time.

B. Find six compound words from the literature in this unit and use them in sentences of your own.

Prewriting
Instructions

Listening and Speaking: Following and Giving Instructions

Listen as your teacher reads aloud this set of instructions for making and bottling toothpowder.

1. Get some ordinary baking soda, some salt, a tablespoon, a teaspoon, and a small jar with a lid.
2. First, wash the jar and the lid in hot, soapy water and dry them with a clean towel.
3. Then measure six tablespoons of baking soda into the jar.
4. Next, add three teaspoons of salt to the jar.
5. Put the lid on the jar.
6. Finally, shake the jar to mix the soda and salt well.

What would happen if you forgot how much baking soda to use? How would the toothpowder taste if you used twice as much salt as the instructions called for? What would happen if you forgot to dry the jar and the lid?

If you don't follow instructions carefully, you may perform a task improperly, get lost, or give incorrect instructions to someone else.

Here are some guidelines to help you follow instructions.

Guidelines for Following Instructions

1. Listen for the words that tell you exactly what to do or state exact amounts or materials to use.
2. Be sure that you understand each step and the order of the steps.
3. Picture each step as you hear it.
4. Ask questions about anything that is not clear.
5. Take notes if you think you will forget something.

When you give instructions to others, remember that they must be clear. Instructions that are not clear will be difficult or impossible to follow. When you prepare instructions, put yourself in your listeners' or readers' shoes.

The first and most important step in giving instructions is to imagine yourself following the steps. When you are telling someone how to do something, picture yourself doing it. (Better yet, actually perform the task yourself to be sure you don't miss an important step.)

When you are giving directions to a place, imagine yourself making the same trip or actually make it yourself. Think carefully about turns, distances, and landmarks.

Remember these guidelines when you give instructions.

Guidelines for Giving Instructions

1. Tell what you are giving instructions for.
2. State routes or methods, amounts, and materials in exact terms.
3. Give the instructions in order, one step at a time.
4. Use order words such as *first, next, then, when, after,* and *finally.*
5. Explain each step so that your listener will be able to picture it clearly.
6. Be sure to include all the steps the listener will need.

Prewriting Practice

A. Listen as your teacher reads a set of instructions. Repeat what you heard to a partner.
B. Give step-by-step instructions for one of the activities below as a partner tries to follow them.

   1. Make a craft project that you can explain well.
   2. Go to a familiar place by an unusual route.
   3. Play a game that you play often.

Could your partner follow the directions?

Thinking: Observing

One important way in which you learn about your world is by **observing.** Observing is different from just looking. When you observe, you concentrate. You make yourself notice things. You stare, you listen, you touch, you smell, and you taste. You try to remember what you observe.

Read Rufus's instructions for making paste:

"My Grandma Mayflower showed me how to make paste when I was four years old."

"How do you do it?" I asked.

"Simple," Rufus said. "You just take a little flour and starch and cook them with a little water till the mixture has a nice pasty feel. Then you can use it to paste pictures in a scrapbook. Or paste up wallpaper."

from "The Toothpaste Millionaire" by Jean Merrill

• How did Rufus learn to make paste?
• Which senses did Rufus use? How do you know?

When you observe something carefully, you understand it better. When you understand it, you are able to explain it to someone else. Therefore, observing not only helps you learn, but it also helps you write about what you learn.

Guidelines for Observing

1. Decide exactly what you want to observe.
2. Concentrate. Notice the details.
3. Notice how things look, sound, feel, smell, and taste.
4. Follow what people do, step by step.
5. Ask yourself *why* people are doing what they are doing.
6. Ask questions if something is not clear.

Prewriting Practice

Work with a partner. Take notes as you observe each other sharpening a pencil or cleaning a chalkboard. Compare notes.

Composition Skills

Instructions

Main Idea of a Paragraph ☑

A paragraph is made up of sentences that tell about one topic. The sentences discuss one main idea about the topic. If you are writing a paragraph of instructions for flying a kite, for example, each sentence should tell about that idea. Should you start telling about how to make a kite in the same paragraph? No, your reader would be confused.

Read this paragraph. Notice that it is indented. What is the topic? What is the main idea?

People with babies were glad to save jars for Rufus, as nobody had thought of a way of instantly recycling baby food jars before. When Rufus put a sign on the bulletin board at school saying he could use the jars, kids brought us hundreds of them.

from "The Toothpaste Millionaire" by Jean Merrill

The topic is *getting baby food jars*. Which of the following sentences best describes the main idea?

1. People with babies had lots of baby food jars.
2. Rufus had no trouble getting baby food jars.
3. Bulletin boards are a good source of information.

The main idea of this paragraph is how Aunt Laurie started a business. Which sentence does not keep to the main idea?

Aunt Laurie decided to start a fabric mail-order business. First, she purchased a list of names and addresses of people who like to sew. I love to sew. Next, she rented a large room where she could store the fabric and prepare orders. Then she bought the fabric from factories. The last thing she did was to prepare a catalog and send it to the people on her mailing list.

Prewriting Practice

A. Read this paragraph. Then choose the sentence below that best describes the main idea.

"Well, you did get one good quote. Remember what your athlete said about the business of running? You can still write something fairly interesting if you find out where he's been in the last few months. It's too late for another interview with him, but you can try the coach at the college. And you can still get to the library."   *from "Interviewing" by Melvin Mencher*

1. The coach may know enough for a story.
2. It's not too late to get some good information.
3. You didn't do your homework.

B. Write the main idea of this paragraph in your own words. Then write the sentence that does not keep to the main idea.

In the frontier days, people could not always go to the drugstore when they were sick. I have been told that my great-grandmother made cough syrup for the whole family. She chopped an onion and put it in a pan with water. Onions always make me cry. Next, she added some sugar and let the liquid simmer. When it turned into syrup, she let it cool. She gave the syrup to anyone who was unlucky enough to cough!

Topic Sentences and Supporting Details ☑

A paragraph usually has one sentence that clearly states the main idea. This sentence is the **topic sentence**. It often comes first in the paragraph, but it can come anywhere. The other sentences give **supporting details** about the main idea. In the paragraph below, the topic sentence is underlined.

To be a good interviewer, you must develop several important skills. Always put the person you are interviewing at ease. Give the person the feeling that you are enjoying the interview. Be courteous at all times.

Read the paragraph below. Which sentence is the topic sentence? Do all the details support the main idea?

Before you begin an interview, choose a private and comfortable setting. This will help to make the situation less formal and more relaxed. Then, after meeting the person you are to interview, engage the person in a bit of small talk. Chatting allows the person to get rid of nervous energy. Finally, introduce an interview question that is easy to talk about. These are just some of the things you can do to get an interview off to a good start.

Prewriting Practice

A. Read the paragraph below and decide what the main idea is. Write a topic sentence that states the main idea. Then write where in the paragraph you would put your topic sentence.

Lace your skates tightly, but not so tightly that they hurt. Stand on the ice with your arms held out slightly, like the sides of an upside-down V. Then bend your knees and stroke forward with one foot. Now bring your feet together and glide!

B. Work with a partner. Write two topic sentences for each of the ideas listed below. Then underline the topic sentence that you and your partner like best.

1. the day that I forgot my homework
2. the day that had a surprise ending
3. a scary night at home

C. Work with a partner. List at least three supporting details for each topic sentence below.

1. Decide on your biking needs to pick out the right bike.
2. A chalkboard should be washed often.
3. One way to stretch is to touch your toes.
4. Flying a kite can be tricky.

Step-by-Step Order ☑

When you write a paragraph, be sure that your sentences are in an order that makes sense. This is especially important for a paragraph of instructions. What would happen if you were giving instructions for baking bran muffins and did not use the correct order? Filling the muffin tin with batter certainly comes before putting the tin in the oven.

When you write a paragraph of instructions, begin by telling what equipment or materials, if any, are needed. After that, use order words such as *first, then, next,* and *finally* to help make the sequence, or order, clear. Order words are useful, but not every sentence needs one.

Read the following passage. The order words are underlined. Notice how they help make the sequence clear.

> "If you want to do a good interview, you have to do some homework. <u>First</u>, learn all you can about the person you are interviewing. Call somebody—like your athlete's coach—who can give you information. Check the newspaper files at the library. <u>While</u> you are getting information, try to guess what your readers would find most interesting. <u>Next</u>, use your information to think of questions that will get the person talking. Try to avoid questions that can be answered 'yes' or 'no'."
>
> *from "Interviewing" by Melvin Mencher*

Some sentences explain, or tell more about, the steps. In the paragraph below, the underlined sentences explain the steps.

> "Then when you start the interview, use your questions to help the person feel at ease. <u>People like to talk about themselves if they think you are really interested.</u> While the person is talking, be sure to listen carefully. You might think of some other good questions to ask. Finally, listen for a good quote or two. <u>Some of the most interesting things are said when the interview is officially over.</u>"
>
> *from "Interviewing" by Melvin Mencher*

Prewriting Practice

A. Use the following sentences to write a paragraph. The topic sentence is underlined. Some of the other sentences begin with order words. Use the order words as clues to put the sentences into an order that makes sense to you.

- Scrambled eggs make a delicious breakfast.
- Use the fork to beat the eggs.
- Remove the eggs from the pan and turn off the stove.
- You will need a mixing bowl, a fork, a frying pan, and a spatula.
- Then pour the beaten egg mixture into the pan.
- Next, break the eggs into the mixing bowl.
- Use the spatula to scramble the eggs, or mix them up, as they cook.
- First, put some margarine in the pan, and heat the pan.
- You will also need two eggs and margarine.

B. Use the following sentences to write a paragraph. First, put the sentences into an order that makes sense to you. Next, add order words such as *first, then,* or *finally.* Remember that not every sentence has to have an order word. Finally, write a topic sentence for the paragraph.

- Empty half the can of cat food into the bowl.
- Wash the cat's bowl and choose a can of cat food from the cabinet.
- Place the bowl on the floor and call the cat.
- Open the can.

Purpose and Audience ☑

Your **purpose** for writing affects what you say and how you say it. Sometimes your purpose is to explain, sometimes to describe. Sometimes it is to persuade someone to do something or to make someone laugh. You write in different ways, depending on your purpose. What would happen if you wrote directions to your house the same way that you write a funny story?

What you say and how you say it also depend on your **audience**. Which directions would you use to tell a classmate how to go to your school's newspaper office? Which directions would you give to a first-time visitor?

Walk to the end of
this hall and take
the stairway. At the
top of the stairs,
take a left. It's
the fifth door on
the right.

It's next door to
Mr. Garcia's room.
Take the stairway
near the art room.

Prewriting Practice

Work with a partner. Think of a game that your partner does not know. Tell the instructions to your partner. Then together figure out how you would give the instructions to a five-year-old child.

The Grammar Connection

Exact Nouns

Using exact nouns will make your writing clearer and more interesting. Which sentence uses exact nouns?

At the store, a person waited in line to pay another person for some things.

At the drugstore, the customer waited in line to pay the clerk for toothpaste and a toothbrush.

Practice Replace the underlined words with more exact nouns.

1. It was amazing that everyone fit into the car.

2. At one store, my mother looked at some furniture.

3. Then we went to the supermarket to buy vegetables.

4. Later Liz bought some clothes for her camping trip.

5. Fortunately, we arrived home before the storm.

Step 1: Prewriting—Choose a Topic

Bryan listed several things he knew how to do. Then he studied his list to select the one he could explain most clearly.

how to draw an animal

It would be better to show this than to explain it.

how to have fun cleaning your room

He knew a lot about this, and it could be fun.

how to make a valentine

Many people already knew how to do this.

how to use a computer

This was too complicated.

how to make a science project

This would be interesting.

He had a really great idea for writing about cleaning his room.

On Your Own

1. **Think and discuss** Make a list of things that you know how to do. Use the Ideas page to help you. Discuss your ideas with a partner.
2. **Choose** Ask yourself these questions about each topic.
   Which one do I know the most about?
   Which one could I explain most clearly?
   Which one would be the most fun to write and to read?
   Circle the topic that you want to write about.
3. **Explore** What will you write? Do one of the activities under "Exploring Your Topic" on the Ideas page.

Ideas for Getting Started

Choosing Your Topic

Topic Ideas

How to
brush your teeth
start a business
care for a pet
make a sandwich
study for a test
make a mask
inflate a bike tire
rake leaves
grow house plants
entertain a young
   child

Ask Yourself

What do I do well?
What do I do often?
What do I especially enjoy doing?
What can I do that I would like to
   explain to others?
What can I do that I can explain
   clearly?
What can I do that others might
   want or need to know how
   to do?
What new thing have I learned?

Exploring Your Topic

Illustrate It

List your steps. Then illustrate
them. Use the pictures to help you
"see" how the task is done. Do you
need to add steps? Would any step
be clearer if it were broken into two
steps? Could any steps be
combined?

1.   **2.**   **3.**

Tell How

Tell a friend, step by
step, how to do the
task. Were your direc-
tions easy to follow?
How can you make
them clearer?

Step 2: Write a First Draft

Bryan decided to write his paper for his classmates. He wanted to make them laugh.

Bryan wrote his first draft. He did not worry about making mistakes. He knew he could correct them later.

Bryan's first draft

Cleaning your room can be fun. ~~See~~ Put all the things on your bed. Try to pick up your books in alpabetical order. Place a wastebasket at the other side. Then crumbel the pieces and shoot them into the basket it is worth two pointes. Toys with wheels can roll to the toy box.

On Your Own

1. **Think about purpose and audience** Ask these questions.
   For whom shall I write my instructions?
   What is my purpose?
   What is the best order for arranging the steps?
   What words will make my instructions the clearest?
   What would be a catchy first sentence?
2. **Write** Remember to keep the steps in order. Write on every other line so that you will have room to add or make changes later. Do not worry about mistakes. Just write the clearest instructions you can for your topic.

Step 3: Revise

Bryan read his first draft. He noticed that some of his steps were out of order. He easily corrected this by moving one sentence. He drew an arrow to show where it should go.

Bryan wanted to find out if his instructions were clear. He read them to Seth.

Reading and responding

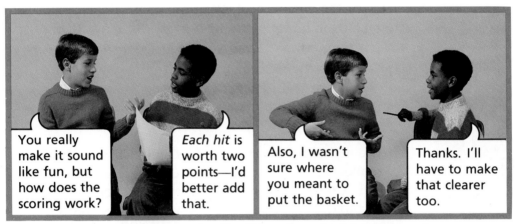

> You really make it sound like fun, but how does the scoring work?

> *Each hit* is worth two points—I'd better add that.

> Also, I wasn't sure where you meant to put the basket.

> Thanks. I'll have to make that clearer too.

Bryan added some details. Even though these instructions were for fun, he wanted them to be clear.

Part of Bryan's revised draft

Cleaning your room can be fun. ~~See~~ if you do it right
First, ~~See~~
Put all the trash things on your bed. Try
to pick up your books in alpabetical
order. Place a wastebasket at the
of the room
other side. Then crumbel the pieces
a hit
and shoot them into the basket. ~~it~~
is worth two pointes. Toys with

Think and Discuss ✓

• What word did Bryan add to make the order clear?
• What words were changed or added? Why?
• Why did he move one sentence?

On Your Own

Revising Checklist

☑ Does my paragraph have a good topic sentence?
☑ Do all the details support the main idea?
☑ Have I used step-by-step order?
☑ Are my instructions written clearly for my audience?

1. **Revise** Make changes in your first draft. Add more order words if needed. To find exact words, use the thesaurus below or the one in the back of the book. Replace words by crossing them out and adding new words above them.

2. **Have a conference** Read your instructions to someone else—a classmate or your teacher. You may want to write down some of your listener's comments.

W R I T I N G
CONFERENCE

Ask your listener:	As you listen:
"Are my steps easy to follow?" "Did I explain each step clearly?" "Where could I add details?"	Can I picture each step? Could I follow these instructions? Would more details make any of the steps clearer?

3. **Revise** Think about your listener's suggestions. Do you have any other ideas? Make those changes on your paper.

Thesaurus

create establish, invent, produce, design
do accomplish, perform
finish end, complete, stop, conclude, close
gather assemble, collect
get earn, obtain, win, acquire, buy
join connect, unite

last finally, at the end
make build, construct, form, manufacture
many several, numerous
price charge, cost, expense
put place, locate, set
start begin, commence
useful handy, helpful
work job, occupation

Step 4: Proofread

Bryan proofread his instructions for mistakes in spelling, capitalization, and punctuation. He used a dictionary to check spelling. He used proofreading marks to make his changes.

Part of Bryan's proofread draft

¶ Cleaning your room can be fun, ~~See~~ *if you do it right*
First, Put all the ~~things~~ *trash* on your bed. Try
to pick up your books in ~~alpabetical~~ *alphabetical* ~~e~~
order. Place a wastebasket at the *of the room*
other side. Then ~~crumbel~~ *crumble* the pieces
and shoot them into the basket, it *a hit*
is worth two ~~pointes~~ *points*. Toys with

Think and Discuss

- Which words did Bryan correct for spelling?
- What word did he capitalize?
- Where did he indent? Why?
- Where did he add an end mark? Why?

On Your Own

1. **Proofreading Practice** Proofread this paragraph. Find two mistakes in forming possessives. Find four other spelling mistakes. Find one run-on sentence and one mistake in paragraph format. Write the paragraph correctly.

   I thought about all my hobbys. I decided two do my science project on my parakeet Rex. First, I observed Rex and took nots. Then I made them into paragraphes and wrote neatly. After that I drew Rexs picture. My two brothers reactions could have been better. I tried again this time it was a success!

Proofreading Marks

⌐ Indent
∧ Add something
⋎ Take out something
≡ Capitalize
/ Make a small letter

2. **Proofreading Application** Now proofread your paper. Use the Proofreading Checklist and the Grammar and Spelling Hints below. You may want to use a colored pencil to make your corrections. Use a dictionary to check spellings.

Proofreading Checklist

Did I

☑ **1.** indent?

☑ **2.** use capital letters correctly?

☑ **3.** use punctuation marks correctly?

☑ **4.** use nouns correctly?

☑ **5.** spell all words correctly?

The Grammar/Spelling Connection

Grammar Hints

Remember these rules from Unit 3 when you use nouns.

- Add *s* or *es* to make most nouns plural. *(hats, boxes)*
- To form a singular possessive noun, add *'s*. *(girl's)*
- To form most plural possessives, add *'* after *s*. *(boys')*

Spelling Hints

- If a word ends with a consonant and *y*, change the *y* to *i* when adding *es*. *(country–countries)*
- Homophones are words that sound alike but have different spellings and meanings. *(sale–sail)*

Step 5: Publish

Bryan neatly copied his revised and proofread draft onto a piece of poster board. He added a title above the draft. Around the border of the paper he drew pictures of himself using these steps to clean his room.

On Your Own

1. **Copy** Write or type your instructions as neatly as possible.
2. **Add a title** Think of a title to catch your reader's interest. Remember to capitalize the first, last, and all important words.
3. **Check** Read over your instructions again to make sure that you have not left out anything or made any mistakes in copying.
4. **Share** Think of a special way to share your instructions.

Ideas for Sharing

- Read your instructions aloud while a classmate acts them out.
- Make a comic strip. Show a character saying your instructions and acting them out.
- Make a booklet. Draw pictures or cut them out of magazines to illustrate each step.

Applying Instructions

Literature and Creative Writing

In "The Toothpaste Millionaire" on pages 110–114, Rufus comes up with the idea of making his own toothpaste. When a friend gets him an interview on a talk show, Rufus's business is off and running.

Have fun using what you have learned about writing instructions to complete one or more of these activities.

Remember these things ☑

Write a topic sentence that tells the main idea.

Write details that support the main idea.

Write the steps in order. Use order words.

Write to suit your purpose and audience.

1. **Pretend that you are your teeth.** Write instructions that explain how to brush you.

2. **Advise others.** In the story "The Toothpaste Millionaire," Rufus starts his own business. If you were Rufus, what advice would you give to others who want to start their own businesses? Write a paragraph that gives instructions about how to set up a successful business.

3. **Launch an advertising campaign.** Rufus has decided to launch a new advertising campaign for his toothpaste. Your job is to give the Zappo Advertising Company instructions on how to conduct this campaign and what information to include.

Writing Across the Curriculum
Computers

A program is a set of instructions written for a computer by a programmer. The instructions must be in the right sequence, or the computer cannot follow them. Programmers make flow charts, or diagrams, to show the steps of the program in sequence. Try doing one or more of the following activities.

The flow chart below presents instructions for washing dishes. Follow the arrows.

Writing Steps

1. Choose a topic
2. Write a first draft
3. Revise
4. Proofread
5. Publish

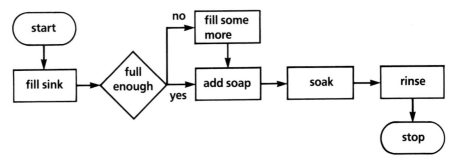

1. **Chart the flow.** The symbols below are used by computer programmers. Use these symbols to develop your own flow chart for a simple home or school chore. Then write an explanation of your chart.

Word Bank

first
next
then
finally
perform
decide

2. **Loading a program.** (Do this only if you know how to use a computer.) Learning to operate a computer is fun, but it can be confusing. That is why computer software comes with documentation. Documentation is a set of instructions for the user. Write documentation telling how to load a program.

Extending Literature
Book Report: Interview

Julia had really enjoyed reading the book *The Toothpaste Millionaire* by Jean Merrill. She decided to share her book with her class by making up an interview with Kate Mackinstrey. Kate is the character who tells the story in the book. Here is Julia's interview with Kate.

JULIA: Kate, how did you get to know Rufus, the boy who made the toothpaste?

KATE: He was the first friend I made when we moved to Cleveland. I was riding my bike to school and accidentally dumped all my books in the street. Rufus stopped traffic so I could pick them up again.

JULIA: Was Rufus already in the toothpaste business?

KATE: No, he got the idea one day when we went to buy toothpaste for his mother. But he was always inventing things. He designed some great saddlebags for his bike. Rufus never dropped *his* books! He even stitched up a set of saddlebags for me.

JULIA: Did you ever dream that your friend would be a millionaire just two years after you met?

KATE: Never! But my father says we should have known. Anyone who could figure exactly how much material you need for a saddlebag could easily make a million dollars' worth of toothpaste.

Think and Discuss
• Who are the characters in the book?
• What did you find out about the characters?
• Why is an interview a good way to share a book?

Share Your Book

Interview a Book Character

1. Decide which character in your book to interview. Choose a character who knows what happened in the story.
2. Decide which parts of the book you will tell about. Choose exciting incidents that will interest your classmates. Ask your character questions about those parts. Before you begin the interview, tell some background information.
3. Write down what the interviewer and the character will say. Ask a classmate to read the part of the interviewer, and you play the part of the book character.
4. Start your interview by having the interviewer introduce you, the character, to the class. Tell the title and author of your book.

Other Activities

• Interview the author of your book. You might ask the author who his or her favorite character in the book is and why. You might also ask the author what his or her favorite part of the story is. Write what the interviewer and the author will say. Then, with a classmate, present your interview.
• Interview the illustrator of your book. Ask the illustrator how he or she decided which parts of the story to illustrate.

 The Book Nook

| **Henry Reed, Inc.**
by Keith Robertson
Henry and Midge's business partnership pays off when they think that they have discovered oil. | **Shoeshine Girl**
by Clyde Robert Bulla
Sarah Ida learns about responsibility by keeping the shoeshine stand open when the owner is ill. |

Runs all day and never walks,
Often murmurs, never talks
It has a bed but never sleeps,
It has a mouth, but never eats.

from Mother Goose

Verbs

Getting Ready We are used to thinking of a verb as a word that shows action. If you say "I run," we all agree that describes an action. Suppose you say, "I sit." It is harder to think of sitting as an action verb, but it is. Suppose you say "I know," or "I am." What kinds of verbs are these? In this unit, you will learn more about verbs and how we put them to work.

ACTIVITIES

Listening Listen as the verse on the opposite page is read. It is a riddle. List all the verbs that tell what the subject does. What verbs tell what the subject does *not* do? Can you guess the answer to the riddle?

Speaking Look at the picture. How many different verbs can you think of for the movement of the water? Have someone list them on the board.

Writing In your journal, make up a riddle of your own about what something does and does not do.

1 Action Verbs

You have learned that the predicate of a sentence tells what the subject is or does. The main word in the predicate is the **verb**. Most verbs are action verbs. An **action verb** shows what the subject does or did.

Jill `pitches` the ball.

The ball `flew` over the plate.

Roberta `swings` at the ball.

Roberta `ran` to first base.

Action verbs can also show action that you cannot see.

The coach `thought` about the players in the field.

Guided Practice What is the action verb in each of the following sentences?

Example: Babe Didrikson performed well in many sports.
performed

1. She learned baseball and basketball as a child.
2. At sixteen she joined an excellent basketball team.
3. She scored a hundred points in one game!
4. Didrikson spent two years on that team.
5. During that same period, she won medals as a swimmer.
6. She also set records as a figure skater.
7. Didrikson entered many track and field events.
8. She broke records in every event.
9. In the 1932 Olympics, she captured three medals.
10. Sports reporters named her the greatest woman athlete.
11. After the Olympics, Didrikson took golf lessons.
12. She soon played in contests against other fine golfers.
13. Didrikson liked golf more than any other sport.
14. She held many championships in golf.

Summing up

▶ An **action verb** shows what the subject does or did.

Independent Practice Write the action verb in each sentence.

Example: Tom enjoys sports events. *enjoys*

15. He watched the Olympic Games on television.
16. Tom wrote about them for the school newspaper.
17. His news story included three different events.
18. All the riders in the bicycle races wore helmets.
19. They raced around the track many times.
20. The runners jumped over the hurdles.
21. They crossed the finish line.
22. The hockey players wore excellent protective clothing.
23. The goalie on the hockey team missed the puck.
24. One player crashed into the wall.
25. Gary passed the puck to Jimmy.
26. Two players from each team slammed into each other.
27. The coach blew his whistle for a time-out.
28. Tom covered the basketball game for the school paper and the local radio station.
29. The basketball team practiced their hoop shots.
30. The cheerleaders yelled the school cheer.
31. John dribbled the ball down the court.
32. Carol passed the ball to Glenn.
33. The crowd roared!
34. The clock ticked the seconds.
35. The referee called a foul against the other team.
36. Marian aimed the ball at the hoop.
37. The ball bounced off the rim of the hoop.
38. The coach paced in front of the bench.
39. Tom and Carla ran down the basketball court.
40. Jane tossed the ball through the net.
41. The buzzer signaled the end of the game.
42. The team carried Jane on their shoulders.

Writing Application: Instructions

Choose a part of a sport or a game, such as running last in a relay race or catching a fly ball. Write a paragraph telling a friend how to perform the action or play the game. Use an action verb in each sentence. Underline the verbs.

For Extra Practice, see p. 177.

2 | Direct Objects

THE CREW

RAISES

THE ANCHOR

Some sentences express a complete thought with only a subject and an action verb.

               action
       subj. verb
The ship sails.

In other sentences, a direct object follows the action verb. A **direct object** is a noun or a pronoun in the predicate that receives the action of a verb.

           action   dir.
      subj.   verb   obj.
The captain steers the big ship.

A direct object answers the questions *what?* or *whom?*

The captain steers the big ship.   (steers what? the ship)

The captain calls the crew.   (calls whom? the crew)

The captain praises them.   (praises whom? them)

Guided Practice What are the action verb and the direct object in each sentence?

Example: The captain ordered the sailors on deck.
          verb: *ordered*   **direct object:** *sailors*

1. Some sailors mopped the deck.
2. Other sailors cooked the stew.
3. A crew member spotted some whales.
4. The whales blew water out of their blowholes.
5. One sailor climbed the mast to the lookout.
6. He carried his binoculars with him.
7. He viewed the whales for a long time.
8. Finally, the sailor left the lookout.
9. He shared his observations with another sailor.
10. He made a sketch of one of the whales.
11. The two friends discussed the whales.

> ▸ A **direct object** is a noun or a pronoun in the predicate that receives the action of the verb.
> ▸ Direct objects follow action verbs only.

Independent Practice

A. Write the action verb in each sentence. Then write the direct object and underline it.

Example: Whales eat tiny plants. *eat* *plants*

12. Some whales sing songs.
13. Whales hold their breath for long periods.
14. They hear sounds under water.
15. They locate objects by sound.
16. Whales use their flippers for balance.

B. Copy the sentences. Underline verbs once and direct objects twice. If there is no direct object, write *no* D.O.

Example: Years ago people hunted whales.
Years ago people hunted whales.

17. Today, people watch whales from boats.
18. My family and I took a trip on one of these boats.
19. We gave our tickets to the captain.
20. He knew interesting facts about whales.
21. We searched the ocean for whales.
22. My brother brought his camera.
23. We saw three whales near the ship.
24. They spouted water through their blowholes.
25. We cheered!
26. Then the whales dived.
27. Their tail fins slapped the water.
28. The water splashed me.

Writing Application: Creative Writing
While diving, you have discovered a friendly sea creature. What does this creature do? What does it eat? Write a paragraph about it. Use action verbs and direct objects.

3 | Main Verbs and Helping Verbs

You know that every sentence has a verb in the predicate. In some sentences, the verb is more than one word. It is made up of a helping verb and a main verb. The **main verb** shows the action in the sentence. The **helping verb** works with the main verb. Helping verbs do not show action. The main verb and the helping verb form a **verb phrase**.

In these sentences, the helping verbs are in yellow, and the main verbs are in blue.

Fran has passed everyone.

She is winning the race.

She will get the prize.

Common Helping Verbs				
am	are	were	shall	has
is	was	will	have	had

Guided Practice What is the main verb in each sentence? What is the helping verb?

Example: The Vikings have practiced for months.

main verb: practiced   *helping verb: have*

1. Their cheerleaders are creating new songs.
2. The football season was planned last summer.
3. The band is practicing every day.
4. The students are getting their tickets.
5. Everyone at school is hoping for another championship season this year.
6. This football team has won the state championship for two years in a row.
7. The coach has trained the players well.

> ▶ A **verb phrase** is made up of a main verb and a helping verb.
> ▶ The **main verb** shows action.
> ▶ The **helping verb** works with the main verb.

Independent Practice

A. Write the verb or the verb phrase in each sentence.

Example: We are watching the game on television. *are watching*

   8. The halfback is tackling the runner.
   9. The runner fumbled the ball.
  10. A player is passing the ball.
  11. A player on the other team caught it.
  12. The quarterback is running for the touchdown.
  13. He had waited for this chance.
  14. His teammates are jumping for joy.
  15. I will go to the game next week.
  16. I always cheer for my favorite team.

B. Write the verb phrase in each sentence. Underline the helping verb once and the main verb twice.

Example: Our friends have come for a visit. _have come_

  17. We had planned a badminton game.
  18. Pedro is practicing his serve.
  19. Sally has played five times this week.
  20. My parents are providing the rackets.
  21. The net is stretched between two posts.
  22. Sally has chosen me for her partner.
  23. Sheila will join us later.
  24. Ron is keeping score for us.
  25. Pedro is hitting fast shots to me.
  26. I have returned most of his shots.

Writing Application: A Description

Pretend that you are a sports announcer. Write a paragraph describing a game that you are watching. Use main verbs and helping verbs in your sentences.

You know that some verbs show action and some verbs are helping verbs.

ACTION VERB: Jennifer runs every day.

HELPING VERB: Jennifer is running now.

A **linking verb** links the subject of a sentence with a word or words in the predicate.

LINKING VERBS: Jennifer is a runner.   She is strong and fast.

When a verb is a linking verb, it does not show action, and it is not a helping verb. It is followed by a word in the predicate that names or describes the subject.

Anna is a lifeguard.   (Anna = lifeguard)

Anna is cheerful.   (*Cheerful* describes Anna.)

Some verbs can be either linking verbs or action verbs.

ACTION: The crowd looked at the divers.

LINKING: The divers looked tired.   (*Tired* describes divers.)

Common Linking Verbs					
am	is	are	was	were	will be
look	feel	taste	smell	seem	appear

Guided Practice What is the linking verb in each sentence? What word or words are linked to the subject by the verb?

Example: The pool is quiet. *is   quiet*

1. The racers seem ready.
2. Ray is an excellent racer.
3. He was a winner last week.
4. Ray's parents are coaches.
5. They are proud of Ray.
6. The race will be quick.

▶ A **linking verb** joins the subject to a word in the predicate that names or describes the subject.
▶ A linking verb does not show action.

Independent Practice

A. Write the verb in each sentence. Then write whether the verb is an action verb or a linking verb.

Example: Gertrude Ederle was a fine swimmer. *was   linking*

7. She swam the English Channel.
8. She was the first woman to swim the channel.
9. Her time was less than fifteen hours.
10. She set a new world record.
11. The English Channel is about twenty miles wide.
12. The Channel is a big challenge for swimmers.

B. Write each sentence and underline the linking verb. Draw an arrow showing the words the verb links.

Example: Elaine is a deep-sea diver.

Elaine is a deep-sea diver.

13. She is careful under water.
14. Usually she seems calm.
15. She was afraid one time.
16. Two big sharks looked hungry.
17. She was just another fish to the sharks.
18. The sharks were fast swimmers.
19. Elaine was a quick thinker.
20. She was very still.
21. Other little fish were the sharks' meals.
22. Elaine was shaky for a long time.

Writing Application: Comparison and Contrast
Write two paragraphs comparing what you were like two years ago and what you are like now. Use linking verbs in your sentences.

For Extra Practice, see p. 180.   **Linking Verbs   149**

5 | Present Tense

Verbs show more than the action in a sentence. They also tell when the action happened.

The ranger sees the campers.

The verb *sees* tells that the ranger is seeing the campers now. A verb that tells what its subject is doing right now is in the **present tense**. Notice that *s* has been added to *see*. You change the form of a verb to show the present tense when a singular noun is the subject.

You do not change the form of verbs when they are used with plural subjects or with *I* or *you*.

The campers wave .   I wave .   You wave .

Rules for Forming the Present Tense	
1. Most verbs: Add *s*.	get – get s play – play s
2. Verbs ending in *s*, *ch*, *sh*, *x*, and *z*: Add *es*.	pass – pass es punch – punch es push – push es mix – mix es fizz – fizz es
3. Verbs ending with a consonant and *y*: Change the *y* to *i* and add *es*.	try – tr ies empty – empt ies

Guided Practice
Which present tense form of the verb in parentheses is correct?

Example: The bird ___. (hatch) *hatches*

1. The stream ___. (flow)
2. The alarm ___. (buzz)
3. The boys ___. (rush)
4. We ___. (talk)
5. Dad ___. (worry)
6. The baby ___. (fuss)

Independent Practice
Write the correct present tense form of each verb in parentheses.

Example: I carefully ____ the weather.   (study)   *study*

7. The sun ____ brightly in the blue sky.   (shine)
8. Only one cloud ____ overhead.   (pass)
9. Roger ____ to the weather report.   (listen)
10. Roger and I ____ the camping trip.   (discuss)
11. Mother ____ a picnic lunch.   (pack)
12. We ____ to the center of the lake.   (row)
13. Mother ____ from the rowboat.   (fish)
14. She ____ for fish in the water.   (watch)
15. I ____ a fish on the end of my line.   (lose)
16. Mother and Roger ____ several trout each hour.   (catch)
17. I ____ a can of worms for bait.   (open)
18. A fish ____ in the water near me.   (splash)
19. Father ____ the boat to shore.   (row)
20. He ____ to the campsite.   (hurry)
21. Father ____ the big fish he caught.   (clean)
22. Mother ____ the shaky table.   (fix)
23. She ____ her hands.   (wash)
24. Father ____ fish on the camp stove.   (fry)
25. The dinner ____ delicious.   (taste)
26. Roger and I ____ the dishes.   (clean)
27. Mother ____ tomorrow's hike with us.   (plan)
28. Father ____ supplies for the hike.   (prepare)

Writing Application: A Story
Imagine that you are fishing and something nibbles on your bait. Write a paragraph in the present tense that tells what happens. Underline the verbs.

For Extra Practice, see p. 181.   **Present Tense**   151

6 | Past Tense

You have learned that verbs in the present tense show what is happening. A verb that shows what has already happened is in the **past tense**.

> Gino liked his grandmother's story.

The verb *liked* is in the past tense. It tells that the action in the sentence happened before now.

There are several ways to form the past tense. You must look at the ending of a verb to see how to form its past tense.

Rules for Forming the Past Tense	
1. Most verbs: Add *-ed*.	play – play**ed** reach – reach**ed**
2. Verbs ending with e: Add *-d*.	believe – believe**d** hope – hop**ed**
3. Verbs ending with a consonant and *y*: Change the *y* to *i* and add *-ed*.	study – stud**ied** hurry – hurr**ied**
4. Verbs ending with a single vowel and a consonant: Double the final consonant and add *-ed*.	stop – stop**ped** plan – plan**ned**

Guided Practice What is the past tense of each verb?

Example: dress *dressed*

1. watch
2. cry
3. scrub
4. store
5. spray
6. review
7. care

8. zip
9. marry
10. yell
11. bake
12. talk
13. dance
14. shop

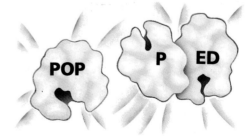

▶ A **past tense verb** shows that something already happened.
▶ Form the past tense of most verbs by adding *-ed.*
▶ If a verb ends with *e,* add *d.* If a verb ends with a consonant and *y,* change the *y* to *i* and add *-ed.* If a verb ends with a vowel and a consonant, double the consonant and add *-ed.*

Independent Practice Write the past tense form of each verb in parentheses.

Example: Jo _____ this story about pirates. (share) *shared*

15. Many years ago, a beautiful ship _____ gold. (carry)
16. The ship _____ many dangers. (face)
17. The brave captain _____ about storms and pirates. (worry)
18. In those days, heavy storms _____ many ships. (destroy)
19. A band of pirates _____ that sea. (sail)
20. The pirates _____ the ship. (attack)
21. They _____ the gold. (grab)
22. Some men _____ the plank. (walk)
23. The pirates _____ the treasure on a beach. (bury)
24. A map _____ where the treasure was hidden. (show)
25. The son of the captain _____ the map. (use)
26. He _____ to find the riches. (hope)
27. Finally, he _____ the huge treasure from his father's ship. (discover)
28. Jo's classmates _____ her story. (enjoy)
29. Vera _____ to read some exciting stories. (want)
30. She _____ at the library after school. (stop)
31. Mr. Lopez _____ several good books. (suggest)
32. Vera _____ to read a mystery and a story about a band of pirates. (decide)

Writing Application: Creative Writing
Imagine that you have found a buried treasure in your neighborhood. What kind of treasure did you find? Where was it? Write a paragraph about how you discovered it. Use past tense verbs in your sentences. Underline the verbs.

For Extra Practice, see p. 182.

7 | Future Tense

Shall we try some?

You know that verbs can tell what is happening now or what has happened in the past. A verb that tells what is going to happen is in the **future tense.**

Derek will bring his new book about birds.

Derek and Gretchen will look for some nests.

To form the future tense of a verb, use the helping verb *will* or *shall* with the main verb.

Shall we invite Melissa?

She will probably come with us.

Guided Practice

A. What is the future tense form of each verb?

Example: perform   *will perform*

1. run
2. think
3. talk
4. check
5. spill
6. count
7. whisper
8. tumble

B. What is the future tense form of each underlined verb?

Example: Birds <u>make</u> homes all over the world.   *will make*

9. Parrots <u>live</u> in hot, steamy jungles.
10. Penguins <u>like</u> very cold climates.
11. Shore birds <u>stay</u> near the water.
12. Many shore birds <u>build</u> nests in the Everglades.
13. Bird watchers <u>study</u> how the birds live.
14. They <u>learn</u> about the birds' actions and habits.
15. The bird watchers <u>watch</u> the birds with binoculars.

Summing up

▸ A **future tense verb** tells what is going to happen.
▸ Use the main verb with the helping verb *will* or *shall* to form the future tense.

Independent Practice

A. Write the tense of each verb below. Then write the future tense form of the verb.

Example: hurries *present* *will hurry*

16. write
17. stop
18. swims
19. prepared
20. surprises
21. decide
22. completed
23. practice
24. delivered
25. recover
26. multiply

B. Write the verb or verb phrase in each sentence. Then write the future tense form of the verb.

Example: Birds have interested people for years.
          have interested *will interest*

27. Each fall, birds leave their summer homes.
28. They move to another place for the winter.
29. Many small birds fly only at night.
30. They eat during the day.
31. Some birds have covered thousands of miles.
32. The barn swallow spends the summer in Alaska.
33. It journeys eight thousand miles to South America.
34. Scientists have measured the speeds of many birds.
35. A scientist wraps a metal band around a bird's leg.
36. The band identifies the bird.
37. Scientists then track the birds' routes.
38. Some scientists have written about their findings.

Writing Application: Writing About Yourself

Picture yourself five years from now. Write a paragraph about what you will be doing. Use the future tense forms of the verbs.

For Extra Practice, see p. 183.

8 | Subject-Verb Agreement

A present tense verb and its subject must **agree** in number. If the subject is singular, use the singular form of the verb. If the subject is plural, use the plural form of the verb. Study the rules for subject-verb agreement in the chart below.

SINGULAR: The race lasts many days.

PLURAL: The sleds move quickly.

Rules for Subject-Verb Agreement	
1. Singular subject: Add *s* or *es* to the verb.	The driver trains his dogs. He teaches one dog to lead. He studies his map.
2. Plural subject: Do not add *s* or *es* to the verb.	The dogs pull the sleds. The drivers and dogs travel far. They work together.
3. I or you: Use the plural form of the verb.	I like your report on dogs. You write well.

Look at the second example for Rule 2. The compound subject *drivers and dogs* is followed by the plural form of the verb. When the parts of a compound subject are joined by *and*, always use the plural form of the verb.

Guided Practice
Which verb in parentheses correctly completes each sentence?

Example: I (like, likes) dogs very much. *like*

1. We (see, sees) dogs every day.
2. Dogs (work, works) with people in many ways.
3. Homes and businesses (keep, keeps) watchdogs.
4. A dog (make, makes) a good partner.
5. Alex (own, owns) a watchdog named Charlie.

▶ A present tense verb and its subject must **agree** in number.
▶ Add *s* or *es* to the verb if the subject is singular.
▶ Do not add *s* or *es* to the verb if the subject is plural or if the subject is *I* or *you*.

Independent Practice
Write the present tense form of the verb in parentheses to complete each sentence.

Example: Mr. Crosby ____ dogs. (raise) *raises*

6. His dogs ____ deaf people. (help)
7. A dog named Tilly ____ for doorbells. (listen)
8. She ____ to the door. (run)
9. Mr. Crosby ____ a dog named Max. (own)
10. He and Max ____ by each morning. (walk)
11. Max and I ____ each other. (like)
12. I often ____ with Max. (play)
13. Mr. Crosby ____ him special tricks. (teach)
14. Max ____ his commands. (follow)
15. Mr. Crosby always ____ Max. (praise)
16. He ____ that Max will help deaf people. (say)
17. Max ____ even tiny sounds. (hear)
18. Sometimes Mr. Crosby ____ to other cities. (travel)
19. Max always ____ his house. (guard)
20. Special dogs ____ many blind people. (assist)
21. You ____ the name for these dogs. (know)
22. We ____ them seeing-eye dogs. (call)
23. Many blind people ____ seeing-eye dogs. (use)
24. They ____ better lives with these dogs. (live)
25. The dogs ____ their owners. (guide)
26. They ____ at red traffic lights. (wait)
27. Seeing-eye dogs ____ blind people through crowds. (lead)
28. A seeing-eye dog ____ a valuable contribution. (make)

Writing Application: Creative Writing
Pretend that you are a seeing-eye dog. Write a paragraph about your experiences. Use present tense verb forms.

For Extra Practice, see p. 184. **Subject-Verb Agreement** 157

9 | Agreement with *be* and *have*

You have already learned that the verbs *be* and *have* can be used as main verbs or as helping verbs. You have also learned that a verb and its subject must agree in number. You must change the forms of the verbs *be* and *have* in special ways to agree with their subjects. The chart below shows the past and present tense forms.

Subject	Form of *be*	Form of *have*
Singular subjects:		
I	am, was	have, had
You	are, were	have, had
He, she, it (or singular noun)	is, was	has, had
Plural subjects:		
We	are, were	have, had
You	are, were	have, had
They (or plural noun)	are, were	have, had

Guided Practice Which form of *be* or *have* in parentheses correctly completes each sentence?

Example: Jeff (is, am) a talented gardener.   *is*

1. I (has, have) helped him in his garden.
2. You (is, are) eating some of his tomatoes.
3. They (was, were) picked this morning.
4. Jeff also (has, have) green peppers in his garden.
5. Becky (has, have) brought us this pumpkin.
6. (Has, Have) you ever seen so many seeds?
7. (Are, Is) you staying for dinner?
8. We (has, have) plenty of food.
9. Molly and Pete (is, are) making pumpkin stew.
10. They (has, have) found an excellent recipe.

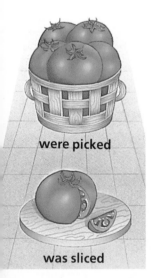

were picked

was sliced

> ▶ Change the forms of the verbs *be* and *have* to make them agree with their subjects.

Independent Practice
Write the verb in parentheses that correctly completes each sentence.

Example: Many fruits (has, have) lots of seeds. *have*

11. Apple trees (was, were) once tiny seeds.
12. I (has, have) seen big trees grow from tiny seeds.
13. Our apple tree (is, are) huge.
14. We (have, has) eaten wonderful apples from that tree.
15. The birds (is, are) gathering in our yard today.
16. Many apples (has, have) fallen on the ground.
17. We (is, are) picking the apples as fast as we can.
18. Jim (have, has) picked a peach from the peach tree.
19. The peach tree (has, have) very few peaches now.
20. Jim (has, have) started a new little tree.
21. I (am, is) watering it every day.
22. Water and rich soil (is, are) needed for growth.
23. Lime trees and lemon trees (is, are) beautiful.
24. Tom and Walt (has, have) a lime tree in Florida.
25. They (has, have) used the limes in fruit salad.
26. Do you (has, have) many trees in your yard?
27. Sophia's yard (is, are) very small.
28. She (has, have) one lilac bush.
29. In the spring, the flowers (has, have) a beautiful smell.
30. My aunt's lilac bush (has, have) white flowers.
31. Sophia's lilacs (is, are) purple.
32. Sophia (has, have) often given me lilacs.

Writing Application: Creative Writing
Imagine that you have planted a garden, but instead of flowers or vegetables, something unusual is coming up. For example, you might be growing shoes. Write a paragraph about your strange garden. Use forms of *be* and *have* in your sentences. Check your sentences for correct subject-verb agreement.

10 | Contractions with *not*

You can combine some verbs with the word *not* to make contractions. A **contraction** is a word formed by joining two words, making one shorter word. An apostrophe (') takes the place of the letter or letters dropped to shorten the word.

Contractions Made with Verbs Plus *Not*

do not	don't	have not	haven't
does not	doesn't	has not	hasn't
did not	didn't	had not	hadn't
is not	isn't	could not	couldn't
are not	aren't	would not	wouldn't
was not	wasn't	should not	shouldn't
were not	weren't	cannot	can't
will not	won't	must not	mustn't

You know that *not* is not a verb. Therefore, it cannot be part of a verb phrase. The *n't* in a contraction is also not part of a verb or a verb phrase.

You may use contractions when you talk with your friends or when you write friendly letters. Do not use contractions in formal reports or business letters.

Guided Practice What are the contractions for the following words?

Example: was not *wasn't*

1. cannot **4.** are not
2. does not **5.** were not
3. is not **6.** has not

Summing up

▶ A **contraction** is the shortened form of one or more words.
▶ Use an apostrophe (') in place of any dropped letters.

Independent Practice

A. Write the contraction for each pair of words.

Example: could not *couldn't*

7. do not
8. should not
9. did not
10. have not
11. had not
12. would not
13. will not
14. must not

B. Write the word or words that form each contraction.

Example: Mary Ann isn't feeling well. *is not*

15. She didn't sleep well last night.
16. She can't go to school today.
17. She wasn't able to eat her breakfast this morning.
18. She couldn't sit up in bed.
19. The doctor said that Mary Ann shouldn't worry.
20. Mary Ann won't be sick for long.
21. Mary Ann shouldn't get out of bed today.
22. We haven't visited her yet.
23. We weren't allowed in her room.
24. I won't forget to make a card for her.
25. I don't want her to feel lonely.
26. I am sad when she isn't well.
27. I don't have any special paper for the card.
28. I mustn't forget to buy some.
29. I won't use any orange crayons.
30. Orange isn't one of Mary Ann's favorite colors.
31. We are glad that Mary Ann won't be sick for long.
32. School isn't as much fun without her.

Writing Application: Writing About Yourself

Have you ever made something that you thought you couldn't do and it turned out great? Write a paragraph about your experience or make one up. Use a contraction from the chart in each sentence.

For Extra Practice, see p. 186.   **Contractions with *not* 161**

11 | Regular and Irregular Verbs

You have learned to form the past tense and to use helping verbs to show that something has already happened. For most verbs, you form the past by adding -*d* or -*ed* to the verb. Verbs that follow this rule are called **regular verbs**.

plant – planted   dare – dared   cry – cried

For some verbs, you do not form the past by adding -*d* or -*ed*. **Irregular verbs** have special forms to show the past.

Irregular Verbs		
Verb	**Past tense**	**Past with helping verb**
bring	brought	(has, have, had) brought
come	came	(has, have, had) come
go	went	(has, have, had) gone
make	made	(has, have, had) made
run	ran	(has, have, had) run
say	said	(has, have, had) said
take	took	(has, have, had) taken
think	thought	(has, have, had) thought
write	wrote	(has, have, had) written

Guided Practice

A. Which of these past tense verbs are regular? Which are irregular?

Example: ran   *irregular*

1. dressed
2. made
3. thought
4. came
5. wanted
6. wrote
7. said
8. tried

B. What is the past form of each verb above when it is used with a helping verb?

Example: ran   *have run*

> ► Add -*d* or -*ed* to **regular verbs** to show the past.
> ► **Irregular verbs** have special forms to show the past.

Independent Practice

A. Write the past tense form of each verb. Then write the past form of the verb when it is used with a helping verb.

Example: go *went   have gone*

  9. bring   **11.** take   **13.** come
10. complete   **12.** dry   **14.** walk

B. Write the correct past form of the verb in parentheses to complete each sentence.

Example: I ____ about a good topic.   (think)   *thought*

15. I ____ to the library for books about bears.   (go)
16. I had ____ a list of the books.   (make)
17. I have ____ that library often.   (visit)
18. I ____ my report in two hours.   (write)
19. I ____ the report to school yesterday.   (take)
20. My teacher ____ to my desk.   (come)
21. She ____ that my report was great!   (say)
22. After school I ____ my report to my sister Joan.   (show)
23. She had ____ home a painting of a palomino.   (bring)
24. We ____ to write a report about horses.   (decide)
25. Joan ____ to use her painting for the cover.   (want)
26. I had ____ a book about horses as a gift.   (receive)
27. We ____ the chapter on palominos.   (study)
28. In the report, we ____ the palomino with other kinds of horses.   (compare)

Writing Application: A Description
Write a paragraph describing a project that you have done in school. Use some irregular verbs from the chart. In some of your sentences, use the past tense form of the verb. In other sentences, use a helping verb with the irregular verb to show the past.

For Extra Practice, see p. 187.

12 | More Irregular Verbs

There are no rules for you to follow when you form the past of irregular verbs. However, certain patterns will help you remember the past forms of some irregular verbs. The chart below groups some of these irregular verbs according to their patterns.

Irregular Verbs

Verb	Past tense	Past with helping verb
ring	rang	(has, have, had) rung
sing	sang	(has, have, had) sung
swim	swam	(has, have, had) swum
begin	began	(has, have, had) begun
tear	tore	(has, have, had) torn
wear	wore	(has, have, had) worn
break	broke	(has, have, had) broken
speak	spoke	(has, have, had) spoken
steal	stole	(has, have, had) stolen
choose	chose	(has, have, had) chosen
freeze	froze	(has, have, had) frozen
blow	blew	(has, have, had) blown
grow	grew	(has, have, had) grown
know	knew	(has, have, had) known
fly	flew	(has, have, had) flown

Guided Practice What is the past tense form of each verb? What form of each verb is used to show the past with a helping verb?

Example: swim *swam* *have swum*

1. fly
2. speak
3. tear
4. steal
5. ring
6. choose
7. begin
8. grow
9. break

▶ Some irregular verbs follow similar patterns to show that something has happened in the past.

Independent Practice

A. Write the correct past tense form of the verb in parentheses to complete each sentence.

Example: Karen and Billy ____ warm clothing to the beach.
(wear) *wore*

10. Rudi and Jessie ____ in the cold water.   (swim)
11. The seagulls ____ high over the cliffs.   (fly)
12. Alex ____ how to tend the campfire safely.   (know)
13. Jessie ____ the bell when dinner was ready.   (ring)
14. After dinner Alex ____ about campfire safety.   (speak)
15. The group leaders ____ branches into small pieces for the fire.   (break)
16. Karen ____ the storytelling.   (begin)
17. Everyone ____ stories to tell.   (choose)
18. Later they ____ their favorite songs.   (sing)

B. Each sentence has a helping verb. Write the correct form of the main verb in parentheses.

Example: The water in the pond had ____ during the night.
(freeze) *frozen*

19. Mr. Lonzo had ____ to us about the cold winter.   (speak)
20. The strong winds have ____ a tent down.   (blow)
21. The snow has ____ some of the tree branches.   (break)
22. Pete has ____ his warmest clothing.   (wear)
23. Penny has ____ a hole in her jacket.   (tear)
24. Mr. and Mrs. Lonzo had ____ the food for lunch.   (choose)
25. The raccoons have ____ some of the food.   (steal)
26. They have ____ bolder since last summer.   (grow)

Writing Application: A Story
Write a story about a camping trip. In each sentence, use a helping verb with an irregular verb from the chart.

For Extra Practice, see p. 188.   **More Irregular Verbs   165**

13 | Verb Phrases with *have*

A main verb can have more than one helping verb. The helping verb *have* is often used with the helping verbs *could,* *would,* *should,* and *must.* The two helping verbs and the main verb form a verb phrase.

These helping verbs are often spoken as contractions.

HELPING VERBS	CONTRACTIONS
could have	could've
would have	would've
should have	should've
must have	must've

Do not use *of* with *could, would, should,* or *must.*

INCORRECT: You should of seen the parade last weekend.

You would of liked the marching band.

CORRECT: You should have seen the parade last weekend.

You would've liked the marching band.

Guided Practice Is the verb phrase in each sentence correct? If not, what should it be?

Example: Jim should of called. *incorrect   should have called*

1. He could of told us about his trip to Utah.
2. Perhaps we should have called him.
3. He must of seen some wonderful places.
4. We would have enjoyed his pictures of the trip.
5. He must of put them in an album by now.

Summing up

▸A verb phrase can have more than one helping verb. Some helping verbs can be contractions.
▸Use *have* or *'ve* with *could, should, would,* and *must.* Do not use *of.*

Independent Practice

A. Write the verb phrase in each sentence.

Example: I should've brought my camera. *should've brought*

6. We could have taken pictures of birds.
7. Larry and I must've seen fifty wild geese.
8. We would have taken some great pictures.
9. You could've come on our hike too.
10. You would've enjoyed it.
11. We should have reminded you about it.
12. You must have seen the posters at school.
13. They would have told you about Elm Point.
14. The posters should've been bigger.

B. Change each verb phrase to include a contraction. Then write the new sentence.

Example: Scientists must have visited Elm Point.
Scientists must've visited Elm Point.

15. They would have learned about wild geese.
16. They could have written about them.
17. I should have checked in the library.
18. Maybe I would have found a good article.
19. I could have read it before the hike.
20. Larry must have studied birds in school.
21. You should have heard him during the hike!
22. You could have learned a lot from him.
23. He must have named ten types of birds.
24. You would have been proud of him.
25. I should have invited Larry for dinner.
26. He would have told some interesting stories.
27. You would have enjoyed them.
28. I should have thought of it before.

Writing Application: A Paragraph

Write a paragraph about something you might have said or done. For example, perhaps you forgot to wish your friend a happy birthday. Use one of these pairs of helping verbs in each sentence: *could have, should have, would have,* or *must have.*

For Extra Practice, see p. 189.   **Verb Phrases with *have*   167**

14 | *teach, learn; let, leave*

Do not confuse the verbs *teach* and *learn*. Their meanings are related but not the same. Also be careful not to confuse the verbs *let* and *leave*. They sound similar, but their meanings are different.

Verb	Meaning	Example
teach	to give instruction	He will teach us history.
learn	to receive instruction	We will learn about Rome.
let	to permit	Let Kevin go with us.
leave	to go away from	We will leave tomorrow.
	to let remain in place	Leave it on the table.

Guided Practice

A. Which is correct in each sentence, *teach* or *learn*?

Example: I would like to ____ more about our city. *learn*

1. This book will ____ you about its history.
2. You can also ____ a lot in the museum.
3. I must ____ to read the subway map.
4. Carol can ____ you that in a few minutes.
5. How can I ____ more about interesting places to visit in the city?
6. People at the information booth will ____ you.

B. Which is correct in each sentence, *let* or *leave*?

Example: Will you ____ me go to the museum with Nate this morning? *let*

7. Don't ____ before breakfast.
8. We should ____ this crowded train go by.
9. Don't ____ your coat on the bench.
10. You should ____ me lead the way.
11. Where did I ____ the map?
12. ____ me search my pockets.

> ▶ Use *teach* when you mean "to give instruction."
> ▶ Use *learn* when you mean "to receive instruction."
> ▶ Use *let* when you mean "to permit."
> ▶ Use *leave* when you mean "to go away from" or "to let remain in a place."

Independent Practice Write the word in parentheses that correctly completes each sentence.

Example: You may (let, leave) your jackets in the coat room. *leave*

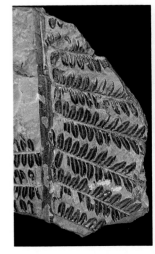

13. (Let, Leave) the museum guide begin her talk.
14. You will (teach, learn) about fossils from her.
15. Fossils (teach, learn) us about early forms of life.
16. Plants and animals (let, leave) their outlines in rocks.
17. Mrs. Avery used to (teach, learn) college students.
18. Please (teach, learn) us about that strange fossil.
19. (Let, Leave) me see that fossil of a fern leaf.
20. What kind of fossil would this plant (let, leave) behind?
21. (Let, Leave) me show you an example of that fossil.
22. We can also (teach, learn) about dinosaurs from fossils.
23. (Let, Leave) us go to the dinosaur room.
24. Will that guide (teach, learn) us about dinosaurs?
25. These computers will (teach, learn) us about them.
26. Will the guide (let, leave) us use the computers?
27. Sam, we promised your mother we would (let, leave) early.
28. How can we (let, leave) before we've seen everything?
29. What did you (teach, learn) today that impressed you?
30. I will (let, leave) you see my notes.
31. I hope we (teach, learn) more about fossils in school.
32. If we (let, leave) now, we won't miss our train.

Writing Application: A Paragraph
Write a paragraph about teaching something to a younger child. Use the present tense of the verbs *let, leave, teach,* and *learn* in your sentences.

For Extra Practice, see p. 190.   *teach, learn; let, leave* **169**

15 | *sit, set; can, may*

NO JUMPING

May I?

You have already learned about some frequently confused verbs. Also be careful not to confuse the verbs *sit* and *set*. Their meanings are different. Do not confuse the verbs *can* and *may*. Their meanings are similar but not the same.

Verb	Meaning	Example
sit	to rest	I will sit in the chair.
set	to place or put	Set the book on the table.
can	to be able	I can ride my bike well.
may	to be allowed	May I go to the park?

Guided Practice

A. Which is correct in each sentence, *can* or *may*?

Example: _____ I bring a friend for lunch?   *May*

1. Alex does not live far away. He _____ get here easily.
2. Yes, you _____ invite Alex.
3. Alex, _____ you reach that jar on the shelf?
4. You _____ sit down now. We are ready to eat.

B. Which is correct in each sentence, *sit* or *set*?

Example: Alex, _____ your gloves on that bench.   *set*

5. No one will _____ there until later.
6. Would you like to _____ near Kim?
7. _____ the puzzle on the worktable.
8. Later you will _____ on the high stools.

Summing up

▶ Use *sit* when you mean "to rest."
▶ Use *set* when you mean "to place or put something."
▶ Use *can* when you mean "to be able to do something."
▶ Use *may* when you mean "to be allowed or permitted."

Independent Practice Write the word in parentheses that correctly completes each sentence.

Example: (Can, May) I do that puzzle with you? *May*

9. Help me (sit, set) up the places.
10. I (can, may) usually find the edges easily.
11. Kim should (sit, set) in the big chair.
12. Alex will (sit, set) a box under her cast.
13. Kim has to (sit, set) with her foot raised.
14. (Can, May) I use your desk lamp for an hour?
15. Please (sit, set) it down on this corner.
16. Do you think we (can, may) finish this puzzle in an hour?
17. Kim (can, may) finish even hard puzzles.
18. Please do not (sit, set) the glass on the table.
19. (Sit, Set) the torn puzzle piece here.
20. I'm not sure if we (can, may) fix it.
21. Where did you (sit, set) the special glue?
22. Is it hard to frame a puzzle, or (can, may) anyone do it?
23. Susan says that we (can, may) use her tools if we are careful.
24. (Can, May) you find them in that messy box?
25. Let's (sit, set) the tools in front of us.
26. (May, Can) you identify all the tools?
27. (Can, May) you find a small screwdriver in that box?
28. (Set, Sit) it with the other tools.
29. (Can, May) we ask Susan to help us?
30. She (may, can) frame pictures and puzzles well.
31. Susan says that she (can, may) help us now.
32. Alex, (sit, set) near Susan to watch what she does.
33. Susan will (sit, set) the glass in the frame.
34. Alex, (can, may) you carefully lift the puzzle?
35. (May, Can) I help Alex place the puzzle in the frame?
36. If we have a hammer, we (can, may) hang the puzzle on the classroom wall today.

Writing Application: Persuasive Letter
Think of an activity you enjoy. Write a letter to convince a friend to try it. Use the verbs *sit*, *set*, *can*, and *may*. Use each verb at least once.

For Extra Practice, see p. 191.　　　　　　　　　　*sit, set; can, may* **171**

Grammar-Writing Connection

Agreement with Compound Subjects

You have learned to vary the lengths of your sentences by combining them. As you know, one way of combining sentences is to form a compound subject.

The two short sentences below each contain a singular subject and the singular form of the verb. Notice that the subject of the longer combined sentence is compound and that it is followed by the plural form of the verb. Remember to use the plural form of the verb when the parts of the compound subject are joined by *and*.

The *earth* has mountains.

The *moon* has mountains.

The *earth* and the *moon* have mountains.

Revising Sentences

Rewrite each group of sentences below as one sentence with a compound subject. Be sure that the verb agrees with the compound subject.

1. The earth travels through space. The moon travels through space.
2. Jupiter is larger than the earth. Saturn is larger than the earth. Uranus is larger than the earth.
3. Mars is similar to the earth in size. Mercury is similar to the earth in size. Venus is similar to the earth in size.
4. Saturn is circled by icy rings. Jupiter is circled by icy rings. Uranus is circled by icy rings.
5. Jupiter also has moons. Saturn also has moons. Uranus also has moons.
6. The United States sends spacecraft to some of the planets. The Soviet Union sends spacecraft to some of the planets.
7. Mars was visited by spacecraft. The moon was visited by spacecraft.
8. The Soviet Union wants to name the moon's features. The United States wants to name the moon's features.

Creative Writing

Imagine living in houses connected together like a honeycomb! This was the idea behind Habitat, designed in the 1960s by Moshe Safdie. Habitat is made up of box-like houses stacked on top of each other. Each house has a rooftop garden and a walkway. In fact, this unusual building is much like a neighborhood floating high in the air.

- In what ways is Habitat different from your own house?
- Of what objects and patterns does this building remind you?

Habitat, Montreal,
Moshe Safdie,
Milton and Joan Mann

Activities

1. **Write a letter to the newspaper.** Imagine that you live in Montreal, Canada, where Habitat was built. Many people have called this building ugly and strange. Others have said that it is beautiful and exciting. What is your feeling? Write a letter to the editor of the *Montreal Messenger,* explaining your position.

2. **Describe the building's inhabitants.** Imagine that many unusual people live in this building. What do they look like? What do they do inside their houses? Do they like to relax or do they keep very busy? Describe one or more of the people who live inside Habitat.

Check-up: Unit 5

Action Verbs (p. 142) Write the action verb in each sentence.

1. A hurricane struck the island.
2. Waves crashed over the rocks near the shore.
3. The wind blew fiercely.
4. Trees bent in the wind.
5. Leaves swirled in the air.
6. Then heavy rains fell.
7. The storm passed quickly.

Direct Objects (p. 144) Write the direct objects.

8. Scientists study the planets.
9. They carefully record all of their observations.
10. Some use special cameras.
11. They take unusual pictures.
12. Others own telescopes.
13. They watch the sky at night.
14. They make important discoveries.

Main Verbs and Helping Verbs (p. 146) Write the verbs in these sentences. Underline the helping verb once and the main verb twice.

15. The sun has risen over the town.
16. A rooster is crowing in the yard.
17. Birds were calling to each other.
18. The children have awakened because of the noise.
19. They are eating fruit and cereal.
20. The day is beginning slowly.
21. Soon the school bus will come for the children.

Linking Verbs (p. 148) Write each sentence and underline the linking verb. Draw an arrow showing the words that the verb links.

22. Canaries are delightful pets.
23. My canary is a good singer.
24. Her songs sound very loud.
25. She looks beautiful to me.
26. Her feathers are yellow.

Present Tense (p. 150) Write the present tense form of each verb.

27. I ___ quickly.   (dress)
28. Alice ___ her long hair.   (fix)
29. The doorbell ___ twice.   (buzz)
30. We ___ to the door.   (hurry)
31. The graduation party ___.   (begin)

Past Tense (p. 152) Write the past tense form of each verb.

32. We ___ the early West.   (study)
33. Few doctors ___ there.   (move)
34. Some doctors ___ to the West with explorers.   (travel)
35. They ___ the wildlife.   (observe)
36. They also ___ the sick.   (treat)

Future Tense (p. 154) Write the future tense form of each verb.

37. Our club ___ a terrific game. (create)
38. Liz and I ___ our ideas.   (share)
39. Stan ___ the board.   (construct)
40. Carlotta ___ the maze.   (draw)
41. Alex ___ the rules.   (write)

Subject-Verb Agreement *(p. 156)*
Write the present tense of each verb.

42. You and I ___ newspapers. (read)
43. An editor ___ stories. (pick)
44. Reporters ___ articles. (write)
45. Photographers ___ interesting pictures. (take)
46. A proofreader usually ___ for errors. (check)

Agreement with *be* and *have*
(p. 158) Write the verb in parentheses that completes each sentence.

47. Hawaii (is, are) made up of many islands.
48. They (was, were) formed long ago by volcanoes.
49. Their beauty (is, are) amazing.
50. I (was, were) in Hawaii last year.
51. (Have, Has) you seen my pictures?

Contractions with *not* *(p. 160)*
Write the word or words that were combined to form each contraction.

52. Aren't you happy with the sketch?
53. I didn't hear your answer.
54. Haven't you seen it yet?
55. Can't you ask about it?
56. Stan hasn't finished it yet.

Regular and Irregular Verbs
(p. 162) Write each sentence, using the past form of each verb.

57. Carlotta ___ the play. (write)
58. Jay had ___ of the idea. (think)
59. Gary ___ the stage set. (make)
60. We ___ our lines well. (say)
61. A large audience ___. (come)

More Irregular Verbs *(p. 164)*
Write the past form of each verb.

62. A cold wind ___. (blow)
63. I had ___ a heavy coat. (wear)
64. The bell ringers ___ an hour ago. (begin)
65. They ___ many bells. (ring)
66. I had ___ the music. (choose)
67. Cleo ___ many songs. (know)

Verb Phrases with *have* *(p. 166)*
Write each sentence, using the correct words in parentheses.

68. He (must of, must have) forgotten.
69. He (should've, should of) told me.
70. Jo (would of, would have) gone.
71. I (could've, could of) asked her.
72. We (would've, would of) had fun.

teach, learn; let, leave; sit, set; can, may *(pp. 168, 170)* Write the word in parentheses that correctly completes each sentence.

73. Ms. Clark will (learn, teach) us.
74. (Set, Sit) the paints on the box.
75. (Set, Sit) on a stool by me.
76. I (may, can) draw well already.
77. (Teach, Learn) us about color.
78. (May, Can) I borrow some paper?
79. (Leave, Let) me help you.
80. We will (learn, teach) about paints.
81. (Sit, Set) your brushes down.
82. (May, Can) we put our work here?
83. (Let, Leave) us come back tomorrow morning.
84. We must (let, leave) now.
85. (Leave, Let) your work overnight.

Enrichment

Latest and Greatest Toy

Pretend that you work for a toy store. You are to design a flyer for *Rodderbonks*, an unusual new toy. What is *Rodderbonks*? You decide! Make it a toy that most children would want. On your flyer, write five sentences that tell why *Rodderbonks* is a superior toy. Use action verbs. Back up your claims with interesting artwork.

Missing Parts

Find a favorite paragraph from a story in your reading or library book. Copy this paragraph onto a piece of paper, leaving out all the verbs and direct objects. Draw a blank where each missing part of speech should be. Exchange papers with a partner. Read the paragraph and write in new verbs and direct objects. Be sure that verb tenses are correct and that all verbs agree with their subjects. Compare the new paragraph with the old one.

The Time of Your Life

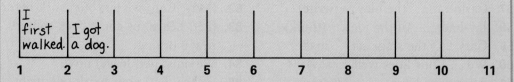

Time lines show important events in history. Make a time line of the important events in your own life. Draw a long line on white paper. Divide the line equally to show the years of your life. Label each year. Then write a short sentence about something important that happened to you that year. Use past tense verbs.

I first walked.	I got a dog.									
1	2	3	4	5	6	7	8	9	10	11

Extra Practice: Unit 5

1 | Action Verbs (p. 142)

● Write an action verb from the box of words to complete each sentence. Use each verb only once.

Example: Carla ____ me for her team. *chose*

1. I ____ at Allison's joke.
2. Sam ____ me a funny story.
3. Laurie ____ the ball to Tony.
4. Kevin ____ to second base.
5. I ____ over a rock in the field.
6. I ____ a hole in my new jeans.
7. Tony always ____ his bike to the game.
8. After the game, we ____ lunch.
9. We also ____ cold drinks.

| tripped |
| ate |
| tore |
| rides |
| sipped |
| ran |
| laughed |
| chose |
| threw |
| told |

▲ Write the action verb in each sentence.

Example: Suzanne Lenglen played tennis well. *played*

10. She won her first Wimbledon competition in 1919.
11. Lenglen changed the game of women's tennis.
12. She turned it into a more exciting game.
13. Long ago, women tennis players wore long dresses.
14. They tapped the ball lightly.
15. Lenglen introduced the short tennis dress.
16. She smashed the ball over the net.
17. She captured six championships in seven years.

■ Read each word. If it is an action verb, use it in a sentence. If it is not an action verb, write *not an action verb*.

Example: leaped *The dancer leaped into the air.*

18. sent	24. sea	30. hurried
19. twig	25. chased	31. shared
20. crawled	26. car	32. constructed
21. sing	27. said	33. skip
22. basket	28. raced	34. pretty
23. hopped	29. threw	35. taped

2 ▍ Direct Objects (p. 144)

● Read each sentence. Then write the answer to each question. The answer will be the direct object.

Example: Hard rain hit the roof.   The rain hit what?   *roof*

1. Thunder scared Glenn.   Thunder scared whom?
2. He shut the windows.   He shut what?
3. He read a book.   He read what?
4. He found the telephone.   He found what?
5. He called his mother.   He called whom?
6. The storm will not hurt him.   It will not hurt whom?
7. He will draw pictures of stormy skies.   He will draw what?

▲ Make two columns. Label them *Action verb* and *Direct object*. Find the action verb and the direct object in each sentence, and write them in the correct columns.

Example: Herman Melville wrote *Moby Dick*.

> **Action verb**   **Direct object**
> *wrote*   *Moby Dick*

8. Melville tells a great story in this book.
9. Men hunt a large white whale.
10. They sail their ship all over the world.
11. Finally, they find the whale.
12. They shoot harpoons at it.
13. During the struggle, the whale sinks their ship.
14. Last year my brother read this book for school.

■ Write a sentence, using each action verb below. Include a direct object in each sentence.

Example: made   *Long ago, people made ships out of wood.*

15. search	**22.** followed
16. carried	**23.** build
17. gathered	**24.** spell
18. chop	**25.** wear
19. dragged	**26.** drew
20. hold	**27.** choose
21. wrote	**28.** covered

3 | Main Verbs and Helping Verbs (p. 146)

● Each sentence contains a helping verb and a main verb. The main verb is underlined. Write the helping verb.

Example: The football team is <u>hoping</u> for a victory. *is*

1. The players have <u>worked</u> hard this season.
2. They have <u>practiced</u> many long hours.
3. It was <u>raining</u> last Saturday.
4. The coach was <u>giving</u> the players good advice.
5. The players were <u>slipping</u> on the muddy field.
6. The quarterback had <u>hurt</u> his shoulder.
7. He is <u>feeling</u> better today.
8. He will <u>play</u> in the game this afternoon.
9. Joan and I are <u>going</u> to the game.
10. The winning team will <u>celebrate</u> tonight.

▲ Write the verb or verb phrase in each sentence.

Example: I am going to every game this season. *am going*

11. We have bought our tickets already.
12. The Eagles have won four games this year.
13. The school newspaper has praised them.
14. We have cheered them from the bleachers.
15. Last year they had hoped for a final victory.
16. Al was throwing a pass in the last game.
17. The Terriers were charging at him.
18. His fumble resulted in a touchdown for them.
19. I am expecting a victory this year.
20. The coach is working very hard.

■ Use each verb phrase in a sentence.

Example: was hired *The new coach was hired yesterday.*

21. is choosing
22. has started
23. will miss
24. is buying
25. had gotten
26. have watched
27. were defeated
28. am memorizing
29. was looking
30. have talked
31. are thinking
32. was wondering

4 | Linking Verbs (p. 148)

● Write *action* or *linking* for each underlined verb below.

Example: Diana Nyad <u>is</u> a long-distance swimmer.   *linking*

1. She <u>completed</u> a sixty-mile swim.
2. She <u>began</u> her swim at Bimini Island.
3. The water <u>looked</u> cold and choppy.
4. She <u>swam</u> to Florida.
5. She <u>saw</u> jellyfish and sharks.
6. She <u>had practiced</u> in a cage with sharks.
7. She <u>was</u> brave.

▲ Write each sentence. Underline the linking verb. Then draw an arrow to connect each subject with the word that names or describes it.

Example: The Olympic Games are exciting.

The Olympic Games <u>are</u> exciting.

8. The athletes are very talented.
9. They seem powerful.
10. The first prize in each event is a gold medal.
11. Mark Spitz was famous during the 1972 Olympic Games.
12. His swimming was excellent.
13. He was a winner of seven gold medals.
14. Perhaps you will be a famous winner too.

■ Write sentences with linking verbs. Use each word or group of words below as the subject of a sentence.

Example: Christopher Columbus
Christopher Columbus was an explorer.

15. Kittens
16. My school
17. An elephant
18. Apples
19. My age next year
20. I
21. The weather today

22. Dinosaurs
23. Abraham Lincoln
24. My future career
25. My favorite building
26. Umbrellas
27. That painting
28. A good writer

5 | Present Tense (p. 150)

● Write the present tense verbs in the sentences below.

Example: Bill collects postage stamps. *collects*

   1. I like stamps too.
   2. Bill and I often go to stamp shows on weekends.
   3. We buy new stamps there.
   4. My cousin Ramon sometimes goes with us.
   5. Bill watches a show about stamps on television.
   6. He never misses this show.
   7. It teaches him a lot about stamps.

▲ Write the correct present tense form of each of the verbs in parentheses.

Example: My mother ____ old chairs. (fix) *fixes*

   8. She ____ new cane seats in them. (put)
   9. First, she ____ the strips of cane in water. (soak)
  10. Next, she carefully ____ the seat. (weave)
  11. Then the cane ____ slowly. (dry)
  12. The new seat ____ tightly. (fit)
  13. Sometimes I ____ my mother with her caning. (help)
  14. While working, we ____ about my day at school. (talk)

■ Write each group of sentences, using the correct present tense form of each underlined verb.

Example: dry: Joan ____ the clothes. We ____ the dishes.
             He ____ his hair.
             Joan dries the clothes. We dry the dishes. He dries his hair.

  15. pay: Pat ____ the bill. He ____ attention.
             We ____ for lunch.
  16. toss: We ____ the ball. He ____ the newspaper.
             I ____ the salad.
  17. mix: I ____ the dough. She ____ the cards.
             Amy ____ the paints.
  18. wash: You ____ the car. He ____ the floor.
             They ____ the windows.

6 | Past Tense (p. 152)

● Write the past tense verbs in the sentences below.

Example: Bonita walked quickly down the hall.   *walked*

1. She carried her pencil with her.
2. Her friends stayed in the classroom.
3. They waited for their turns.
4. Bonita finally reached the cafeteria.
5. Mr. Wong called her to a special table.
6. She picked up the paper with the list of names.
7. She marked an X beside one name.
8. She voted for Terry for president of the school.

▲ Write the past tense form of each verb in parentheses.

Example: Inez ____ an adventure on TV.   (watch)   *watched*
9. Later she ____ the plot to us.   (explain)
10. We ____ her description of the scenery.   (enjoy)
11. She ____ the main character very well.   (describe)
12. People ____ this pirate "Blackbeard."   (call)
13. Blackbeard ____ his black beard.   (braid)
14. Blackbeard ____ along the coast of Virginia.   (sail)
15. He and his men ____ many ships.   (rob)
16. Blackbeard once ____ to stop stealing.   (promise)
17. He ____ for just a few weeks.   (stop)
18. The people finally ____ him.   (punish)

■ Rewrite these sentences, using verbs in the past tense.

Example: People write many stories about Captain Kidd.
   People wrote many stories about Captain Kidd.

19. At first, Captain Kidd works for the British king.
20. Kidd captures French ships.
21. He also chases pirates.
22. He carries the pirates' treasures back to England.
23. He and his men save some of the treasure for themselves.
24. They bury the treasure in a secret place.
25. Captain Kidd dies in 1701.
26. People search for his treasure without success.

7 | Future Tense (p. 154)

● Write the future tense form of each verb below.

Example: cry   *will cry*

1. read	**5.** ride	**9.** begin
2. hope	**6.** pull	**10.** wish
3. steal	**7.** come	**11.** worry
4. want	**8.** grow	**12.** catch

▲ Write the verb in each sentence. Then write the future tense form of the verb.

Example: We have fed the birds every winter for many years.
have fed   will feed

13. We hang pieces of fat in special bags.
14. Chickadees and woodpeckers like this food.
15. Woodpeckers flew to our feeder last winter.
16. The fat has kept them warm on cold days.
17. We buy seeds for the cardinals and sparrows.
18. Often we mix grain with the seeds.
19. Cardinals have eaten at our feeder many times.
20. They survive the long, cold winter.
21. Blue jays always reach the feeder before the other birds.
22. Sometimes they chase the other birds away.

■ Answer these questions by writing full sentences. Use the future tense form of each underlined verb.

Example: Where are we <u>going</u>?   *We will go to the park.*

23. What birds do we expect to <u>see</u>?
24. Where do these birds <u>build</u> their nests?
25. Do they <u>travel</u> south for the winter?
26. What foods do they <u>eat</u>?
27. Is anyone going to <u>bring</u> seeds for them?
28. Have you <u>read</u> any books about birds?
29. Has Ted <u>designed</u> a birdhouse?
30. What color is he <u>painting</u> it?
31. When is he <u>hanging</u> it in the apple tree?
32. Are you going to <u>help</u> him?

8 | Subject-Verb Agreement (p. 156)

● Write whether the subject and the verb in each sentence are *singular* or *plural*.

Example: Some dogs work on farms and ranches.   *plural*

1. They watch the cattle and sheep.
2. Annie Dalton lives on a ranch with her dog.
3. She calls her dog Judd.
4. Annie and Judd work together.
5. Judd takes care of many sheep and cattle.
6. Sometimes the sheep and cattle wander away.
7. Judd brings them back.

▲ Write each sentence. Use the correct present tense form of the verb in parentheses.

Example: Some dogs _____ sleds over ice and snow.   (pull)
            Some dogs pull sleds over ice and snow.

8. The sleds _____ supplies.   (carry)
9. My friend in Canada _____ dog sleds.   (use)
10. He _____ the sleds out of wood.   (make)
11. Each sled _____ seven to ten strong dogs.   (need)
12. A lead dog _____ the others.   (guide)
13. The other dogs _____ the lead dog.   (follow)
14. A person _____ on the back of the sled.   (ride)
15. The lead dog _____ the commands of that person.   (obey)

■ If the subject and the verb agree in number, write *correct*. If they do not agree, rewrite the sentence correctly.

Example: You knows a lot about working dogs.
            You know a lot about working dogs.

16. I read books and articles about them.
17. You and I often goes to the library.
18. The librarian also enjoy books about dogs.
19. She usually puts books about dogs on that shelf.
20. The books on this topic teaches me interesting things.
21. The librarian and her helper ask me about the books.
22. We talks about different kinds of working dogs.

9 | Agreement with *be* and *have* (p. 158)

● The subjects and the verbs agree in the sentences below. For each sentence, write *singular* or *plural*.

Example: Potatoes and carrots are vegetables.   *plural*

1. A vegetable is part of a plant.
2. A carrot plant has only one root.
3. I am eating a carrot.
4. This carrot was once a root.
5. We have eaten flower buds too.
6. We were eating cauliflower last night.
7. The flower buds of cauliflower are delicious.
8. Melissa has brought us cauliflower from her garden.

▲ Write each sentence, using the verb in parentheses that agrees with the subject.

Example: A banana (has, have) seeds.   *A banana has seeds.*

9. You (has, have) a ripe banana.
10. I (has, have) looked for the seeds in this banana.
11. The banana seeds (was, were) tiny.
12. Sam (was, were) cutting open a watermelon.
13. The watermelon (has, have) many seeds.
14. White seeds and black seeds (is, are) in a watermelon.
15. We (is, are) saving these seeds.
16. I (has, have) planted some in pots already.

■ Read each sentence below. If the subject and the verb agree, write *correct*. If not, rewrite the sentence correctly.

Example: These tomatoes is ripe.   *These tomatoes are ripe.*

17. I is going to pick them this afternoon.
18. This morning we has a bad storm.
19. The wind and the rain has damaged my plants.
20. You has offered your help in the garden.
21. We is tying the plants to strong stakes.
22. We are protecting them from the wind and the rain.
23. Too much water are bad for plants.
24. High winds are dangerous too.

10 || Contractions with *not* (p. 160)

● Write the contraction in each sentence.

Example: Some doctors don't treat people.   *don't*

1. We can't go to them when we are sick.
2. Haven't you ever met an animal doctor?
3. Animals aren't always healthy.
4. I don't like to see my dog sick.
5. Shouldn't you take your cat to the doctor?
6. My dog's doctor isn't far from your house.
7. Why don't you take your cat to Dr. Strong?

▲ Write each sentence, using a contraction in place of the underlined word or words.

Example: My cat Molly is not feeling well.
        My cat Molly isn't feeling well.

8. Molly has not eaten any food.
9. This morning she did not want to play.
10. She will not stay sick if Dr. Strong treats her.
11. Dr. Strong does not want to hurt you, Molly.
12. You should not be afraid of Dr. Strong.
13. I cannot make you feel better by myself.
14. Thanks to Dr. Strong, you are not sick any more.

■ Answer each question by writing a sentence that contains a contraction with *not*.

Example: Does your pony have a cold?
        My pony doesn't have a cold.

15. Do you know an animal doctor named Dr. Strong?
16. Have you forgotten that dogs need shots every year?
17. Has your cat seen a doctor lately?
18. Can you please show me the best way to get to Dr. Strong's office?
19. Will that bus go to his office?
20. Has your goldfish stopped coughing yet?
21. Could a lion get the chicken pox?
22. Do you have office hours on Tuesday evenings?

11 ┃ Regular and Irregular Verbs (p. 162)

● Write each verb or verb phrase. Then write whether it is *regular* or *irregular*.

Example: have thought   *have thought   irregular*

1. walked
2. has written
3. had stamped
4. said
5. had gone
6. had discovered
7. brought
8. have taken
9. tried
10. had needed

▲ Write each sentence, using the correct form of the verb in parentheses to show past time.

Example: In school we have ___ about deer.   (learn)
In school we have learned about deer.

11. People have ___ about them in books.   (write)
12. One book ___ the different kinds of deer.   (discuss)
13. A famous photographer had ___ the pictures.   (take)
14. A deer once ___ past me in the mountains.   (run)
15. My sister ___ a deer while it slept.   (observe)
16. My teacher ___ that deer rest most of the day.   (say)
17. She once ___ several deer in the evening.   (follow)
18. She ___ them as they grazed.   (watch)

■ Rewrite each sentence, using the past with a helping verb.

Example: The polar bear ran twenty-five miles per hour.
The polar bear has run twenty-five miles per hour.

19. The brown bear gathered acorns and berries.
20. A mother bear brought her cubs to the stream.
21. They hungrily looked for fish.
22. The black bear searched for honey.
23. Angry bees swarmed around the bear.
24. My teacher wrote a book about animals.
25. He studied polar bears in Greenland.
26. In class he said many interesting things about them.
27. He also shared his photographs with us.
28. I enjoyed the pictures of the cubs most of all.

12 | More Irregular Verbs (p. 164)

● Write the past tense form of each verb below. Then write the form that is used to show the past with a helping verb.

Example: know   *knew*   *have known*

1. sing	**5.** fly	**9.** grow
2. wear	**6.** tear	**10.** freeze
3. choose	**7.** speak	**11.** swim
4. blow	**8.** ring	**12.** begin

▲ Write each sentence, using the correct form of the verb in parentheses to show past time.

Example: I ____ my Lions hat to the baseball game.   (wear)
         I wore my Lions hat to the baseball game.

13. I have ____ into a great fan of the Lions.   (grow)
14. We ____ "The Star Spangled Banner" at the game.   (sing)
15. Then the game ____.   (begin)
16. A great hit ____ into center field.   (fly)
17. The next batter ____ a base.   (steal)
18. He ____ the league record for stealing bases.   (break)
19. The manager ____ to the pitcher.   (speak)
20. We had ____ an exciting game.   (choose)
21. I ____ we would have a great time.   (know)

■ Each sentence below uses the past tense form of a verb. Rewrite these sentences, using the past form with a helping verb.

Example: Strong winds blew over the beach.
         Strong winds had blown over the beach.

22. Sand flew against our beach house.
23. Harsh winds tore off the shutters.
24. The door broke in the storm.
25. We knew about all the damage.
26. Jim spoke to us about repairs.
27. We wore old clothes for painting.
28. We chose a soft shade of yellow paint.
29. We began our work early in the day.
30. We sang many lively songs during the day.

13 | Verb Phrases with *have* (p. 166)

● Write the verb phrases that are in the sentences below.

Example: You should've seen the lovely sunset last night.
should've seen

 1. I must have taken five pictures of it.
 2. You would've loved the pink clouds.
 3. I could have watched that sunset forever.
 4. There must've been four shades of red in it.
 5. Perhaps I should have taken more pictures.
 6. I could've hung them in my room.
 7. I could have written a poem about the sunset too.
 8. The pictures would have illustrated the poem.

▲ Write each sentence, using the correct word or words shown in parentheses.

Example: You (should have, should of) seen the movie.
You should have seen the movie.

 9. Tim (must of, must have) told you about it.
10. The whole school (would've, would of) liked it.
11. We (could have, could of) gone together.
12. Tim (should of, should've) told Ms. Brooks.
13. She (would of, would have) provided a school bus.
14. Tim (must've, must of) forgotten.
15. You (could've, could of) learned more about England.

■ If the verb phrase is incorrect, rewrite the sentence correctly. If the verb phrase is correct, write *correct*.

Example: Karen must of taken a course in photography.
Karen must have taken a course in photography.

16. We should've gone to the course too.
17. We should of looked in the paper for an announcement.
18. The paper would of told us about the course.
19. Perhaps I should have asked Karen about it.
20. She must've gotten a new camera for the course.
21. She could of used mine.
22. I would of given it to her.

14 | *teach, learn; let, leave* (p. 168)

● Write the correct word to complete each sentence.

Example: (Let, Leave) me use your camera.
> *Let me use your camera.*

1. Where did Jon (let, leave) the extra film?
2. You can (learn, teach) someone to take good pictures.
3. Did you (learn, teach) from someone?
4. My Aunt Maria (lets, leaves) me use her camera.
5. She can (learn, teach) you about cameras.
6. (Leave, Let) your phone number on the note pad.
7. Will she (teach, learn) me how to focus more quickly?

▲ If the underlined word is correct, write *correct*. If it is incorrect, write the word that should replace it.

Example: Please <u>learn</u> Paul about photography.   *teach*

8. It is exciting to <u>learn</u> a new student.
9. <u>Let</u> me show you how to focus.
10. I will <u>let</u> the instructions in your bag.
11. Will I ever <u>teach</u> enough to take good pictures?
12. I won't <u>let</u> you give up now.
13. Don't <u>let</u> the lens cap on the camera.
14. <u>Learn</u> us how to use the flash.
15. Will you <u>leave</u> us take your picture?

■ Answer each question by writing a complete sentence containing one of the words in parentheses.

Example: Where will you put your equipment?   (let, leave)
> *I will leave it in the closet.*

16. Are you allowed to take pictures in here?   (let, leave)
17. Who will show us how to take portraits?   (teach, learn)
18. Are you permitted to use Sara's darkroom?   (let, leave)
19. Will you allow Dan to enlarge that photo?   (let, leave)
20. What did you find out about taking pictures on very cloudy days?   (teach, learn)
21. What else does Kim want to know?   (teach, learn)
22. Who has to go home early?   (let, leave)

15 | *sit, set; can, may* (p. 170)

● Write the correct word to complete each sentence.

Example: People (may, can) easily make bookends.
People can easily make bookends.

1. (Sit, Set) the glue bottle on the bench.
2. (May, Can) we use your good saw?
3. Nellie (can, may) cut the wood correctly.
4. Now she will (set, sit) one piece next to the other.
5. You (can, may) watch if you are quiet.
6. Please (sit, set) on the other side of the bench.
7. (Can, May) you brush the glue neatly on the wood?

▲ If the underlined word is correct, write *correct*. If it is incorrect, write the word that should replace it.

Example: <u>May</u> you move this heavy chair for me?   *Can*

8. Please do not <u>set</u> anything on that table.
9. Everyone needs to <u>set</u> for a while.
10. Maybe you <u>can</u> find two more chairs.
11. When will you be able to <u>sit</u> down?
12. No one <u>may</u> see the wall from the couch.
13. <u>Can</u> I move to that empty seat?
14. Alex will <u>sit</u> the screen in the corner.

■ Answer each of the following questions by writing a sentence. Use the word in parentheses that better fits the meaning of your answer.

Example: Where will Arthur put the box?   (sit, set)
Arthur will set the box on the green bench.

15. Is there room on that bench for my friend?   (sit, set)
16. Is Erin allowed to ride the bus alone?   (can, may)
17. How well does Jan read a map?   (can, may)
18. Where is an empty seat for me?   (sit, set)
19. Are people permitted to stand?   (can, may)
20. Where should Carlos put his suitcase?   (sit, set)
21. Do most people face the front or the back?   (sit, set)
22. Do you know how to get to the movies by bus?   (can, may)

O nce upon a time there was a man who had a meadow which lay high up on the hillside and in the meadow was a barn, which he had built to keep his hay in. . . .

translated by George Webbe Dasent
from "The Princess on the Glass Hill"

Story

Getting Ready In this unit, you will read a story and later write one of your own. When you write a story, your imagination can come to life. Your story can take place long ago, in the future, or at the present time. You can make up characters or base them on people you know. Start now to think about stories you could write.

ACTIVITIES

Listening

Listen as the story beginning on the opposite page is read. What happens next? As a class, make up the next sentence. Take turns adding sentences. Can you tell the whole story?

Speaking

Look at the picture. How many story ideas can you and the class get from this one photograph? How many different settings does it suggest? What kinds of characters might there be? What could happen? List as many ideas as you can. Save them until it is time to write your story.

Writing

In your journal, begin a story of your own about this photograph. Will it be a memory or a fantasy?

LITERATURE

What qualities make a person worthy to be a king?

The Needle in the Haystack

By John Hamma

Once in another time, there lived a King and Queen who had no children. The King worried about who would take his place when he grew too old to rule, so he asked his chief counselor what to do.

"Why not adopt a son, Your Majesty, and teach him the laws of the land?" his counselor suggested.

"But how will I find the right boy?" the King asked.

"Look for one who shows honesty, patience, and perseverance," the counselor told him. "It will be like looking for a needle in a haystack, but if you search wisely and well, I am certain you will find someone worthy."

"That's it!" the King exclaimed. "A needle in a haystack! Who would be more patient and persevering

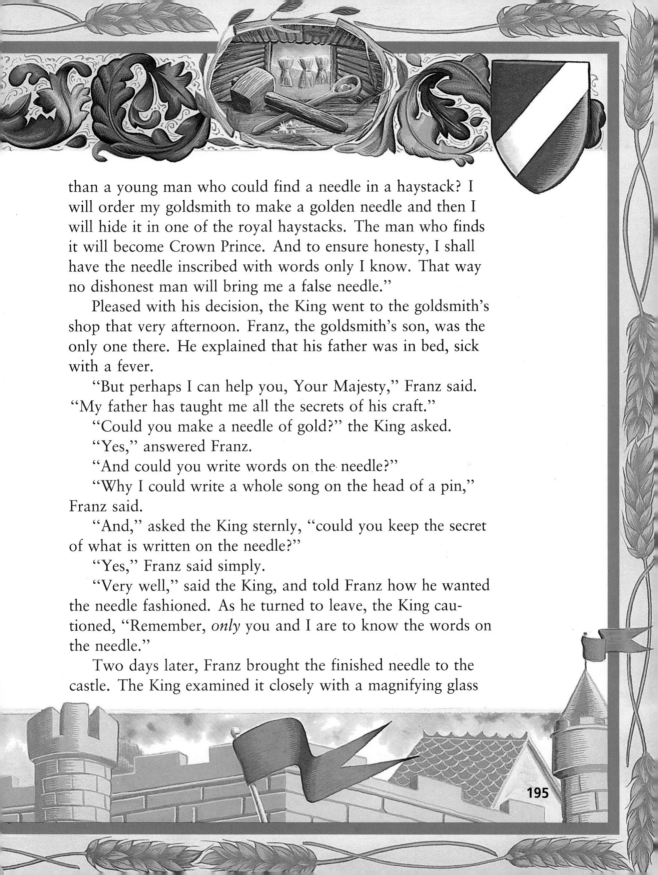

than a young man who could find a needle in a haystack? I will order my goldsmith to make a golden needle and then I will hide it in one of the royal haystacks. The man who finds it will become Crown Prince. And to ensure honesty, I shall have the needle inscribed with words only I know. That way no dishonest man will bring me a false needle."

Pleased with his decision, the King went to the goldsmith's shop that very afternoon. Franz, the goldsmith's son, was the only one there. He explained that his father was in bed, sick with a fever.

"But perhaps I can help you, Your Majesty," Franz said. "My father has taught me all the secrets of his craft."

"Could you make a needle of gold?" the King asked.

"Yes," answered Franz.

"And could you write words on the needle?"

"Why I could write a whole song on the head of a pin," Franz said.

"And," asked the King sternly, "could you keep the secret of what is written on the needle?"

"Yes," Franz said simply.

"Very well," said the King, and told Franz how he wanted the needle fashioned. As he turned to leave, the King cautioned, "Remember, *only* you and I are to know the words on the needle."

Two days later, Franz brought the finished needle to the castle. The King examined it closely with a magnifying glass

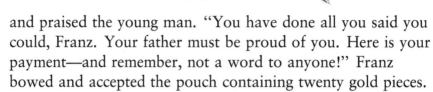

and praised the young man. "You have done all you said you could, Franz. Your father must be proud of you. Here is your payment—and remember, not a word to anyone!" Franz bowed and accepted the pouch containing twenty gold pieces.

That night the King set out secretly to hide the needle, and the next afternoon he ordered Joseph, his first minister, to appear before him in his private audience chamber. After Joseph had bowed at the King's feet and kissed his hand several times, the King said, "Last night I placed a golden needle in one of the royal haystacks. Today you will post a proclamation, inviting all young men between the ages of eighteen and twenty-five to search for this needle three days hence. The one who finds and brings the needle to me will become heir to the throne."

"Right away, Your Majesty," Joseph said, and after several more bows, he left the room. He rubbed his hands and smacked his lips in glee as he walked into the courtyard. Eavesdropping does have its benefits, he thought. What a good thing I saw young Franz hand the golden needle to the King yesterday. It has given me the chance I've been waiting for. I shall see to it that my son, Joseph II, will present a golden needle to the King and be pronounced heir. Through him I shall rule the kingdom.

First Joseph had to determine which haystack the King had visited. He questioned the farmers who worked the fields surrounding the castle, until finally he found an old man who said

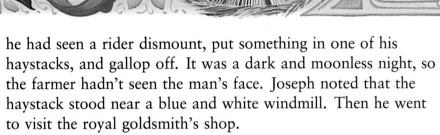

he had seen a rider dismount, put something in one of his haystacks, and gallop off. It was a dark and moonless night, so the farmer hadn't seen the man's face. Joseph noted that the haystack stood near a blue and white windmill. Then he went to visit the royal goldsmith's shop.

He found Franz fashioning a bird out of spun silver and complimented him upon the excellence of his work. Franz thanked him politely and asked, "How may I help you, Your Excellency?"

"I am here on the King's business," Joseph said. "You are the one who made the golden needle for His Majesty, are you not?"

Franz said nothing. He intended to keep his promise to the King.

Joseph read his silence correctly. "I know that the King has sworn you to secrecy, so you need not answer. Just listen. The King has lost the needle. He was drinking from a well of fresh mountain water, and the needle fell in. He now requests that you make an exact duplicate."

Franz nodded, and Joseph's eyes glinted with guile as he placed twenty gold pieces on the counter. "Can you have it ready for me by tomorrow afternoon?"

Again, Franz nodded.

"I see I need not caution you about keeping my visit a secret. If word got out that the King had lost the needle, the kingdom would be in an uproar."

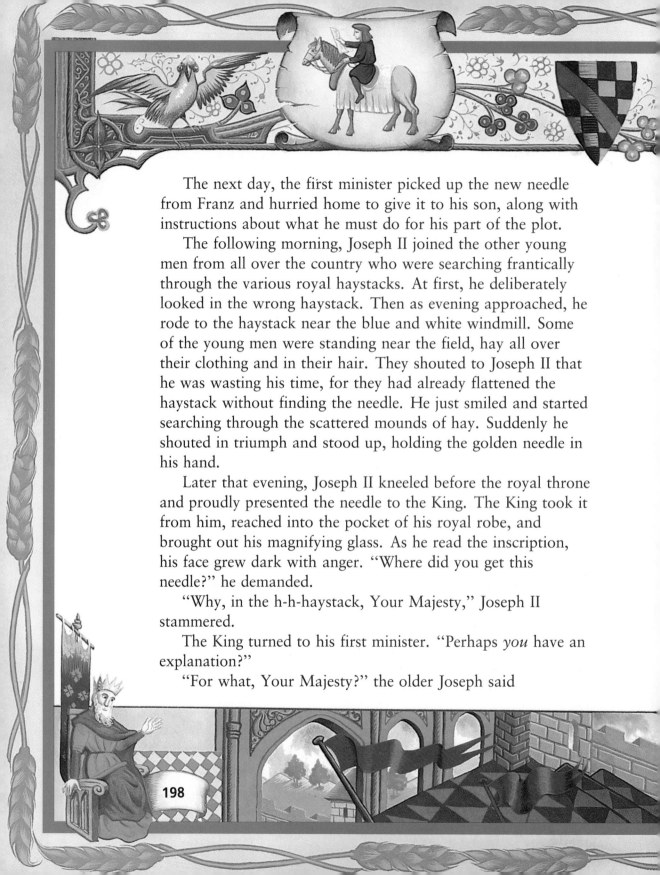

The next day, the first minister picked up the new needle from Franz and hurried home to give it to his son, along with instructions about what he must do for his part of the plot.

The following morning, Joseph II joined the other young men from all over the country who were searching frantically through the various royal haystacks. At first, he deliberately looked in the wrong haystack. Then as evening approached, he rode to the haystack near the blue and white windmill. Some of the young men were standing near the field, hay all over their clothing and in their hair. They shouted to Joseph II that he was wasting his time, for they had already flattened the haystack without finding the needle. He just smiled and started searching through the scattered mounds of hay. Suddenly he shouted in triumph and stood up, holding the golden needle in his hand.

Later that evening, Joseph II kneeled before the royal throne and proudly presented the needle to the King. The King took it from him, reached into the pocket of his royal robe, and brought out his magnifying glass. As he read the inscription, his face grew dark with anger. "Where did you get this needle?" he demanded.

"Why, in the h-h-haystack, Your Majesty," Joseph II stammered.

The King turned to his first minister. "Perhaps *you* have an explanation?"

"For what, Your Majesty?" the older Joseph said

198

innocently, trying to hide the tremor in his voice.

"Come here," the King commanded, "and read this."

The first minister read the tiny script on the needle: *Exact duplicate of first needle: Patience, Perseverance, Honesty.* Color drained from his face, and he awaited judgment.

The next day, Franz heard that the first minister and his family had been banished from the kingdom and the needle search called off. His heart sank. Surely this had something to do with the second needle he had made without consulting the King!

He was prepared for the worst when he heard a knock on the door and saw the King standing outside with his royal guard. But to his surprise, the King gave him a friendly smile as he entered the shop.

"No doubt you have heard that I have called off the contest," the King said to Franz, "and that I have banished the first minister for trying to trick me with the second needle?"

"Yes, Your Majesty," Franz answered in a low voice.

"I have called off the contest for three reasons," the King continued. "The first reason is that everybody knows by now which haystack the needle is in. Secondly, the contest was not a good idea; the hay is ruined—scattered all over the field, and I will have to have my royal harvesters gather more. And finally, I have found my heir."

"You have?" Franz asked.

"Yes," said the King. "You."

"Me?" Franz looked at the King as if he had gone mad.

"Yes, you," repeated the King firmly. "It took patience and perseverance to craft the needle and honesty not to betray a confidence. And more importantly, you are intelligent. You knew that if I had truly lost the needle, the words "exact duplicate" would not matter, and if I had not lost it, the words would reveal a trickster to me. I am proud to make you my royal heir and son."

And so Franz, the goldsmith's son, came to be the King's heir, and in time he ruled the kingdom with patience, perseverance, honesty—and intelligence.

Think and Discuss

1. What qualities did the King want his heir to have? How would these qualities make his heir a good ruler?
2. What did Joseph ask Franz to do? How was his trick discovered?
3. The main idea of a story is called the **theme**. Which of the following best states the theme of this story? Explain your answer.

   a. Haystacks sometimes contain needles.
   b. Wealth does not guarantee happiness.
   c. Goodness is sometimes rewarded.

RESPONDING TO LITERATURE

The Reading and Writing Connection

Personal Response Are the qualities you would want in a friend the same ones that would make a good king? Write one or two paragraphs explaining why they are the same or why they are different.

Creative Writing During the search for the needle, hay was scattered all over the field. Write a journal entry from the point of view of a piece of hay. Tell about your experience on the day of the search.

Creative Activities

Draw Choose a moment in the story that is not illustrated in your book. Then draw or paint the scene. Identify the moment by writing a sentence from the story under your illustration.

Act Out What might have happened if Franz had forgotten to inscribe the words *exact duplicate* on the needle? How would the story have been different? Choose three partners and decide how to change the story to include this event. Take the roles of the King, Joseph, Joseph II, and Franz. Rehearse your version of the story, and act it out for your classmates.

Vocabulary

The word *plot* has several different meanings. In the story, you read about Joseph's *plot*, or secret plan, to trick the king. Use a dictionary or a thesaurus to find other meanings for *plot*.

Looking Ahead

Story You have just read a fairy tale. Some other kinds of stories are mysteries, adventures, and science fiction. In the following composition lessons, you will write a story. Think about the kind of story you would like to write.

VOCABULARY CONNECTION

Using Context Clues

When you read an unfamiliar word, try to figure out its meaning by using the **context**—the surrounding words and sentences. What words in the context help you understand the meaning of *examined*?

> Two days later, Franz brought the finished needle to the castle. The King **examined** it closely with a magnifying glass. . . .
>
> *from "The Needle in the Haystack" by John Hamma*

The words *closely* and *magnifying glass* give you the idea that *examined* means "looked at closely and carefully."

Sometimes context clues can be found in other sentences.

> Carved into the stone was a four-word message. It was the **inscription** the woodcutter had been seeking.

The words *four-word message* probably gave you an idea that *inscription* means "a short message."

Vocabulary Practice

A. Use context clues to figure out the meaning of each underlined word from "The Needle in the Haystack."

1. I turned the <u>duplicate</u> key! It was an exact copy.
2. I entered the <u>chamber</u>, the most beautiful room in the castle.
3. If caught, I'll be <u>banished</u> from the kingdom. The queen will never allow me to return.

B. Write sentences, using five hard words from "The Needle in the Haystack." Include context clues for the meaning of each hard word. Then ask a classmate to figure out the meaning of each word, using your sentences.

Prewriting
Story

Listening: Predicting Outcomes

Speakers and writers often give you clues, or bits of information, about what will happen next in their stories. When you hear or read a story, you put together the storyteller's clues to make a **prediction**. You guess in advance what the **outcome**, or the results of the story events, will be. Including clues in your stories will keep your listeners or readers interested in learning more, so that they can figure out the outcomes.

Read this passage and look for clues about the outcome.

> Later that evening, Joseph II kneeled before the royal throne and proudly presented the needle to the King. The King took it from him, reached into the pocket of his royal robe, and brought out his magnifying glass. As he read the inscription, his face grew dark with anger.
> *from "The Needle in the Haystack" by John Hamma*

- What did you predict would happen after you read the first sentence? What clue helped you?
- What later clue changed your prediction of the outcome?

Follow these guidelines to help you predict outcomes.

Guidelines for Predicting Outcomes

1. Listen for information and clues provided by the author.
2. Base your prediction on the clues and your experience.
3. Change your prediction as new information is provided.

Prewriting Practice

Listen to your teacher read a story. Use the guidelines to help you predict what will happen in the story. Discuss possible outcomes. Which one is most likely? Why?

Thinking: Imagining

Have you ever read a story such as "The Needle in the Haystack" and wondered, "How did the writer think of that?" Good writers know how to *imagine*—to set their thoughts free to create ideas.

One way to think of new ideas is to write down words that pop into your head. Write each word on a separate piece of paper. Then combine any two or three words. Write down all the ideas that spring to mind. Look at this list of words.

needle	gold	haystack	telephone	wheels	pink
mouse	feather	lamp	bracelet	apple	cliff

What story ideas might come to you if you picked *feather– pink–telephone?* What if the words you chose were *lamp* and *wheels?* What if you picked *mouse–apple–bracelet?*

Stir your imagination by asking questions. Ask *Who? What? Where? When? How? Why?* and *What if?* Here are some examples.

> *Where* might you discover a pink telephone and a feather?
> *Why* might a pink feather be sitting beside a telephone?
> *What if* the telephone had been ringing when a bird flew by?
> *Who* might have been calling?

• What questions might the author of "The Needle in the Haystack" have asked to expand his story idea?

Guidelines for Imagining

1. List twelve words that pop into your head.
2. Combine the words on your list to make story ideas.
3. Ask *Who? What? Where? When? How? Why? What if?*

Prewriting Practice

Follow the imagining guidelines to think of story ideas. Jot down your ideas.

Composition Skills
Story

Plot ☑

You probably know that the events of a story make up the **plot**. A plot, however, is more than just a series of events. It is a series of events that center on a problem. There are three main parts to a plot.

Beginning: The plot begins with a problem. In "The Needle in the Haystack," the problem is that the King wants an heir.

Middle: The main part of the plot tells what happens as the result of the opening situation. Complications arise. In "The Needle in the Haystack," the complications are caused by Joseph. While the King is making plans for a fair contest, Joseph is making his own plans to cheat.

End: The end tells how the original problem and the resulting complications are solved. At the end of "The Needle in the Haystack," all loose ends are tied up. Franz ruins Joseph's plan, and Joseph is banished. The King is so pleased with Franz that he makes him the Crown Prince.

Prewriting Practice

A. Make a plot outline of another story that you have read.

   1. **Beginning:** Tell what the opening problem was.
   2. **Middle:** Tell what happened as a result of the problem.
   3. **End:** Tell how the problem was solved.

   Write two sentences for each part. Leave out the details.

B. Work with a group of classmates to brainstorm problems for stories that you could write.

C. Choose one problem from Practice B. Make a plot outline based on that problem. Use the heads **Beginning, Middle,** and **End.** Write only the main points. Leave out the details.

Setting and Characters ☑

Besides plot, the two most important parts of any story are its setting and its characters. The **setting** tells the time and the place of a story. A story can be set in the past, the present, or the future. It can take place in a big city or in a jungle, in France or in China, on the moon, or in an imaginary place.

When you write a story, you may not want to tell everything about your setting. Instead you may decide to provide clues and have your reader draw conclusions. Where does "The Needle in the Haystack" take place? Read the following sentence. What clues does the author give about the setting?

> Once in another time, there lived a King and Queen who had no children.
>
> *from "The Needle in the Haystack" by John Hamma*

- Does the story take place in the past or in the future?
- What clue tells you that the story takes place in a kingdom?

The **characters** in a story can be people, animals, or imaginary creatures. You can use three methods to tell what your characters are like.

1. Tell what the characters think and do.

2. Have one character tell about another.

3. Have the characters speak.

- We learn many things about Franz in the story. Which method did the author use to tell you that Franz is worried about the King's visit? that the King thinks Franz is intelligent?

When you write a story, try to *show* what your characters are like or what they feel. Read this sentence about Joseph.

> Color drained from his face, and he awaited judgment.
>
> *from "The Needle in the Haystack" by John Hamma*

- What is Joseph feeling?
- How do you know? What clues did the author give?

Prewriting Practice

A. Here are two ideas for story settings. On a separate piece of paper, add five more ideas to each list.

TIME	PLACE
present time	hotel
the year 2000	small town

B. Choose a setting from Practice A or make one up. Write several sentences that show rather than tell about the setting. Then ask a classmate to figure out the setting.

C. Make up a story character. Is your character shy? brave? selfish? kind? Choose two of the three methods from page 206 to tell what your character is like. For each method, write two or three sentences about your character.

D. Now think about what your character is feeling. Is your character happy? sad? excited? worried? Write three or four sentences that *show* rather than tell what your character is feeling. Give your reader clues.

The Grammar Connection

Verb Tenses

Be careful not to change from one tense to another in the same sentence or paragraph. Read the paragraph below, noticing the underscored verbs. Can you follow the paragraph easily?

> Ray <u>walked</u> down the stairs of his front porch and <u>sees</u> his friend Marcus. Marcus <u>ran</u> up to Ray and <u>says</u> he <u>had</u> two tickets for the basketball game. They <u>decide</u> they <u>wanted</u> to go. They <u>asked</u> their parents, and their parents <u>say</u> yes. The boys <u>leave</u> for the game.

Practice The paragraph above is confusing because the verbs change from one tense to another. Decide whether you want the action to take place in the past or the present. Then rewrite the paragraph correctly.

The Writing Process
How To Write a Story

Step 1: Prewriting—Choose a Topic

Scott listed some ideas he had for stories. Then he thought about which one would be best.

A boy gets lost on Mars

He couldn't think of enough things that would happen.

Abe Lincoln visits Disney World

He had never been to Disney World.

Two friends discover a rare old book

He couldn't think of a good ending for this.

The adventures of a piece of paper

He thought he could write a good story about this.

Moving West in a covered wagon

He would have to study some history to write about this.

He circled the paper idea.

On Your Own

1. **Think and discuss** Make a list of story ideas of your own. Use the Ideas page to help you. Discuss your ideas with a partner.
2. **Choose** Ask yourself these questions about each topic.
   Would this make an interesting story to write and read?
   Do I know enough about the setting?
   Could I think of a good ending for this story?
   Circle the idea you want to use for your story.
3. **Explore** What will you write? Do one of the activities under "Exploring Your Topic" on the Ideas page.

Ideas for Getting Started

Choosing Your Topic

Story Ideas

A king who becomes
  invisible
A gold watch that
  stops time
Two friends who start
  a club
A family's lost dog
The adventures of a
  pair of roller skates
A duck rescued by a
  boy

Picture This!

Do you see
a story in
this picture?
Think about
it! Write it!

Exploring Your Topic

Outline It!

To get started, outline your plot.
Here is Scott's outline.

*Beginning: Paper is in store.
Boy buys paper and takes
it home.
Middle: Boy makes and
plays with kite. Kite is
eventually thrown out.
End: Paper is recycled.*

Talk About It

Tell your story to
someone. Does the
ending work? Are
your characters inter-
esting enough? Did
you get more ideas?

Step 2: Write a First Draft

Scott decided to write his story for his friends. He thought they would like his idea of having a piece of paper tell its own story.

Scott wrote his first draft. He did not worry about making mistakes. He would have a chance to correct them later.

The beginning of Scott's first draft

> Two years ago I was just a sheet of paper in a rack at a store. ~~I~~ My life wasn't so bad until a boy came in. ~~He saw~~ The next thing I knew I was in a bag. It herd him say that he was going to make a penut kite out of it. He would fly it with uncle jim. That sounded scary!

On Your Own

1. **Think about purpose and audience** Ask yourself these questions.

   For whom shall I write my story?

   What is my purpose? Do I want my reader to laugh? feel frightened? learn a lesson?

2. **Write** Use details to show plot, character, and setting. Write on every other line so that you will have room to add or make changes later. Do not worry about mistakes. Just write your story.

Step 3: Revise

Scott read his first draft. He thought the boy should have a name. He also decided to add some more details about the sheet of paper. He made some changes in his first draft.

Scott wanted to know what someone else thought of his idea. He read the whole story to Elena.

Reading and responding

I like the first part when the paper was talking.

Oh—I *had* started out that way!

Could you have the paper tell the whole story?

Great idea!

Scott thought about Elena's comments and made some changes. He also used dialogue to show what the boy said.

Part of Scott's revised beginning

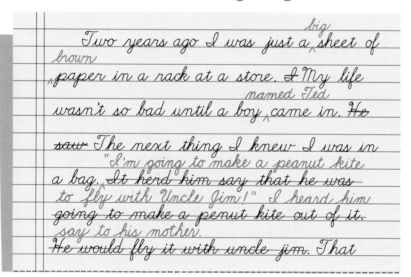

Think and Discuss ✓

• What details did Scott add?
• Where did he add dialogue?
• What other changes did he make? Did they improve the story?

The Writing Process 211

On Your Own

Revising Checklist

☑ Have I used details to show the setting clearly?
☑ How could I show more about my characters?
☑ Does the plot have a beginning, a middle, and an end?
☑ Does the ending of the story work?

1. **Revise** Make changes in your first draft. If you need to find exact words, use the thesaurus below or the one in the back of the book. Replace words by crossing them out and adding new words above them. Add details and dialogue.

2. **Have a conference** Read your story to someone else. Make notes about your listener's remarks.

Ask your listener:	As you listen:
"Can you see the setting clearly?" "What more could I show about the characters?" "Can you follow the plot?" "Does the ending work?"	Can I see the setting and the characters in my mind? Can I follow the plot? Does the ending fit? What else would I like to know about the story?

3. **Revise** Think about your listener's suggestions. Do you have any other ideas? Make those changes on your paper.

Thesaurus

boast brag, crow
bold daring, audacious
brave courageous, valiant, fearless
change convert, transform
decide determine, resolve
faithful loyal, true
fake fraud, phony, impostor

hide conceal, bury
moment instant
necessary essential, required
opponent competitor, rival
pull drag, haul, tow
shake quake, shiver, shudder, tremble
warning alarm, signal

Step 4: Proofread

Scott proofread his story for mistakes in spelling, capitalization, and punctuation. He used a dictionary to check spelling. He used proofreading marks to make his changes.

Scott's proofread ending

> ⁊ Well, that's ^my the story. Maybe you're
> ~~wondring~~ wondering how ^it got back to the store
> without even a ^wrinkle ~~rinkle~~. You see, ^it was
> ~~resycled~~ recycled and made into a birthday card.
> ≡now ^it lives in the Card Rack. It's so
> nice here. Oh, no! I've been spotted!

Think and Discuss

- Which words did Scott correct for spelling?
- Which verb was changed to agree with its subject?
- Where did Scott indent? Why?
- Why did he add an apostrophe?

On Your Own

1. **Proofreading Practice** Proofread this paragraph. Find two mistakes in forming contractions. Find four other spelling mistakes. Find one run-on sentence and one mistake in paragraph format. Write the paragraph correctly.

```
Sharon hurryed out of the station
wagon! Her family's mountin vacation
was finaly beginning. She lugged her
heavy suitcase up the rocky hill she
shouldve worn her sneakers! Her hair
was in her eyes, and she didnt see
the old cabin until she got to the
top. When she saw it, she droped her
suitcase and groaned.
```

Proofreading Marks

⁊ Indent
∧ Add something
⍓ Take out something
≡ Capitalize
/ Make a small letter

2. **Proofreading Application** Now proofread your paper. Use the Proofreading Checklist and the Grammar and Spelling Hints below. You may want to use a colored pencil to make your corrections. Use a dictionary to check spellings.

Proofreading Checklist

Did I

☑ **1.** indent?

☑ **2.** use capital letters correctly?

☑ **3.** use punctuation marks correctly?

☑ **4.** use verbs correctly?

☑ **5.** spell all words correctly?

The Grammar/Spelling Connection

Grammar Hints

Remember these rules from Unit 5 when you use verbs.

- Use apostrophes in contractions. *(isn't, could've)*
- Use *have* or *'ve*, not *of*, with *could*, *should*, *would*, and *must*. *(could have, could've, would have, would've)*

Spelling Hints

- When you add a suffix that begins with a consonant, do not change the spelling of the base word. *(unusual–unusually, soft–softness)*
- If a verb ends with a consonant and *y*, change the *y* to *i* when adding *-ed*. *(carry–carried, try–tried)*

Step 5: Publish

Scott added a title to his story. Then he shared his story by making a brown paper kite like the one in his story. He put it on the bulletin board beside the finished copy of his story.

On Your Own

1. **Copy** Write or type your story as neatly as possible.
2. **Add a title** Think of a title to catch your reader's interest. Remember to capitalize the first, last, and all important words.
3. **Check** Read over your story again to make sure that you have not left out anything or made any mistakes in copying.
4. **Share** Think of a special way to share your story.

Ideas for Sharing

- Divide your story into three parts. Have two friends help you read your story aloud as though it is a news story on the radio.
- Make a story book and illustrate the events.
- Make a model of your story setting in a cardboard box.

Applying Story Writing

Literature and Creative Writing

"The Needle in the Haystack" is a fairy tale set in an imaginary kingdom. A childless king decides that whoever finds the needle he has hidden in a haystack will become his heir. The first minister tries to trick the King, but he is outwitted by the goldsmith's son.

Have fun using what you have learned about writing stories to complete one of the following activities.

> **Remember these things** ☑
> Give your story a plot that is centered on a problem.
> Include a setting and characters.

1. **The joke's on the joker.** Write a story in which one character tries unsuccessfully to outwit another by playing a joke or making a bargain that is not really a bargain.

2. **Find the object.** Write a story that centers on a small object like the needle. It could be a pen, a ring, a photo, or anything you choose.

3. **What did the needle see?** Write a story from the point of view of the needle. Include the needle's opinion of the King's plan and its feelings about being part of it.

Writing Across the Curriculum
Science

The wonders and mysteries of science have inspired many people to write stories based on science. These stories are usually very imaginative, and the writers have a good understanding of scientific principles.

Try doing one or more of these activities.

1. **Become another part of nature.** Imagine that you are an inanimate object—something that is not alive. For example, you might be a rock, a river, or a cloud. How were you formed? In what ways do you change? Do you touch people's lives? Write a story about your life.

Writing Steps
1. Choose a topic
2. Write a first draft
3. Revise
4. Proofread
5. Publish

Word Bank
flow
motion
force
cycle
transform

2. **Tell the news.** Imagine that you are a newspaper reporter covering the story of a pet that has taken on the characteristics of another animal. For example, perhaps a cat is suddenly able to fly. Write the story and give it an exciting headline.

3. **Weight doesn't matter.** This morning you awake as usual, only to find that there is no gravity. The force that keeps everything on the earth is no longer working! What do people do? Write a story about what happens.

Extending Literature
Book Report: Play

Sandy enjoyed reading "The Needle in the Haystack." She liked stories in which the characters caused their own good or bad luck. At the library, she found a book called *Aesop's Fables*. The fables had such good endings that Sandy wanted her classmates to read them. She decided to produce one fable as a play. Sandy wrote this play and acted it with three friends.

NARRATOR: You are about to see a play version of "The Wind and the Sun." This fable was told by a wise man named Aesop. Aesop's fables are stories that teach lessons. This fable takes place one beautiful autumn day on a country road. The characters are the Sun, the Wind, and a Traveler. Here are the Sun and the Wind.

WIND (waving arms): Look at that, Sun! Leaves fly and trees bend when I walk by. I'm much stronger than you are!

SUN (smiling quietly): Oh, no, I'm afraid you're wrong.

WIND (looking insulted): Huh! Let's see you prove it! (Traveler enters wearing a heavy coat. It is unbuttoned.)

TRAVELER (looking around): What a great day for traveling!

SUN (to Wind): I think I can prove it. Let's see who is strong enough to make this Traveler take off that coat.

WIND: Ha! I'll go first. You go stand behind that cloud and watch me! I'll have that coat off in a hurry!

NARRATOR: So the contest begins. Who will win? What will the contest *really* prove? Read the fable!

Think and Discuss

• What kind of a story is a fable?
• What do you think the answers are to the narrator's questions?

Share Your Book

Write a Play

1. Decide which part of the book you want to share. Choose a part in which the characters talk to one another.
2. Write a short script for your play. Don't give away the ending of the story. Add stage directions in parentheses to explain how the characters sound and move.
3. Use a narrator to explain what the play is about, or write a short introduction. Include the title and the author's name.
4. Read the play to your class, using a different voice for each character. If you decide instead to present the play with several friends, make a copy of the play for each actor.

Other Activities

- Make masks for the different characters. If you are reading the parts yourself, make the masks out of stiff cardboard and mount them on flat sticks. Then you can hold up the proper mask as each character speaks.
- Use chairs and other props to make the play more realistic for the audience. You may want to have each character wear a simple costume.
- Print a program and make copies for the audience. Include the title and the author's name. Give the time and the place of the action. List the characters and the names of the actors.

 # The Book Nook

The Cat-King's Daughter	Stoneflight
by Lloyd Alexander	*by Georgess McHargue*
Margot, a talking cat, helps the princess convince her father, the King, to let her marry her true love.	Jamie is upset about spending the summer in New York until she learns to fly on a stone griffin.

Language and Usage

The gray sea and the long black land;
And the yellow half-moon large and low. . . .

Robert Browning
from "Meeting at Night"

Adjectives

Getting Ready Have you ever wanted or used a camera to capture the glorious colors of a sunrise or sunset? Adjectives are like word cameras. They are the words that describe colors and sizes and shapes. They tell which one, what kind, and how many. Adjectives help you capture how the world around you looks and feels. In this unit, you will learn how you can use adjectives to make your writing more vivid and more correct.

ACTIVITIES

Listening   Listen as the poem on the opposite page is read. Listen for the six adjectives. What are they?

Speaking   Look at the picture. How many adjectives can your class think of to describe it? Have a class "secretary" write your list on the board. Then circle the adjectives that do the best job.

Writing   In your journal, write your thoughts about moonlight. Describe how it is different from sunlight.

A word that describes a noun or a pronoun is called an **adjective**.

1. **Adjectives tell what kind.**	Spotted fawns were resting. They looked peaceful
2. **Adjectives tell how many.**	Three elephants were eating. Monkeys did several tricks.

Adjectives appear in a variety of places in a sentence. They may come before the noun they are describing.

Powerful lions stared boldly at us.

Adjectives may also come after a linking verb.

Giraffes seemed gentle and shy.

When two or more adjectives are listed together, you should usually use a comma to separate them.

Large, colorful parrots screeched.

When one of these adjectives tells how many, do not use a comma.

Two white geese honked loudly.

Guided Practice
What are the adjectives in each sentence? (Do not include *a, an,* or *the*.)

Example: Several graceful zebras played in the tall grass.
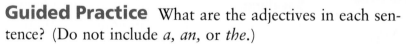
Several   graceful   tall

1. The two cubs are small and playful.
2. One enormous hippo swam in deep water.
3. The beautiful, proud peacock has many feathers.
4. The owls have speckled wings and sharp claws.
5. We were curious about three alligators.
6. They were resting on a long, smooth rock.

> ▸ An **adjective** is a word that describes a noun or a pronoun.
> ▸ An adjective tells what kind or how many.

Independent Practice Write each sentence. Underline each adjective. Do not include *a, an,* or *the.* Then draw an arrow from the adjective to the noun that it describes.

Example: The famous zoo has many interesting animals.

The famous zoo has many interesting animals.

7. The giraffes have long legs and knobby knees.
8. The striped tiger sits in a shady spot.
9. Two chimpanzees performed funny tricks.
10. Several monkeys are cute and frisky.
11. One cage is filled with colorful birds.
12. The noisy birds were sitting in the small trees.
13. The green and blue parrot has a hooked bill.
14. The crocodiles have long, narrow snouts and big teeth.
15. Three gentle deer graze beneath the fir trees.
16. Five young kangaroos drink from the shallow pond.
17. The old, brown bear protects the small cubs.
18. The heavy elephant has a slow, swaying walk.
19. A camel with two humps is watching the people.
20. The large, powerful gorilla is sleeping.
21. The lion with a thick, sandy mane gave a mighty roar.
22. Six black and white penguins marched in two rows.
23. The playful seals pose for the happy photographer.
24. Two graceful zebras jumped over the large boulders.
25. The swift cheetah has strong legs.
26. The wooly goat is a stubborn animal.

Writing Application: Instructions
Imagine that you are a zoo keeper. Write instructions for caring for one of your favorite animals. Use adjectives in each sentence.

For Extra Practice, see p. 241.   **What Is an Adjective?**

2 | Articles and Demonstrative Adjectives

a magazine   a tie

an orange shirt   an interesting hat

an alarm clock

Two special kinds of adjectives are articles and demonstrative adjectives. They are used before a noun or before another adjective.

A, an, and *the* are **articles**. *A* and *an* refer to any person, place, or thing. *The* refers to a particular one.

Let's take a trip. (any)   It's time for the trip. (particular)

This, that, these, and *those* are **demonstrative adjectives**. A demonstrative adjective tells which one. *This* and *these* refer to nouns close to the speaker or writer. *That* and *those* refer to nouns farther away.

This trip will be long.   Please pass me that book.

Articles:		
a	Use before singular words that begin with a consonant sound.	a jet a high step
an	Use before singular words that begin with a vowel sound.	an engine an hour
the	Use before singular and plural words.	the plans
Demonstrative adjectives:		
this, that	Use before singular words.	this seat
these, those	Use before plural words.	those pens

Guided Practice Which word correctly completes each sentence?

Example: I am flying in (a, an) huge plane. *a*

1. I am sitting in (a, an) aisle seat.
2. (Those, That) man should fasten his seat belt.
3. We are flying over (a, the) state of New York.
4. (This, That) magazine is old, but that one is new.
5. (These, Those) clouds are far away.

> ▶ *A, an,* and *the* are special adjectives called **articles**. *A* and *an* refer to any person, place, or thing. *The* refers to a particular person, place, or thing.
> ▶ *This, that, these,* and *those* are demonstrative adjectives. They tell which one.

Independent Practice Write the word in parentheses that correctly completes each sentence.

Example: I took (a, an) bus to the train station.   *a*

6. I rushed to (a, the) nearest window.
7. My train left the station before (that, those) train.
8. I sat in (a, the) first car of the train.
9. (Those, These) cars behind me were more crowded.
10. My seat has a better view than (this, that) seat over there.
11. I put my suitcase on (a, an) empty shelf.
12. One of (a, the) conductors took my ticket.
13. (This, That) seat feels uncomfortable when the train goes fast.
14. I ask the conductor for (a, an) pillow.
15. My train is moving faster than (these, those) buses over there.
16. (A, The) engine's noise is very loud.
17. The loud screech of the brakes sounds exactly like (an, a) elephant's call.
18. (This, That) window next to me rattles when we go fast.
19. (That, This) loudspeaker near me is broken.
20. I can hear the conductor's voice from (that, this) loudspeaker down the aisle.
21. The conductor is announcing (a, the) next station.
22. I will be at my friend's house in (a, an) hour.

Writing Application: A Paragraph

Imagine that you are flying in a hot-air balloon. Who are the people that are traveling with you? Write a paragraph about them and the things that you see around and below you. Use articles and demonstrative adjectives in your sentences.

For Extra Practice, see p. 242.
Articles and Demonstratives   225

3 | Comparing with Adjectives

You know that adjectives describe nouns. One way they describe is by comparing people, places, or things. To compare two people, places, or things, add *-er* to the adjective. To compare three or more, add *-est*.

ONE PERSON: My brother is tall .

TWO PERSONS: My mother is taller than my brother.

THREE OR MORE: My father is tallest of all.

Highest

Higher

High

Rules for Comparing with Adjectives	
1. Most adjectives: Add *-er* or *-est* to the adjective.	bright bright**er** bright**est**
2. Adjectives ending with e: Drop the e and add *-er* or *-est*.	safe saf**er** saf**est**
3. Adjectives ending with a consonant and *y*: Change the *y* to *i* and add *-er* or *-est*.	busy bus**ier** bus**iest**
4. One-syllable adjectives that end with a single vowel and a consonant: Double the consonant and add *-er* or *-est*.	flat flat**ter** flat**test**
5. Some adjectives with two or more syllables: Use *more* or *most* instead of *-er* or *-est*.	careful **more** careful **most** careful

Guided Practice Which form of each adjective do you use to compare two people, places, or things? Which form do you use to compare more than two?

Example: angry *angrier angriest*

1. small	**3.** helpful	**5.** curious	**7.** wise
2. strange	**4.** red	**6.** shaky	**8.** great

> ▸ Add *-er* to most adjectives to compare two.
> ▸ Add *-est* to most adjectives to compare more than two.
> ▸ Use *more* and *most*, not *-er* and *-est*, with long adjectives.

Independent Practice Write the correct form of each adjective in parentheses to complete each sentence correctly.

Example: Roberto is the ____ child in my family. (friendly)
friendliest

 9. His school grades are ____ than mine. (high)
10. Maria is the ____ person in my family. (energetic)
11. Of all the children, she is the ____ in student government at Central Elementary School. (active)
12. Her campaign posters are always ____ than those of the other students. (interesting)
13. I am ____ than Maria. (artistic)
14. Art is my ____ subject of all. (enjoyable)
15. My new poster is ____ than my last one. (large)
16. Of the two posters, this one was the ____. (complex)
17. Of all my projects, it has taken the ____ time. (long)
18. That was the ____ cartoon I could find. (funny)
19. The blue letters are ____ than the red letters. (fat)
20. The white glue is ____ than the clear glue. (sticky)
21. Of all the posters on the bulletin board, mine is the ____. (colorful)
22. My next poster will be ____ than this poster. (simple)
23. I will use ____ colors than I did this time. (few)
24. The message on my next poster will be ____ than the one on this poster. (short)
25. My last painting was the ____ piece of art that I have ever made. (attractive)
26. My next painting will be even ____. (beautiful)

Writing Application: Comparison and Contrast
Write a paragraph comparing yourself to other members of your family. Be sure to use correct adjective forms in your comparisons.

For Extra Practice, see p. 243.   **Comparing with Adjectives   227**

4 | Comparing with *good* and *bad*

The adjectives *good* and *bad* have special forms for making comparisons. These words do not take the endings *-er* and *-est* or use the words *more* and *most* to make comparisons.

GOOD: The dress rehearsal of our play was good .

Our first performance was better .

Our last performance was best .

BAD: I had a bad case of stage fright.

It was worse in the second act.

The worst stage fright came just before my entrance.

Comparing with *good* and *bad*		
Describing one person, place, or thing	good	bad
Comparing two persons, places, or things	better	worse
Comparing three or more persons, places, or things	best	worst

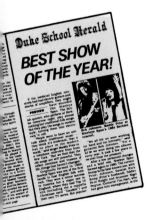

Guided Practice
What is the correct form of *good* or *bad* in each sentence?

Example: This play was (better, best) than the last play.   *better*

1. Sarah gave a very (good, better) performance.
2. The musical was the (better, best) show of the three.
3. Mary had a (bad, worst) cough.
4. Her coughing grew (bad, worse) in the last speech.
5. Her coughing was the (bad, worst) thing that happened on-stage.
6. Of the four singers, Merle was the (best, good).
7. The costumes were (better, good) this year than last year.
8. The dancing in this show was the (good, best) ever.

▶ The adjectives *good* and *bad* have special forms for making comparisons.
▶ Use *better* and *worse* to compare two.
▶ Use *best* and *worst* to compare more than two.

Independent Practice

A. Write the correct form of *good* for each sentence.

Example: Linda thought the concert was very ____. *good*

9. Our seats were ____ than the seats that we had last time.
10. Mark thought the clarinet section was the ____ of all.
11. The musicians' new outfits looked ____ than the old ones.
12. What is the ____ concert you have ever heard?
13. This year's songs were much ____ than last year's.
14. The audience reaction was ____ than it was last year.
15. The new conductor is ____ than the last one.
16. She knows that she has the ____ musicians in town.
17. Each rehearsal was ____ than the previous one.
18. This concert was the ____ of all ten.
19. Next year's concerts should be just as ____.

B. Write the correct form of *bad* for each sentence.

Example: This trumpet player is ____ than that one. *worse*

20. Ona's performance was ____ than yours.
21. It was her ____ performance of the year.
22. The former conductor was ____ than the present one.
23. Last year's attendance was ____ than this year's.
24. Even very ____ weather didn't keep people away this year.
25. The musicians felt that this was a very ____ year.
26. They thought it was their ____ season in ten years.
27. However, the concerts did not get one ____ review.
28. Even the ____ concert of the season was well attended.

Writing Application: Comparison and Contrast

Write a paragraph comparing three similar events, such as three school assemblies or plays. Use forms of *good* and *bad*.

For Extra Practice, see p. 244.   **Comparing with *good* and *bad*   229**

5 | Proper Adjectives

You have learned that a proper noun names a particular person, place, or thing. An adjective formed from a proper noun is called a **proper adjective**. Like a proper noun, a proper adjective is capitalized.

PROPER NOUN: Those geese are from Canada .

PROPER ADJECTIVE: They are Canadian geese.

Proper noun	Proper adjective
Italy	Italian cooking
Mexico	Mexican rug
Switzerland	Swiss watch
South America	South American bird

Notice that the proper adjective *South American* is two words that describe one thing. When a proper adjective is two words, capitalize both words.

South American Scarlet Macaw

Guided Practice How would you form a proper adjective from the underlined noun to complete each sentence? Use your dictionary if you need help.

Example: Food from Spain is ____ food. *Spanish*

1. People from Russia are ____ people.
2. Travelers from America are ____ tourists.
3. The ____ Highway runs through Alaska.
4. People in Germany are proud of ____ cars.
5. A company in Japan makes ____ watches.

> ### Summing up
>
> ▶ A **proper adjective** is formed from a proper noun.
> ▶ A proper adjective begins with a capital letter.

Independent Practice

A. Write the proper adjective in each sentence correctly.

Example: I sent a letter to my british pen pal. *British*

6. We rode on a turkish train last summer.

7. Have you ever tasted polish bread?

8. The weather is hot on the greek islands.

9. A danish student named Jette visited our school.

10. Have you ever been to a canadian campground?

11. My aunt owns a beautiful chinese painting.

12. I have a swiss flag in my collection.

13. Have you ever been to a vietnamese restaurant?

14. Do you know any japanese words?

15. I have a beautiful moroccan robe.

B. Write the proper adjective that comes from the proper noun in parentheses. Use your dictionary if you need help.

Example: Storms are very common over the ____ Channel.
(England) *English*

16. The ____ city of Paris is very beautiful. (France)

17. Canada is a ____ country. (North America)

18. Kangaroos run wild on the ____ plains. (Australia)

19. ____ ranchers raise cattle. (Brazil)

20. People ski in the ____ Alps. (Austria)

21. Oil is found in the ____ desert. (Saudi Arabia)

22. ____ meatballs are delicious. (Sweden)

23. Do you know any ____ songs? (Hawaii)

24. The ____ city of Cairo is often hot. (Egypt)

25. I have a beautiful ____ shirt. (Greece)

26. My sister owns some lovely ____ pottery. (Mexico)

27. Sandra is an excellent ____ teacher. (Germany)

28. My aunt once stayed in a ____ village. (Spain)

Paris

Eiffel Tower

Writing Application: A Paragraph

Many things we use in the United States, such as cars and watches, come from other countries. Write a paragraph about things you use that were made in other countries. Use a proper adjective in each sentence.

For Extra Practice, see p. 245.   **Proper Adjectives 231**

Grammar-Writing Connection

Expanding Sentences with Adjectives

One way to improve your writing is to answer the questions your reader might ask. Adjectives answer the questions, what kind? how many? and which one? The sentence below does not contain any adjectives.

> A pilot flew the jet across the continents.

Your reader might ask, which pilot? what kind of jet? or how many continents? The following sentence, which contains three adjectives, answers these questions.

> An expert pilot flew the jumbo jet across three continents.

Notice that the adjectives provide important information, which makes the sentence more meaningful. The adjectives also make the sentence more interesting.

Revising Sentences

Rewrite the sentences below, adding adjectives to them. Answer the questions that your reader might ask.

1. Jets arrived at the airport.
2. A runway had been built near the terminal.
3. Airports are often located near cities.
4. Noise from planes can disturb people.
5. My aunt flew across the ocean on a jet.
6. Passengers on her flight enjoyed the trip.
7. Attendants served both breakfast and dinner.
8. They gave the passengers pillows and blankets.
9. My aunt read magazines and watched a movie.
10. The passengers were greeted by friends and relatives at the airport in Switzerland.
11. My aunt stayed with a friend in a village.
12. Her friend showed her mountains, lakes, and cities.

Creative Writing

Claude Monet's quick paintbrush has caught forever the floating clouds, sunlight, and swaying flowers of a long-ago moment.

• How would the picture be different if it were painted in sharper detail? Would you like it better?

Wild Poppies,
Claude Monet,
Musée du Louvre

Activities

1. **Write an advertisement.** Imagine that this field is called Poppy Park. Would you want to walk in the park? Write an advertisement, explaining why Poppy Park is a beautiful place to visit.
2. **Describe your impressions.** Pretend that you are standing in this field. What are you seeing? hearing? smelling? Try to capture the moment in words. Write a detailed paragraph.
3. **Make up a poem.** Have you ever been in a large space like a field or an empty lot? Perhaps you have been alone on a lake or an ocean? How did you feel—lonely? free? unimportant? Describe your feelings in a poem.

Check-up: Unit 7

What Is an Adjective? *(p. 222)* Write each adjective and the noun that it describes. (Do not include *a, an,* or *the.*)

1. Denmark is a small kingdom.
2. It is in northern Europe.
3. Denmark lies between two seas.
4. It has many islands.
5. Denmark has mild, damp weather.
6. Little farms cover the land.
7. The white houses have red roofs.
8. Beautiful Copenhagen is the capital.
9. It is a lively, modern city.
10. Danes look cheerful and friendly.
11. Tivoli Gardens is a huge park.
12. It is an exciting place.
13. The park has colorful buildings.
14. They glow with bright lights.
15. There is an outdoor stage.
16. Concerts sound delightful.
17. People sail boats on a large lake.
18. Hans Christian Andersen was a famous writer.
19. He wrote wonderful tales.
20. People around the world read them in many languages.
21. One character is a little mermaid.
22. There is a charming statue of her.
23. The bronze mermaid sits on a rock.
24. She looks at the great, blue sea.
25. Denmark has lovely beaches.
26. People sometimes stay in pretty cottages at the seashore.
27. Many families enjoy holidays there.
28. The blue lakes are also popular.

Articles and Demonstrative Adjectives *(p. 224)* Write the word in parentheses that completes each sentence correctly.

29. (A, The) island has a good market.
30. (This, That) is an indoor market over there.
31. I like (this, that) open-air market better than that one.
32. (An, The) island is known for its excellent pottery.
33. (An, A) vase will be a nice gift.
34. Look at (these, those) vases back there.
35. Are they any nicer than (those, these) right here?
36. Here is (an, a) unusual vase.
37. (The, A) one in my hand is lovely.
38. Did you see (that, this) green one on the far table?
39. I still like (that, this) one in my hand the best.

Comparing with Adjectives *(p. 226)* Write the correct form of each adjective in parentheses.

40. Gorillas are (big) than other apes.
41. Of all the apes, gorillas are the (gentle).
42. They are (fast) than their enemies.
43. They are also (brave) than most monkeys.
44. Chimpanzees are (intelligent) than other apes.
45. They are also the (noisy).

Comparing with *good* and *bad* (p. 228) Write the correct form of *good* or *bad* for each sentence.

46. I used to be a very (bad) cook.
47. I now have a very (good) cookbook.
48. My meals are (good) than before.
49. The (good) one of all was ravioli.
50. It was (good) than spaghetti.
51. Some of the recipes were very (bad).
52. The (bad) dish that I ever made was bean loaf.
53. It tasted (bad) than beans do.
54. Jo bakes very (good) bread.
55. The (good) one of all is nut bread.
56. My rolls are also (good).
57. They taste (good) than bread.
58. This one looks the (good).
59. Your fruit salad is always (good) than mine.
60. This apple looks very (bad).
61. It is (bad) than that one.
62. That store has very (good) fruit.
63. The vegetables are even (good) than the fruit.
64. I know a recipe for a very (good) vegetable stew.
65. Joe's diner is (bad) than Harry's.
66. That's the (bad) place around.
67. I know a very (good) restaurant.
68. Is it (good) than Rick's?
69. It's the (good) one in town!
70. Does it have very (good) chili?
71. I had very (good) chili there.
72. Was it (good) than the soup?
73. It was (good) than Rick's chili.
74. It was the (good) chili ever.

Proper Adjectives (p. 230) Write the proper adjective that comes from the proper noun in parentheses. You may use your dictionary.

75. Is that (Denmark) furniture?
76. Do you like (Italy) shoes?
77. I sometimes make (Mexico) tacos.
78. Do you know any (Israel) dances?
79. The (Africa) continent is large.
80. Liz wore a (Norway) folk dress.
81. Katya had a (Greece) hat.
82. We studied the (Egypt) pyramids.
83. I heard some (Russia) music.
84. You will enjoy the (France) shops.
85. I love (Switzerland) cheese.
86. Elephants roam the (Kenya) plains.
87. I have an (Ireland) sweater.
88. The (Rome) ruins are interesting.
89. I liked that (Poland) song.
90. Ben has an (Iceland) blanket.
91. Joe visited (Germany) castles.
92. (Scotland) wool feels warm.
93. I just saw an (Australia) movie.
94. A new (Britain) museum opened.
95. We saw a (Hungary) folk dance.
96. Is that a (Paris) perfume?
97. (Japan) noodles are tasty.
98. Was he an (America) composer?
99. Is this a (Hawaii) pineapple?
100. Sue climbed the (Chile) mountain.
101. We loved the (England) cliffs.
102. Famous (Austria) horses performed.
103. The (China) silk was yellow.
104. That is (Portugal) pottery.
105. This (India) shirt is handmade.
106. They explored a (Bolivia) jungle.

Cumulative Review

Unit 1: The Sentence

Kinds of Sentences *(p. 16)* For each sentence, write *declarative, interrogative, imperative,* or *exclamatory.* If a group of words is not a sentence, write *fragment.*

1. Have you ever been to a factory?
2. This afternoon our class.
3. We will learn about paper making.
4. Look at this box of pressed wood.
5. How huge the machines are!

Subjects and Predicates *(pp. 18, 20)* Write each sentence. Draw a line between the complete subject and the complete predicate. Underline the simple subject once and the simple predicate twice.

6. Dragonflies live near fresh water.
7. These insects dart through the air.
8. Their long, thin bodies fly high.
9. Their large eyes hunt for insects.
10. Four shiny wings beat rapidly.

Imperative Sentences *(p. 24)* For each sentence, write *declarative* or *imperative.* Then write the simple subject.

11. Eat more carrot sticks.
12. Carrots are good for you.
13. Don't cook the carrots.
14. Raw carrots taste better.
15. Have carrots with your lunch.

Conjunctions *(p. 26)* Choose the correct conjunction in parentheses.

16. Lively otters swim (and, but) play.
17. They slide on mud (or, but) snow.
18. Cubs are blind at birth, (but, or) their eyes open after a month.
19. Otters (and, or) minks are related.

Combining Sentences *(pp. 28, 30, 32)* Combine each group of sentences, using the conjunction given. Form a compound subject, a compound predicate, or a compound sentence.

20. Frogs swim in water.   (or)
    Frogs jump on land.
21. Tadpoles are baby frogs.   (but)
    They look like tiny fish.
22. Some frogs croak loudly.   (and)
    The sound is heard a mile away.
23. Ducks are enemies of frogs.   (and)
    Otters are enemies of frogs.

Run-on Sentences *(p. 34)* Write each of the following run-on sentences correctly.

24. Mallards are wild ducks lakes and rivers are their homes.
25. Plants supply most of their food some plants are found under water.
26. The male duck has a green head its chest is rust its belly is white.
27. Female ducks look different they are brown.

Unit 3: Nouns

Common and Proper Nouns (p. 88)
List common and proper nouns.

28. A trip to Australia is exciting.
29. This continent is an island.
30. Sydney is the largest city.
31. Kangaroos roam the vast plains.
32. Farmers raise sheep and cattle.

Plural Nouns (pp. 84, 86) Write the plural of each underlined noun.

33. I made the <u>lunch</u> for the <u>party</u>.
34. I heard the <u>recipe</u> on the <u>radio</u>.
35. First, put the <u>fish</u> in the <u>dish</u>.
36. Add the <u>potato</u> and the <u>peach</u>.
37. Pour the extra <u>juice</u> in the <u>glass</u>.
38. Bake the <u>loaf</u> in the <u>oven</u>.

Possessive Nouns (pp. 90, 92) Rewrite each phrase, using a possessive noun.

39. the spots of leopards
40. the size of the gorilla
41. the manes of the lions
42. the feathers of the ostrich
43. the grins of the monkeys

Unit 5: Verbs

Action Verbs (p. 142) Write the action verb in each sentence.

44. The colonists fought the British.
45. They won their independence.
46. They called a meeting in 1787.
47. The members argued all summer.
48. Finally, they formed a new nation.

Direct Objects (p. 144) Write the direct objects.

49. Dr. Dian Fossey studied gorillas.
50. This scientist watched their interesting behavior.
51. She wrote several interesting books about them.
52. Each gorilla has a personality.
53. Gorillas do not harm other animals.
54. They eat only plants.

Main Verbs and Helping Verbs (p. 146) Write the verbs in these sentences. Underline the helping verbs once and the main verbs twice.

55. I am starting a stamp collection.
56. I will collect stamps from many countries.
57. The first stamps were sold in 1840.
58. Stamps have honored great people.
59. Some stamps have become extremely valuable.
60. A very rare stamp was sold for one million dollars in 1981.

Linking Verbs (p. 148) Write each sentence and underline the linking verb. Then draw an arrow showing the words the verb links.

61. This beach is my favorite place in the summer.
62. The blue ocean looks calm today.
63. The gentle waves sound pleasant.
64. The cool breeze smells fresh.
65. I am an excellent swimmer.
66. The water tastes salty.

Cumulative Review, *continued*

Verb Tenses *(pp. 150, 152, 154)*

Change each underlined verb to the tense shown in parentheses. Write the new sentences.

67. Leah <u>will study</u> a problem.   (past)
68. She <u>asks</u> a question.   (past)
69. She <u>hopes</u> for an answer.   (past)
70. Leah <u>planned</u> a complex experiment.   (present)
71. She <u>has mixed</u> chemicals. (present)
72. The chemicals <u>fizzed</u>.   (present)
73. Leah <u>discovers</u> something. (future)

Subject-Verb Agreement *(p. 156)*

Write the correct present tense form of each verb in parentheses.

74. A wolf (look) like a skinny dog.
75. Its cry (sound) sad.
76. Wolves (roam) the Arctic hills.
77. Their fur (keep) them warm.
78. They (live) in family groups.

Agreement with *be* and *have*

(p. 158) Write the verb in parentheses that correctly completes each sentence.

79. My relatives (is, are) visiting.
80. We (have, has) enjoyed their visit.
81. Uncle Jake (is, are) an athlete.
82. His stories (is, are) exciting.
83. His bike club (have, has) races.
84. He (have, has) crossed the Rockies.

Contractions with *not* *(p. 160)*

Write the contraction for the underlined word or words below.

85. Sam <u>has not</u> arrived yet.
86. I <u>cannot</u> imagine where he is.
87. We <u>should not</u> start the meeting.
88. We <u>do not</u> have his notes.
89. Sam <u>is not</u> usually late.
90. Maybe his bus <u>was not</u> on time.
91. <u>Do not</u> call his office.
92. He <u>will not</u> still be there.
93. We <u>should not</u> worry yet.
94. We <u>have not</u> waited long.

Irregular Verbs *(pp. 162, 164)*

Write the correct forms of the verbs in parentheses to show the past.

95. Joe (run) for club president.
96. He had (run) once before.
97. The members (know) him well.
98. The club had (grow) in size.
99. Joe (speak) to the members.
100. He had (wear) a good suit.
101. The speech had (begin) well.
102. Joe (say) the club was great.
103. He had even (write) a poem.
104. Joe (sing) the club song.
105. Then he (make) many promises.
106. The club members (choose) Joe.
107. The job (begin) right away.
108. Soon Joe (know) his mistake.
109. He had (make) too many promises.

Verb Phrases with *have* *(p. 166)*
Write the correct words to complete these sentences.

110. Mom (must of, must have) heard.
111. I (should have, should of) asked.
112. Dad (could've, could of) told her.
113. She (might of, might've) agreed.
114. We (should of, should've) talked.
115. We (would've, would of) laughed.

teach, learn; let, leave; sit, set; can, may (pp. 168, 170) Write the word in parentheses that correctly completes each sentence.

116. (Can, May) you play checkers well?
117. I will (teach, learn) you to play.
118. Please (sit, set) the board here.
119. I will (sit, set) over there.
120. (Let, Leave) the box on the table.
121. This time (let, leave) me have the red pieces.
122. I (learn, teach) games from Amy.

Unit 7: Adjectives

What Is an Adjective? *(p. 222)*
Write each sentence. Underline each adjective. Then draw an arrow from the adjective to the noun it describes.

123. Java is a tropical island.
124. The climate is warm and wet.
125. Java has a long rainy season.
126. The island has active volcanoes.
127. Healthy plants grow in rich soil.
128. The main crop is rice.

Articles and Demonstrative Adjectives *(p. 224)* Write the word in parentheses that correctly completes each sentence.

129. (A, An) ivy plant is a nice gift.
130. Look at (those, these) back there.
131. I like (these, those) right here.
132. I'll buy (a, the) one in my hand.
133. (This, That) plant across the room is for my aunt.

Comparing with Adjectives *(p. 226)*
Write the correct form of each adjective in parentheses.

134. Al's voice is (low) than mine.
135. He has the (deep) voice of all.
136. Flo's solo is (long) than Bob's.
137. Mine is the (short) of all.
138. This is our (nice) show ever.

Comparing with *good* **and** *bad*
(p. 228) Write the correct form of *good* and *bad*.

139. I've had a (bad) cold.
140. This is the (bad) time of year.
141. Your cold is (bad) than mine.
142. I'm (good) than I was yesterday.
143. Soup is the (good) cure of all.

Proper Adjectives *(p. 230)* Write the proper adjective that comes from the proper noun in parentheses.

144. One man wore an (Africa) robe.
145. The (Poland) acrobat has talent.
146. The (Austria) mountains are high.
147. That (Finland) knit hat is warm.
148. I love spicy (India) foods.

Enrichment

Using Adjectives

Inviting Menus

Pretend that you own a restaurant. Design a menu for it. Describe each menu item with adjectives that will tempt your customers. Use adjectives that appeal to the senses. **Extra!** Now pretend that you are a customer who has just had a meal. React to the food in writing. Use the adjectives *good, better, best, bad, worse,* and *worst* in your sentences.

Spin the Globe

Players—2. **You need**—paper and a globe or large map. **How to play**—Spin the globe or spread out the map. Close your eyes. Point to a spot on the globe or map. Say the proper noun for where you have landed. (If water, try again.) Write a sentence, using the proper adjective formed from the proper noun. Continue until you have 5 sentences. Keep track of the time. **Scoring**—The one who writes 5 correct sentences in the shortest time wins.

Adjective Add-On

Players—2. **How to play**—One player picks a letter, such as *c,* and says a noun beginning with it, such as *cat.* The other player scores points for each adjective that describes the noun. All words must begin with the same letter.

cute, cautious, calico cat

Now the second player chooses a letter and a noun. **Scoring**—2 points for each adjective. The player with the most points wins.

Extra Practice: Unit 7

1 | What Is an Adjective? (p. 222)

● Write the adjectives in the sentences below. (Do not include *a,*
an, or *the.*)

Example: Lions have large teeth and loud roars.   *large   loud*

1. They have soft, brown fur.
2. Male lions have thick manes.
3. They look proud and fierce.
4. Female lions are gentle mothers.
5. They take good care of the little cubs.
6. The cubs have pretty, spotted coats.

▲ Write these sentences. Underline the adjectives. Then draw an
arrow from the adjectives to the nouns or pronouns described.

Example: Many wild animals play funny games.

Many wild animals play funny games.

7. Young raccoons play with small pieces of wood.
8. Black bears roll down the steep hills.
9. They are big and clumsy.
10. Old, gray otters slide down the muddy banks.
11. Two squirrels enjoy a fast game of tag.
12. Four lively elephants play with a large ball of clay.

■ Rewrite each sentence, adding two or more adjectives. Draw
an arrow from the adjectives to the nouns described.

Example: Alligators have bodies and teeth.

Alligators have long, green bodies and sharp teeth.

13. The snakes ran through the grass.
14. A monkey swings from a tree.
15. A giraffe nibbles leaves.
16. The bird made a nest out of twigs.
17. The woodpecker and the squirrel seem hungry.
18. The robin finds a worm in the ground.

2 | Articles and Demonstratives (p. 224)

● Copy the sentences below. Underline the articles once and the demonstrative adjectives twice. Not every sentence contains both articles and demonstrative adjectives.

Example: We took that airplane to the city of Boston.
We took that airplane to the city of Boston.

1. The sky was bright blue outside the window.
2. I saw a group of puffy clouds.
3. Those clouds looked like cotton.
4. I fastened the seat belt before the flight.
5. During that flight, I tried to read a book.
6. Our plane landed an hour after lunch.

▲ Write the word in parentheses that correctly completes each sentence.

Example: Boston is (a, an) interesting city.   *an*

7. I am having (a, an) good visit in Boston.
8. We are riding in one of (the, a) swan boats.
9. The driver pedals the boat like (a, an) bicycle.
10. (Those, These) ducks on the other side of the pond are cute.
11. (That, This) bridge over there looks old.
12. I will remember (this, those) day in Boston for a long time.

■ To complete each sentence, write an article or a demonstrative adjective as indicated in parentheses.

Example: May I look at _____ book on the shelf above you?
(demonstrative adjective)   *that*

13. Are _____ books on your desk mysteries?   (article)
14. Please hand me _____ stack of mysteries from the bottom shelf. (demonstrative adjective)
15. _____ book that I am carrying is very heavy.   (demonstrative adjective)
16. These books are more neatly stacked than _____ books over there.   (demonstrative adjective)
17. Is there _____ book cart in this room?   (article)
18. Could we get a book cart from _____ room down the hall? (demonstrative adjective)

3 | Comparing with Adjectives (p. 226)

● Complete each sentence by writing the correct form of the adjective in parentheses.

Example: Crows are _____ than robins.   (loud)   *louder*

1. A peacock is _____ than a turkey.   (colorful)
2. Of all birds, ostriches are the _____.   (tall)
3. Swans are _____ than ducks.   (large)
4. Geese are _____ than swans.   (noisy)
5. Hummingbirds are the _____ birds of all.   (small)
6. Eagles are _____ than hawks.   (powerful)
7. Blue jays are _____ than robins.   (bold)

▲ Complete each sentence by writing the correct form of the adjective in parentheses.

Example: Bees are _____ than wasps.   (chunky)   *chunkier*

8. They are _____ than ants.   (large)
9. They are _____ than flies.   (interesting)
10. Their _____ job of all is to spread pollen.   (important)
11. Pollen is _____ than sand.   (fine)
12. It is _____ than powder.   (sticky)
13. Bees are the _____ insects of all.   (busy)
14. They are also the _____.   (helpful)

■ Write an adjective to complete each sentence. Include adjectives that take *-er* and *-est* and adjectives that use *more* and *most*. If the adjective compares two, write *two*. If it compares more than two, write *more than two*.

Example: This book is the _____ of all.
  This book is the hardest of all.   *more than two*

15. Your calendar is _____ than mine.
16. Of all the chairs, this one is the _____.
17. This table is _____ than the one in the dining room.
18. Joseph's desk is _____ than Pauline's desk.
19. That is the _____ bulletin board in the school.
20. Our class is _____ than yours.
21. The blue sweater is _____ than the red one.
22. This invention is the _____ of all.

4 | Comparing with *good* and *bad* (p. 228)

● Read each sentence below. If the underlined adjective compares two, write *two*. If it compares more than two, write *more than two*. Write *none* if the sentence contains no comparison.

Example: Rob is a <u>good</u> trumpet player.   *none*

1. Rob is a <u>better</u> trumpet player than Paul.
2. Rob practices every day, and he loves <u>good</u> music.
3. Yesterday was a very <u>bad</u> day for Rob.
4. The afternoon was <u>worse</u> than the morning.
5. Rob took his <u>best</u> trumpet to school in the morning.
6. He had a <u>bad</u> fall after lunch.
7. It was Rob's <u>worst</u> fall, and he dented his trumpet.

▲ Write the adjective that correctly completes each sentence.

Example: Our band is the (better, best) school band.   *best*

8. It is (better, best) than the Oak School band.
9. We have several (good, best) musicians in the band.
10. We are (better, best) musicians than marchers.
11. We are very (bad, worst) marchers.
12. Al is the (worse, worst) marcher of all.
13. His marching is (worse, worst) than mine.
14. We could win an award for the (worse, worst) marching band in the state.

■ Write full sentences to compare each pair of items. Use a form of *good* or *bad* in each sentence.

Example: a sweater and a jacket
    On a cold day, a jacket is better than a sweater.

15. cats and dogs
16. science and social studies
17. today's weather and yesterday's weather
18. your favorite book and all other books
19. this morning and this afternoon
20. your least favorite food and all other foods
21. swimming and diving
22. your favorite hobby and all other hobbies

5 | Proper Adjectives (p. 230)

● Write each phrase, using a proper adjective made from the noun in parentheses.

Example: ____ hotel (West Germany)   *West German hotel*

1. ____ dance   (Mexico)
2. ____ village   (England)
3. ____ poetry   (Greece)
4. ____ restaurant   (Sweden)
5. ____ desert   (Africa)
6. ____ castle   (Austria)
7. ____ seacoast   (Ireland)
8. ____ food   (Japan)

▲ Write each sentence, using a proper adjective made from the noun in parentheses. Use your dictionary if you need help.

Example: Oslo is the ____ capital.   (Norway)
          Oslo is the Norwegian capital.

9. Paris is the ____ capital.   (France)
10. Madrid is the ____ capital.   (Spain)
11. Budapest is the ____ capital.   (Hungary)
12. New Delhi is the ____ capital.   (India)
13. Bern is the ____ capital.   (Switzerland)
14. Lima is the ____ capital.   (Peru)
15. Belgrade is the ____ capital.   (Yugoslavia)
16. Stockholm is the ____ capital.   (Sweden)
17. Dublin is the ____ capital.   (Ireland)

■ Answer each question by writing a sentence that contains a proper adjective. Use your dictionary if you need help.

Example: Have you ever been to a beach in Puerto Rico?
          I went to a Puerto Rican beach last year.

18. Did you see a car that was made in Japan?
19. Was Abraham Lincoln a President of the United States?
20. Do you have a sweater from Denmark?
21. Have you met my cousin from Poland?
22. Have you studied the history of Rome?
23. Have you ever heard music from Ireland?
24. Do you have a pen pal from South America?
25. Have you ever seen any painting by artists from Italy?
26. Have you hiked through the wilderness of Canada?

Literature and Writing

Blinding wild snow
blows, whirls and
drifts about me . . .
in this world alone

CHORA

Description

Getting Ready How do you describe a place to someone who hasn't been there?

"It's a great place! There's a big lake and lots of interesting things to do. It was, well, how can I tell you?"

It isn't easy to find the words that will bring a special time and place to life. In this unit, you will read some good descriptions and work with describing words. Then you will write a description of your own. Start thinking now of some special place or object or person that you might write about.

ACTIVITIES

Listening
Listen as the haiku on page 246 is read. Shut your eyes and try to imagine the scene. Which words describe the snow? Which words tell how the poet feels?

Speaking
Look at the picture. How is it different from what the poem describes? How would you describe it now, as it looks *after* the storm? Have someone list words that tell what you see and feel.

Writing
In your journal, write your own description of snow, either from snow you have seen or snow you imagine.

LITERATURE

Have you ever felt afraid and then relieved when every-thing turned out fine? Why was Sam so scared?

I Hole Up in a Snowstorm

By Jean George

Sam Gribley wanted to try living on his own in the woods. His father agreed to the experiment. Summer had been fine. Winter was the test.

"I am on my mountain in a tree home that people have passed without ever knowing that I am here. The house is a hemlock tree six feet in diameter, and must be as old as the mountain itself. I came upon it last summer and dug and burned it out until I made a snug cave in the tree that I now call home.

"My bed is on the right as you enter, and is made of ash slats and covered with deerskin. On the left is a small fireplace about knee high. It is of clay and stones. It has a chimney that leads the smoke out through a knothole. I chipped out three other knotholes to let fresh air in. The air coming in is bitter cold. It must be below zero outside, and yet I can sit here inside my tree and write with bare hands. The fire is small, too. It doesn't take much fire to warm this tree room.

"It is the fourth of December, I think. It may be the fifth. I am not sure because I have not recently counted the notches in the aspen pole that is my calendar. I have been just too busy gathering nuts and berries, smoking venison, fish, and small game to keep up with the exact date.

"The lamp I am writing by is deer fat poured into a turtle-shell with a strip of my old city trousers for a wick.

"It snowed all day yesterday and today. I have not been outside since the storm began, and I am bored for the first time since I ran away from home eight months ago to live on the land.

"I am well and healthy. The food is good. Sometimes I eat turtle soup, and I know how to make acorn pancakes. I keep my supplies in the wall of the tree in wooden pockets that I chopped myself.

"Every time I have looked at those pockets during the last two days, I have felt just like a squirrel, which reminds me: I didn't see a squirrel one whole day before that storm began. I guess they are holed up and eating their stored nuts, too.

"I wonder if The Baron, that's the wild weasel who lives behind the big boulder to the north of my tree, is also denned up. Well, anyway, I think the storm is dying down because the tree is not crying so much. When the wind really blows, the whole tree moans right down to the roots, which is where I am.

"Tomorrow I hope The Baron and I can tunnel out into the sunlight. I wonder if I should dig the snow. But that would mean I would have to put it somewhere, and the only place to put it is in my nice snug tree. Maybe I can pack it with my hands as I go. I've always dug into the snow from the top, never up from under.

"The Baron must dig up from under the snow. I wonder where he puts what he digs? Well, I guess I'll know in the morning."

When I wrote that last winter, I was scared and thought maybe I'd never get out of my tree. I had been scared for two days—ever since the first blizzard hit the Catskill Mountains. When I came up to the sunlight, which I did by simply poking my head into the soft snow and standing up, I laughed at my dark fears.

250

Everything was white, clean, shining, and beautiful. The sky was blue, blue, blue. The hemlock grove was laced with snow, the meadow was smooth and white, and the gorge was sparkling with ice. It was so beautiful and peaceful that I laughed out loud. I guess I laughed because my first snowstorm was over and it had not been so terrible after all.

Then I shouted, "I did it!" My voice never got very far. It was hushed by the tons of snow.

I looked for signs from The Baron Weasel. His footsteps were all over the boulder, also slides where he had played. He must have been up for hours, enjoying the new snow.

Inspired by his fun, I poked my head into my tree and whistled. Frightful, my trained falcon, flew to my fist, and we jumped and slid down the mountain, making big holes and trenches as we went. It was good to be whistling and carefree again, because I was sure scared by the coming of that storm.

I had been working since May, learning how to make a fire with flint and steel, finding what plants I could eat, how to trap animals and catch fish—all this so that when the curtain of blizzard struck the Catskills, I could crawl inside my tree and be comfortably warm and have plenty to eat.

During the summer and fall I had thought about the coming of winter. However, on that third day of December when the sky blackened, the temperature dropped, and the first flakes swirled around me, I must admit that I wanted to run back to New York. Even the first night that I spent out in the woods, when I couldn't get the fire started, was not as frightening as the snowstorm that gathered behind the gorge and mushroomed up over my mountain.

I was smoking three trout. It was nine o'clock in the morning. I was busy keeping the flames low so they would not leap up and burn the fish. As I worked, it occurred to me that it was awfully dark for that hour of the morning. Frightful was leashed to her tree stub. She seemed restless and pulled at her

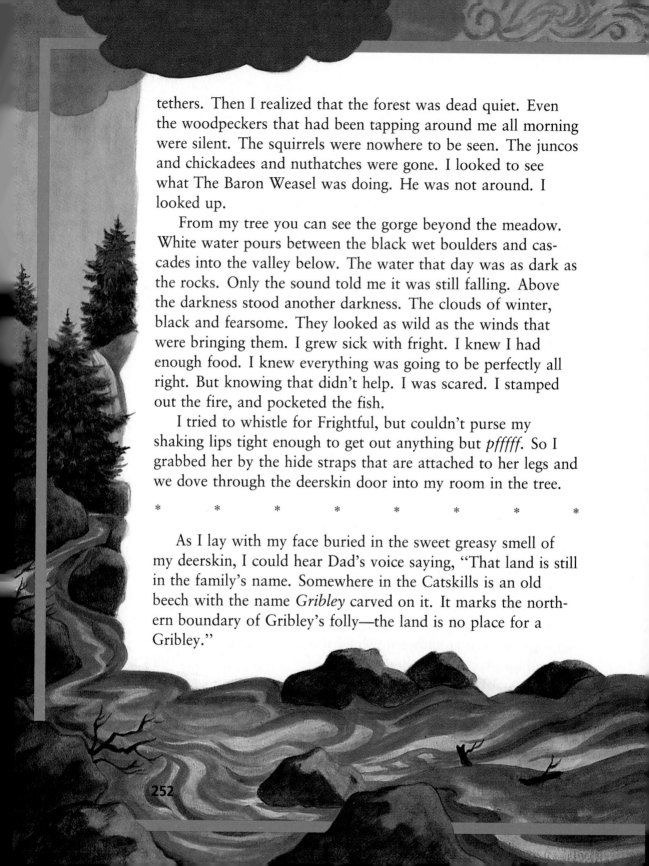

tethers. Then I realized that the forest was dead quiet. Even the woodpeckers that had been tapping around me all morning were silent. The squirrels were nowhere to be seen. The juncos and chickadees and nuthatches were gone. I looked to see what The Baron Weasel was doing. He was not around. I looked up.

From my tree you can see the gorge beyond the meadow. White water pours between the black wet boulders and cascades into the valley below. The water that day was as dark as the rocks. Only the sound told me it was still falling. Above the darkness stood another darkness. The clouds of winter, black and fearsome. They looked as wild as the winds that were bringing them. I grew sick with fright. I knew I had enough food. I knew everything was going to be perfectly all right. But knowing that didn't help. I was scared. I stamped out the fire, and pocketed the fish.

I tried to whistle for Frightful, but couldn't purse my shaking lips tight enough to get out anything but *pfffff*. So I grabbed her by the hide straps that are attached to her legs and we dove through the deerskin door into my room in the tree.

*   *   *   *   *   *   *   *

As I lay with my face buried in the sweet greasy smell of my deerskin, I could hear Dad's voice saying, "That land is still in the family's name. Somewhere in the Catskills is an old beech with the name *Gribley* carved on it. It marks the northern boundary of Gribley's folly—the land is no place for a Gribley."

252

"The land is no place for a Gribley," I said. "The land is no place for a Gribley, and here I am three hundred feet from the beech with *Gribley* carved on it."

I fell asleep at that point, and when I awoke I was hungry. I cracked some walnuts, got down the acorn flour I had pounded, with a bit of ash to remove the bite, reached out the door for a little snow, and stirred up some acorn pancakes. I cooked them on a top of a tin can, and as I ate them, smothered with blueberry jam, I knew that the land was just the place for a Gribley.

This story is from the first chapter of *My Side of the Mountain*, by Jean George. Sam's adventure in living alone on the mountain continued.

Think and Discuss

1. What frightened Sam? Why did he later think his fears were silly?

2. **Imagery** is the use of words to create images, or mental pictures. Imagery helps you picture how something looks, sounds, smells, tastes, or feels. For example, *the whole tree moans right down to the roots* helps you *hear* the sounds of the forest in Sam's description of the snowstorm. Some images appeal to several senses at once. For example, *the curtain of blizzard* helps you *see* and *feel* the thickness of the snow. What other examples can you find on page 251 of the story? To which senses do they appeal?

3. Sam was proud of the way he survived alone in the woods. He also enjoyed his life there! Do you think he chose a good way to live? Why or why not? What would be some of the advantages or disadvantages to such a life?

Deer at Dusk

By Elizabeth Coatsworth

I stood so still
It wasn't I who scared them.
I was in the house, so it couldn't have been I,
But suddenly the three deer went
        leaping across the pasture,
Their white tails flashing and
        their heads held high,
Over the wall and into the woods they
        went soaring,
Running as swallows fly.

Think and Discuss

1. What scene does the poem describe? From whose point of view is it described?

2. A **simile** is a comparison between two different things, using the word *like* or *as*. The following simile compares a flame to a trapped moth: "The flame trembled and flapped like a trapped moth." What is the simile in this poem?

3. What does the simile add to the poem? How would the poem be different if the word *running* were used by itself in the last line?

Haiku

By Kyorai

Weeping . . . willows
   Kneel here by
   The waterside
Mingling long green hair

Haiku

By Buson

Ah leafless willow . . .
   Bending over
   The dry pool
Of stranded boulders

Think and Discuss

1. A **haiku** is a short Japanese poem, usually about nature. Traditional haiku have three lines and seventeen syllables. (The haiku on this page were translated.) A haiku gives one picture, or image, and creates a mood. Describe the picture and feeling you get from each haiku.

2. How are the willows in the two haiku alike? What details show you that the first and the second haiku take place during different seasons?

3. **Personification** is the use of human qualities to describe something that is not human. In the first haiku, the trees are described as if they were people—weeping, kneeling, and having long hair. What example of personification do you find in the second haiku? Why do you think the poet uses personification in the two haiku?

Snow Toward Evening

By Melville Cane

Suddenly the sky turned gray,
The day,
Which had been bitter and chill,
Grew soft and still.
Quietly
From some invisible blossoming tree
Millions of petals cool and white
Drifted and blew,
Lifted and flew,
Fell with the falling night.

Think and Discuss

1. What two things happened before the snow began?
2. A **metaphor** compares two very different things without using the word *like* or *as*. A metaphor says that one thing *is* another: "Her face was a thundercloud." Sometimes, however, a metaphor simply suggests the comparison: "The car horns kept squawking all night." The car horns are compared to squawking birds or chickens. What is the snowstorm being compared to in this poem? Why is this a good comparison?
3. The metaphor in "Snow Toward Evening" shows how very different things are surprisingly alike in some ways. What metaphors would you create to describe a rainstorm? a sandstorm?

RESPONDING TO LITERATURE

The Reading and Writing Connection

Personal Response In "I Hole Up in a Snowstorm," Sam turned a hemlock tree into a secret hide-out. What would be your special place? It could be a place you know or one you make up. Describe it.

Creative Writing In each haiku that you read, the poet described a single image from nature. Write a haiku of your own, creating a single picture, or image, of something else from nature.

Creative Activities

Draw On page 248 in "I Hole Up in a Snowstorm," Sam describes his tree room. Read the description and draw a floor plan of the room. Then listen and check your plan as a classmate reads the paragraph.

Telling How Sam tells how he survived in the mountains. Think of something you would like to know more about that might help you survive in the woods. For example, how do you start a fire from flint and steel, or which berries are safe to eat? Read about your subject and share your information in a talk.

Vocabulary

The weasel that Sam knows lives in a den. Different animals have different types of homes. Name as many animals as you can that live in each type of home listed below.
nest burrow lair hive

Looking Ahead

Description In the following composition lessons, you will write a description. Sam describes a winter scene: "the meadow was smooth and white, and the gorge was sparkling with ice." Which words create a clear picture?

VOCABULARY CONNECTION

Homophones

Can you find two words that sound the same and are spelled differently in the passage below?

 My bed is on the right as you enter. . . . It must be below zero outside, and yet I can sit here inside my tree and write with bare hands.

from "I Hole Up in a Snowstorm" by Jean George

Right meaning "the opposite of left" and *write* meaning "to form letters or words" sound the same but have different spellings and meanings. These words are called **homophones**.

Homophones and Their Meanings

your	belonging to you	**its**	belonging to it
you're	you are	**it's**	it is
to	in the direction of	**there**	in that place
too	also	**their**	belonging to them
two	the number 2	**they're**	they are

Vocabulary Practice

A. Write each sentence, using the correct homophone.

1. Jay goes (too, to, two) the mountains every fall.
2. He likes to hike (through, threw) thick forests.
3. On (one, won) trip he saw a huge black (bare, bear).
4. (Its, It's) never dull in the mountains.

B. Each of these words from "I Hole Up in a Snowstorm" is part of a homophone pair. Write another homophone to complete each pair. Use each pair in one sentence.

5. no   6. knew   7. here   8. ate   9. bored

Prewriting
Description

Listening and Speaking: Poetry

In poetry, the sounds of words are very important. Understanding how those sounds work can help you with all kinds of descriptive writing. Sounds help to carry a poem along and add to its mood and meaning. A poem can gush, rage, gurgle, or hiss. It can whisper or shout. When you listen to a poem or recite it, notice the sounds that work closely together.

One sound effect used in poetry is **alliteration,** the repetition of beginning sounds. Listen to the following lines. Which sound is repeated?

I stood so still
It wasn't I who scared them.
from "Deer at Dusk" by Elizabeth Coatsworth

Did you hear the repeated sound of *s*? By repeating this soft, hushed sound, the poet creates a stillness you can hear and feel.

Onomatopoeia is the use of words that imitate sounds. Which line below has onomatopoeia?

1. Mockingbirds swoosh through the pines.
2. Mockingbirds fly through the pines.

- What sound do you hear in the word *swoosh*?
- Does the word *fly* create the same effect?

Rhyme is the repetition of ending sounds. Listen to the four lines below. Which words rhyme?

Suddenly the sky turned gray,
The day,
Which had been bitter and chill,
Grew soft and still.
from "Snow Toward Evening" by Melville Cane

Did you hear the rhyming sounds of *gray* and *day*? of *chill* and *still*? Each pair is linked together in sound and also in meaning. The linking of *gray* and *day* suggests a kind of chain reaction: When the sky turned to gray, the day changed. The linking of *chill* and *still* emphasizes the sudden change: The day was bitter and chill; now it is soft and still.

Rhythm is the pattern of stresses or beats in a line of poetry. Often rhythm supports the mood or meaning of a poem. Listen to the rhythm in the following lines. Tap it out with your fingers silently. Notice the patterns of stress.

Drifted and blew,
Lifted and flew,
Fell with the falling night.
from "Snow Toward Evening" by Melville Cane

The rhythm of the first two lines, TUM-Ti-Ti-TUM/TUM-Ti-Ti-TUM, suggests the flitting movement of drifting petals. The rhythm of the last line, TUM-Ti-Ti-TUM-Ti-TUM, suggests the way the snow finally settles on the ground and stays for a while—just as night does.

Prewriting Practice

A. With a partner, take turns reading the poem "Deer at Dusk." Find examples of alliteration and onomatopoeia. Emphasize these sound effects as you read the poem.

B. Play with alliteration. Think of words that begin with the same sounds. Put them together to describe other words.

   Examples: crisp, clear air   raging, roaring storm

C. Play with onomatopoeia. Think of three sounds made by each item below. Write words that imitate the sounds.

   Example: typewriter—clack, clatter, tap
              an old car   a ball being hit   a marching band

D. Listen for rhythm as your teacher reads part of a poem. Then listen to the lines again. Write the rhyming words.

Thinking: Classifying Likenesses and Differences

One way to describe something is to show how it is like or different from something else. When you show the likenesses between two things, you are **comparing.** When you show differences, you are **contrasting.** You begin a comparison or a contrast by **classifying,** or grouping, the ways in which two items are alike or different.

How are snow and rain alike and different? Look at the descriptions of snow in "I Hole Up in a Snowstorm" and in "Snow Toward Evening." Next, think about rainy days that you have experienced. How are they alike and different?

Look at the lists below. Notice that similes, exact words, and sense words are included in the lists.

LIKENESSES
Both *rain* and *snow*
1. come from clouds
2. are cool and tingly
3. make the world glisten
4. refresh and clean the air

DIFFERENCES
Rain
1. makes a noisy clatter
2. seeps in or leaves puddles
3. is clear like glass
4. looks like tears

Snow
1. drifts in quietly
2. piles up
3. is white when clean
4. looks like falling stars

Prewriting Practice

A. Classify the likenesses and differences between the items in one of the pairs below. Make one list of likenesses and one list of differences.

   1. a maple tree and a willow
   2. a white-tailed deer and a moose

B. Compare and contrast two similar but different things in your home, such as two chairs, two lamps, or two pets. Make one list of likenesses and another of differences.

Using Sense Words ☑

Your five senses are always busy seeing, smelling, hearing, tasting, and touching. Use them all to develop your ability to observe. Then think of sense words that describe how the thing you are observing looks, smells, tastes, sounds, and feels.

Read the following descriptions. Notice the senses Sam uses to describe the sounds of a winter night, a meal made of cattail roots, and his first fire.

1. . . . the trees cry out and the limbs snap and fall, and the wind gets caught in a ravine and screams until it dies.

2. . . . the fibers are tough and they take more chewing to get the starchy food from them than they are worth. However, they taste just like potatoes . . . .

3. Out of dead tinder and grass and sticks came a live warm light. . . . It stood tall and bright and held back the night.

from My Side of the Mountain *by Jean George*

- Which senses did Sam use to make his observations?
- What are the sense words in each description?

The following list shows other sense words.

SIGHT: red, golden, bright, dusty, sudsy, twisted, wiggly, brick, wooden, pointed, clean, sparkling, five, large, slender

SOUND: booming, chiming, loud, whispering, silent, laughing, crackling, screeching, clanging, hooting, quiet, rattling

SMELL: flowery, piny, sweet, sour, gingery, spicy, soapy, musty

TASTE: salty, peppery, bitter, spicy, sweet, sour, spoiled, tangy

TOUCH: sandy, brittle, fuzzy, sharp, stinging, icy, slippery, sticky, damp, prickly, dry, velvety, cuddly, crusty

Try to use all your senses as often as you can.

Prewriting Practice

Turn on your senses and tune in the world. First, look outside. How would you describe the things that you see? When you go outside, how does the outside air smell? Next, listen. What kinds of sounds do you hear? Now, notice sensations. How does your arm feel on your desk? How does your pen feel to the touch? Finally, what tastes do you remember from your last meal? Write down your observations, using sense words.

Using Exact Words ☑

If you want to describe something or someone, what tools do you need besides alert senses and close observation? Exact and vivid words are among your most important tools. They give exact meaning and create a clear or vivid mental picture.

Compare the descriptions below. Which one describes the swim more vividly?

1. I climbed down the rocks and went into the pool. It was very cold. But when I got out and put on my trousers and sweaters, which I thought was a better way to carry clothes than in a pack, my skin felt funny and I felt energetic. I went up the bank and fell on my face in some flowers.

2. I scrambled down the rocks and slipped into the pool. It was so cold I yelled. But when I came out on the bank and put on my two pairs of trousers and three sweaters, which I thought was a better way to carry clothes than in a pack, I tingled and burned and felt coltish. I leapt up the bank, slipped, and my face went down in a patch of dogtooth violets.

from My Side of the Mountain *by Jean George*

The second paragraph describes the swim vividly. *Scrambled* and *slipped* are more exact than *climbed* and *went*.

• Compare the two paragraphs. What other words and details make the second paragraph more exact and vivid?

Prewriting Practice

Replace the words in italics with more exact words that give a clear and vivid picture of a summer shower. Write the new sentences and share them with a partner.

1. The sun was bright and the air was *uncomfortable*.
2. Suddenly the sun *went* behind the clouds.
3. Soon it was *raining*, but I didn't mind.
4. I watched the storm from a *dry place*.
5. The rain made a *nice* sound.
6. The air smelled *good* from the rain.
7. Then I was startled by a *noise*.
8. I noticed a bird *flying* over the trees.
9. Soon my cat joined me in the shelter and *sat* beside me.
10. I patted her *soft* fur, and she grew calm and content.

The Grammar Connection

Exact Adjectives and Adverbs

You can use adjectives and adverbs to write descriptions that will let your readers see, hear, taste, smell, and feel whatever you want. Look at how adjectives and adverbs can change the meaning of sentences.

The excited girl walked happily into the cheerful classroom.
The exhausted girl walked slowly into the noisy classroom.

Practice Write each of these sentences twice. Use different adjectives and adverbs to create two different pictures with each sentence.

1. The ____ boy went ____ to the ____ kitchen.
2. The ____ ____ car moved ____.
3. The ____ tree looked ____ and ____
4. My ____ shoes are ____ and ____.
5. The ____ friends hiked ____ and ____.
6. The ____ doorbell sounds ____.
7. The ____ fans cheered ____ and ____.

Choosing Details ☑

The variety of details you can use to describe someone or something is almost endless. How would you describe the street where you live? First decide on your purpose: How do you feel about your street? What impression do you want your reader to have? Then choose details that support your purpose.

The details listed below all describe a winter scene. However, two different impressions of the scene can be formed from this list. What are they?

1. gorge—sparkling with ice
2. snow—stark, cold, lifeless
3. branches—empty, broken arms
4. hemlock grove—laced with snow
5. waterfall—swollen with anger
6. meadow—smooth and white

- Which details create a joyful and beautiful impression?
- What other impression of the scene can be formed from this list? Which details support that purpose?

Now read the following passage. Notice which details the author chooses to describe Sam's relief and amazement when he came out of his tree home after the blizzard.

> The sky was blue, blue, blue. The hemlock grove was laced with snow, the meadow was smooth and white, and the gorge was sparkling with ice. It was so beautiful and peaceful that I laughed out loud.
> *from "I Hole Up in a Snowstorm" by Jean George*

- Do all the details fit the author's purpose? Why?

Prewriting Practice

For each item, write two details that create an impression of fear and two details that create an impression of excitement.

balloon ride   surprise visit   tree climbing   new baby

Organizing Your Description ☑

Suppose you wanted to describe a room so that a blind-folded person could walk through it without bumping into anything. First, you would have to think about where the things in the room are placed. The way things are arranged in a space is called **spatial order.**

When you write a description, you can use spatial order to organize your details. In this way, you help your reader to picture what you are describing. You can arrange your details from right to left, left to right, top to bottom, bottom to top, near to far, or far to near. Choose the arrangement that fits your details best.

Notice how Sam uses spatial order to guide you through his tree room.

> "My bed is on the right as you enter, and is made of ash slats and covered with deerskin. On the left is a fireplace about knee high."
>
> *from "I Hole Up in a Snowstorm" by Jean George*

• How are the details organized?
• Certain words and phrases can help show spatial order. What words or phrases has the author used to help show the order here?

Here are some words and phrases you can use to show spatial order.

above	inside	alongside
across	outside	beside
below	closer	next to
opposite	farther away	in front of
nearer	on the left	on the right
behind	beyond	at the top
higher	lower	at the bottom

When you are using spatial order to describe a place, try to use exact words such as those in the above list.

Spatial order is not the only way to organize details in a description. Sometimes certain details will be more important than others. They may be more striking, or they may support the impression better. Then you can organize your details in **order of importance.** You can go from the most to the least important detail, or from the least to the most important.

Here is Sam's description of the approaching storm. Think about the purpose of the description as you read the details.

> From my tree you can see the gorge beyond the meadow. White water pours between the black wet boulders and cascades into the valley below. The water that day was as dark as the rocks. Only the sound told me it was still falling. Above the darkness stood another darkness. The clouds of winter, black and fearsome. They looked as wild as the winds that were bringing them. I grew sick with fright.
>
> *from "I Hole Up in a Snowstorm" by Jean George*

- What are the two main details? Which is more important? Why?
- In what order are the details arranged?
- How does the order fit the writer's purpose?

These words and phrases help show the order of details.

to begin with	next	then	more important
first	another	finally	most important

Prewriting Practice

A. List the details that describe a room that you know. Arrange the details in spatial order. Then tell how you have arranged them—for example, from left to right or from front to back.

B. Think of a place that makes a strong impression. It can be beautiful or ugly, cheerful or gloomy. List the details that describe it. Then arrange the details from most to least important. Share the list with a partner and see if your partner agrees with your arrangement.

The Writing Process
How to Write a Description

Step 1: Prewriting—Choose a Topic

Lian made a list of all the things she could think of to describe. Then she thought about her list.

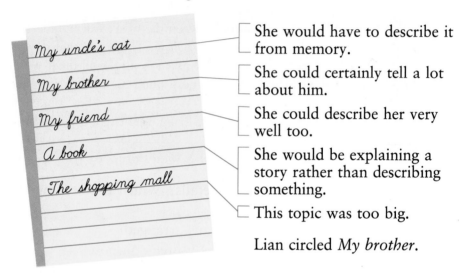

My uncle's cat — She would have to describe it from memory.

My brother — She could certainly tell a lot about him.

My friend — She could describe her very well too.

A book — She would be explaining a story rather than describing something.

The shopping mall — This topic was too big.

Lian circled *My brother*.

On Your Own

1. **Think and discuss** Make a list of the things you can describe. Use the Ideas page to help you. Discuss your ideas with a partner.
2. **Choose** Ask yourself these questions about each topic.
   Could I look at this before I write?
   Could I describe this in detail?
   Could I describe this clearly?
   Would I enjoy writing about this?
   Would someone else enjoy reading about this?
   Circle the topic you want to use for your description.
3. **Explore** What will you write? Do one of the activities under "Exploring Your Topic" on the Ideas page.

Ideas for Getting Started

Choosing Your Topic

Topic Ideas

The first snow
An unusual tree
My pet
My favorite clothes
My friend
My bike
My favorite car
The river
My room
My back yard

Description Starters

Read these starters for ideas.
Yesterday I found the perfect present for my friend's birthday. It was . . .
You wouldn't believe how my brother keeps his room. It . . .
Last week I found a really peculiar insect. It had . . .
I'm always a little nervous when my cousin comes to visit. She . . .

Exploring Your Topic

Cluster

Write your topic in the middle of a piece of paper. Around it write the parts of the thing you are describing. Then write words that describe the parts. Here is the cluster Lian made about her brother.

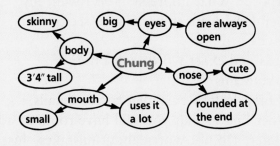

Talk About It

Make your topic into a riddle. Describe it to a friend in detail. Have your friend guess what it is. Do you need to add any details?

Step 2: Write a First Draft

Lian decided to write her description for her mother. She knew her mother would enjoy it.

Lian wrote her first draft. She did not worry about making mistakes. She would have a chance to correct them later.

Lian's first draft

- Which of her five senses did Lian use?
- What details help to paint a clear picture in your mind?
- Which words could be more exact?

> My bruther Chung is short and cute. He has a cute nose that is rounded at the end and ~~it~~ big eyes that ~~are always~~ stay open from erly morning til night. He is less than four feet tall and very skinny. His mouth is sort of small but, he never stops using it!

On Your Own

1. **Think about purpose and audience** Ask yourself these questions.

    For whom shall I write this description?

    What is my purpose? What impression do I want my reader to have? Do I want my reader to see this as beautiful? new?

    What sense words and exact words can I use?

    How do I feel about this?

2. **Write** Write your first draft. Remember to use details. Write on every other line so that you will have room to add or make changes later. Do not worry about mistakes. Just write your description.

Step 3: Revise

Lian read her first draft. She noticed that she hadn't described the color of Chung's eyes. She added that detail.

Lian wanted to know if she had described her brother
clearly. She read her description to Christopher.

Reading and responding

> Your brother does sound cute. Is he younger than you?

> Yes. I'll add that! Is there anything else?

> I think the part about his height should come at the beginning.

> Oh, I see where it should go. Thanks!

Lian thought about Christopher's comments and made
some changes. Then she came up with an idea for describing
Chung's mouth more vividly. She also changed a word to one
that was more exact.

Part of Lian's revised draft

little
My brother Chung is short and cute.
short
He has a cute nose that is rounded at
brown
the end and it big eyes that are always
stay open from erly morning til night.
He is less than four feet tall and very
as small as a broken crayon
skinny. His mouth is sort of small but,

Think and Discuss

- Why did Lian move a sentence?
- How did she make her description of Chung's mouth clearer?
- What other details did she add? Why?

On Your Own

Revising Checklist

☑ Have I used sense words and exact words? Could I use more?

☑ Have I chosen details that fit my purpose?

☑ Have I ordered the details in a way that makes sense?

☑ What details could I add?

1. **Revise** Make changes in your first draft. If you need to find exact words, use the thesaurus below or the one in the back of the book. Replace words by crossing them out and adding new words above them. Add necessary details and be sure they are well organized.

2. **Have a conference** Read your description to someone else—a classmate or your teacher.

WRITING
CONFERENCE

Ask your listener:	**As you listen:**
"Can you picture what thing I am describing?" "Which parts help you see it best?" "Where isn't it clear?" "Could I add details?"	Can I picture this clearly in my mind? Which parts are most vivid? What more would I like to know?

3. **Revise** Think about your listener's suggestions. Do you have any other ideas? Make those changes on your paper.

Thesaurus

active energetic, lively
calm peaceful, tranquil
clean spotless
clear transparent
cold chilly, cool, icy
dark dim, murky
dull blunt
fat plump, stout

little tiny, small, miniature
pretty beautiful, lovely
quick fast, hasty, rapid, swift, speedy
sharp pointed
shiny bright, gleaming, glistening
thin skinny, slender

Step 4: Proofread

Lian proofread her description for mistakes in spelling, capitalization, and punctuation. She used a dictionary to check spelling. She used proofreading marks to make her changes.

Lian's proofread draft

> little brother
> My ^brother Chung is short and cute.
>   short
> He has a ^cute nose that is rounded at
>   brown
> the end and ~~it~~ big eyes that ~~are always~~
>   early   till
> stay open from erby morning tib night.
> He is less than four feet tall and very
>   as small as a broken crayon,
> skinny. His mouth is ^sort of small but,
> he never stops using it!

Think and Discuss

- Which words did Lian correct for spelling?
- Where did she take out a comma? Why?
- Where did she add one? Why?

On Your Own

1. Proofreading Practice Proofread this paragraph. Find two mistakes in making comparisons with adjectives. Find four other spelling mistakes and one wrong punctuation mark. Write the paragraph correctly.

> Yesterday was gloomy. Today was even worst. The sky was gray. The bildings were gray. The river was gray. The grown was gray. The smoke was the grayer of all. The only things that weren't gray were the city lites. I felt as if my whole. life had turned into a gray bored.

Proofreading Marks

- ¶ Indent
- ∧ Add something
- ℓ Take out something
- ≡ Capitalize
- / Make a small letter

The Writing Process 273

2. **Proofreading Application** Now proofread your paper. Use the Proofreading Checklist and the Grammar and Spelling Hints below. You may want to use a colored pencil to make your corrections. Use a dictionary to check spellings.

Proofreading Checklist

Did I

☑ **1.** indent?

☑ **2.** use capital letters correctly?

☑ **3.** use punctuation marks correctly?

☑ **4.** use adjectives correctly?

☑ **5.** spell all words correctly?

The Grammar/Spelling Connection

Grammar Hints

Remember these rules from Unit 7 for using adjectives.

- Use *-er* to compare two and *-est* for three or more. *(Nick is taller than Ting. Stan is tallest of all.)*
- Use *more* and *most* with long adjectives. *(Liz is more thoughtful than Sue. Alicia is most thoughtful of all.)*
- *Good* and *bad* have special forms for comparing. *(good—better—best, bad—worse—worst)*

Spelling Hint

- The (ī) sound is often spelled *i*, *igh*, or *i*-consonant-*e*. *(mild, right, bike)*

Step 5: Publish

Lian added a title to her description. Then she made a poster with a snapshot of Chung at the top and her description of him below it. She shared her poster with her mother and Chung.

On Your Own

1. **Copy** Write or type your description as neatly as possible.
2. **Add a title** Think of a title to catch your reader's interest. Remember to capitalize the first, last, and all important words.
3. **Check** Read over your description again to make sure that you have not left out anything or made any mistakes in copying.
4. **Share** Think of a special way to share your description.

Ideas for Sharing

- Make a card. Put your description on the front and a drawing inside.
- Read your description to your classmates. Have them draw what they see in their minds.
- Write your description as a rebus, using magazine pictures for some of the words.

Applying Description

Literature and Creative Writing

In "I Hole Up in a Snowstorm," on pages 248-253, Sam Gribley describes the mountain where he lives, the hemlock grove, and his tree room. He explains how he kept himself alive in the woods and how he survived his first snowstorm.

Have fun using what you have learned about writing descriptions to complete one or more of the following activities.

> **Remember these things** ☑
> Use sense words.
> Use exact and vivid words.
> Choose details that support your point of view.
> Organize your description in the most effective way.

1. **Describe a place.** Sam described the gorge that he saw from his tree. What do you see from your front door? Do you look out onto a street with many houses, or do you see fields and trees? Describe the view.

2. **Describe an outdoor person.** Do you know someone who spends most of the time outdoors —working or playing? What does this person look like? How does he or she dress? move? talk?

3. **Describe an object.** Sam described the lamp that he made for his tree room. He used it at night and during the storm when clouds covered the sun. Think of an object that is important to you and describe it in detail.

Writing Across the Curriculum
Social Studies

We know what our country was like in the past because explorers and travelers wrote descriptions in their letters and journals.

Choose one or more of the following activities.

1. **Describe your discovery.** Imagine that you are a Spanish explorer in the New World. You are bringing seeds for two new vegetables back to your family in Spain. How will you describe the vegetables to your family? How do the vegetables taste, look, smell? Can you compare them to anything your family has eaten? Write a description.

Writing Steps
1. Choose a topic
2. Write a first draft
3. Revise
4. Proofread
5. Publish

2. **Go back in time.** Look at the picture of the early New England village. Imagine that you are a colonist living in the village. Write a description of the village for a friend who still lives in England.

Word Bank
cabin
stockade
chimney
guard
shutters
stocks

3. **Look to the future.** The way we live now will be history in the future. Write a description of your classroom or your cafeteria so that someone in the future could picture it. What do you see? What sounds can you hear? What do you smell?

Gabriel enjoyed reading "I Hole Up in a Snowstorm." He liked books about different kinds of courage. When Gabriel read *The House of Dies Drear* by Virginia Hamilton, he decided to share his book by making an advertisement. He told about an exciting part of the story and drew a picture of it. He was careful not to tell too much. Here is his advertisement.

THE HOUSE OF DIES DREAR

Virginia Hamilton

Thomas and his family move into a strange old house with secret passages left over from the days of the Underground Railroad. Thomas stumbles into a passage, and in the dark and damp tunnel, he hears strange, non-human sounds. He cries out in fear.

Is Thomas brave enough to go on? What happens next? Read *The House of Dies Drear* by Virginia Hamilton.

Go to your bookstore or library today!

Think and Discuss

- What do you learn about the book from the advertisement?
- What information about the book does the picture give?
- Why is this a good way to share a book?

Share Your Book

Make an Advertisement

1. Choose an exciting or interesting part of your book. Tell enough to make readers want to know more about what happens. Be careful not to tell the ending of the book.
2. Draw a picture to help make the advertisement exciting. You might illustrate the incident you tell about, or you might show what the characters look like. Your picture might also suggest the story's mood—for example, mysterious or sad.
3. Be sure to include the title and the author's name.

Other Activities

- Write and present a radio announcement to advertise your book. Time your announcement to thirty seconds.
- Make a billboard advertisement for your book. On a large sheet of paper, draw a picture of an exciting part of the book. Include the title and the author's name. Describe your book, using such words as *funny, exciting,* and *mysterious.*
- Write a poem based on the feelings of a character in the story. Pretend that the character is writing the poem. Remember the various ways poets create sound effects and word pictures. Try to use them in your poem.

 # The Book Nook

House of Wings	Bridge to Terabithia
by Betsy Byars	*by Katherine Paterson*
Sammy spends the summer with his grandfather, who keeps geese and an owl in the house. The summer has an effect on Sammy.	The special friendship of Jess and Leslie ends sadly, but their imaginary kingdom, Terabithia, lives on in an unexpected way.

Mechanics

A comma hung above the park,
a shiny punctuation mark;
we saw it curving in the dark
the night the moon was new.

A period hung above the bay,
immense though it was far away;
we saw it at the end of day
the night the moon was full.

Aileen Fisher
from "Comma in the Sky"

Capitalization and Punctuation

Getting Ready   In this unit, you will be studying the many rules for capitalizing and punctuating. These rules will help you make your writing clear and correct. It would take you three times as long to read a book if there were no clues to tell you where one sentence ended and another began. When you capitalize and punctuate correctly, you are helping your readers get your message.

ACTIVITIES

Listening   Listen as the poem is read. What part of the poem does the picture illustrate?

Speaking   Look at the picture. With your class, make up sentences about it that end with periods, question marks, and exclamation points. Make up sentences about it that have words that should be capitalized. Make up sentences that use quotation marks.

Writing   Would you ever live on this island? In your journal, write a dialogue for and against.

1 | Capitalizing and Punctuating Sentences

You know that every sentence must begin with a capital letter and end with an end mark. Without capital letters and end marks, sentences run together. With them, your reader knows where one sentence ends and another begins.

INCORRECT: we will join you later we are waiting for Cory

CORRECT: We will join you later. We are waiting for Cory.

End marks tell whether you are making a statement (.), asking a question (?), giving a command (.), or showing strong feeling (!).

DECLARATIVE: The concert is on Sunday.
INTERROGATIVE: Are you going?
IMPERATIVE: Buy your tickets early.
EXCLAMATORY: What a terrific band we have!

Guided Practice
How should these sentences be written correctly? Be sure to separate any run-on sentences.

Example: the band is practicing our school song has two verses.
The band is practicing. Our school song has two verses.

1. each class has music once a week
2. what a chorus we make
3. will you come to the concert
4. listen to us sing the song was written by our music teacher
5. what a funny song that is has he written any others
6. he also wrote the music for the school play
7. what talent he has
8. when is the next concert I'd like to go to it
9. the concert is on Tuesday we will be ready
10. please buy me two tickets my sister will go with me
11. she takes guitar lessons what a great voice she has too
12. come to our house she will play for you

> ▶ Begin every sentence with a capital letter.
> ▶ Use a **period** to end a declarative sentence or an imperative sentence.
> ▶ Use a **question mark** to end an interrogative sentence.
> ▶ Use an **exclamation point** to end an exclamatory sentence.

Independent Practice Write each sentence correctly.
Separate any run-on sentences. Add capital letters and end marks.

Example: open your music books can you sing this song
Open your music books. Can you sing this song?

13. the band played a march
14. who wrote that march
15. John Philip Sousa composed many popular marches
16. how sharp the band looks
17. keep your chin up keep your back straight
18. march in step with the other players
19. the band played songs from the musical *The Music Man*
20. my favorite song is from that musical
21. how many trombone players are in our band there are six
22. what a loud noise the cymbals make
23. do you know any other marching songs look in the book
24. have you heard of the composer Charles Ives
25. he also wrote marching songs
26. he is a famous American composer he wrote over 150 songs
27. do you know the names of other American composers
28. I like the music of Aaron Copland he won a Pulitzer Prize
29. he used songs of the American West in his music
30. listen to his music for the ballet *Rodeo*
31. what an exciting piece of music it is
32. does it remind you of cowhands it makes me want to dance

Writing Application: Persuasive Writing
Write a paragraph in which you persuade your parents to let you go to a school concert. Include the four types of sentences. Use capital letters and end marks correctly.

For Extra Practice, see p. 304.   **Capitalizing and Punctuating**

2 | Proper Nouns and Proper Adjectives

As you know, proper nouns name specific persons, places, and things. Always begin a proper noun with a capital letter. If a proper noun is two words, capitalize both words. If it is three or more words, capitalize only the important words.

Capitalizing Proper Nouns		
People	Queen Victoria	Lewis Carroll
Places and things	Norway Lake Ontario Tulsa	Mount Whitney Wisconsin Avenue Gulf of Mexico
Days, months, and holidays	Monday Columbus Day	July New Year's Day
Buildings and companies	Sears Tower Langley Company	Fogg Art Museum Colorado College

Proper adjectives are adjectives made from proper nouns. Like proper nouns, proper adjectives begin with capital letters. If a proper adjective is two words, capitalize both words.

England	English landscape
Japan	Japanese painting
South America	South American music

Guided Practice Which nouns and adjectives should be capitalized?

Example: Who was wolfgang mozart?   *Wolfgang Mozart*

1. He was a famous composer from austria.
2. He was born in January 1756 in the city of salzburg.
3. He and his sister anna maria were gifted pianists.
4. Their father, leopold, took them on european concert tours.
5. Young wolfgang performed for empress maria theresa.

> ► Capitalize proper nouns and proper adjectives.
> ► If a proper noun is two words, capitalize both. If it is three or more words, capitalize each important word.
> ► If a proper adjective is two words, capitalize both.

Independent Practice Write the proper nouns and the proper adjectives. Capitalize them correctly.

Example: The composer johann strauss is called the waltz king.
Johann Strauss   Waltz King

6. At nineteen he conducted his own orchestra in vienna.
7. Thousands of austrian people gathered to hear him play his dance music.
8. He later conducted summer concerts in russia.
9. News of his fame traveled across the atlantic ocean.
10. The american people were eager to see and hear him.
11. People in boston and new york invited him to visit.
12. Some bostonians offered him a large sum of money.
13. In massachusetts he conducted a huge orchestra.
14. He also wrote a german opera.
15. One of his biggest fans was a pianist from hamburg, germany.
16. That musician was johannes brahms.
17. As a child, he had studied violin and cello with his father, johann jacob.
18. At twenty he gave concerts with a hungarian violinist.
19. He met the great composers franz liszt and robert schumann.
20. The university of cambridge gave brahms a special degree.
21. Children loved him and called him uncle brahms.
22. For more than one hundred years, babies in europe and in the united states have fallen asleep to one of his songs.

Writing Application: Writing About Yourself

If you could travel anywhere in the world, where would you go? Whom would you take with you? Write a paragraph about the places and the things that you would like to see. Use proper nouns and proper adjectives.

For Extra Practice, see p. 305.   **Proper Nouns and Adjectives   285**

3 | Commas in a Series

An end mark tells your reader where to stop. A comma (,) tells your reader where to pause. Commas help make the meaning of a sentence clear. Commas may also change the meaning of a sentence.

> Beth, Ann, John, Paul, and I are in the same class.
> Beth Ann, John Paul, and I are in the same class.

Each sentence above contains a series. A **series** is a list of three or more items in a sentence. A comma is used after each item except the last. A conjunction, such as *and* or *or,* is used before the last item in a series.

> Sara writes poems, short stories, <u>and</u> plays.
> Her newest play will have two, three, <u>or</u> four characters.
> The play takes place under a tree, on a porch, <u>and</u> in a classroom.

Do not use a comma if a sentence lists only two items, for the sentence does not contain a series.

> Sara writes poems and short stories.

Guided Practice Where are commas needed in the following sentences?

Example: My class has written directed and produced a musical.
My class has written, directed, and produced a musical.

1. Frank Lisa and Saito are in charge of tickets and food.
2. Everyone will sing dance or play an instrument.
3. Our costumes will be red blue and gold.
4. Teachers will sit in the first second and third rows.
5. Parents friends and relatives will also be in the audience.
6. The performances will be on Thursday Friday and Saturday in the school auditorium.
7. My parents brothers and sisters will come on Thursday.
8. Karl Sandra and Peter found the props made the scenery and planned the costumes.

> ▶ A **series** is a list of three or more items in a sentence.
> ▶ Use commas to separate the items in a series. Put a comma after each item except the last one.
> ▶ Use *and* or *or* before the last item in a series.

Independent Practice Copy each sentence that includes a series. Add commas where they are needed. For each sentence that does not have a series, write *none*.

Example: The play is about a child a detective and a gold ring.
The play is about a child, a detective, and a gold ring.

 9. Ted Janet and Alex are in the play.
10. Costumes props and lights were planned by the art teacher.
11. Marci and Miguel will control the lights.
12. Ted wears glasses and a black beard.
13. A magnifying glass a ring a book and a hatbox are props.
14. We built painted and set up the scenery.
15. The cast joins hands steps forward and bows at the end.
16. The audience will applaud the actors dancers and musicians.
17. Yoshiko and Ken visited a school for the performing arts.
18. Students learn to sing dance act and juggle.
19. Students also take courses in English science and history.
20. Dance students learn ballet tap folk and jazz dancing.
21. Yoshiko wants to be a pianist or a conductor.
22. Ken wants to be an actor a director or a writer.
23. They observed classes rehearsals and sports activities.
24. They spoke to students and teachers.
25. Theater students study speech movement and acting.
26. Other classes teach art set design and lighting.
27. The students paint scenery build sets and sew costumes.
28. In this school, the students study hard practice long hours and love it all!

Writing Application: A Description
Write a paragraph about a play that you have given, seen, or read. Use a series in three of your sentences.

For Extra Practice, see p. 306.

4 | More Uses for Commas

Words such as *yes, well,* and *no* are called **introductory words** when they begin a sentence. Always use a comma after an introductory word.

Yes, I play the drums.   Well, will you play for us?

No, I can't play now.

The name of a person who is spoken to, or addressed, is called a **noun in direct address.** Use a comma or commas to set off a noun in direct address from the rest of the sentence.

Myra, will you play the piano for us?
Place your sheet music here, Myra.
Thank you, Myra, for doing a good job.

Sometimes you may use introductory words and nouns in direct address in the same sentence.

Yes, Myra, you are ready for the concert.

Cynthia, have you finished yet?

Guided Practice Where are commas needed in the following sentences?

Example: No I don't know which instrument I should play Jo.
No, I don't know which instrument I should play, Jo.

1. Well do you like the tuba?
2. Yes I like the tuba.
3. I think Paul that you should try it.
4. Well the music room is closed today Jo.
5. I have permission Paul to use it.
6. Yes Ilona you may come too.
7. Ilona what instrument do you play?
8. I play the piano Paul.
9. Well Jo will you show me how to play the tuba?
10. Yes Paul I will show you a few notes.
11. I am sure Paul that you will soon play very well.
12. Ilona will you play a song for us on the piano?

> ▶ **Introductory words** are words such as *yes*, *no*, and *well* when they begin a sentence. Use a comma after these words.
> ▶ A **noun in direct address** is the name of a person who is spoken to. Use commas to set off a noun in direct address.

Independent Practice Write each sentence correctly. Add commas where they are needed.

Example: Yes Cynthia you play the piano very well.
Yes, Cynthia, you play the piano very well.

13. Mother may I take piano lessons?
14. Well I took piano lessons in the first grade.
15. Yes I will let you take lessons.
16. Carol you must promise to practice.
17. Yes Mother I will practice every day.
18. Do you know what a metronome is Carol?
19. Yes a metronome helps you keep time to the music.
20. The metronome ticks at a steady beat Mrs. Jacobs.
21. You just play in time to the metronome Carol.
22. Mrs. Jacobs could I use a metronome?
23. Well I will bring one to class next week.
24. Carol the music teacher would like to see you.
25. I need more practice Mrs. Jacobs.
26. No you are doing very well today Carol.
27. Do you think Carol that this music is too hard for you?
28. No Mrs. Jacobs I am learning it.
29. Well take your time Carol.
30. You should remember Carol to look at the music.
31. Do you think Mrs. Jacobs that I will ever play well?
32. Yes Carol in time you will be an excellent piano player.

Writing Application: Instructions

You are in charge of a committee to make up posters for a school concert. Write instructions for making the poster. Begin each sentence with an introductory word. Use a noun in direct address in at least three of your sentences.

For Extra Practice, see p. 307.

5 | Interjections

An **interjection** is a word or words that show feeling or emotion.

Common Interjections			
Hurray	Hey	Oh, no	Well
Good grief	Ah	Oops	Whew
Goodness	Oh	Ouch	Wow

If the interjection shows strong feeling, it is followed by an exclamation point and stands alone.

Wow! That boat is big!

Good grief! The sails are huge.

If the interjection shows mild feeling, it is followed by a comma and begins the sentence.

Ah, the breeze is nice.

Well, let's go sailing!

Guided Practice What is the interjection in each sentence?

Example: Hey, this boat needs a few repairs.   *Hey*
Goodness! Let's begin work immediately.   *Goodness*

1. Good grief! Can we repair it in time for the race?
2. Oh, I hope so!
3. Oops! The sail is torn!
4. Wow! That's a long rip!
5. Oh, no, I found another hole.
6. Well, we'll just have to mend the tears.
7. Hey! Where are the sewing supplies?
8. Whew! Someone remembered to bring the sewing box.
9. Ouch! That needle is sharp!
10. Hurray! The sail is as good as new!
11. Ah, that was a job well done.
12. Oh, no! Here's another rip we missed!

> ▶ An **interjection** is a word or words that show feeling.
> ▶ Use an exclamation point or a comma after an interjection.

Independent Practice
Write each sentence. Add the punctuation after each interjection.

Example: Whew The big day is here at last!
Whew! The big day is here at last!

13. Ah there's nothing like a windy day for a race!
14. Well let's get everything ready.
15. Oops We forgot the life jackets.
16. Oh, no The race begins in an hour!
17. Hey The jackets are in the boat!
18. Whew Now we don't have to go back.
19. Wow Look at the markers along the race course!
20. Good grief It's getting windier.
21. Oh the race may be delayed a bit.
22. Hey It seems to be getting calmer.
23. Hurray Everyone is ready to begin!
24. Wow Our little catboat is zipping along.
25. Ah don't you just love sailing?
26. Goodness Do you suppose we might win?
27. Hey Look out for that rock just ahead!
28. Oh, no We may hit it!
29. Good grief Turn the rudder now!
30. Whew We missed it by inches.
31. Hurray Give the skipper a cheer!
32. Well we may still have a chance to win.

Writing Application: A Dialogue
Imagine that you and a friend are watching an exciting sports event, such as a baseball game, a tennis match, or a diving meet. Write the dialogue that might take place between you and your friend as you watch the event. Use at least five interjections in your dialogue.

For Extra Practice, see p. 308.

6 | Quotations

In written conversation, a **direct quotation** gives a speaker's exact words. You set off a quotation with **quotation marks** and capitalize the first word.

Study the statement and the command in quotation marks.

> Heidi announced, "My aunt works in a fire tower."
> "Tell me what she does," said Josh.

A comma separates the quoted statement or command from the speaker's name whether the name comes before or after the quotation.

Sometimes you write quotations that are questions or exclamations. When the speaker's name comes first, use a comma before the quotation. When the name comes last, use a question mark or an exclamation point to end the quotation. Use a period after the name.

> Heidi asked, "Would you like to interview her?"
> "I certainly would!" exclaimed Josh.

Some quotations are divided. If the quotation is one sentence, use commas to separate the speaker's name from the quotation. If the quotation is two sentences, use a period after the name. Capitalize the first word of the second sentence.

> "Do you think," asked Josh, "that we could see the tower?"
> "I know that we can," replied Heidi. "Let's call my aunt."

Guided Practice Where would you use capital letters and punctuation marks in these sentences?

Example: Jean said there was a terrible earthquake in 1906
Jean said, "There was a terrible earthquake in 1906."

1. Peter added it happened in San Francisco
2. Sara asked did it last long
3. it did not last long, but there were fires answered Peter
4. over the years said Jean the city has been rebuilt
5. how beautiful San Francisco is now exclaimed Sara

> ▶ A **direct quotation** gives a speaker's exact words.
> ▶ Set off a quotation with quotation marks. Begin each quotation with a capital letter. Place end punctuation inside the quotation marks. Use commas to separate most quotations from the rest of the sentence.

Independent Practice Write each sentence. Use punctuation marks and capital letters correctly.

Example: did you see the fire on Tenth Street asked Holly
"Did you see the fire on Tenth Street?" asked Holly.

6. Ralph said ten fire engines arrived in fifteen minutes
7. Ira exclaimed it destroyed an entire block of buildings
8. one firefighter was slightly injured said Holly
9. Ira said the people living in the buildings escaped unhurt
10. tell me what will happen to them said Ralph
11. other people are giving them food and clothes replied Holly
12. Ira added they're staying in schools for now
13. the mayor is looking for housing for them said Holly
14. it was the biggest fire I have ever seen exclaimed Ralph
15. the street was blocked off said Holly how did you see it
16. well said Ralph we watched the fire from Eighth Street
17. once said Holly there was a fire in our basement
18. did you have to leave your building asked Ralph
19. for fifteen minutes said Holly we stood outside in the cold
20. it was a small fire she added nothing was ruined
21. I am glad said Ralph that we have fire drills in school
22. Holly said my mother once walked down twenty flights of stairs during a fire drill
23. how tiring that must have been exclaimed Ralph
24. remember to avoid elevators during a fire advised Holly

Writing Application: A Conversation
You and a friend are sitting at a campfire. Write a conversation that you might have. Use direct quotations in all of your sentences.

For Extra Practice, see p. 309.

7 | Abbreviations

An **abbreviation** is a shortened form of a word. An abbreviation usually begins with a capital letter and ends with a period. Use abbreviations only in special kinds of writing, such as addresses and lists.

Common Abbreviations				
Titles	Mr.	Mister	Dr.	Doctor
	Mrs.	married woman	Jr.	Junior
	Ms.	any woman	Sr.	Senior
Businesses	Co.	Company	Ltd.	Limited
	Corp.	Corporation	Inc.	Incorporated
Days	Tues.	Tuesday	Wed.	Wednesday
Months	Feb.	February	Aug.	August
Addresses	Ave.	Avenue	Rte.	Route
	Apt.	Apartment	P. O.	Post Office
States	CA	California	NJ	New Jersey
	TX	Texas	IN	Indiana

Notice that state abbreviations are two capital letters that are not followed by a period. For a list of abbreviations, see the Capitalization, Punctuation, and Usage Guide.

Initials are a special kind of abbreviation. Initials most often stand for a person's first or middle name. Some names have both a first and a middle initial.

E. B. White wrote *Charlotte's Web*.   (E. B. = Elwyn Brooks)

Guided Practice What abbreviations and initials would you use for the underlined words?

Example: Gordon Shoe Company   Co.

1. Doctor Ann Hubbell
2. Robert Stanton, Junior
3. 132 Willow Street
4. Honolulu, Hawaii 96815
5. Thursday, March 5, 1928
6. Mister Alan Wells Blake

> ▸ An **abbreviation** is a shortened form of a word.
> ▸ An abbreviation usually begins with a capital letter and ends with a period.

Independent Practice

A. Write these groups of words, using the correct abbreviations and initials for the underlined words.

Example: 325 University <u>Road</u>   *325 University Rd.*

7. <u>Mister</u> Barnett
8. Davis <u>Corporation</u>
9. <u>Leah Susan</u> Baker
10. Ellis, <u>Kansas</u> 67637
11. <u>Apartment</u> 2
12. 184 Pine <u>Avenue</u>
13. Jay, <u>Florida</u> 32565
14. Monaco <u>Incorporated</u>
15. <u>Post Office</u> Box 36

16. <u>Sunday</u>, <u>October</u> 3, 1935
17. Richard Greene, <u>Senior</u>
18. Modern Designs, <u>Limited</u>
19. Sunset <u>Boulevard</u>
20. <u>Thomas</u> James Carey
21. Brooklyn, <u>New York</u> 11235
22. <u>Friday</u>, <u>April</u> 28, 1947
23. Cooper Stamp <u>Company</u>
24. <u>Mister Ronald Gary</u> Payne

B. Write these addresses, using the correct abbreviations and initials for the underlined words.

Example: <u>Doctor</u> Theresa Ruiz   *Dr. Theresa Ruiz*
581 Verde <u>Drive</u>   *581 Verde Dr.*
Austin, <u>Texas</u> 78759   *Austin, TX 78759*

25. Wombolt Fabrics <u>Corporation</u>
820 Market <u>Street</u>
Philadelphia, <u>Pennsylvania</u> 19102

26. <u>Mister Steven Lane</u> Bingham
<u>Post Office</u> Box 12
Rindge, <u>New Hampshire</u> 03461

Writing Application: A Story

You are writing a story in which the main character receives a secret message. Write the message, using abbreviations from the list in your Capitalization, Punctuation, and Usage Guide.

For Extra Practice, see p. 310.

8 | Titles

There are special ways for writing the titles of books, poems, and other written works. Capitalize the first, last, and all important words in a title. Do not capitalize words such as *a, in, and, of,* and *the* unless they begin or end a title.

"The Ways of Trains"   The Treasure Is the Rose

When titles of books, magazines, newspapers, and movies are used in printed materials, they appear in italics: *Prince Caspian.* Because you cannot write in italics, you should always underline these titles in your writing.

My sister reads The Washington Post every morning.
Have you finished the book Abel's Island?

Some titles are set off by quotation marks. Put quotation marks around the titles of short stories, songs, articles, book chapters, and most poems.

I recited the poem "Take Sky."
My sister showed me the article "Wonder of Words."

Guided Practice How would you write these titles?

Example: the necklace   (short story)
         "The Necklace"

1. cricket   (magazine)
2. water life   (book chapter)
3. a fox at midnight   (book)
4. this old man   (song)
5. portland press herald   (newspaper)
6. the wind and the sun   (short story)
7. the black stallion   (movie)
8. rudolph is tired of the city   (poem)
9. in search of the castaways   (book)
10. endangered animals   (article)
11. beautiful ohio   (song)
12. island of the blue dolphins   (book)

> ▶ Capitalize the first, last, and all important words in a title.
> ▶ Underline the titles of books, magazines, newspapers, and movies.
> ▶ Put quotation marks around the titles of short stories, songs, articles, book chapters, and most poems.

Independent Practice

A. Write each title correctly.

Example: the wind has wings   (poem)   "The Wind Has Wings"

13. cobblestone   (magazine)
14. animals with pouches   (book chapter)
15. rocky mountain news   (newspaper)
16. the web in the grass   (book)
17. the air we breathe   (article)
18. the last piece of light   (short story)
19. an edge of the forest   (book)
20. national velvet   (movie)
21. up a road slowly   (book)
22. thirteen ways of looking at a blackbird   (poem)

B. Write these sentences correctly.

Example: Stan and I started the magazine the green light.
    Stan and I started the magazine The Green Light.

23. I had been reading the book sand and sea.
24. The chapter shore birds gave me an idea for a story.
25. I wrote the short story the flight of one gull.
26. Liz's poem the fog at moon bay is on page three.
27. Stan wrote the article animals we love.
28. My class puts out the newspaper everything in the news.
29. The article light and bright is about our magazine.
30. I wrote a movie review of fantasia.

Writing Application: A Paragraph

If you could create a library, what would you put in it? Write a paragraph. Include titles of books, stories, and poems.

For Extra Practice, see p. 311.

Grammar-Writing Connection

Combining Sentences with a Series

You have learned that when three or more items are listed in a sentence, the list is called a series. Sometimes you can use a series when you combine two or more sentences into a single sentence. Each of the three sentences below contains one item.

Most people enjoy parks.
Most people enjoy museums.
Most people enjoy zoos.

Notice that the following combined sentence is much smoother than the three separate sentences.

Most people enjoy parks, museums, and zoos.

Revising Sentences

Rewrite each group of sentences as one sentence with a series.

1. Mammals live in zoos. Reptiles live in zoos. Birds live in zoos.
2. Animals are caged in zoos. Animals are cared for in zoos. Animals are protected in zoos.
3. Zoos protect animals from hunters. Zoos protect animals from diseases. Zoos protect animals from natural disasters. Zoos protect animals from their natural enemies.
4. Baby giraffes have been born in zoos. Baby gorillas have been born in zoos. Baby monkeys have been born in zoos. Baby cheetahs have been born in zoos.
5. Zoos in the United States provide homes for animals of all kinds. Zoos in Great Britain provide homes for animals of all kinds. Zoos in France provide homes for animals of all kinds. Zoos in Africa provide homes for animals of all kinds.
6. Animals have been observed. Animals have been studied. Animals have been photographed.
7. The tourists visited the Washington Zoo. The tourists visited the Bronx Zoo. The tourists visited the San Diego Zoo.

Creative Writing

Let's take an imaginary boat ride through the city of Venice, Italy. The painter Canaletto will be our guide. Here is a typical sight: grand palaces surrounded by canals.

- Which part of the painting contains the most detail? the least?
- Would you like the painting better without the boats? Explain.

View of the Riva degli Schiavoni, Canaletto
The Toledo Museum of Art, Toledo, Ohio

Activities

1. **Write a postcard or a letter.** Imagine that you are gliding through the canals of Venice on a long boat, or gondola. Write to your friend, describing your boat ride and your impressions of Venice.
2. **Write a dialogue.** What if two boats got in each other's way? Write a funny dialogue in which each navigator claims the right of way.

Check-up: Unit 9

Capitalizing and Punctuating Sentences *(p. 282)* Write each sentence. Separate any run-on sentences.

1. Everglades National Park is a swamp it is in Florida
2. have you ever visited a swamp
3. how remarkable it is
4. small clumps of high land are called hummocks they are covered with trees
5. take a nature walk with a ranger observe the unusual birds
6. what a great time you will have
7. go to the Ten Thousand Islands you can reach the area by boat
8. do you smell the salt air
9. how pleasant it is

Proper Nouns and Proper Adjs. *(p. 284)* Write the proper nouns and the proper adjectives. Capitalize them correctly.

10. Who was john muir?
11. He was an american who loved nature and wildlife.
12. He came to the united states from scotland when he was eleven.
13. The sierra mountains thrilled him.
14. He crossed the alaskan glaciers.
15. He went with his dog, stickeen.
16. He persuaded president roosevelt to protect the wilderness.
17. He helped set up yosemite national park in California.
18. He also explored asian lands.

Commas in a Series *(p. 286)* Write each sentence. Use commas to separate the items in a series.

19. Men women and children enjoy the Rocky Mountains in Colorado.
20. The mountains lakes and glaciers are beautiful.
21. Once people hunted buffalo deer and elk there.
22. Arrowheads pots and tools remain.
23. The slopes are cold windy and dry.
24. Moss primroses and sunflowers grow.
25. Chipmunks squirrels and gophers live there too.
26. Beavers build dams make lodges and gather food.
27. You might see bluebirds hawks owls or meadowlarks.

More Uses for Commas *(p. 288)* Write each sentence. Add commas where needed.

28. Well here we are in speech class.
29. Fred please give your speech first.
30. Is it about the Ritz Theater Fred?
31. Yes Mr. Stone it is.
32. No it won't be torn down.
33. Do you like the idea Fred?
34. Fred stand up straight.
35. Yes look at the audience.
36. Remember to speak clearly Fred.
37. Well that speech was very good.
38. Jane do you agree with Fred?
39. No Mr. Stone I don't.

Interjections *(p. 290)* Write each sentence. Underline the interjections. Add the correct punctuation after each interjection.

40. Hurray The parade boats are beginning to come down the river!
41. Hey Look at the variety of boats!
42. Ah how I'd love to cruise around on one of them.
43. Goodness Boats have come a long way since log dugouts.
44. Whew They couldn't have been very sturdy.
45. Oh let's pick our favorite boat.
46. Good grief That one is as big as a house!
47. Well it's a houseboat.
48. Wow Wouldn't it be fun to live on the water?

Quotations *(p. 292)* Write each sentence. Use punctuation marks and capital letters correctly.

49. have you read about the volcano asked Don
50. no answered Tony what happened
51. Mt. Ridley blew up said Don
52. were many people hurt asked Tony
53. it happened in a wilderness area replied Jo no one was hurt
54. several campers got out just in time she added
55. what a miracle that was said Tony
56. mud flowed down the Jones River Jo continued the river flooded
57. help is on its way she added
58. rescue workers are in the area said Don families are out of danger

Abbreviations *(p. 294)* Write these groups of words, using initials or abbreviations for the underlined words.

59. Duxbury, <u>Massachusetts</u> 02332
60. <u>Post Office</u> Box 35
61. <u>Friday</u>, <u>March</u> 10, 1989
62. <u>Doctor</u> Peter Denny
63. Richard Allman, <u>Senior</u>
64. Revere <u>Corporation</u>
65. <u>Anna</u> <u>Christina</u> Smithson
66. <u>Mister</u> James <u>William</u> Carson
67. Terry Douglas <u>Company</u>
68. 33 Cleary <u>Boulevard</u>
69. <u>Apartment</u> 2B
70. San Antonio, <u>Texas</u> 78284
71. <u>Sunday</u>, <u>December</u> 8, 1917
72. 11221 Vista <u>Drive</u>
73. Durham, <u>North Carolina</u> 27108

Titles *(p. 296)* Write each of the following titles correctly.

74. pioneer press   (newspaper)
75. you are my sunshine   (song)
76. children of the year   (article)
77. julie of the wolves   (book)
78. the goat well   (short story)
79. popular science   (magazine)
80. how to eat a poem   (poem)
81. mary poppins   (movie)
82. a new age begins   (chapter)
83. sports illustrated   (magazine)
84. georgia on my mind   (song)
85. the little prince   (book)
86. the wall street journal   (newspaper)
87. using the camera   (chapter)
88. trial by wilderness   (book)

Enrichment

Using Capitalization and Punctuation

Topnotch Titles

Think of poems, stories, and books that you have read this year. Which had the best titles? Write down at least three of these titles, punctuating them correctly. Ask a friend which title seems most interesting. What does your friend think it means? Does your friend want to read the poem, story, or book?

Animal Talk

You are in charge of making buttons to urge people not to pollute the forest. Draw five large circles on cardboard. Inside each circle, draw a forest animal. Under each picture, write a statement by the animal.

"I can't find clean water to wash my food," says Rob Raccoon.

Cut out your buttons and give them to friends.

LICENSE PLATES

Players—3. **You need**—paper. **How to play**—Pretend that you are on a trip across the country. On your way, you see license plates from many different states. One player "sees" a license plate and calls out the state. The second player must then spell the state correctly on paper. The third player must write the correct abbreviation for the state. The second player now calls out a new state. **Scoring**—1 point for each state; 2 points for each state spelled correctly; 5 points for each correct abbreviation. The player with the most points wins.

Inventors' Convention

Pretend that you are attending an inventors' convention. While there, you see these four crazy inventions:

refrigercycle   vitapaste
plantifier   zoomotel

Write a short paragraph about each invention. Tell the inventor's name, when and where the product was invented, and what the product is supposed to do. Be sure to capitalize and punctuate your paragraphs correctly.

> The <u>musikite</u> was invented by Melody Raines of Kansas City, Kansas, on April 16, 1988. This toy/instrument plays jazz, rock, or classical music. As the musikite rises higher in the sky, the tune it plays changes!

Ballooning

What do you think Dara might be saying? How about Fred, Max, and Zina? Write down what you might see in a speech balloon for each child. Use one of the interjections below in each statement. Be sure to punctuate your statements correctly.

Ouch Hurray Hey Oh, no
Good grief Ah Wow Whew
Oh Goodness Oops Well

1 | Correct Sentences (p. 282)

● Each sentence is missing a capital letter or an end mark. Write each sentence correctly.

Example: How hard we practice   *How hard we practice!*

1. The spring concert is in just two weeks
2. will you sing any new songs?
3. you know many of the new songs.
4. Think about the words and the music
5. Who will try out for the solo parts
6. What a lovely voice Rita has
7. please sing the last verse one more time.

▲ Write the sentences correctly. Separate run-on sentences.

Example: contact Allan he has details about the concert
          Contact Allan. He has details about the concert.

8. the concert will be held on Saturday
9. will your school take part
10. what a musical night it will be
11. how many school bands will we hear
12. we heard thirty-five bands last year
13. how the music filled the air what a great concert that was
14. don't miss the concert buy your tickets now

■ Rewrite each sentence below as the kind of sentence shown in parentheses. Write the new sentences correctly.

Example: The tickets were sold quickly.   (exclamatory)
          How quickly the tickets were sold!

15. Will the concert begin on time?   (declarative)
16. The audience is large tonight.   (exclamatory)
17. Will Mr. Case record the entire concert?   (declarative)
18. Francis Scott Key wrote the national anthem.   (interrogative)
19. How well the chorus performed!   (interrogative)
20. Did you listen to the words of our class song?   (imperative)

2 | Proper Nouns and Proper Adjs. (p. 284)

● Write the underlined proper nouns and proper adjectives. Capitalize them correctly.

Example: Are these paintings by <u>mary cassatt</u>? *Mary Cassatt*

1. She was an <u>american</u> artist.
2. She was born in <u>pittsburgh</u>.
3. Her father was president of the <u>pennsylvania railroad</u>.
4. Her art education began in the <u>united states</u>.
5. Later she went to <u>europe</u>.
6. She studied with <u>italian</u> and <u>spanish</u> artists.
7. She became friends with a <u>french</u> artist named <u>degas</u>.
8. You can see paintings by <u>cassatt</u> at the <u>museum of fine arts</u>

▲ Write the proper nouns and the proper adjectives. Capitalize them correctly.

Example: When was the artist pablo picasso born? *Pablo Picasso*

9. He was born on october 25, 1881.
10. He spent his childhood in the spanish city of barcelona.
11. The academy of arts was his first art school.
12. Later he studied art in madrid.
13. He moved to paris in 1903.
14. Although born in spain, he is considered a french painter.
15. Some of his works were influenced by african art.
16. His paintings hang in european and american museums.

■ Write each sentence, using capital letters correctly.

Example: The city of lakeville is sponsoring an art contest.
　　　　　The city of Lakeville is sponsoring an art contest.

17. I read about it in a newsletter from the blake art museum.
18. Paintings must be turned in by the first monday in may.
19. The judges are franko pallo and maria romano.
20. They are well-known italian artists.
21. Paintings will be displayed in the lobby of city hall.
22. The regal company donated all the prize money.
23. First prize is a scholarship to the hamilton school of art.
24. The awards will be presented by mayor lewis.

3 | Commas in a Series (p. 286)

● Copy the sentence that is correct in each pair.

Example: The show was held on Monday Tuesday and Wednesday.
The show was held on Monday, Tuesday, and Wednesday.
The show was held on Monday, Tuesday, and Wednesday.

1. We watched laughed and clapped.
   We watched, laughed, and clapped.
2. We saw string puppets, finger puppets, and hand puppets.
   We saw string puppets finger puppets and hand puppets.
3. Jack Rita and I played with the string puppets.
   Jack, Rita, and I played with the string puppets.
4. We made hand puppets from bags, felt, or yarn.
   We made hand puppets from bags felt or yarn.
5. Theo made the stage from a large box, curtains, and wallpaper.
   Theo made the stage from a large box curtains and wallpaper.

▲ Write these sentences correctly.

Example: Choose between <u>The Wizard of Oz</u>, and <u>Peter Pan</u>.
Choose between <u>The Wizard of Oz</u> and <u>Peter Pan</u>.

6. Will you play the Tin Man the Lion or the Scarecrow?
7. You can try out for the play on Sunday Monday or Tuesday.
8. Julie Stan and Amy are making the costumes.
9. Peter and Rob designed built and painted the sets.
10. Memorize your lines learn the songs and be on time.
11. Relax smile and enjoy yourself on stage.

■ Rewrite each sentence to include a series. Use commas correctly in your sentences.

Example: Use music and movement in your performance.
Use music, movement, and costumes in your performance.

12. Pretend that you are a flower or an earthworm.
13. Now decide whether your world is a tiny garden or a forest.
14. Actors and dancers work long hours.
15. Courage and hard work can lead to success.
16. The day of the performance was windy and cold.
17. People wore rubber boots and heavy coats.
18. The auditorium was filled with cheers and joy.

4 | More Uses for Commas (p. 288)

● Copy each sentence. Then underline the introductory word or the noun in direct address and the commas.

Example: You play the piano so well, Carla.
You play the piano so well, Carla.

1. Well, I practice two hours a day.
2. Your flute has a beautiful sound, Leo.
3. Matt, do you also play the flute?
4. I don't have time for flute lessons, Amy.
5. Yes, the recorder is an easy instrument to learn.
6. I think, Amy, that we should play together.
7. No, I have never heard that tune.

▲ Write the sentences. Add commas where they are needed.

Example: Yes Olivia I would like to play in a band.
Yes, Olivia, I would like to play in a band.

8. Yes it would be a lot of fun.
9. Tia what instrument would you choose?
10. Well I would choose a guitar like my dad's.
11. I think Scott that my dad will let me use his guitar.
12. No he does not play very much anymore.
13. Mr. Garcia is a good music teacher Ruby.
14. I don't think Olivia that I can stay for the concert.
15. Yes I will play for you now Ruby.

■ Write the sentences. Add commas where needed. Underline introductory words once and nouns in direct address twice.

Example: No Becky I have never been to the ballet.
No, Becky, I have never been to the ballet.

16. My grandfather took me to the ballet last year Linda.
17. Yes Linda the dancers are very graceful.
18. Louis would you like to square-dance tonight?
19. How do you know what steps to do Meryl?
20. Well Lenny one person calls out directions.
21. Do you think Meryl that the caller ever makes mistakes?
22. I am certain Lenny that the caller sometimes gets confused.

5 | Interjections (p. 290)

● Copy each sentence. Then underline the interjection and the punctuation that follows it.

Example: Hey! Look under that bush!
Hey! Look under that bush!

1. Oh, no! The bird flew away!
2. Goodness! What do you think it was?
3. Oh, I think it might have been a lark.
4. Oops! I forgot to bring my binoculars!
5. Ah, that's too bad.
6. Wow! Look at the tiny speckled eggs in this nest!

▲ Write the sentences. Add the correct punctuation after each interjection.

Example: Ouch I just got a splinter from this birdhouse.
Ouch! I just got a splinter from this birdhouse.

7. Goodness The woodpeckers should love that!
8. Oh it's just a hollowed-out log with a roof.
9. Well it will seem cozy to a bird.
10. Oh, no I forgot to put a perch on the front!
11. Hurray It's finished!
12. Ah it looks great in that tree.
13. Oops Is that a squirrel I see peeking out?

■ Write the sentences, using the interjection in parentheses. Add the correct punctuation after the interjection.

Example: ___ An ostrich can run extremely fast! (Goodness)
Goodness! An ostrich can run extremely fast!

14. ___ it can run faster than I can! (Well)
15. ___ That's good, because it can't fly. (Whew)
16. ___ Did you know that some ostriches are taller than my dad? (Good grief)
17. ___ Your dad is over six feet tall! (Wow)
18. ___ Can you imagine the size of an ostrich egg? (Hey)
19. ___ it must be enormous! (Oh)
20. ___ what a scrambled egg that would make! (Ah)

6 | Quotations (p. 292)

● Write each sentence correctly. Use capital letters and quotation marks where they are needed.

Example: do you know any riddles? asked Lois.
"Do you know any riddles?" asked Lois.

1. Tim answered, what is black, white, and read all over?
2. it is a blushing zebra, guessed Lois.
3. that's not right, but it's a good guess, said Tim.
4. Tim exclaimed, it's a newspaper!
5. what has teeth but can't eat? asked Lois.
6. Tim replied, a comb has teeth but can't eat.
7. next time I'll fool you! exclaimed Lois.

▲ Write each sentence correctly. Use punctuation marks and capital letters where they are needed.

Example: our town has a volunteer fire department said Norma
"Our town has a volunteer fire department," said Norma.

8. Seth added my father is a volunteer firefighter
9. how does he know when there is a fire asked Jean
10. the volunteers use a phone chain answered Seth
11. Jean asked are there many big fires in your town
12. we're lucky said Norma that we've never had a big fire
13. I hope that we never do exclaimed Seth

■ Rewrite each sentence. Move the speaker's name to the position shown in parentheses.

Example: Jo asked, "Is volunteer firefighting a new idea?"   (end)
"Is volunteer firefighting a new idea?" asked Jo.

14. Lee said, "Volunteers were used in ancient Egypt."   (end)
15. "They were also used in early America," he added.   (beginning)
16. Stan asked, "Were there big fires then?"   (end)
17. "Yes," answered Sue, "they often destroyed towns."   (end)
18. "The wooden buildings burned easily," Lee added.   (beginning)
19. "To stop the spread of fire, firefighters often blew up buildings," said Sue.   (middle)
20. "How strange that is!" exclaimed Jo.   (beginning)

7 | Abbreviations (p. 294)

● Write the words that the underlined abbreviations stand for.

Example: 465 Highland <u>Ave.</u>   *Avenue*

1. Orlando, <u>FL</u> 32859
2. <u>Wed.</u>, <u>Dec.</u> 3, 1835
3. <u>Dr.</u> Linda Chang
4. DeMarco Tire <u>Co.</u>
5. 36 Park <u>Dr.</u>
6. <u>Aug.</u> 25, 1912
7. Frank Dolan, <u>Jr.</u>
8. <u>Rte.</u> 114
9. <u>P. O.</u> Box 50
10. <u>Mr.</u> Peter Jackson
11. Healthy Foods, <u>Inc.</u>
12. Birmingham, <u>AL</u> 35294

▲ Rewrite these groups of words, using abbreviations or initials for the underlined words.

Example: 139 Palmer <u>Road</u>, Sherwood, <u>Connecticut</u> 06143
        139 Palmer Rd., Sherwood, CT 06143

13. <u>Post Office</u> Box 15, Hattiesburg, <u>Mississippi</u> 39406
14. <u>Sunday</u>, <u>January</u> 7, 1949
15. Boats Afloat, <u>Incorporated</u>
16. <u>Mister</u> Benjamin <u>Montgomery</u> Thompson, <u>Junior</u>
17. <u>Thursday</u>, <u>September</u> 12, 1928
18. <u>Doctor</u> Maria <u>Carmen</u> Perez
19. Maxwell Hamilton Photo Color <u>Company</u>
20. 14 Hamlet <u>Street</u>, <u>Apartment</u> 7, Ithaca, <u>New York</u> 14853

■ Follow the directions for each item. You may make up some of the information. Use abbreviations and initials.

Example: Write the name of your best friend's father.
        Mr. S. D. Merrick, Sr.

21. Write the day and the date.
22. Write your complete home address.
23. Write the name of a company that makes computers.
24. Write an address that includes a post office box number.
25. Mark Rand, Sr., has a son with the same name. Write his name.
26. Write the day and date of your birthday this year.
27. Write the address of one of your friends.
28. Write the day and date that school began this year.

8 | Titles (p. 296)

● Each title below should be underlined or enclosed in quotation marks. Write the titles correctly.

Example: The White Horse   (poem)   "The White Horse"

1. Treasure Island   (movie)
2. The Borrowers   (book)
3. Oklahoma!   (song)
4. Dreams   (poem)
5. Boys' Life   (magazine)
6. Summertime   (chapter)
7. The Necklace   (short story)
8. The New Yorker   (magazine)
9. Autumn Woods   (poem)
10. Miami News   (newspaper)
11. A Clever Judge   (short story)
12. The Yearling   (book)

▲ Write these titles correctly.

Example: on a night of snow   (poem)   "On a Night of Snow"

13. how thor found his hammer   (short story)
14. home on the range   (song)
15. the philadelphia inquirer   (newspaper)
16. swift things are beautiful   (poem)
17. the wizard of oz   (movie)
18. the princess on the glass hill   (short story)
19. a tale of two cities   (movie)
20. the old farmers' almanac   (magazine)
21. crossing kansas by train   (poem)
22. when morgan had a horse   (book)

■ Rewrite each sentence, correcting the title.

Example: I just finished the article life in the mountains.
            I just finished the article "Life in the Mountains."

23. The book Heidi is about a girl in the Swiss Alps.
24. My favorite chapter is called in the pasture.
25. The magazine national geographic has interesting articles.
26. Listen to the poem the river is a piece of sky.
27. On our camping trip, we sang this land is your land.
28. The magazine consumer reports taught me a lot about tents.
29. Alexandra and I just saw the movie the sound of music.
30. My teacher read us a humorous poem called cheers.
31. Susan is reading the book the trumpet of the swan.
32. I will write my book report on the incident at hawk's hill.

I write long letters and do not know anyone
to send them to.
Most tender things speak in my heart
And I can only say them to the bamboos
in the garden.

from "The Garden of Bamboos"
A Southeast Asian Song

Persuasive Letter

Getting Ready Have you ever tried to persuade someone to go with you somewhere? Did that person try to persuade you *not* to go (or to go somewhere else)? Who won? The person with the most reasons? The person with the *best* reasons? Sometimes people write letters to persuade others about their point of view. In this unit, you will learn how to write persuasive letters.

ACTIVITIES

Listening   The quotation on the opposite page is from a poem. Listen as it is read. What is this person saying about letters?

Speaking   Look at the picture. Would you consider this a quiet, beautiful place to be or a boring place to be? What reasons would you use to persuade someone that you were right? Have someone write your reasons on the board.

Writing   In your journal, write a letter to the gardener with the reasons why you do or do not like this garden. Is it perfect or could it be improved?

LITERATURE

Can you find out what a person is like through a few short letters?

Sarah, Plain and Tall

By Patricia MacLachlan

Anna and her little brother Caleb lived on a prairie farm with their father. Caleb couldn't remember their mother, who had died a day after he was born, but Anna remembered how their parents used to sing.

Papa might not have told us about Sarah that night if Caleb hadn't asked him the question. After the dishes were cleared and washed and Papa was filling the tin pail with ashes, Caleb spoke up. It wasn't a question, really.

"You don't sing anymore," he said. He said it harshly. Not because he meant to, but because he had been thinking of it for so long. "Why?" he asked more gently.

Slowly Papa straightened up. There was a long silence, and the dogs looked up, wondering at it.

"I've forgotten the old songs," said Papa quietly. He sat down. "But maybe there's a way to remember them." He looked up at us.

"How?" asked Caleb eagerly.

Papa leaned back in the chair. "I've placed an advertisement in the newspapers. For help."

"You mean a housekeeper?" I asked, surprised.

Caleb and I looked at each other and burst out laughing, remembering Hilly, our old housekeeper. She was round and slow and shuffling. She snored in a high whistle at night, like a teakettle, and let the fire go out.

"No," said Papa slowly. "Not a housekeeper." He paused. "A wife."

Caleb stared at Papa. "A wife? You mean a mother?"

Nick slid his face onto Papa's lap and Papa stroked his ears.

"That, too," said Papa. "Like Maggie."

Matthew, our neighbor to the south, had written to ask for a wife and mother for his children. And Maggie had come from Tennessee. Her hair was the color of turnips and she laughed.

Papa reached into his pocket and unfolded a letter written on white paper. "And I have received an answer." Papa read to us:

Dear Mr. Jacob Witting,

I am Sarah Wheaton from Maine as you will see from my letter. I am answering your advertisement. I have never been married, though I have been asked. I have lived with an older brother, William, who is about to be married. His wife-to-be is young and energetic.

I have always loved to live by the sea, but at this time I feel a move is necessary. And the truth is, the sea is as far east as I can go. My choice, as you can see, is limited. This should not be taken as an insult. I am strong and I work hard and I am willing to travel. But I am not mild mannered. If you should still care to write, I would be interested in your children and about where you live. And you.

Very truly yours,
Sarah Elisabeth Wheaton

P.S. Do you have opinions on cats? I have one.

No one spoke when Papa finished the letter. He kept looking at it in his hands, reading it over to himself. Finally I turned my head a bit to sneak a look at Caleb. He was smiling. I smiled, too.

"One thing," I said in the quiet of the room.

"What's that?" asked Papa, looking up.

I put my arm around Caleb.

"Ask her if she sings," I said.

Caleb and Papa and I wrote letters to Sarah, and before the ice and snow had melted from the fields, we all received answers. Mine came first.

Dear Anna,

Yes, I can braid hair and I can make stew and bake bread, though I prefer to build bookshelves and paint.

My favorite colors are the colors of the sea, blue and gray and green, depending on the weather. My brother William is a fisherman, and he tells me that when he is in the middle of a fog-bound sea the water is a color for which there is no name. He catches flounder and sea bass and bluefish. Sometimes he sees whales. And birds, too, of course. I am enclosing a book of sea birds so you will see what William and I see every day.

Very truly yours,
Sarah Elisabeth Wheaton

Caleb read and read the letter so many times that the ink began to run and the folds tore. He read the book about sea birds over and over.

"Do you think she'll come?" asked Caleb. "And will she stay? What if she thinks we are loud and pesky?"

"You *are* loud and pesky," I told him. But I was worried, too. Sarah loved the sea, I could tell. Maybe she wouldn't leave there after all to come where there were fields and grass and sky and not much else.

"What if she comes and doesn't like our house?" Caleb asked. "I told her it was small. Maybe I shouldn't have told her it was small."

"Hush, Caleb. Hush."

Caleb's letter came soon after, with a picture of a cat drawn on the envelope.

Dear Caleb,

My cat's name is Seal because she is gray like the seals that swim off shore in Maine. She is glad that Lottie and Nick send their greetings. She likes dogs most of the time. She says their footprints are much larger than hers (which she is enclosing in return).

Your house sounds lovely, even though it is far out in the country with no close neighbors. My house is tall and the shingles are gray because of the salt from the sea. There are roses nearby.

Yes, I do like small rooms sometimes. Yes, I can keep a fire going at night. I do not know if I snore. Seal has never told me.

Very truly yours,
Sarah Elisabeth

"Did you really ask her about fires and snoring?" I asked, amazed.

"I wished to know," Caleb said.

He kept the letter with him, reading it in the barn and in the fields and by the cow pond. And always in bed at night.

One morning, early, Papa and Caleb and I were cleaning out the horse stalls and putting down new bedding. Papa stopped suddenly and leaned on his pitchfork.

"Sarah has said she will come for a month's time if we wish her to," he said, his voice loud in the dark barn. "To see how it is. Just to see."

Caleb stood by the stall door and folded his arms across his chest.

"I think," he began. Then, "I think," he said slowly, "that it would be good—to say yes," he finished in a rush.

Papa looked at me.

"I say yes," I told him, grinning.

"Yes," said Papa. "Then yes it is."

And the three of us, all smiling, went to work again.

The next day Papa went to town to mail his letter to Sarah. It was rainy for days, and the clouds followed. The house was cool and damp and quiet. Once I set four places at the table, then caught myself and put the extra plate away. Three lambs were born, one with a black face. And then Papa's letter came. It was very short.

Dear Jacob,

I will come by train. I will wear a yellow bonnet. I am plain and tall.

Sarah

"What's that?" asked Caleb excitedly, peering over Papa's shoulder. He pointed. "There, written at the bottom of the letter."

Papa read it to himself. Then he smiled, holding up the letter for us to see.

Tell them I sing was all it said.

Will Sarah decide to stay? To find out, read the rest of the book *Sarah, Plain and Tall*.

Sarah, Plain and Tall is based on a real-life Sarah. When the author was a little girl, her mother often told her the story of a woman who came to the prairie from the coast of Maine to marry a member of their family and be a mother to the man's children. Years later, the author decided to write this story as a picture book. Instead, the story grew into a different form. The words make their own pictures.

Think and Discuss

1. Did Anna and Caleb feel that Sarah's letters helped them know what she was like? Give reasons for your answer.

2. What questions did Anna ask Sarah in her first letter? What questions did Caleb ask? How did you know from Sarah's return letters that they had asked her these questions?

3. The author introduces the **character** Sarah by having her describe herself in four personal letters. Reread each letter. What do you find out about Sarah? What does she look like? What kind of person do you think she is?

4. What would you want to know about a pen pal that you couldn't find out through letters? What kinds of things would Anna and Caleb *not* be able to find out about Sarah from her letters?

Writing

By Olivia Castellano

A girl, pencil in hand,
writes alone on a squeaky desk.
She loves the feel of wood on flesh
as the thin yellow stick moves
methodically on three expert fingers,
and settles into the ridges
of her calloused, grateful hand.

Say that she loves the freedom
all for the taking of wood to wood:

she gallops away
on a yellow horse
cutting pathways
through a wide, white forest.

Think and Discuss

1. The poem "Writing" has three parts, or **stanzas**. The first stanza describes a girl who is writing. The second stanza describes her feelings. What does the third stanza describe?

2. **Literal language** is the use of words with their ordinary meaning. **Figurative language** goes beyond the ordinary meaning of words. It requires you to use your imagination to figure out the author's meaning. In the poem, the pencil is referred to as a "thin yellow stick" and as a "yellow horse." Which of these is figurative?

3. Why did the poet compare the movement of the pencil to a galloping horse? What comparison would you make to describe the movement of your pencil?

RESPONDING TO LITERATURE

The Reading and Writing Connection

Personal Response Anna, Caleb, and their father first learned about Sarah from her letter of introduction. If you were going to visit a family you had never met, what things would you tell about yourself in a letter? Make a list.

Creative Writing Imagine moving away from a place that you love. Write a poem about leaving the colors, sights, and sounds you value. Use figurative language to compare your leaving with something else, like the sun setting at twilight.

Creative Activities

Illustrate Use one side of your paper to draw a picture of Sarah's house on the Maine coast. Base your picture on the descriptions in her letters. Use the other side to draw a picture showing where you live.

Discuss Sarah lived on the coast of Maine. Find Maine on a map of the United States. Now locate Wyoming. If Sarah were going to Wyoming by train, what route might she travel? What states, mountains, and rivers would she cross? Describe the route to a partner.

Vocabulary

Anna described Caleb as "loud and pesky." What is the meaning of the word *pesky*? What other words could Anna have used for *pesky*? If you had to choose two words to describe yourself, what would they be?

Looking Ahead

Persuasive Letter Later in this unit, you will be writing a persuasive letter. Sarah wants Anna, Caleb, and their father to like her. How does she try to persuade them in her letters?

VOCABULARY CONNECTION

A **prefix** is a word part that you add to the beginning of a word. This word is called the **base word**. Look at the word with a prefix in the passage below.

> Papa reached into his pocket and **unfolded** a letter written on white paper.
> *from "Sarah, Plain and Tall" by Patricia MacLachlan*

A prefix changes the meaning of the base word. The prefix *un-* means "not." *Unfolded* means "not folded."
Each prefix has its own meaning.

Prefix	Meaning	Example
mis-	wrong, incorrectly	misspell—to spell incorrectly
re-	again	remake—to make again
pre-	before, in advance	preschool—before school

Vocabulary Practice

A. Copy each underlined word. Then underline the prefix and write the meaning of the word.

1. Cal had <u>misplaced</u> his book about Maine.
2. He <u>rechecked</u> his desk, closet, and bookcase.
3. He looked in the most <u>unusual</u> places.
4. His father helped him <u>review</u> his activities.
5 They were <u>unlucky</u> in their search.

B. Add a prefix to each of these words from "Sarah, Plain and Tall." Check your words in a dictionary. Then use each new word in a sentence of your own.

6. build   7. willing   8. read   9. written   10. washed

Listening: Telling Fact from Opinion

When you say something like "I think cats make good pets," you are stating your **opinion**. An opinion is your thought or feeling about something. When you say something like "I am tall," you are stating a **fact**. A fact is information that can be proved true. Compare the statements below.

> 1. "Sarah has said she will come for a month's time if we wish her to," he said, his voice loud in the dark barn.
> 2. "I think," he began. Then, "I think," he said slowly, "that it would be good—to say yes. . . ."
> *from "Sarah, Plain and Tall" by Patricia MacLachlan*

• Which statement is an opinion? Which is a fact? Why?

Often people will try to persuade you to agree with their opinions. You need to be able to tell whether they are supporting their opinions with facts or whether they are just piling on more opinions. Use these guidelines to help you.

Guidelines for Telling Fact from Opinion

1. Ask whether the statement can be proved true. If it can, it is a fact.
2. Ask whether the statement is a feeling or a belief. If so, it is an opinion.
3. Be alert for words such as *best, worst, should,* and *I think.* They signal opinions.

Prewriting Practice

Number a paper from 1 to 10. Listen as some sentences are read. After each one, write *F* for fact or *O* for opinion.

Thinking: Analyzing and Evaluating

Every day you must **analyze** and **evaluate** things people tell you and things you read. When you analyze information, you take it apart in your mind and study each part. Then you evaluate it—you make a judgment about its value or worth.

People try to persuade you to do things all the time. Advertisements try to persuade you to buy certain products. Here are some guidelines for analyzing and evaluating persuasion.

Guidelines for Analyzing and Evaluating

1. **Separate facts from opinions.** Facts state information you can prove to be true. Opinions, however, tell what a person thinks or feels about something.

   FACT: Sarah is from the coast of Maine.
   OPINION: Sarah will like the children.

2. **Question opinions that are not backed up by facts.** If someone fails to give you facts to support an opinion you are being urged to share, question the opinion.

3. **Watch for overgeneralizations.** A **generalization** is a general statement about something, based on facts. An **overgeneralization** is a very broad, general statement that does not follow from the facts. Look at these statements.

   FACT: Jacob Witting found a wife through an ad he placed in our newspaper.
   FACT: Jacob's neighbor Hal also found a wife through an ad in our paper.
   GENERALIZATION: Some pioneer farmers have found wives through ads in our paper.
   OVERGENERALIZATION: Any pioneer farmer can find a wife by advertising in our paper.

4. **Be sure that each statement agrees with the others.** Two statements that do not agree cannot both be true.

   Come to the prairie for a carefree life.
   Prairie life is good in spite of the hardships.

5. **Look out for exaggeration.** A statement that goes beyond the truth is an **exaggeration.** An exaggeration says that something is greater than it is.

   Our soil is so rich that your corn will grow to the sky.

   Keep the guidelines in mind as you read the following letter.

Dear Paul,

    <u>Sarah, Plain and Tall</u> is the best book ever written! You've just got to read it.
    The beginning is the most interesting part of the book. It tells about a prairie farm family. The father advertises for a wife, and Sarah answers the ad. She writes to Anna and Caleb, the father's children. Through their letters, the children learn that Sarah can do millions of things. She can braid hair, make stew, bake bread, build bookshelves, and paint. Sarah can do anything!
    About halfway through, the story really gets interesting. To learn why, just get the book!

             Your friend,
             Heidi

- What facts and opinions are stated in this letter?
- Are Heidi's opinions backed up by facts?
- What overgeneralization has Heidi made?
- Which two statements do not agree?
- Where does Heidi exaggerate?

Prewriting Practice

With a partner, take turns trying to persuade each other to read a favorite book. Then evaluate each other's arguments.

Writing Business Letters ☑

Business letters are usually written to people you do not know. They have many purposes—to request information, to order a product, to express an opinion, to persuade someone to do something.

A business letter has six parts. The body should be brief. It should give all necessary details in polite, formal language.

<table>
<tr><td>HEADING</td><td>314 Winter Avenue
Brewster, MA 02631
March 30, 1990</td></tr>
<tr><td>INSIDE ADDRESS</td><td>Editor, Children's Books
Harper & Row Publishers, Inc.
10 East 53rd Street
New York, NY 10022</td></tr>
<tr><td>GREETING</td><td>Dear Sir or Madam:</td></tr>
<tr><td>BODY</td><td>I hope you will publish more books like <u>Sarah, Plain and Tall</u>. This book taught me about life on the prairie. It showed me how people lived long ago and made me want to read more about the period. I shared the book with friends.
Please continue publishing excellent stories about the past.</td></tr>
<tr><td>CLOSING

SIGNATURE</td><td>Sincerely,
Eva Lopez
Eva Lopez</td></tr>
</table>

- What are the six parts of a business letter?
- What information does each part of the letter give?
- What is the purpose of this letter?
- What opinion does Eva express? What are her reasons?
- Does Eva's language suit a business letter? Explain.
- Notice how Eva signed her name. Why didn't she use just "Eva"?

Guidelines for Writing Business Letters

1. Use all six parts of the business letter. Use a colon (:) after the greeting. If you do not know whose name to use, use the name of the business or "Dear Sir or Madam."
2. Be businesslike. Keep your language polite and formal.
3. Make your point briefly and clearly.
4. Include all necessary details.
   a. **To request information:** State what information you want, why you want it, and when you need it.
   b. **To order a product:** Identify the item. Tell where you saw it. Give the price, the number you want, and other information such as size, color, and amount enclosed.
   c. **To express an opinion or to persuade someone:** State your opinion clearly. Give good reasons for it.

Prewriting Practice

A. The following section of a business letter has errors in capitalization and punctuation. Make up an inside address and add your own heading, closing, and signature. Then rewrite the letter correctly.

```
dear Avon bookstore,
    Three weeks ago I ordered a copy of Sarah,
Plain and Tall by Patricia MacLachlan. I told
you that I had to have the book in two weeks.
It still has not come, and I do not need it
now. Please return the $8.25 I sent you.
```

B. Rewrite this following section of a business letter. Take out the sentence that does not belong. Change any language that is not formal or polite.

> On July 24 I sent you a great ad and asked
> you to put it in your newspaper. I wanted to
> give away three of my cat's new kittens. You
> should see the gray one--it's the greatest! Cuz
> you left out my phone number, no one could call
> me. You'd better run the ad again next week,
> and I won't be paying for it!
>
> Your friend,
>
> *Larry Stokes*
>
> Larry Stokes

The Grammar Connection

Capitalization and Punctuation in Business Letters

When you write business letters, be especially careful to capitalize and punctuate the parts correctly. Capitalize the names of people, businesses, streets, cities, and months as well as the first word of the greeting and the closing. Remember to abbreviate state names by using two capital letters. Use commas between the city and the state, between the day and the year, and after the closing. Use a colon after the greeting.

18 Walker Road	Davis Corporation
Hartford, CT 06117	4321 Avers Street
April 24, 1990	Laredo, TX 78041
Dear Davis Corporation:	Sincerely yours,

Practice The letter parts below contain many errors. Find the errors and rewrite the parts correctly.

14 Wayne drive	Fine fabrics company
brockton mA 02401	29 South street
february, 12 1990	peoria IL, 61602
dear fine Fabrics company	Yours, Truly

Stating and Supporting an Opinion ☑

"P.S. Do you have opinions on cats?" Sarah asks Jacob at the end of a letter. You probably have opinions about many things. However, persuading someone to believe one of your opinions requires more than just speaking your mind. You must state your opinion clearly and support it with reasons.

Suppose you were asked to write about your opinion of Sarah as a mother for Anna and Caleb. First, you would state your opinion in a topic sentence. Then you would list reasons.

OPINION: Sarah would make a good mother for Anna and Caleb.
REASONS: **1.** She is interested in children.
       2. She braids hair, makes stew, and bakes bread. (important to Anna)
       3. She sings and can keep a fire going at night. (important to Caleb)
       4. She has other interests to share: She loves the sea, has a cat, paints, and builds bookshelves.

• Do you find the reasons convincing? Why or why not?

How do you know which reasons to choose to persuade someone of your opinions? Suppose you would like to go to a weekend swimming camp in Maine. You are probably excited by the thought of racing across the clear, cool lake. Would these reasons persuade your friends to go with you? Would the same reasons convince a parent to go as a sponsor?

When you want to be persuasive, choose reasons that appeal to your audience—the person or persons you want to persuade. For example, the chance to do things with their children might convince parents to go on a weekend trip more than the reasons stated above.

Suppose you chose the following reasons to persuade your parents to let you have a cat.

1. Caring for a cat would teach me to be responsible.
2. I would learn a lot about cats.
3. Our whole family would enjoy having a cat.

• Would these reasons persuade the audience? Explain.

➡

Composition Skills   329

Prewriting Practice

A. Write a sentence stating your opinion on one of the topics below. List at least three supporting reasons, and save your list.

   1. playing baseball at morning recess
   2. taking dancing lessons

B. Tell a partner your opinion from Practice A. Try to convince your partner of your view, using the reasons you listed. Was your partner convinced? How could you change your argument to make it better? Save your list.

C. Practice choosing reasons to suit your audience. In "Sarah, Plain and Tall," Sarah said that her cat, Seal, liked dogs —most of the time. First, persuade Sarah that Seal will be fine with the dogs. Then persuade Seal. With a partner, take turns making each argument and being the audience.

Ordering Your Reasons ☑

As you organize your reasons, picture the audience you are trying to persuade. Then choose an order that will be convincing to them. There are two basic ways to order your reasons.

1. from the most important to the least important
2. from the least important to the most important

If you heard that *Sarah, Plain and Tall* was going to be on TV, how might you persuade your parents to let you stay up to watch it? If you decided to write down your reasons in order of their importance to you, your list might look like this.

```
1.  Sarah, Plain and Tall is one of
    my favorite books.
2.  My favorite actor is in the show.
3.  Most of my friends will be watching it,
    and I want to be part of the discussions.
4.  It would give me a good essay topic.
```

   • What was the most important reason to the writer?
   • What order would be more appealing to parents?

The paragraph below is in an order that will be more convincing to parents. The most important reason is given first.

> I would really like to stay up to watch <u>Sarah, Plain and Tall</u> on TV. I can compare the TV version with the book, and that will make a good topic for my school essay. Most of my friends will be watching, and I want to be able to talk about it with them. Also, <u>Sarah, Plain and Tall</u> happens to be one of my favorite books. I hope you will agree that I should watch this program.

- Why did the writer think the first reason would be the most important one to her parents?
- Which reason was left out? Why?

The writer could also have arranged the reasons from least important to most important. In your writing, use that order when you want to build to your most important reason.

> I would really like to stay up to watch <u>Sarah, Plain and Tall</u> on TV. It is based on one of my favorite books. Most of my friends will be watching, and I want to be able to talk about it with them. Most important, I can compare the TV version with the book, and that will make a good topic for my school essay. I hope you will agree that I should watch this program.

- How is this paragraph different from the first paragraph?

Prewriting Practice

Take out the list of supporting reasons you saved from Prewriting Practice A on page 330. Decide on your audience, and order these reasons from most to least important.

The Writing Process
How to Write a Persuasive Letter

Step 1: Prewriting—Choose a Topic

Joshua made a list of topics he might want to write about in a persuasive letter. Then he thought about his list.

TV stations should have more kids' shows

He couldn't think of enough good reasons.

We should have a shorter school year

There wasn't much hope for this.

There should be a national Children's Day

He was excited about this topic, and he had lots of ideas.

Our city should have a zoo

He had some good arguments for this too.

Joshua circled *Children's Day.*

On Your Own

1. **Think and discuss** Make a list of ideas for a persuasive letter. Use the Ideas page to help you. Discuss your ideas with a partner.
2. **Choose** Ask yourself these questions about each topic.
   To whom shall I write this letter?
   Do I really care about this topic?
   Can I think of enough good reasons for my opinion?
   Circle the topic you want to write about in your letter.
3. **Explore** What will you write? Do one of the activities under "Exploring Your Topic" on the Ideas page.

Ideas for Getting Started

Choosing Your Topic

Topic Ideas

Letters are better than phone calls

The best place to live is near the ocean

Everyone should learn to cook

Endangered animals should be protected

Schools should teach bicycle safety

My favorite book should be required reading

I should have a later bedtime

Letter Starters

Answer these questions for ideas.

What do you think everyone (or no one) should do?

What would you like to change?

What makes you really happy or excited?

What isn't fair?

What makes you really annoyed?

What do you sometimes argue about?

What should happen more often?

Exploring Your Topic

1-2-3

Write your topic at the top of your paper. List all the reasons you can think of to support your opinion. Review your list. Cross out any reasons that would not persuade your audience. Do you want to add any reasons? Number your reasons in the best order for your letter.

Take Sides

Debate your topic with a friend. You argue your opinion and have your friend take the other side. Did you think of any new reasons?

Step 2: Write a First Draft

Joshua decided to write his letter to his congresswoman. He thought she might help him do something about his idea.

Joshua wrote his first draft. He did not worry about making mistakes. He would have a chance to correct them later.

Part of Joshua's first draft

Dear Congresswoman Stevens:

~~Why~~ I think we should have a national Children's Day. We have Mother's day and father's Day to show appreciashun for what our parents do. We kids dezerve ~~the~~ to be appreciated for what we do. We work hard at school and do stuff at home. We try hard to make our parents prowd. Let's have a day with presents and nothing to do!

On Your Own

1. **Think about purpose and audience** Ask these questions.
   To whom shall I write this letter?
   What is my purpose? How can I state it clearly?
   What reasons can I think of to support my opinion?
   Which reasons would best convince my audience?
   How should I order my reasons?
2. **Write** Stick to the reasons for your opinion. Leave out any unrelated ideas. Write on every other line so that you will have room to add or make changes later. Do not worry about mistakes. Write the most persuasive letter you can.

Step 3: Revise

Joshua read his first draft. He replaced a word with one that was more businesslike.

Joshua wanted to know if the letter would be convincing to his congresswoman. He read it to Andrew and asked him what he thought.

Reading and responding

It's a good idea, but tell more about the work kids do at home.

Oh, I know what to add! Is there anything else?

Well, *I* agree with your last point, but it won't convince *her*!

I see what you mean. Thanks!

Joshua thought about Andrew's comments and made some changes. He also added a sentence at the end.

Part of Joshua's revised draft

Children's Day. We have Mother's day and

father's Day to show appreciashun for what

our parents do. We ~~kids~~ *children* dezerve ~~the~~ to be

appreciated for what we do. We work hard at

school ~~and do stuff at home~~ *perform errands and chores and do homework.* We try hard to

make our parents prowd. Let's have a day

~~with presents and nothing to do!~~ *especially for children. We deserve it!*

Think and Discuss ✓

- Which word did Joshua change? Why?
- What details did he add?
- Which sentence did he change? Why?
- What sentence did he add?

On Your Own

Revising Checklist

☑ Did I state my opinion clearly?
☑ Do all my reasons support my opinion?
☑ Have I stated my reasons in the best order?
☑ Is my language appropriate for a business letter?

1. **Revise** Make changes in your first draft. Cross out sentences that do not support your opinion. Add reasons and details. If you need to find exact words, use the thesaurus below or the one in the back of the book. Replace words by crossing them out and adding new words above them.

2. **Have a conference** Read your letter to a classmate or your teacher.

W R I T I N G
CONFERENCE

Ask your listener:	As you listen:
"Have I stated my opinion clearly?" "Are my reasons good ones? Should I leave out any or add more?" "Are my reasons in a good order?"	Do I understand clearly what is being asked? Would I be persuaded by this letter? Are there enough good reasons to support the opinion?

3. **Revise** Think about your listener's suggestions. Do you have any other ideas? Make those changes on your paper.

Thesaurus

appreciation gratitude, recognition
choice selection, preference, alternative
danger hazard, risk, peril
deserve merit, be worthy
education knowledge, training

effect consequence, result
give offer, supply, present, provide
grateful appreciative, thankful
protect guard
see notice, observe, view
think believe, consider

Step 4: Proofread

Joshua proofread his letter for mistakes in spelling, capitalization, and punctuation. He used a dictionary to check spelling. He used proofreading marks to make his changes.

Part of Joshua's proofread draft

Dear Congresswoman Stevens:

~~Why~~ I think we should have a national

Children's Day. We have Mother's ḏay and

appreciation
father's Day to show ~~appreciashun~~ for what
‗
children deserve
our parents do. We ∧kids ~~dezerve~~ ~~the~~ to be

appreciated for what we do. We work hard at
perform errands and chores, and do homework.
school∧~~and do stuff at home~~. We try hard to
proud
make our parents ~~prowd~~. Let's have a day
especially for children. We deserve it!
∧~~with presents and nothing to do!~~

Think and Discuss

- Which words did Joshua capitalize? Why?
- Which words did he correct for spelling?
- Where did he add commas? Why?

On Your Own

1. Proofreading Practice Proofread this part of a business letter. Find one mistake in capitalization. Find five spelling mistakes, one wrong punctuation mark, and two missing commas. Write the paragraph correctly.

Dear Rosie's Pizza parlor,
    I think your resturant should have two kinds of crust different kinds of sawces and a salid bar. Most of the other pizza places offer these choises, and I think you should. It would help your bussiness.

Proofreading Marks

- ⌐Ͱ Indent
- ∧ Add something
- ℰ Take out something
- ‗ Capitalize
- / Make a small letter

2. **Proofreading Application** Now proofread your letter. Use the Proofreading Checklist and the Grammar and Spelling Hints below. You may want to use a colored pencil to make your corrections. Use a dictionary to check spellings.

Proofreading Checklist

Did I
- ☑ **1.** use proper format for my letter?
- ☑ **2.** use capital letters correctly?
- ☑ **3.** use punctuation marks correctly?
- ☑ **4.** spell all words correctly?
- ☑ **5.** sign my full name?

The Grammar/Spelling Connection

Grammar Hints

Remember these rules from Unit 9 for using commas.

- Use commas to separate the items in a series. Put a comma after each item except the last one. *(Ken bought five tomatoes, a bunch of carrots, and a green pepper.)*
- Use commas to set off the name of a person being spoken to directly. *(Thank you, Ken, for shopping.)*

Spelling Hint

- The (ô) sound is often spelled *aw*, *au*, or *a* before an *l*. *(fawn, haunt, bald)*

Step 5: Publish

Joshua copied his letter neatly on plain stationery. Then he addressed the envelope, added a stamp, and mailed the letter to his congresswoman. He hoped he would soon get a reply telling what she thought of his idea.

On Your Own

1. **Copy** Write or type your letter as neatly as possible. Be sure you have the correct heading and inside address.
2. **Check** Read over your letter again to make sure you have not left out anything or made any mistakes in copying.
3. **Share** Mail your letter.

Ideas for Sharing

- If your idea might interest many people, send a copy to the newspaper in your school or town.
- Write your opinion and reasons on separate pieces of paper. Then make a mobile. Put your opinion in the center and hang the reasons from it.

Applying Persuasive Letter

Literature and Creative Writing

In "Sarah, Plain and Tall," on pages 314-319, Anna and Caleb live with their father on a prairie farm. Their house has been empty of song since their mother died. When their father advertises for a new wife, he receives a reply from Sarah, who lives in Maine. After several letters pass between Sarah and the family, Sarah decides to come for a visit—"just to see." Anna, Caleb, and their father are delighted.

Have fun using what you have learned about writing letters to complete one or more of these activities.

Remember these things ☑
Use appropriate language and letter parts. State your opinion clearly. Put your reasons in the order that will be most convincing.

1. **Write to Sarah.** Imagine yourself as Anna or Caleb. Write a letter persuading Sarah to come and visit you and your family.
2. **Write to a celebrity.** Write a letter persuading a famous actor to visit your school to help spark enthusiasm for the drama program.
3. **Write to the governor.** Suppose that the governor of your state is holding a forum to discuss the interests and concerns of children. Write a letter persuading the governor to include you on a panel of twelve fifth graders.

Writing Across the Curriculum
Physical Education

Interest in physical fitness has grown in recent years. Magazines and newspapers publish many articles on sports and recreational activities. More and more people are realizing the importance of exercise. They often express their interests and concerns in letters to newspapers and government officials.

Try doing one or more of these activities.

1. Write for a sponsor. Many teams have sponsors that help pay for uniforms and equipment. Write a letter asking a local business to sponsor one of your school teams. Give good reasons for this business to sponsor your team.

Writing Steps
1. Choose a topic
2. Write a first draft
3. Revise
4. Proofread
5. Publish

2. Write to the mayor. Does your community have enough parks, bike paths, hiking trails, swimming pools, and sports fields? Write a letter to your mayor to request an additional recreational area. Give strong reasons for your request.

Word Bank
reason
enjoy
safety
facilities
conservation
leisure

3. Write to a sports star. Write a letter asking a sports personality to visit and talk with a group in your community. Will you ask this person to speak on a special topic? What reasons will you give for coming to your group?

Paloma enjoyed the book *Sarah, Plain and Tall.* She lived in the East and liked stories about people going West. When she read *The Little House on the Prairie* by Laura Ingalls Wilder, she realized just how important letters were in the days before telephones. Letters were the only way people had to keep in touch with faraway relatives and friends! Paloma shared her book by writing this imaginary letter to one of the characters.

23 Suffolk Street
Sag Harbor, NY 11963
April 18, 1990

Dear Mary Ingalls,

I just read The Little House on the Prairie by Laura Ingalls Wilder. It must be great to live on the prairie where the sky is so wide! When you walk with your sister Laura, and she acts as your eyes, can you picture the flowers and the birds from her wonderful descriptions? You and your family still get newsy letters from your relatives back East, but your little house in the big woods must seem far away.

Will your family stay in the prairie or move farther West? I can't wait to read the next book in the series!

Sincerely,
Paloma
Paloma

Think and Discuss
- What did you learn about the book from this letter?
- What did you learn about the setting of the book?
- What did you learn about the characters?

Share Your Book

Write to a Book Character

1. Choose a character in the book to receive your letter.
2. Choose one part of the book to write about in your letter. You might tell the character what he or she did that you liked, or you might ask the character some questions.
3. Write your letter. Tell enough about the book to get other people interested. Include the title and the author's name.

Other Activities

• Make a telephone call to a friend who likes the same kinds of books you do. Tell your friend why you think he or she will enjoy the book. Tell just enough to make your friend want to read it.

• Write an imaginary letter from your book character to your class. What kinds of questions would this person have about your life and times? Try to think and write as your book character might think and write.

• Make a model of the setting of your book. You might want to show the house where your book character lived or the site of some important event in the story.

 The Book Nook

By the Great Horn Spoon *by Sid Fleischman* Young Jack Fogg and Praiseworthy, the butler, go West to the 1849 California Gold Rush. Their adventures are hilarious!	**Farmer Boy** *by Laura Ingalls Wilder* Almanzo Wilder works hard on his father's farm in upstate New York. (When Almanzo grows up, he meets and marries Laura Ingalls.)

I'm Nobody! Who are you?
Are you—Nobody—too?
Then there's a pair of us!
Don't tell! they'd banish us—you know!

Emily Dickinson

Pronouns

Getting Ready When you tell about something you and a friend have done, you do not keep repeating your names. That would be very awkward. Instead, you use pronouns such as *me, I,* and *us.* In this unit, you will learn more about using pronouns to help you write and speak effectively.

ACTIVITIES

Listening Listen as the poem on the opposite page is read. Listen for the pronouns. What are they?

Speaking Look at the picture. With your classmates, describe the scene. In your discussion, use pronouns and have a class "secretary" write on the board a list of the pronouns you use. What pronouns did you use for the people, the beach, and the water? What other pronouns did you use?

Writing In your journal, write about being alone and being with other people.

1 | Subject Pronouns

You know that a noun names a person, a place, or a thing. A **pronoun** is a word that takes the place of a noun. A **subject pronoun** takes the place of a noun as the subject of a sentence.

NOUN	SUBJECT PRONOUN
Carl watches the swimmers.	He watches the swimmers.
Rope divides the lanes.	It divides the lanes.
Jean and Susan practice.	They practice.

Subject pronouns also appear after forms of the linking verb *be*. Study the following examples.

The lifeguard today is he .

Yesterday the lifeguards were Tara and I .

Go in for Carla.

Subject Pronouns		
Singular: I	**Plural:**	we
you		you
he, she, it		they

Guided Practice

A. What are the subject pronouns in these sentences?

Example: She and I ate egg rolls.   *She   I*

1. They ate rice and fish.
2. We like Chinese food.
3. It is very tasty.
4. The biggest eater was he.
5. You helped the cooks.
6. The cooks were Tim and I.

B. What subject pronouns could replace the underlined words?

Example: <u>Leo and Emily</u> cooked.   *They*

7. <u>Leo</u> bought the fruit.
8. <u>Emily</u> fixed chicken.
9. <u>The chicken</u> was broiled.
10. <u>The apples</u> were juicy.
11. <u>Bill and I</u> ate the most.
12. The dishwasher was <u>Pa</u>.

> ▶ A **pronoun** is a word that replaces a noun.
> ▶ The **subject pronouns** are *I, you, he, she, it, we,* and *they.*
> ▶ Use subject pronouns as subjects and after forms of the verb *be.*

Independent Practice Write these sentences, using subject pronouns to replace the underlined words.

Example: <u>Mark</u> swims in swim meets.   *He swims in swim meets.*

13. Last year <u>Arnie</u> was the lifeguard.
14. The new lifeguard is <u>Jenny</u>.
15. <u>Linda</u> has won many swimming medals.
16. <u>Ed and Jocelyn</u> perform in many events.
17. <u>Conrad, Sally, and I</u> played water basketball.
18. <u>Arthur and Pablo</u> watched from the side.
19. <u>Janie</u> skimmed the ball well.
20. <u>Leroy</u> threw the ball through the floating hoop.
21. <u>The floating hoop</u> fell over.
22. <u>Sam</u> put the hoop back in place.
23. The fastest players were Tina and <u>Tony</u>.
24. <u>Uncle Ted and Lily</u> cheered.
25. <u>Melissa</u> went to get the ball.
26. <u>The ball</u> had landed in the other swimming pool.
27. The best players <u>were Conrad and Tina</u>.
28. After the game, <u>both teams</u> climbed out of the pool.
29. Volunteers for cleanup were Nicole and <u>Alan</u>.
30. <u>Conrad</u> and <u>Sally</u> handed out the towels.
31. <u>Conrad</u> lost his eyeglasses.
32. Alan and <u>Nicole</u> found the glasses.
33. <u>The glasses</u> were under the diving board.
34. The heroes of the day were <u>Alan</u> and <u>Nicole</u>.

Writing Application: A Letter
Write a letter to a friend or a relative. Tell about a sports activity in which you participated. Use subject pronouns.

For Extra Practice, see p. 365.   **Subject Pronouns   347**

2 | Object Pronouns

You have learned that subject pronouns can replace nouns that are subjects and nouns that follow forms of the linking verb *be*. **Object pronouns** can replace nouns used after action verbs or after words such as *to, for, with, in,* or *at*. The object pronouns are *me, you, him, her, it, us,* and *them.*

NOUN

Mrs. Stone drove Clyde .

Clyde waved to Mary and Alice .

OBJECT PRONOUN

Mrs. Stone drove him .

Clyde waved to them .

You and *it* may be subject pronouns or object pronouns.

SUBJECT PRONOUN

You are a good driver.

It is my favorite car.

OBJECT PRONOUN

We thank you for the ride.

I like to ride in it .

Be careful not to confuse subject pronouns with object pronouns. Study this chart.

Subject pronouns		Object pronouns	
I	we	me	us
you	you	you	you
she, he, it	they	her, him, it	them

Guided Practice Which pronoun in parentheses is correct? Is it a subject pronoun or an object pronoun?

Example: Adam sketched (us, we).

  us object pronoun

1. Liz asked (he, him) for a picture.
2. Adam sketched Liz and (I, me).
3. He gave a picture to (us, we).
4. Adam and (she, her) saw Dave and Bob.
5. Adam drew Liz and (they, them).

> ▶ The **object pronouns** are *me, you, him, her, it, us,* and *them.*
> ▶ Use object pronouns after action verbs and words such as *to* and *for.*
> ▶ *It* and *you* may be subject pronouns or object pronouns.

Independent Practice Write these sentences, using the correct pronouns.

Example: Lois and Tony planned a camping trip for (us, we).
Lois and Tony planned a camping trip for us.

6. Beth went with (they, them) to the store.
7. Max helped (I, me) with the packing.
8. (We, Us) drove with (they, them) to the mountains.
9. Lois and Tom told (us, we) about the campground.
10. They had chosen the campground for Beth and (me, I).
11. Max had gone with (they, them) before.
12. At the campsite, Lois sent (he, him) for wood.
13. I helped (her, she) with the tent.
14. (They, Them) had chosen a spot high in the mountains.
15. (We, Us) pitched the tent for a good view of (they, them).
16. The next day, Lois took Beth and (me, I) for a swim.
17. That night Max helped (her, she) build a campfire.
18. Lois praised (him, he) for his good work.
19. On the second day, Tom took Max and (me, I) on the boat.
20. (Me, I) love to fish with (he, him).
21. Tom also showed (us, we) many different birds.
22. On the third day, Tom took Beth and (me, I) on a hike.
23. (We, Us) followed the trail markers.
24. Everyone spotted (they, them) easily.
25. That night Paul played his guitar for (us, we).
26. (We, Us) told (he, him) the names of our favorite songs.

Writing Application: Writing About Yourself

Write about an outdoor activity that you have enjoyed with friends. Write a paragraph, using a pronoun in each sentence. Underline subject pronouns once and object pronouns twice.

For Extra Practice, see p. 366.

3 | Using *I* and *me*

I always go last

You have learned to use the subject pronoun *I* as a subject or after forms of the linking verb *be*. You have also learned to use the object pronoun *me* after action verbs or words such as *to, for, with, in,* or *at.* You may have trouble, however, deciding whether to use *I* or *me* with nouns or other pronouns. To help you decide, say the sentence with only *I* or *me*.

Diana and I ride the bus.	I ride the bus.
Who chose Paul and me ?	Who chose me ?
Is Leo coming with Paul and me ?	Is Leo coming with me ?

When you use *I* or *me* with nouns or other pronouns, always name yourself last.

| Scott and I invited Rosa. | Rosa met Scott and me . |
| He and I saw Rosa. | Rosa waited for him and me . |

Guided Practice

A. Which words in parentheses correctly complete each of these sentences?

Example: (Lisa and I, I and Lisa) visit Daria.
 Lisa and I

1. Daria teaches a game to (Lisa and me, me and Lisa).
2. Lisa reminds (me and Daria, Daria and me) of another game.
3. (Daria and I, I and Daria) learned it in school.
4. Daria invites (me and Lisa, Lisa and me) for lunch.

B. Does *I* or *me* correctly complete each sentence?

Example: _____ usually skate on Saturdays. *I*

5. Nat and _____ played ice hockey last Saturday.
6. Nat waved to Dad and _____.
7. The coach and _____ discussed my weak points.
8. He told _____ about the need for safety.
9. Who will skate with Nat and _____?

▶ Use *I* as the subject of a sentence and after forms of *be.*
▶ Use *me* after action verbs or words like *to, in,* and *for.*
▶ When using the pronouns *I* and *me* with nouns or other pronouns, name yourself last.

Independent Practice Write these sentences, using the correct words in parentheses.

Example: Todd and (I, me) practice our skating every week.
Todd and I practice our skating every week.

10. (Me, I) always ride my bike to the rink.
11. Kate called to (Nate and me, me and Nate).
12. She and (me, I) talked for a few minutes.
13. Kate asked Todd and (me, I) about our progress.
14. Todd and (I, me) laughed about our falls.
15. Kate gave some good advice to Todd and (me, I).
16. (He and I, I and he) thanked her for her help.
17. Todd and Lennie followed (I, me) onto the ice.
18. Todd, Lennie, and (me, I) practiced for an hour.
19. (I and Lennie, Lennie and I) wear the same skates.
20. Todd skated behind Lennie and (I, me).
21. Amy met (me and Lennie, Lennie and me) at the rink.
22. She and (me, I) learned to skate at the same time.
23. Amy complimented (I, me) on my skating.
24. (I and she, She and I) both like speed skating.
25. Todd and Amy raced (me, I) around the rink.
26. Lennie cheered for (I, me).
27. (I and Lennie, Lennie and I) will race together next week.
28. Todd and Amy have asked (I, me) to their house.
29. They will walk home, and (me, I) will ride my bike.
30. (Amy and I, I and Amy) look through sports magazines for pictures of famous skaters.

Writing Application: Creative Writing
Imagine that you are a famous speed skater or figure skater. You are skating with a partner in an ice show. Write a paragraph about this experience. Use *I* and *me* correctly.

For Extra Practice, see p. 367.

4 | Possessive Pronouns

As you know, possessive nouns show ownership. A **possessive pronoun** can replace a possessive noun. Some possessive pronouns appear before a noun.

Paul's pen is black.   His pen is black.

Other possessive pronouns stand alone and replace nouns in a sentence.

The blue notebook is Kate's .   The blue notebook is hers .
Their folders are full.   Theirs are full.

Two Kinds of Possessive Pronouns

Possessive pronouns used with nouns		Possessive pronouns that stand alone	
my	My book is green.	mine	The green book is mine.
your	Clean your desk.	yours	Yours is messy.
his	His bike is blue.	his	The red bike is his.
her	This is her house.	hers	Hers is the gray house.
its	Its coat is shaggy.	its	Its is the shaggy coat.
our	Those are our pens.	ours	Those pens are ours.
your	Take your sweaters.	yours	Leave yours here.
their	Their hats are red.	theirs	Those hats are theirs.

FREE KITTENS!
Take your pick!

Guided Practice Which possessive pronoun in parentheses correctly completes each sentence?

Example: The students finished (their, theirs) reports.   *their*

1. Rosa read (her, hers) report about Carlsbad Caverns.
2. Was the report about the pioneer village (your, yours)?
3. (My, Mine) report was about our trip to the zoo.
4. Flo called (my, mine) the best.
5. (Her, Hers) was about a visit to the museum.
6. Tomorrow we will make covers for (our, ours) reports.

▸ A **possessive pronoun** shows ownership.
▸ Use *my, your, his, her, its, our,* and *their* before nouns.
▸ Use *mine, yours, his, hers, its, ours,* and *theirs* to replace nouns in a sentence.

Independent Practice Write each sentence, using the correct possessive pronoun in parentheses.

Example: (My, Mine) class is publishing a newspaper.
My class is publishing a newspaper.

7. (It, Its) title is The Roundup.
8. (Our, Ours) stories will be printed with headlines.
9. The article about the Special Olympics will be (your, yours).
10. Michele is glad that the cartoons are (her, hers).
11. (Her, Hers) story about the bird feeder is on page two.
12. The story about the woodcarvings is (mine, my).
13. Kiki and Toby wrote (their, theirs) story about butterflies.
14. The article on subways was also (theirs, their).
15. (Mine, My) article was not as long as that one.
16. Mia wrote (her, hers) about the new museum.
17. For (their, theirs) article, Carl and Paula interviewed Molly.
18. (Her, Hers) favorite hobby is gardening.
19. Iris reviewed (her, hers) favorite movies.
20. I also wrote about (my, mine).
21. Nancy wrote about (her, hers) most embarrassing moment.
22. The funniest story was (her, hers).
23. I hope the award for the best newspaper will be (our, ours).
24. We are already planning (our, ours) next issue.
25. The success of (your, yours) baseball team will be the big story on page one.

Writing Application: A Description
Write a description of a person or a place in your town. Remember to use sense words and exact words in your description. Also include three possessive pronouns that appear before nouns and three possessive pronouns that stand alone.

5 | Contractions with Pronouns

You have learned that a contraction is a shortened form of two words. An apostrophe (') replaces any letters dropped when the words are combined.

You can make contractions by combining pronouns and the verbs *am, is, are, will, would, have, has,* and *had.* Study the following chart of contractions.

Pronoun + verb	Contraction	Pronoun + verb	Contraction
I am	I'm	I have	I've
he is	he's	he has	he's
it is	it's	it has	it's
you are	you're	you have	you've
they are	they're	they have	they've
I will	I'll	I had	I'd
you will	you'll	you had	you'd
we would	we'd	we had	we'd

Notice that some contractions look the same but are formed from different words.

he is, he has = he's   we had, we would = we'd

Guided Practice

A. What is the contraction for each word pair?

Example: we have   *we've*

1. you will   3. he had   5. you have
2. we would   4. I am   6. they will

B. What pronoun and verb make up each contraction? Some have two answers.

Example: she's   *she is   she has*

7. I'll   9. you'd   11. they're
8. we're   10. he's   12. she'd

> ▶ You can combine pronouns with the verbs *am, is, are, will, would, have, has,* and *had* to form contractions.
> ▶ Use an apostrophe in place of the dropped letter or letters.

Independent Practice

A. Write contractions by combining these pronouns and verbs.

Example: you had   *you'd*

13. it is   **19.** I have
14. I will   **20.** she will
15. he had   **21.** they would
16. she is   **22.** I am
17. we have   **23.** we had
18. it has   **24.** he would

B. Write the words that were combined to form the contraction in each sentence.

Example: We'll visit my grandparents' farm.   *We will*

25. I'm a farmer every summer.
26. It's fun to pitch hay.
27. You'll enjoy riding in Grandpa's tractor.
28. He's working in the corn fields.
29. I've often gone with Pete to milk the cows.
30. He's worked on the farm for three years.
31. Maybe he'll show you how to milk a cow.
32. I'd go with you the first time.
33. It's not hard to learn.
34. Now we're going to weed the garden with Grandma.
35. She's already fed the chickens and pigs today.
36. What a big breakfast they've eaten!
37. If you'd like to feed them tomorrow, ask Grandma.
38. She'll show you what to do.

Writing Application: A Description

Write a paragraph describing people on vacation. Include at least five contractions from the chart.

For Extra Practice, see p. 369.
          Contractions with Pronouns

6 Double Subjects

You know that every sentence must have a subject. Sometimes people incorrectly use a double subject—a noun and a pronoun—to name the same person, place, or thing.

INCORRECT	CORRECT
<u>Mary</u> <u>she</u> is my sister.	Mary is my sister.
	She is my sister.
Her <u>hat</u> <u>it</u> is pretty.	Her hat is pretty.
	It is pretty.

Mary, she is my sister.

Mary and *she* should not both be used as subjects. The subject *hat* should not be used with *it*. Use only a noun or a pronoun to name a subject.

Guided Practice What is the unnecessary word in each sentence?

Example: My parents they own a shoe store. *they*

1. My father he waits on customers.
2. My mother she arranges the shoes.
3. People they like our store.
4. The shoes they are beautiful.
5. The store it is on Elm Street.
6. My brother and sister they work there too.
7. Uncle Ted he helps at the store on weekends.
8. Our shop it is open six days a week.
9. My brother he makes window displays.
10. My sister she writes newspaper ads.
11. The ads they are very clever.

Summing up

▶ Do not use a double subject—a noun and a pronoun—to name the same person, place, or thing.

Independent Practice Each sentence has a double subject. Write each sentence correctly.

Example: Paul Newman and Joanne Woodward they are married.
Paul Newman and Joanne Woodward are married.

12. Paul Newman he is an actor.
13. Joanne Woodward she is also an actor.
14. Paul he directed a television movie.
15. *See How She Runs* it was the name of the movie.
16. Joanne Woodward she starred in that movie.
17. Joanne and Paul they filmed the movie in Boston.
18. The movie it was about a big race.
19. Their daughter she was also in that movie.
20. Ozzie Nelson and Harriet Nelson they worked together too.
21. The Nelsons they had a show on television.
22. The show it was called *Ozzie and Harriet*.
23. Their sons they were named David and Ricky.
24. The two boys they were on the show too.
25. The show it was on television for many years.
26. George Burns he is a comedy writer and an entertainer.
27. Gracie Allen she acted, sang, and danced.
28. In the 1920s, Gracie she joined George's comedy act.
29. Gracie she was a talented comedian.
30. After three years, Gracie and George they were married.
31. The Burnses they started their own radio show.
32. That show it was on the air for nearly twenty years.
33. In the 1950s, television it became more popular than radio.
34. Gracie and George they decided to move their show from radio to television.
35. Their show it was on television twice a week.
36. Many people they found the Burnses funny.
37. Gracie she also painted pictures for a hobby.
38. George he has been in many movies over the years.

Writing Application: A Paragraph
Imagine that you are a member of a famous family. Write a paragraph describing what you and your family do. Be careful not to use any double subjects in your sentences.

For Extra Practice, see p. 370.　　　　　　　　　**Double Subjects 357**

7 Using *we* and *us* with Nouns

Sometimes you need a noun after the pronoun *we* or *us* to make clear whom you are talking about.

We girls took our places on the field.

The pronouns must be the same as if they were alone. Use *we* with noun subjects or after linking verbs.

We girls threw the ball.   The best players are we girls .

Use the pronoun *us* with a noun that follows an action verb or a word such as *to, for, with,* or *at.*

The girls threw it to us boys .   They will not beat us boys .

To help you decide whether *we* or *us* is correct, read the sentence without the noun.

We friends watch the game.   We watch the game.

The coach talks to us players .   The coach talks to us .

Guided Practice Which word is correct in each sentence?

Example: Mr. Locke invited (we, us) neighbors.   *us*

1. (We, Us) friends played softball.
2. The winners were (us, we) girls.
3. (Us, We) parents watched the game.
4. Steve came with (we, us) boys.
5. The cooks were (we, us) brothers.
6. (Us, We) girls brought our dog.
7. Your dog chased (we, us) joggers.
8. (We, Us) neighbors thanked Mr. Locke.
9. Luisa drove (us, we) boys home.
10. Mr. Locke reminded (we, us) girls about our dog.
11. Sam invited (us, we) brothers to his house.
12. The last guests were (us, we) boys.
13. (Us, We) boys helped Mr. Locke put the chairs back.

Independent Practice Write each sentence, using *we* or *us.*

Example: The show was planned by ____ girls.
The show was planned by us girls.

14. The girls wrote songs for ____ singers.
15. ____ singers practiced all week.
16. Lois chose ____ dancers.
17. The actors were ____ boys.
18. The parents arrived before ____ teachers.
19. Were ____ friends the last to arrive?
20. The crowd cheered ____ jugglers.
21. They laughed at ____ clowns.
22. The next performers were ____ singers.
23. Alice waited for ____ musicians.
24. ____ drummers were on time.
25. Who made the costumes for ____ dancers?
26. The teachers were proud of ____ girls.
27. The helpers were ____ students.
28. The funniest pictures were taken by ____ brothers.
29. The most experienced photographers were ____ teachers.
30. What long hours ____ girls worked!
31. The parents complimented ____ singers.
32. ____ performers thanked the parents for the flowers.
33. May ____ reporters speak to the performers?
34. A party is planned for ____ performers.
35. ____ dancers are not tired yet!
36. ____ musicians will bring our instruments.

Writing Application: A Description
Write a paragraph about a store or a shopping mall. In each sentence, use the pronoun *we* or *us* with one of the following nouns: *shopkeepers, parents, children, friends,* and *customers.*

For Extra Practice, see p. 371.   **Using *we* and *us* with Nouns**

Grammar-Writing Connection

Using Pronouns Well

When you use pronouns, be sure that your reader can tell whom or what they refer to. In the paragraph below, the pronoun *it* is not clear.

ORIGINAL: It is a country in Europe. It has a varied climate and a beautiful landscape. Many people visit France each year.

In the revised paragraph, the pronoun *it* refers clearly to the noun *France*. Notice that the paragraph is clear because the noun comes before the pronoun.

REVISED: France is a country in Europe. It has a varied climate and a beautiful landscape. Many people visit France each year.

Revising Sentences

Rewrite the sentences below so that the pronouns refer clearly to nouns that come before them.

1. For many years, it was a major power in Europe. It continues to play a leading role in world affairs. France is also a leading producer of farm goods and automobiles.
2. Most of them raise dairy animals. The farmers use much of the milk to make butter and cheese. Their cheese is sold throughout the world.
3. They work off the French coasts. They also sail to Iceland and New-foundland. The fishing crews catch many kinds of fish.
4. He is elected for a term of seven years. He is the most important public official. The president of France has many special powers.
5. It is the capital of France. It is a favorite place for tourists to visit. Paris has beautiful buildings, shops, parks, and museums.
6. She visited Paris last spring. She especially enjoyed the wide streets and beautiful parks. Aunt Leona would like to go back to Paris someday.
7. They are attracted to France for many reasons. They explore the valleys, the mountains, and the beaches. Tourists also enjoy visiting the old walled cities and the castles.

Creative Writing

One night the artist Georgia O'Keeffe leaned against her ranch house ladder. She looked out at the bright moon and dark desert mountains. The next day she painted the simple shapes and bold colors she had seen. The result was this painting, *Ladder to the Moon*. Like many of her pictures, it praises nature's beauty.

- What is the picture's mood?
- How would the mood change if more things were added?

Ladder to the Moon, Georgia O'Keeffe
Private Collection

Activities

1. **Describe the sky.** Imagine that you can climb up this ladder and paint whatever you want in the sky. What will you add—stars, spaceships, floating houses? Write a paragraph describing your newly painted sky.

2. **Write a good-by note.** Suppose that this ladder appears outside your window one night. It is ready to carry you anywhere. Write a good-by note explaining what has happened, where you are going, and what you hope to see and do.

3. **Write a poem.** What would it be like to hang above the world on a floating ladder? How would the world below look to you? What sounds might you hear? Write a poem describing your imaginary experience.

Check-up: Unit 11

Subject Pronouns *(p. 346)* Write subject pronouns to replace the underlined words.

1. Todd and I are studying dinosaurs.
2. Dinosaurs lived on Earth long ago.
3. Almira and Jeb read about them.
4. A dinosaur could be very large.
5. Jody and Carrie drew pictures.
6. You and Sue visited a museum.
7. Jay and Mary and Paul went too.
8. The museum had dinosaur bones.
9. The museum guide was Mr. Ross.
10. The dinosaurs mysteriously disappeared from Earth.
11. Scientists think about the reason.
12. You and I wonder about it too.

Object Pronouns *(p. 348)* Replace underlined words with pronouns.

13. Kristin spoke to Chet in Swedish.
14. I asked Kristin about the words.
15. Chet said hello to Tim and me.
16. Then he said a word in Swedish.
17. Paul read some French poems.
18. We did not understand the words.
19. We asked Paul about the meaning.
20. I'll speak Dutch to you and Tanya.
21. Ask Greta about that song.
22. Mia knows the song in Italian.
23. She will teach it to Paula and me.
24. I'll teach some Greek words to Tim.
25. Now you can greet Eleni in Greek.
26. I just saw Eleni with Lucy.

Using *I* and *me* *(p. 350)* Write the words that correctly complete these sentences.

27. (Me, I) love to play table tennis.
28. (Terry and I, I and Terry) entered a contest last week.
29. Terry and (me, I) had trained hard.
30. The first and second games went to (me and her, her and me).
31. (She and I, I and she) played well.
32. Luis kept score for her and (I, me).
33. (Me, I) play with Terry every day.
34. The games are good practice for (Terry and me, me and Terry).
35. (I, Me) play with my family too.
36. My sisters play (my father and me, me and my father).
37. No one can beat him and (me, I).

Possessive Pronouns *(p. 352)* Write the possessive pronoun that correctly completes each sentence.

38. Al and Lily rode (their, theirs) bikes in the race.
39. We rode (our, ours) too.
40. The green bike is (my, mine).
41. (Your, Yours) bike is blue.
42. (Her, Hers) has a silver seat.
43. The red bikes are (their, theirs).
44. (My, Mine) bike passed the test.
45. The safety award was (him, his).
46. That yellow bike is (her, hers).
47. Is this repair kit (your, yours)?
48. (My, Mine) air pump is at home.
49. (Him, His) tire needs air.

Contractions with Pronouns
(p. 354) Write the words that were combined to form each contraction.

50. We've come to Washington, D.C.
51. We're at the Air and Space Museum.
52. I'm enjoying the museum.
53. I've been here with my family.
54. I'd studied Lindbergh earlier.
55. He'd flown across the ocean.
56. We'd studied him at school.
57. You've heard of him.
58. You'd love his airplane.
59. You'll see it today.
60. It's called the *Spirit of St. Louis*.
61. We'll meet Jenny later.
62. She's seen the movie already.
63. She's looking at the moon exhibit with Alexander.
64. He's also interested in rockets.
65. He's been reading about them since last summer.
66. I'll like this movie.
67. It's shown on a huge wall.
68. I've seen the other film.
69. You'll learn about different kinds of flights.
70. I'd like to see the special show.
71. It's about the stars and planets.
72. You'd like Dr. Hernando.
73. He's used many special effects.
74. We'll sit in a special dark room.
75. They've always shown the stars and planets overhead.
76. You'll see the volcano on Mars.
77. It's like traveling in space.
78. They've just made a new film.
79. They're showing it next month.

Double Subjects *(p. 356)* Each sentence has one unnecessary subject. Write each sentence correctly.

80. Dr. Lee she is an animal doctor.
81. Pet owners they bring their animals to her.
82. Pets they need check-ups.
83. A hurt animal it needs treatment.
84. Dr. Snow he works at the animal hospital.
85. The doctors they work together.
86. My mother and I we found Andi.
87. Andi he had hurt a paw.
88. Dr. Lee she put a cast on it.
89. Andi and the doctor they like each other very much.
90. The cast it will be removed soon.
91. Soon Andi he will be well again.

Using *we* and *us* with Nouns
(p. 358) Write *we* or *us* to correctly complete each sentence.

92. ____ performers are ready.
93. Those blue costumes are for ____ actors.
94. ____ actors know our lines.
95. The singers are ____ children.
96. Get the armor for ____ knights.
97. ____ royal guards stand here.
98. Are there hats for ____ ladies?
99. ____ musicians go to the ball.
100. Play music for ____ princesses.
101. When do ____ princes arrive?
102. Follow ____ kings on the stage.
103. ____ kings sit near the queens.
104. Everyone watches ____ jugglers.
105. How great ____ dancers will be!
106. Look at ____ magicians.

Enrichment

Using Pronouns

Lost and Found

Pretend that you run the school's Lost and Found. Five students have recently lost things. You must file a report on each claim. Write five sentences to identify the owners of the lost items. Use possessive pronouns. Draw pictures of the items.

Maria Romano says that the notebook with unusual animal stickers is hers.

Pronouns with Style

Choose a paragraph from a short story or novel. Read the paragraph and notice how many pronouns are used. Now rewrite the paragraph, substituting a common or proper noun for each pronoun. Write an explanation of which version is better and why.

Healthy Riddles

You are designing posters for the cafeteria to encourage students to eat healthy food. First, think up a riddle about a healthy food. Use the homophones *its* and *it's* in your riddle. Then write the riddle on the poster. Draw pictures as clues.

It's orange, red, and purple but mostly green.
In a bowl on the table, it's usually seen.
With oil and vinegar I like it best.
Its sparkle shows up when it's properly dressed.

Answer: It is a salad.

364

Extra Practice: Unit 11

1 | **Subject Pronouns (p. 346)**

● Copy these sentences. Then underline the subject pronouns.

Example: I went to the cookout with Becky and Diego.
I went to the cookout with Becky and Diego.

1. First, we swam in the pool with Gina and Andrew.
2. Then Diego and I made a fruit salad.
3. It was full of watermelon, apples, and pears.
4. We ate, and then Becky suggested a game of softball.
5. The best hitters were she and Margie.
6. The slowest runners were Scott and I!

▲ Write these sentences. Use subject pronouns to replace the underlined words.

Example: Johnny Weissmuller was a famous swimmer.
He was a famous swimmer.

7. Johnny was the star of the 1924 Olympic Games.
8. The Olympic Games were in Paris that year.
9. His greatest race was the hundred-meter freestyle.
10. Two onlookers were my grandmother and my grandfather.
11. Weissmuller and other swimmers have been in movies.
12. The star of many Tarzan movies was Weissmuller.
13. His best fans are my grandparents and I.

■ Write these sentences. Use subject pronouns to fill the blanks.

Example: Lars and ____ often watch movies on TV.
Lars and she often watch movies on TV.

14. ____ and I have seen Esther Williams in many movies.
15. In one movie, ____ played a swimming princess.
16. Did ____ like that movie the best?
17. For many years, the most famous woman swimmer was ____.
18. Was ____ in movies with her husband, Fernando Lamas?
19. Before his movie career, ____ was in swimming races.
20. What terrific swimmers ____ and ____ were!

2 | Object Pronouns (p. 348)

● Complete the second sentence in each pair. Write it correctly. (Use the object pronoun that replaces the underlined word or words in the first sentence.)

Example: I camped with <u>Alex and Carlos</u>. I camped with ____.
    I camped with them.

1. We slept in <u>a tent</u>. We slept in ____.
2. Alex gave some oranges to <u>Carlos and me</u>. Alex gave some oranges to ____.
3. We peeled and ate <u>the oranges</u>. We peeled and ate ____.
4. I found <u>an interesting rock</u>. I found ____.
5. I saved the rock for <u>my sister</u>. I saved the rock for ____.
6. My father said to me, "The rock will delight <u>Rosa</u>!" My father said to me, "The rock will delight ____!"

▲ Write these sentences, using the correct pronouns.

Example: We took Bob and (she, her) on a camping trip.
    We took Bob and her on a camping trip.

7. Last night, the rangers showed a film to (we, us).
8. Leah thanked (them, they) for the show.
9. They gave some maps to Bob and (she, her).
10. The maps showed (we, us) interesting places in the park.
11. Bob asked (them, they) about Old Faithful, the geyser.
12. They gave a picture of the geyser to Leah and (him, he).
13. They also told (we, us) how Old Faithful was formed.

■ Write these sentences, replacing the words in parentheses with pronouns.

Example: (The students) met (Gustave and me).   *They met us.*

14. (Gustave) questioned (the students) about their bicycle trip.
15. Their answers will help (Gustave) with his own trip.
16. (Gustave's sister) will go with (Gustave).
17. Gustave and his sister will invite (several friends).
18. Have you known Gustave and (his sister) for a long time?
19. I have known (Gustave's sister and Gustave) for two years.
20. Their parents had a graduation party for (Gustave and me).

3 || Using *I* and *me* (p. 350)

● Use *I* or *me* to complete the second sentence in each pair. Then write the second sentence.

Example: We washed the car. Eva and ____ washed the car.
Eva and I washed the car.

1. The water splashed us. The water splashed Eva and ____.
2. Later we saw Dad. Later Eva and ____ saw Dad.
3. He asked us about his clean car. He asked Eva and ____ about his clean car.
4. We did not say a word. Eva and ____ did not say a word.
5. Dad had not seen us. Dad had not seen Eva and ____.
6. We had surprised him! Eva and ____ had surprised him!
7. Dad thanked us. Dad thanked Eva and ____.

▲ Write each sentence, using *I* or *me* correctly.

Example: My brother and ____ built a doghouse for Willy.
My brother and I built a doghouse for Willy.

8. Willy was happy, but Tom and ____ were even happier.
9. Willy used to sleep with my brother and ____.
10. My bed is too narrow for a big dog and ____.
11. Willy and ____ barely fit in.
12. My brother and ____ did not want Willy on our beds.
13. Tom and ____ thought of the doghouse idea.
14. Uncle Nick gave some wood to my brother and ____.
15. The builders of the doghouse were Tom and ____.

■ Rewrite each incorrect sentence. If a sentence contains no mistakes, write *correct*.

Example: Me and Larry like to take pictures of animals.
Larry and I like to take pictures of animals.

16. May Larry and I take a picture of your dog?
17. Will your dog pose for I and Larry?
18. I and some other students took these pictures.
19. Last summer my cousin Larry took this shot of I and a horse.
20. My sister took this picture for Larry and me.
21. It shows him and I at the zoo.
22. In this picture, me and my cat are sitting on the sidewalk.

● ▲ ■ **Three levels of practice   367**

4 | Possessive Pronouns (p. 352)

● Copy the sentences. Then underline the possessive pronouns.

Example: Your report on the school play is excellent.
Your report on the school play is excellent.

1. In fact, yours was the best report in the class.
2. The librarians in our town are having a puppet show.
3. Will you write a report on their puppet show?
4. You can write about the story and its characters.
5. My neighbor is one of the women in charge of the show.
6. Her job is to sell tickets.
7. Sam has already bought his ticket.
8. This ticket is mine, and that one is yours.

▲ Write these sentences, using the correct possessive pronouns.

Example: (My, Mine) aunt works for a newspaper.
My aunt works for a newspaper.

9. Many people in (our, ours) city read that newspaper.
10. Please let me borrow (your, yours) copy of the paper.
11. Samantha is reading (my, mine).
12. Hoshi and Umeko took (their, theirs) to the beach.
13. My aunt's name appears with (her, hers) stories.
14. The story on the front page is (her, hers).
15. Many writers begin (their, theirs) careers in school.
16. (Your, Yours) stories are in (our, ours) school paper.

■ Rewrite these sentences, using possessive pronouns.

Example: The students' news stories are written carefully.
Their news stories are written carefully.

17. Our newspaper is the best school paper in the city.
18. Hernando and Shani work on the newspaper's staff.
19. Shani's photographs often appear with Hernando's stories.
20. This photograph of the baseball team is Shani's.
21. Hernando's story comes before my story.
22. Azami and Bret wrote about Azami and Bret's class trip.
23. I will write a story about my class trip.
24. Our class trip is Monday. When is your class trip?

5 | Contractions with Pronouns (p. 354)

● Write the pronouns and verbs that make up these contractions.

Example: I'd   *I had   I would*

1. she'll	**6.** you've	**11.** it's
2. I'm	**7.** we're	**12.** you'd
3. I've	**8.** they'll	**13.** they're
4. you'll	**9.** you're	**14.** we'd
5. I'll	**10.** they've	**15.** he's

▲ Write the contractions in these sentences. Then write the words that make up each contraction.

Example: She'll have a great summer.   *She'll   She will*

16. She's at a farm camp.
17. Perhaps you've heard of the camp.
18. It's called Longacre Farm.
19. She's wanted to go there for a long time.
20. I'll tell you about the camp.
21. First, you'll want to know about the staff members.
22. They're teachers and college students.
23. They've bought a large farm with animals.
24. You're probably wondering about the campers' activities.
25. They'll work in the fields and care for the chickens, the cows, and the pigs on the farm.
26. We've visited the camp.
27. It's the best farm camp in the state.
28. You'd like Longacre Farm!
29. I'm probably going there next summer with my brother.
30. We've already written to the camp.

■ Write contractions that combine these pronouns and verbs. Then write a sentence, using each contraction.

Example: we have   *we've   We've made a colorful poster.*

31. you are	**36.** I had	**41.** I have
32. they will	**37.** we are	**42.** you will
33. I am	**38.** she is	**43.** it is
34. they had	**39.** I will	**44.** he would
35. he has	**40.** they would	**45.** it has

6 | Double Subjects (p. 356)

● Write the word that should not appear in each sentence.

Example: Jane Goodall she is a famous scientist.   *she*

1. This scientist she worked with her mother at first.
2. Jane and her mother they were a good team.
3. Their work it took them to Africa.
4. Jane she learned a lot about chimpanzees.
5. A photographer he came to Africa.
6. His name it was Hugo van Lawick.
7. He and Jane they worked together.
8. In 1964 Jane she married Hugo.

▲ Each sentence has a double subject. Write each of the sentences correctly.

Example: Robert Browning he was a poet.
         Robert Browning was a poet.

9. His home it was in England.
10. Elizabeth Barrett she was an English poet too.
11. Robert Browning he wrote her a letter in 1845.
12. The letter it praised her poetry.
13. Elizabeth and Robert they became good friends.
14. In 1846 Robert he was married to Elizabeth.
15. Their poetry it is enjoyed by many people today.
16. Many students they study their poems.

■ Rewrite each sentence that has a double subject. If a sentence is correct, write *correct*.

Example: Franklin Roosevelt he became President in 1933.
         Franklin Roosevelt became President in 1933.

17. His wife she was named Eleanor.
18. The Roosevelts worked together.
19. Eleanor she traveled all over the world to help people.
20. Her goal it was to give all people equal rights.
21. President Roosevelt worked for human rights too.
22. The President he died in 1945.
23. Eleanor Roosevelt she continued to work for human rights.
24. Many people they have written books about the Roosevelts.

7 | Using *we* and *us* with Nouns (p. 358)

● Copy each sentence. Then underline the pronoun and the noun that are used together.

Example: The school supports us athletes.
The school supports us athletes.

1. We girls play basketball every Wednesday afternoon.
2. The reporter talked to us coaches about the teams.
3. We teammates help each other.
4. Come with us girls to the game this week.
5. We friends cheer loudly.
6. Last week we boys joined the drama club.
7. Mr. Diaz spoke to us beginners.
8. We students learned about the coming events.

▲ Write each sentence, using the correct word in parentheses.

Example: (We, Us) friends have a club. *We friends have a club.*

9. Jog with (we, us) girls in the park.
10. (Us, We) boys will meet you near the bridge.
11. (We, Us) people will ride bikes around the pond.
12. The fastest swimmers in the race were (us, we) boys.
13. (Us, We) girls are excellent divers.
14. Beth followed (we, us) skiers downhill.
15. (We, Us) skiers compete locally.

■ Write the sentences, using *we* or *us* with the underlined words.

Example: The girls will debate the boys on Friday.
The girls will debate us boys on Friday.

16. The club members spoke to Mr. Alessi.
17. Mr. Alessi gave advice to the students.
18. The debaters took opposing views of the issue.
19. They tried to persuade the listeners.
20. The boys argued well.
21. The speakers were evenly matched.
22. The material was thoroughly prepared by the teammates.
23. Mr. Alessi talked to the judges.
24. Finally, the judges announced the winners.

C oronado and his conquistadores introduced the Spanish horse to southwestern America. As time passed, some of the horses strayed to the wild. Today, a hundred generations later, the scattered offspring of these horses can still be found in some of our western states.

Otis Hays, Jr.
from "The Spanish Horse"

Research Report

Getting Ready Most of us know a little about a lot of things and know quite a lot about a few things. We do not begin to know all we could, not even about our favorite things! A research report is a good way to gain expert knowledge about a topic. In this unit, you will read a report and write a report of your own. Start thinking about the topic you might want to explore.

ACTIVITIES

Listening Listen as the paragraph on the opposite page is read. What information does the writer give you? What other questions do you have that the writer has *not* answered? List at least three of these questions.

Speaking Look at the picture. It shows a group of wild horses. What do you really know about how these horses live? Where can you check your facts and find more information?

Writing   What other ideas for a research report can you get from this picture? List them in your journal.

How did ponies first come to Assateague?

Before Misty

By Marguerite Henry

A wild, ringing neigh shrilled up from the hold of the Spanish galleon. It was not the cry of an animal in hunger. It was a terrifying bugle. An alarm call.

The captain of the *Santo Cristo* strode the poop deck. "That stallion again!" he muttered under his breath as he stamped forward and back, forward and back.

Suddenly he stopped short. The wind! It was dying with the sun. It was spilling out of the sails, causing them to quiver and shake. He could feel his flesh creep with the sails. Without wind he could not get to Panama. And if he did not get there and get there soon, he was headed for trouble. The Moor ponies to be delivered to the viceroy of Peru could not be kept alive much longer. Their hay had grown musty. The water casks were almost empty. And now this sudden calm, this heavy warning of a storm.

He plucked nervously at his rusty black beard as if that would help him think. "We lie in the latitude of white squalls," he said, a look of vexation on his face. "When the wind does strike, it will strike with fury." His steps quickened as he made up his mind. "We must shorten sail."

Cupping his hands to his mouth he bellowed orders: "Furl the topgallant sail! Furl the coursers and the main-topsail! Shorten the fore-topsail!"

The ship burst into action. From forward and aft all hands came running. They fell to work furiously, carrying out orders.

The captain's eyes were fixed on his men, but his thoughts raced ahead to the rich land where he was bound. In his mind's eye he could see the mule train coming to meet him when he reached land. He could see it snaking its way along the Gold Road from Panama to the seaport of Puerto Bello. He could almost feel the smooth, hard gold in the packs on the donkeys' backs.

His eyes narrowed greedily. "Gold!" he mumbled. "Think of trading twenty ponies for their weight in gold!" He clasped his hands behind him and resumed his pacing and muttering. "The viceroy of Peru sets great store by the ponies, and well he may. Without the ponies to work the mines, there will be no more gold." He clenched his fists. "We must keep the ponies alive!"

His thoughts were brought up sharply. That shrill horse call! Again it filled the air about him with a wild ring. His beady eyes darted to the lookout man in the crow's-nest, then to the men on deck. He saw fear spread among the crew.

Meanwhile, in the dark hold of the ship a small bay stallion was pawing the floor of his stall. His iron shoes with their sharp rims and turned-down heels threw a shower of sparks, and he felt strong charges of electricity. His nostrils flared. The moisture in the air! The charges of electricity! These were storm warnings—things he knew. Some inner urge told him he must get his mares to high land before the storm broke. He tried to escape, charging against the chest board of his stall again and again. He threw his head back and bugled.

From stalls beside him and from stalls opposite him, nineteen heads with small pointed ears peered out. Nineteen pairs of brown eyes whitened. Nineteen young mares caught his anxiety. They, too, tried to escape, rearing and plunging, rearing and plunging.

But presently the animals were no longer hurling themselves. They were *being* hurled. The ship was pitching and tossing to the rising swell of the sea, flinging the ponies forward against their chest boards, backward against the ship's sides.

A cold wind spiraled down the hatch. It whistled and screamed above the rough voice of the captain. It gave way only to the deep *flump-flump* of the thunder.

The sea became a wildcat now, and the galleon her prey. She stalked the ship and drove her off her course. She slapped at her, rolling her victim from side to side. She knocked the spars out of her and used them to ram holes in her sides. She clawed the rudder from its sternpost and threw it into the sea. She cracked the ship's ribs as if they were brittle bones. Then she hissed and spat through the seams.

376

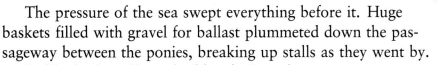

The pressure of the sea swept everything before it. Huge baskets filled with gravel for ballast plummeted down the passageway between the ponies, breaking up stalls as they went by.

Suddenly the galleon shuddered. From bow to stern came an endless rasping sound. The ship had struck a shoal. And with a ripping and crashing of timber the hull cracked open. In that split second the captain, his men, and his live cargo were washed into the boiling foam.

The wildcat sea yawned. She swallowed the men. Only the captain and fifteen ponies managed to come up again. The captain bobbed alongside the stallion and made a wild grasp for his tail, but a great wave swept him out of reach.

The stallion neighed encouragement to his mares, who were struggling to keep afloat, fighting the wreckage and the sea. For long minutes they thrashed about helplessly, and just when their strength was nearly spent, the storm died as suddenly as it had risen. The wind calmed.

The sea was no longer a wildcat. She became a kitten, fawning and lapping about the ponies' legs. Now their hooves touched land. They were able to stand! They were scrambling up the beach, up on Assateague Beach, that long, sandy island which shelters the tidewater country of Virginia and Maryland. They were far from the mines of Peru.

The ponies forgot the forty days and forty nights in the dark hold of the Spanish galleon. They forgot the musty hay. They forgot the smell of bilge water, of oil and fishy odors from the cooking galley.

The seasons came and went, and the ponies adopted the New World as their own. They learned how to take care of themselves. When summer came and with it the greenhead flies by day and the mosquitoes by night, they plunged into the sea, up to their necks in the cool surf. The sea was their friend. Once it had set them free; now it protected them from their fiercest enemies.

378

With each season the ponies grew wiser. And with each season they became tougher and more hardy. Horse colts and fillies were born to them. As the horse colts grew big they rounded up mares of their own, and started new herds that ranged wild—wild as the wind and the sea that had brought them there long ago.

Years went by. And more years. Changes came to Assateague. The red men came. The white men came. The white men built a lighthouse to warn ships of dangerous reefs. They built a handful of houses and a white church. But soon the houses stood empty. The people moved their homes and their church to nearby Chincoteague Island, for Assateague belonged to the wild things—to the wild birds that nestled on it, and the wild ponies whose ancestors had lived on it since the days of the Spanish galleon.

To learn more about the ponies that live in Assateague, read the rest of the book *Misty of Chincoteague*.

Think and Discuss

1. Wild ponies have lived on Assateague for hundreds of years. How did they first get there?

2. Why were the ponies on board the *Santo Cristo*? Where were they being taken?

3. To what animal is the sea compared during the storm? after the storm? Why does the comparison fit the events in the story?

4. **Fiction** is writing made up from an author's imagination. The people, things, and events told about need not be real. **Nonfiction,** on the other hand, tells about people and things that really exist, and events that have really happened. "Before Misty" is fiction, but it tells about a real event. What event do you think this was? What parts of this story do you think are *not* real?

379

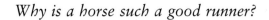

Why is a horse such a good runner?

A Horse's Body

By Joanna Cole

When you look at a horse, you see a large, beautiful animal with long legs, hard hoofs, and a big barrel chest.

Its long legs are made up of elongated, or stretched out, leg bones. The part of the leg that you can see is actually made of only the shin, foot, and toe bones. But these bones are much longer than the same ones in other animals. The parts of the leg that would equal the human thigh and hip are hidden within the body of the horse.

The horse is perfectly suited for running. When it runs, its stiff spine does not move. Only its legs are in motion. They are moved like levers by powerful muscles at the top of each limb, thus giving the horse a very long stride.

A horse's legs are built so that it can stand with hardly any effort. Because its joints will stay in place without using muscle power, a horse can doze easily while standing up. But to sleep more soundly, it must lie on the ground. Then the horse's stiff spine makes getting up and down very difficult.

Like its legs, a horse's feet are also perfect for running over flat land. Although prehistoric horses had several toes, the foot of a modern horse is actually an enlarged single toe encased in a tough hoof. On the outside is a covering called the hoof wall, which grows downward and is always being replaced like a fingernail.

Bare hoofs are tough enough for a wild horse that lives on a grassy plain. But the hoofs of a riding horse get more wear than those of a wild horse.

A riding horse has to carry a heavy person on its back. It may have to run on hard roads and for longer periods than it would in nature. Therefore, many horses need metal shoes to keep their hoofs from getting too worn down. The shoes are put on with nails, but they don't hurt because the nails are driven into a part of the hoof wall that has no feeling.

The horse is a grass eater. And since the tough fibers in grasses are harder to eat and digest than other plants, the horse has a special digestive system.

Its sharp front teeth are used for biting off grass, and the large rear teeth, or molars, grind it up. A horse also needs very large jaw muscles because it chews from twenty to thirty pounds of hay a day.

Although a horse has a wide range of vision, it cannot see things very sharply. Instead, it notices movement and is ready to run at the first hint of danger.

A horse focuses its eyes by raising and lowering its head. This may seem like nervousness, but actually the horse is only trying to see better.

A horse can hear sounds several miles away, not only with its ears but also through its legs. Vibrations from the ground travel up the leg bones, so a horse can detect something large moving a quarter of a mile away.

Because they can hear sounds so far away, horses get nervous when a storm is coming—long before human ears can hear it. For this reason, some people have thought horses could "predict" the weather through ESP.

A horse usually keeps its ears facing front, but it can turn them a full 180 degrees. It can pinpoint any sound exactly with these swivel ears.

The horse's velvet-soft muzzle is the center of its sense of touch. The muzzle is covered with extra-sensitive bristles, each one connected to a cluster of nerves at its root. A horse can tell a lot about the size and position of its food through these hairs.

A horse sometimes is able to understand what a rider wants even before the rider gives the signal. This is because the person's muscles make small movements before giving the signal, movements that he is not aware of. Through its skin, the horse can feel these tiny muscle twitches, and a rider sometimes gets the feeling that the horse can read his mind.

But whether a horse is destined for riding, racing, or working, it will always have the special body of an animal that was born to run.

To learn more details about horses, read the rest of the book *A Horse's Body*.

Think and Discuss
1. Why is a horse's body so well suited to running?
2. **Expository writing** is a type of nonfiction that explains how things are, how they work, what they mean, and why they are important. "A Horse's Body" is an example of expository writing. Which types of information about horses does it give you? Give an example of each type.
3. Horses are not usually thought of as guard animals. Would a horse make a good watchdog? Explain.

RESPONDING TO LITERATURE

The Reading and Writing Connection

Personal Response To describe a horse to someone who has never seen one before, what information would you give? Write a paragraph telling what a horse looks like.

Creative Writing Make up the words for a song about the last voyage of the *Santo Cristo*. In your song, tell about the storm, the sinking of the galleon, and the escape of the fifteen ponies.

Creative Activities

Make a Map Assateague Island lies off the coast of Virginia. Find this area on a map of the United States. Then draw a map that shows the coastline, the two islands Chincoteague and Assateague, and the ocean. Label these parts of your map. Then show the Spanish galleon on the water and the ponies swimming ashore.

Imitate Animal Sounds On the *Santo Cristo*, the stallion's neigh was an alarm. With a partner, imitate this sound. Then imitate the sound a bird, a dog, or a cat might make when it is in danger, when it is angry, and when it is hungry.

Vocabulary

"A Horse's Body" names some parts of that animal's body. Here are the names of six more parts: fetlock, coronet, hock, barrel, forelock, withers. Look in an encyclopedia to find out where each part is located on a horse. Then draw a horse and label each part.

Looking Ahead

Research Report Finding facts is an important part of planning for a research report. Turn to page 381 of "A Horse's Body." List facts to answer the questions *What does a horse eat?* and *How does it eat?*

VOCABULARY CONNECTION

Suffixes

A **suffix** is a word part added to the end of a base word.

> Only its legs are in motion. They are moved like levers by
> power**ful** muscles. . . .
>
> *from "A Horse's Body" by Joanna Cole*

Each suffix has its own meaning. The suffix *-ful* means
"full of." *Powerful* means "full of power."

Suffix	Meaning	Example
-able	can be	wear**able**—can be worn
-er	one who does	walk**er** —one who walks
-ish	like, somewhat	green**ish**—somewhat green
-less	without	fear**less**—without fear
-ness	quality of	kind**ness**—quality of being kind

A word can have both a prefix and a suffix.

un + manage + able = unmanageable

Adding the prefix *un-* and the suffix *-able* to the base word
manage changes its meaning to "cannot be managed."

Vocabulary Practice

A. Copy each underlined word. Then underline the suffix and
write the meaning of the word.

I was (1) <u>careful</u> on the trail. I didn't want to fall off the horse
and look (2) <u>foolish</u>. Luckily my clothes were (3) <u>washable</u>.

B. Add a suffix from this lesson to each of these words.

4. kitten   **5.** work   **6.** smooth   **7.** fear   **8.** think

Listening and Speaking: Interviewing

Suppose you need facts for a research report on horses. One way to get information is to **interview** an expert on horses. An interview is an organized way of asking questions to get information. Use the following interviewing guidelines.

Guidelines for Interviewing

1. Before the interview, plan the questions you will ask. Choose *who, what, where, when, why,* and *how* questions that will encourage the person to respond fully. Do not ask questions that call for a *yes* or *no* answer.
2. Write your questions in an order that makes sense. Leave plenty of space between questions so you can take notes on the answers during the interview.
3. At the interview, state your purpose right away.
4. Ask your questions clearly and politely.
5. Give the person time to answer each question completely. Listen carefully to each response.
6. Take notes on important facts. If you want to repeat something the person said, write the person's exact words in quotation marks.
7. Ask questions if you do not understand something.

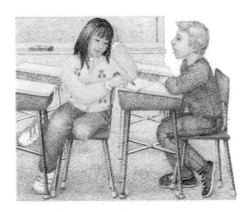

Now read the following notes, taken at an interview with a woman who raises horses on a ranch.

QUESTION: *Where* is your ranch?
      —in the state of Montana

QUESTION: *What* kind of horses do you raise?
      —Arabians

QUESTION: *Who* buys your horses?
      —circuses and rodeos
      —owners of riding stables
      —people who love horses

QUESTION: *Why* do you raise horses?
      —good living
      —"I love these animals."

QUESTION: *How* do you feel when you sell one of your horses?
      —very sad
      —"Every horse is a friend, almost like a part of the family."

- What kinds of questions did the interviewer ask?
- Do any of the questions call for *yes* or *no* answers? Why?

Prewriting Practice

A. Make up five more questions you could ask for the above interview. Share your questions with a partner.

B. Remember that interviewing is one of several ways you can get facts for a report. Choose one of the following ideas and try out your interviewing skills. Write six questions to ask. Remember to follow the interviewing guidelines. You may wish to share the results of your interview with the class.

1. Interview a veterinarian. Find out about the work one of these animal doctors does and what training is needed to become one.

2. Interview a librarian. Find out the titles and authors of fiction and nonfiction books about horses and how popular such books are with readers.

3. Interview someone at home. Find out about a special interest or talent of a friend or a family member.

Thinking: Identifying Causes and Effects

A drought strikes the western plains. What happens? Many ranch animals die from the lack of water and grass. When you explain why something happens, you explain its **cause.** The drought is the cause of ranch animals dying. When you explain what happens as a result of something, you explain the **effects.** The death of many ranch animals is an effect of the drought.

You will probably write many research reports about causes and effects. Study each of these causes and its effect.

CAUSE	EFFECT
A bee buzzed in the horse's ear.	The horse reared up.
Horses have good memories.	They are easily trained.

• What other effects can you think of for each cause?

Read this passage. Can you identify any causes and effects?

A horse sometimes is able to understand what a rider wants even before the rider gives the signal. This is because the person's muscles make small movements before giving the signal, movements that he is not aware of. Through its skin, the horse can feel these tiny muscle twitches, . . .

from "A Horse's Body" by Joanna Cole

• Which sentence is the topic sentence? Does it state a cause or an effect?
• Do the other sentences state causes or effects?

Prewriting Practice

Each sentence below states a cause. Write at least one effect for each cause.

1. Lian noticed that her pony's leg was swelling.
2. Horses shed their thick winter coats in the spring.
3. My horse performed well in the contest.
4. A horse can hear sounds from any direction.

Composition Skills
Research Report

Finding Facts ☑

You know that you could get facts for a research report on horses by interviewing an expert: a breeder, trainer, a horse owner, a jockey, or a ranch hand. However, you could also find facts for your report at the library. A library provides information on almost every subject. Study this list of nonfiction materials.

Nonfiction books give facts about real people, things, places, and events. You can find a nonfiction book by looking in the library card catalog. Every book has a title card, an author card, and a subject card. The cards are arranged alphabetically in the card catalog.

Reference books are special kinds of nonfiction books. Dictionaries, encyclopedias, atlases, and almanacs are all reference books. Look for them in the reference section of a library.

1. A **dictionary** is a book that gives the spellings, pronunciations, and meanings of words in alphabetical order. Some dictionaries contain information such as biographical facts.

2. An **encyclopedia** is a set of books with articles giving basic information about many subjects. The books and the articles in them are arranged in alphabetical order.

3. An **almanac** is a book of facts that is published every year. It contains articles, lists, and tables that give up-to-date information on many subjects.

4. An **atlas** is a book of maps and tables that gives information about places. There are different types of atlases. A road atlas, for example, gives information on highways, streets, and roads in a given area. A world atlas gives information on every part of the world. An encyclopedia may contain maps, but an atlas will provide more detailed information.

Newspapers and **magazines** contain the most up-to-date information. If you are looking for facts about a recent event, look in the newspapers published the next day and in the news magazines published the week following the date of the event. Libraries also have old issues of newspapers and magazines.

To get the most out of a reference work, follow these guidelines.

1. Choose the reference work that has the type of information you want.
2. Check the accuracy of your facts in more than one reference work of the same type.
3. Choose the source with the most recent information on your topic.

Prewriting Practice

Decide whether you would look for the answer to each question in a dictionary, encyclopedia, atlas, almanac, newspaper, or nonfiction book. Then write the name of the source beside the number of each question.

1. What river runs through the city of Minneapolis?
2. What is the definition of *quarter horse*?
3. What do some animal trainers think about horse training?
4. What are some different kinds of horses?
5. What are the two pronunciations of *February*?
6. Which horses won prizes at the horse show yesterday?
7. How many miles is it from Boston to Denver?
8. Which country in the world produced the most wheat last year?
9. How many horses were there in the United States last year?
10. What explorer discovered the Pacific Ocean?

Taking Notes ☑

Taking notes can help you remember what you have read. When you take notes, write down key words that will help you recall information. Write notes in your own words.

➡

Suppose you are going to write a report on the Appaloosa horse. You would want to know how the Appaloosa is different from other horses. When you read, then, you will take notes that answer that question. Read the paragraph below and the notes that follow.

> Several traits set the Appaloosa apart from other horses. All Appaloosas have a light-and-dark pattern, especially on the face. The eye of most horses is completely dark. But Appaloosas have a white area, or sclera, around the dark iris, just as people do. This gives the horse a somewhat "wild-eyed" look that has nothing to do with the animal's spirit.
>
> *from* Horses of America *by Dorothy Hinshaw Patent*

QUESTION: How is the Appaloosa's face different from that of
             other horses?

NOTES: —light-dark pattern
           —eye has white area, like a person's
           —wild-eyed expression

- Do the notes give the key facts that answer the question?
- What fact from the paragraph was left out of the notes? Why?
- Who wrote the paragraph on which the notes were taken?

Prewriting Practice

Read this next passage about the Appaloosa. Write notes to answer the question *What does the body of an Appaloosa look like?*

The hooves of Appaloosas are usually striped up and down with dark and light. Most of the time, a large area of the body is one color, while the rear part is white with irregular spots. Some Appaloosas are white with spots all over their bodies. A few are dark with white spots. The mane and tail on an Appaloosa tend to be thin and wispy.

from Horses of America *by Dorothy Hinshaw Patent*

Making an Outline ☑

Making an outline will make your writing easier. You can use it as a plan for your writing. An outline helps you sort out your main ideas and the facts that support them. It also helps you plan the best order for your ideas. You can make an outline from notes.

Read the following notes and the outline that was made from them.

What kind of horse is the draft horse?
—breeds such as Shire, Clydesdale, Percheron, Belgian, Suffolk
—type of heavy horse—one of 3 main horse groups
—strongest, tallest, heaviest type of horse

What kinds of work do they do?
—earliest horses used by knights during Middle Ages
—pulled coaches, wagons, hauled loads
—today still used on farms to pull plows, do other farm work
—used for heavy farm work before tractors, trucks

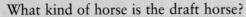

Draft Horses Title

I. Kind of horse **Main Topic**
  A. Type of heavy horse—one of 3 main groups **Subtopic**
  B. Strongest, tallest, heaviest type of horse
  C. Breeds such as Shire, Clydesdale, Percheron, Belgian, Suffolk
II. Kinds of work they do
  A. Earliest horses used by knights during Middle Ages
  B. Used for heavy farm work before tractors, trucks
  C. Pulled coaches, wagons, hauled loads
  D. Today still used on farms to pull plows, do other farm work

• How is the outline the same as the notes? How is it different?
• Has the order of any facts been changed?
• Why is the new order better?

The outline is made up of main topics and subtopics. A **main topic** starts with a Roman numeral and a period. A main topic tells a main idea. The questions in the notes were turned into main topics in the outline.

QUESTION: What kind of horse is the draft horse?
MAIN TOPIC: Kind of horse

A **subtopic** starts with a capital letter and a period. Subtopics give the supporting details that tell about the main topics. They are always listed under a main topic. The first word of a main topic or subtopic always begins with a capital letter. An outline also has a title.

Prewriting Practice

Write an outline from the notes below. Put the notes in an order that makes sense. Give your outline a title.

What is the earliest
known form of the horse?
—found in N. America, Europe
—called *Eohippus*
—lived over 55 million
   years ago

What did this animal look
like?
—very small, 10 to 20 in. high
—several toes each foot
—short neck, arched back
—very different from horse today

Writing a Paragraph from an Outline ☑

Each section of an outline is about one main idea, just as a paragraph is. To write a paragraph from an outline section, first read the title of the outline. Then read and think about the main topic and the subtopics. Think about the main idea.
Read the following title and outline section below.

Small Horses

   I. Chincoteague pony
      A. Usually 12 to 13 hands high
      B. Manes and tails long and thick
      C. At one time coats mostly solid color
      D. Now pintos common

• What is the main idea of this outline section?

The main idea is how the Chincoteague pony looks. Once you have thought about the main idea, you can write a topic sentence for your paragraph.

Topic Sentence   Remember that the topic sentence states the main idea. Read this topic sentence.

> The Chincoteague pony is a small horse.

Does this topic sentence state the main idea? Yes, but it states only the main idea. You can also include other information about the topic in a topic sentence to make it more interesting. Read this topic sentence.

> The Chincoteague pony is a small horse that is usually be-
> tween 12 and 13 hands high.

This expanded topic sentence states the main idea and includes a fact from the first subtopic in the outline section. It is more interesting.

The Paragraph   After you have written a topic sentence, complete the paragraph with sentences that give supporting details. The subtopics in the outline give these details. Write the subtopics in complete sentences. Remember that if you used information from a subtopic in your topic sentence, you should not write another sentence for that subtopic.

Try to write interesting sentences. You can combine the details from two subtopics in one sentence. You may want to add words that will make the details clearer.

Read the paragraph that was written from the outline section on page 392.

> The Chincoteague pony is a small horse that is usually between 12 and 13 hands high. The manes and tails of these ponies are long and thick. At one time, these ponies had coats of mostly solid color, but pinto markings are now much more common.

• Which facts in the outline are included in each sentence?
• Which details were combined from two subtopics into one sentence?

Prewriting Practice

Write a paragraph from the following outline section. Write a good topic sentence. Write the supporting details in the sub-topics in complete sentences. Try to make your sentences interesting.

Imaginary Animals

I. Unicorn
    A. Head and body of a horse
    B. Horn with a spiral in it in middle of its head
    C. Body and horn all white
    D. Hind legs of antelope and tail of lion

Writing Openings and Closings ☑

When you write a report, think about how you will begin and end it. A good introduction will capture your reader's interest and tell what the report is about. Keep your introduction brief. Lead into your topic in a way that will make your reader want to keep reading. Read these introductions.

1. A horse has a body that suits it for running. This report tells about the body of a horse.

2. What is the secret behind a horse's grace and power as a runner? A study of the parts of a horse's body will give you the answer to this question.

• Which introduction is better? Why?

Write a conclusion to let your reader know that the report is finished. In your closing, sum up the main ideas in your report. Keep the conclusion brief. Now read this closing.

But whether a horse is destined for riding, racing, or working, it will always have the special body of an animal that was born to run.

from "A Horse's Body" by Joanna Cole

• Is this a good conclusion? Why or why not?

Prewriting Practice

A. Read each pair of introductions for a report and each pair of conclusions. With a partner, discuss which introduction and conclusion are better and why.

1. Clever Hans is my topic. This horse did interesting things.
2. A horse answers questions and does arithmetic. Impossible? The owner of Clever Hans the horse said his pet could.

1. Clever Hans was certainly an unusual animal. I'm sure you will agree because of the facts given in this report.
2. As you discovered, Clever Hans was not so smart after all. The owner gave his horse signals he was not aware of making.

B. Think about the main ideas in "A Horse's Body." Then write your own introduction and conclusion.

The Grammar Connection

Writing Clearly with Pronouns

When you write, be sure your reader can tell what noun a pronoun replaces.

UNCLEAR: They say that a horse should be groomed daily.
CLEAR: Experts say that a horse should be groomed daily.

Do not use *they* unless its meaning is clear. Use a noun instead.

Sometimes a pronoun can seem to replace more than one noun. Again, use a noun instead of the pronoun so that your reader can understand exactly what you mean.

UNCLEAR: Use a comb for the mane. Keep it clean.
CLEAR: Use a comb for the mane. Keep the mane clean.

Practice Rewrite each sentence so that it is clear. Use a noun instead of a pronoun if necessary.

1. Horses have large eyes. They are oval.
2. They say that a horse can move each eye separately.
3. Horses have short ears. They move to pick up sounds.
4. A horse needs a comfortable stall. It should be kept dry.

The Writing Process
How to Write a Report

Step 1: Prewriting—Choose a Topic

Maria made a list of topics that interested her. Then she thought about which one would make the best report topic.

California — This topic was too big.

The finest breed of horse — This would be a matter of opinion, not fact.

The art of paper making — She'd like to learn to do this, but not write about it.

The Civil War — There was too much to say about this topic too.

Robert E. Lee — She would like to write about a person.

Maria circled *Robert E. Lee* on her list.

On Your Own

---

1. **Think and discuss** Make a list of topics you might choose for your report. Use the Ideas page to help you. Discuss your ideas with a partner.
2. **Choose** Ask yourself these questions about each topic.
   Is this topic too broad? Do I need to narrow it?
   Can I fit the facts about this topic into a short report?
   Can I find enough information on this topic?
   Circle the topic you want to write about.
3. **Explore** What will you write? Do both of the activities under "Exploring Your Topic" on the Ideas page.

Ideas for Getting Started

Choosing Your Topic

Topic Ideas

The sea horse
Wild horses
Louisa May Alcott
Grizzly bears
The Alamo
Box kites
The Boston Tea Party
Martin Luther King, Jr.
Cross-country skiing
Niagara Falls

Brainstorm

On a sheet of paper, make a list of as many things that you are curious about as you can. Do not stop to think about whether an idea would make a good or bad topic. Just write everything that comes to mind until you can't think of anything else. Then look over your list. Do you see a good topic idea for your report?

Exploring Your Topic

Question It

What do you want to learn about your topic? Make a list of questions. Circle those you will answer in your report. Here are Maria's.

What was Lee's early life like?
What did he do before he became a Confederate commander?
What did he do as a Confederate commander?
What were Lee's later years like?

Talk About It

Could you narrow your topic more? Tell a friend your questions. Together make up three more questions about one question on your list. Would one of these questions make a good report in itself?

Step 2: Plan Your Report

Maria thought about what she wanted to know about Robert E. Lee. She wrote four questions she wanted to answer. Here are her first two questions.

What was Lee's early life like?

What did he do before he became a Confederate commander?

Maria looked in some library books and encyclopedias to find the facts to answer her questions. Each time she found a fact, she entered it on a note card. She wrote only one fact on each card. Here are two note cards, one for information from an encyclopedia and one for information from a book. Notice that Maria wrote on each card where she got her information. Later she would list these sources at the end of her report.

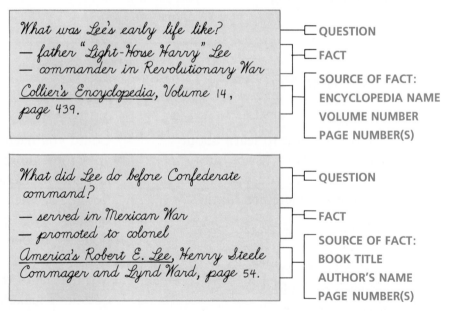

Maria made an outline from her notes.

1. She organized her cards into four groups. Each group answered one of her questions.
2. She decided on an order for the cards for each question.
3. She turned her four questions into main topics.
4. She wrote the facts that answered the questions as subtopics.

Part of Maria's outline

I. Lee's early life
  A. Born January 19, 1807
  B. Father — "Light-Horse Harry" Lee
      Revolutionary War commander
  C. Married Mary Custis — great granddaughter
      of Martha Washington — 1831
  D. Served in Mexican War
  E. Was devoted to Virginia
II. Lee's life before Confederate command
  A. Superintendent of West Point — 1852
  B. Offered Union field command
      — turned it down
  C. Great devotion to Virginia made
      him fight for the Confederacy

Think and Discuss ✓

- What are Maria's main topics?
- What are her subtopics?
- Why did Maria circle a subtopic and draw an arrow?

On Your Own

1. **Write questions** Use the questions you chose in "Exploring Your Topic" or write three or four questions that your report will answer.

2. **Do research** Find books or encyclopedia articles. Take notes that answer your questions. Write on note cards. Write the question at the top of the card. Include the title, author, and page numbers for a book. Write the title, volume number, and page numbers for an encyclopedia article.

3. **Make an outline** Turn your questions into main topics. Write the facts that answer each question as subtopics. Check your outline. Are the main topics in the best order? Does each subtopic tell about the main topic under which it is listed?

Step 3: Write a First Draft

Maria decided to write her report for her grandfather. She wrote one paragraph for each main topic in her outline. For each paragraph she wrote a topic sentence that stated the main idea. She wrote the subtopics in complete sentences. Maria did not worry about making mistakes. She would correct them later.

The beginning of Maria's first draft

Think and Discuss

- What is the topic sentence in the first paragraph?
- What facts did Maria include in this part of her report?
- What details could be clearer?

> Robert E. Lee was born on January 19, 1807, on a ~~farm~~ plantation in Virginia. His father was a commander in the Revolutionary War. He was referred to as "Light-Horse Harry." From his earliest days, Lee was devoted to his home state of Virginia. In 1831, he married Mary Custis, the great-granddaughter of Martha Washington.

On Your Own

1. **Think about purpose and audience** Ask these questions.
   What do I want my reader to learn? How much information should I include?
   What facts may need explanation?
2. **Write** Write your first draft from your outline. Write on every other line so that you will have room to add or make changes later. Do not worry about mistakes.

Step 4: Revise

Maria read her first draft. She thought she needed a more interesting sentence to introduce her report. She decided her third sentence would also make a good introduction. She moved it to the beginning of her report.

Maria wanted to know if her report would seem clear to someone else. She read it to Kristen.

Reading and responding

MARIA: Is there enough information?

KRISTEN: Yes! I learned lots of new facts about Lee.

MARIA: Were all the facts clear?

KRISTEN: Well, was Lee or his father called "Light-Horse Harry"?

Maria changed the sentence about "Light-Horse Harry" to show that the nickname belonged to Lee's father. Then she checked to make sure her other facts were still clear.

Part of Maria's revised draft

> He
> ~~Robert E.~~ Lee was born on January
> 19, 1807, on a ~~farm~~ plantation in
> referred to as "Light-Horse Harry,"
> Virginia. His father, was a commander
> in the Revolutionary War. ~~He was~~
> ~~referred to as "Light-Horse Harry."~~ From
>   Robert E.
> his earliest days, Lee was devoted to his
>   Robert
> home state of Virginia. In 1831, he
> married Mary Custis, the great-

Think and Discuss ✔

- How did Maria make it clear who "Light-Horse Harry" was?
- Why did she move a sentence?
- What words did she replace? Why?

On Your Own

Revising checklist

☑ Does my opening catch my reader's interest?

☑ Have I written only facts and left out opinions?

☑ Are the facts explained clearly? Are they in an order that makes sense?

☑ Does my closing sum up the main ideas in my report?

1. Revise Make changes in your first draft. Add details. Circle any fact that is out of order. Draw an arrow to show where it goes. If you need to find exact words, use the thesaurus below or the one in the back of the book. Replace words by crossing them out and adding new words above them.

2. Have a conference Read your report to a classmate or your teacher. Make notes about your listener's remarks.

WRITING CONFERENCE

Ask your listener:	**As you listen:**
"How could I improve the opening?" "Which facts were unclear or out of order?" "How could I improve the closing?"	I must listen closely. Are the facts clear? Did I hear any opinions? Do I have questions that the report doesn't answer? Was it interesting?

3. Revise Think about your listener's suggestions. Do you have any other ideas? Make those changes on your paper.

Thesaurus

chief main, principal	**opposite** contradictory, contrary
examine investigate	**real** actual, true
example case, instance	**same** equal, identical
further more, additional	**source** cause, origin
meaning significance, sense	**while** as long as

Step 5: Proofread

Maria read her report for mistakes in spelling, capitalization, and punctuation. She used a dictionary to check spellings. She used proofreading marks to make her changes.

Part of Maria's proofread report

> Lee spent his remaining years ^as^ at
> president of ~College.~ it
> washington ~Colledge.~ After his death ~he~ ^e^
> renamed
> was ~renamd~ Washington and Lee
>
> University in his honor. Robert Edward
> ∧Lee
> Lee died on October 12, 1870. He wanted
> peacefully
> the North and South to work together. ∧
> Throughout
> ~Thruout~ his life he served his beloved
> Virginia
> ~state,~ both in crisis and in peace. ←

Think and Discuss

- Where did Maria add a period? Why?
- What words did she correct for spelling?
- What word did she capitalize? Why?
- What word did she change? Why?

On Your Own

1. **Proofreading Practice** Proofread this paragraph. Find one mistake in the use of a pronoun. Find one run-on sentence and five spelling mistakes. Write the paragraph correctly.

   Makeng balloons is a simple but interesting process. First, the liquid latex is colored then the molds are dipped in the liquid. The balloons dry as them move threw the factory. Next, stiff brushs roll down the openings. Last, they are rimoved from the molds and seald in bags.

Proofreading Marks

⁋ Indent
∧ Add something
ℐ Take out something
≡ Capitalize
╱ Make a small letter

2. Proofreading Application Now proofread your report. Use the Proofreading Checklist and the Grammar and Spelling Hints below. You may want to use a colored pencil to make your corrections. Use a dictionary to check spellings.

Proofreading Checklist

    Did I

☑ **1.** indent?

☑ **2.** use capital letters correctly?

☑ **3.** use punctuation marks correctly?

☑ **4.** use pronouns correctly?

☑ **5.** spell all words correctly?

The Grammar/Spelling Connection

Grammar Hints

Remember these rules from Unit 11 when you use pronouns.

- Use *it* as a subject or object pronoun. *(A seagull perched on the roof. It took off gracefully. We watched it.)*
- Use *they* as a subject pronoun. Use *them* as an object pronoun. *(The girl and boy played near the water. They made sand castles until their mother called them.)*

Spelling Hint

- When a word ends with *e*, the *e* is usually dropped when adding *-ed* or *-ing. (saved, riding)*

Step 6: Publish

Here is the way Maria shared her report with her grand-father. She cut a large piece of white paper in the shape of a plantation house and wrote her report on it. Then she glued the report onto a map of Virginia.

On Your Own

1. **Copy** Write or type your report as neatly as possible.
2. **Give it a title** Think of a good title. Write it above the first line of your report.
3. **List your sources** At the end of your report list all the sources from which you got information.
4. **Check** Read over your report again to make sure you have not left out anything or made any mistakes in copying.
5. **Share** Think of a special way to share your report.

Ideas for Sharing

- Make a slide show to use as you read your report aloud.
- Place your report on a large travel poster to illustrate it.
- Make a collage of class report topics. Write some questions that are answered. Add pictures.

Applying Research Reports

Literature and Creative Writing

"Before Misty" tells the story of the Spanish galleon *Santo Cristo* carrying a cargo of ponies to the New World. In the fierce storm that sank the galleon off the coast of Assateague Island, fifteen ponies survived and swam to the island. Since that time, ponies have lived there. "A Horse's Body" presents factual information about the body of the horse.

Use what you have learned about writing research reports to do one or more of the following activities.

<table>
<tr><td>

Remember these things ☑
Use the library to find facts.
Take notes.
Make an outline.
Write the report from the outline.
Write a good opening and closing.

</td><td>

1. **Report on the horse.** Do library research to find out when and how horses were brought to North America. Who brought them? Why?

2. **Explain how to care for a horse.** What must a horse owner do to take care of a horse every day? Find out. Then write a report on two or three of these daily responsibilities.

3. **Report on a particular animal.** A horse runs easily. A cat is an excellent climber. Think of an animal that interests you. Do some research on it. Tell how the animal uses its special features in its everyday life.

</td></tr>
</table>

Writing Across the Curriculum
Health

The health of individuals and of whole communities often depends on sharing information. The quality of our air and water, the food we eat, and the cure of diseases concern everyone. Much research is done in the health field, and the information is usually shared in reports.

Choose one or more of the following activities.

1. **Find out about your body.** Report on one system of your body. How does it work? What does it do? Make a class booklet of all your reports.

2. **Report on the water.** Fluoride is a natural substance found in water. Some communities add fluoride to their drinking water. Find out why. What does fluoride do? How much is usually added? What are its effects? Does your water contain fluoride? Share your information with your class.

Writing Steps
1. Choose a topic
2. Plan
3. Write a first draft
4. Revise
5. Proofread
6. Publish

Word Bank
fluoridate
substance
natural
enamel
resistant
caries

3. **Report on vaccinations.** Diseases such as smallpox and diphtheria were once common. Now vaccinations can prevent their occurrence. Find out about one type of vaccination given in your school. What disease does it protect against? When was the vaccine discovered? Who discovered it?

Toshio really liked reading "Before Misty." He had read some stories about the Chincoteague ponies before but did not know how they had come to be there. Toshio read another book by Marguerite Henry, *King of the Wind*. He decided to share this book by making a book jacket. On the outside of the jacket, he drew a picture. On the inside flaps, he wrote about the book. Here is how the inside of the book jacket looked when he finished.

King of the Wind

by Marguerite Henry

    This is the true story of a horse who lived in the 1700s. He became the ancestor of Man o' War and many other famous Arabian horses. The story begins in Morocco, moves to France, and ends in England on the estate of the Earl of Godolphin.

    The horse, who is called Sham, is cared for by a stable boy who cannot speak. The boy's name is Agba and he loves the horse very much. When Sham is sent to France as a gift for the king, Agba goes with him. Agba stays with the horse through hard times and danger. It's an exciting story!

Think and Discuss

- What did you learn about the story from the book jacket?
- Why is this a good way to share a book?

Share Your Book

Make a Book Jacket

1. Fold down a flap about three inches wide on each end of a large piece of drawing paper. Paste lined paper on each flap.
2. On the left flap, print the title of your book and the author's name. Below this, tell about interesting parts of the book. Use both flaps.
3. Draw a picture on the front of the jacket. Print the title and the author's name on this side also.
4. Share your book jacket with your class by showing the illustration and reading the information you have written.

Other Activities

- Make a collage for your book. From magazines and newspapers, cut out words and pictures of people and places that represent the characters and setting of your book. Arrange your cutouts on a large piece of paper and paste them down. Include the title and author of your book in your collage.
- Imagine that you are the illustrator of your book. Draw pictures of interesting characters and events in the story.
- Research the names of other books written by the same author and interesting facts about the author's life.

 **The Book Nook**

Justin Morgan Had a Horse *by Marguerite Henry* A schoolteacher takes a weak colt in payment for a debt, and young Joel Goss raises it.	**Blind Colt** *by Glen Rounds* A blind colt depends on his other senses to survive on a western ranch until a handicapped boy trains him.

Far, far will I go,
Far away beyond the high hills,
Where the birds live,
Far away over yonder, far away over yonder.

Eskimo

Adverbs and Prepositions

Getting Ready Have you ever gone on a long trip? Did you write a letter to a friend that told how far away you were and how long it took you to get there? Words that tell where and when are usually adverbs and prepositions. You will learn how to use these important words.

ACTIVITIES

Listening

Listen as the poem on the opposite page is read. The words *far* and *away* are used as adverbs. The word *beyond* is used as a preposition.

Speaking

Look at the picture. Make up a class poem about going to the mountains shown in the background. Your first line could be *Over the shining river*. Have someone write your poem on the board as you make it up.

Writing

Is there a faraway place that you want to visit? In your journal, write down your thoughts about that place. Where is it? Why do you want to go there?

1 | Adverbs

You have learned that an adjective describes a noun or a pronoun. A word that describes a verb is an **adverb**. Adverbs tell how, when, or where an action happens.

HOW: The plane landed <u>smoothly</u> at the airport.

WHEN: <u>Soon</u> Jeff would see his grandparents at the gate.

WHERE: They were waiting for him <u>there</u>.

Many adverbs end with *-ly*. Some are included in these lists of common adverbs.

HOW	WHEN	WHERE
fast	tomorrow	here
hard	later	inside
together	again	far
happily	often	upstairs
quietly	first	downtown
secretly	next	somewhere
slowly	then	forward

Guided Practice What adverb describes the underlined verb in each sentence? Does it tell how, when, or where?

Example: Tina <u>waited</u> patiently.   *patiently   how*

1. She <u>stood</u> outside.
2. Soon her brother <u>arrived</u>.
3. He cheerfully <u>greeted</u> her on the porch.
4. Keith and Tina <u>hurried</u> downtown.
5. They easily <u>found</u> Grove Street Park.
6. They <u>ate</u> their picnic lunch there.
7. Then they <u>watched</u> the parade from the corner.
8. A boy in a robot costume <u>walked</u> awkwardly toward them.
9. Tina and Keith immediately <u>recognized</u> their friend Stan.
10. They excitedly <u>waved</u>.

> ▶An **adverb** is a word that tells how, when, or where.
> ▶Adverbs can describe verbs.
> ▶Many adverbs end with -*ly*.

Independent Practice

A. Write the adverbs in the sentences below. Then write whether the adverb tells how, when, or where.

Example: Mrs. Janis often visits the art museum. *often when*

11. Yesterday she took Ramiz and Leslie.
12. The bus traveled far.
13. Finally, they reached the museum.
14. Ramiz went downstairs for an art class.
15. Everyone quietly watched the painter.
16. He worked carefully and skillfully.
17. His artwork was recently shown at the museum.
18. People looked curiously at his unusual paintings.

B. Copy each sentence below. Underline the adverb and draw an arrow to the verb it describes.

Example: The children planned a special trip today.

The children planned a special trip today.

19. Eagerly they approached the house.
20. The doorbell buzzed loudly.
21. Soon the wooden door opened.
22. The children went inside.
23. They hugged their grandmother tightly.
24. She sent Olaf upstairs.
25. He brought the photo album down.
26. Joyfully they shared the family pictures.

Writing Application: A Persuasive Letter

You have just visited a park or museum. Write a letter to convince a friend to visit the park or museum. Use adverbs that tell how, when, and where.

For Extra Practice, see p. 438.

2 | Comparing with Adverbs

You know that you can use adjectives to compare people, places, or things. You can use adverbs to compare actions. Like adjectives, adverbs have special forms for comparisons. To compare two actions, add *-er* to most short adverbs. To compare three or more actions, add *-est* to most short adverbs.

ONE ACTION: Amy will finish the book soon .

TWO ACTIONS: Amy will finish sooner than Jessie will.

THREE OR MORE: Amy will finish soonest of all.

Rules for Comparing with Adverbs		
1. Most short adverbs: Add *-er* or *-est* to the adverb.	late later latest	early earlier earliest
2. Most adverbs of two or more syllables: Use *more* or *most* with the adverb.	often more often most often	quickly more quickly most quickly

Guided Practice What form of each is used to compare two actions? What form is used to compare three or more?

Example: loudly *more loudly* *most loudly*

1. sadly
2. near
3. softly
4. cleverly
5. politely
6. hard
7. firmly
8. fast
9. powerfully

Summing up

▶ To compare two actions, use *-er* or *more* with an adverb.
▶ To compare three or more actions, use *-est* or *most*.
▶ Use *-er* and *-est* with most one-syllable adverbs.
▶ Use *more* and *most* with most adverbs of two or more syllables.

Independent Practice

A. For each adverb, write the form for comparing two and the form for comparing three or more.

Example: peacefully *more peacefully* *most peacefully*

10. bitterly
11. early
12. harshly
13. cozily
14. sweetly
15. low
16. simply
17. joyfully
18. rudely
19. long
20. carelessly
21. late
22. awkwardly
23. clearly
24. straight
25. successfully

B. Write each sentence using the correct form of the adverb.

Example: Matt lives ____ to the pond than Jon does.   (near)
Matt lives nearer to the pond than Jon does.

26. Does Adam swim ____ than Barb does?   (often)
27. I get into the water ____ than Lois does.   (slowly)
28. Tracy jumps into the water ____ of us all.   (quickly)
29. Of everyone, Chris splashes ____.   (noisily)
30. Josh always swims ____ than I do.   (straight)
31. I do the side stroke ____ than I do the crawl.   (easily)
32. Ron dives ____ than Stan does.   (deep)
33. Arlene dives ____ of all the swimmers.   (skillfully)
34. Of all the boys, Adam swims ____ underwater.   (fast)
35. Sara swims ____ of everyone in the group.   (gracefully)
36. Tom swam ____ than I did in the race.   (swiftly)
37. Of everyone, Alex swam the ____.   (fast)
38. Beth threw the beach ball ____ than Paula did.   (high)
39. Paula passed the beach ball ____ of all.   (accurately)
40. Josh went home ____ than Gail did.   (soon)
41. My hungry dog left the pond ____ than I did.   (eagerly)
42. Gail and Beth stayed in the water ____ of all.   (long)

Writing Application: A Paragraph

Write a paragraph comparing three different kinds of animals. Use adverbs to compare their actions.

For Extra Practice, see p. 439.   **Comparing with Adverbs**

3 | Adjective or Adverb?

Many adverbs are formed by adding *-ly* to an adjective. These words look similar and are easy to confuse. Be careful to use them correctly in a sentence.

INCORRECT: Robert writes clear . (adjective)

CORRECT: Robert writes clearly . (adverb)

Remember to use an adjective to describe a noun or a pronoun. Use an adverb to describe a verb.

ADJECTIVE: Heather draws beautiful designs.

ADVERB: She also paints beautifully.

The words *good* and *well* are also often confused. *Good* is always an adjective. Use *good* before a noun or after a linking verb. Do not use *good* when you mean "healthy."

ADJECTIVE: Sam has a good vocabulary. His stories are good.

Use *well* as an adverb to describe a verb. Use it as an adjective to mean "healthy."

ADVERB: Sam describes buildings well.

ADJECTIVE: Because Todd ate too fast, he is not well now.

Guided Practice Which word in parentheses correctly completes each sentence?

Example: The ballet company performed (good, well).   *well*

1. The dancers' movements were (beautiful, beautifully).
2. The star ballerina smiled (bright, brightly).
3. She spun (rapid, rapidly) on her toes.
4. Then she leaped (graceful, gracefully) into the air.
5. The male lead also gave a (good, well) performance.
6. The audience clapped (loud, loudly) at the end of the show.

Summing up

> ▸ Use adjectives to describe nouns or pronouns. Use adverbs to describe verbs.
> ▸ Do not confuse *good* and *well*. *Good* is always an adjective. *Well* is an adverb unless it means "healthy."

Independent Practice

A. Write the adjective or the adverb in parentheses that correctly completes each sentence.

Example: James is carving a small statue of a lion (skillful, skillfully). *skillfully*

7. His special tools for carving are (sharply, sharp).
8. At first, the wood changed (quick, quickly).
9. James cut the wood (expert, expertly).
10. The statue took shape (slow, slowly).
11. The lion's strong features became (clearly, clear).
12. James sanded the rough areas (careful, carefully).
13. Then he (proud, proudly) examined his statue.

B. Write the word in parentheses that correctly completes each sentence. Then label it *adjective* or *adverb*.

Example: Christine does (good, well) in class. *well   adverb*

14. She expresses herself (good, well) in writing.
15. Her grades on her stories and poems are very (well, good).
16. Christine's mystery stories are particularly (well, good).
17. She develops the characters (good, well).
18. Detective O'Malley is a (good, well) main character.
19. In her stories, Christine hides the clues (well, good).
20. Detective O'Malley's guesses are always (well, good).
21. Colorful words describe the action (good, well).
22. Christine's stories hold my attention (good, well).

Writing Application: A Story

Write the first paragraph of a story about a detective. Use adverbs and adjectives in your sentences. Include *good* and *well*. Underline each adjective once and each adverb twice.

For Extra Practice, see p. 440.   **Adjective or Adverb?**

4 | Negatives

Words that mean "no" or "not" are called **negatives**.

She has no more tickets.   There are none left.

You have learned to form a contraction from a verb and *not*. These contractions are also negatives. The letters *n't* stand for *not*. The word *not* is an adverb.

We won't be able to go to the show.

She couldn't get tickets.

Here is a list of some other common negatives.

not	nowhere	nobody	aren't	haven't
never	nothing	no one	doesn't	wouldn't

A sentence should have only one negative. Using double negatives in a sentence is usually incorrect.

INCORRECT	CORRECT
Ralph <u>hasn't</u> <u>no</u> homework.	Ralph hasn't any homework.
	Ralph has no homework.
<u>Isn't nobody</u> at home?	Isn't anybody at home?
	Is nobody at home?
I <u>haven't</u> bought <u>nothing</u>.	I haven't bought anything.
	I have bought nothing .

Guided Practice Which word in parentheses correctly completes each sentence?

Example: Didn't you (ever, never) see a three-ring circus? *ever*

1. Isn't (anybody, nobody) watching the high-wire act?
2. Look! There isn't (anything, nothing) underneath the wire.
3. Our friends at home (had, hadn't) none of the fun.
4. Didn't (any, none) of them have tickets for the circus?
5. Not one of us (would, wouldn't) have missed it.

Independent Practice

A. Write the sentences correctly. Underline the negative word.

> Example: My friends haven't (any, no) extra money.
> *My friends haven't any extra money.*

 6. They (have, haven't) nothing to spend.
 7. Isn't (anyone, no one) working this summer?
 8. There (is, isn't) no work in the neighborhood.
 9. Annie and Jo haven't (anywhere, nowhere) to go.
10. Can't you think of (any, no) ideas for earning money?
11. We haven't (ever, never) tried.

B. Rewrite each sentence once, correcting the double negative. (There are two ways to correct each sentence.)

> Example: Why isn't nobody having a yard sale?
> *Why isn't anybody having a yard sale?*

12. Didn't you never plan a yard sale?
13. Aren't none of you delivering newspapers?
14. There isn't nobody weeding gardens.
15. Debra hasn't looked nowhere for a job.
16. Ted hasn't had no luck.
17. He can't find a job nowhere in the neighborhood.
18. Doesn't nobody in the neighborhood need help?
19. Hasn't no one thought of washing cars?
20. We couldn't think of nowhere to have a car wash.
21. Why didn't no one ask the principal for advice before the end of school?
22. Didn't anyone never think of the school yard?

Writing Application: A Letter

Have you ever enjoyed studying a topic that you didn't think you would like? Write a letter to your teacher about this experience. Use at least three negatives.

For Extra Practice, see p. 441.   **Negatives   419**

5 | Prepositions

Small words that we use all the time can make a big difference in meaning.

Sula found it on the shelf.

Sula found it under the shelf.

The words *on* and *under* show very different relationships between *found* and *shelf*. Words that show relationships between other words are called **prepositions**.

Common Prepositions				
about	before	except	of	through
above	behind	for	off	to
across	below	from	on	under
after	beside	in	out	until
along	by	inside	outside	up
around	down	into	over	with
at	during	near	past	without

A preposition relates some other word in the sentence to the noun or the pronoun that follows the preposition. The noun or the pronoun that follows a preposition is the **object of the preposition**.

I liked the book with the blue cover.   Sula gave it to me.

Guided Practice The object of the preposition is underlined in each sentence. What is the preposition?

Example: Scientists study tools from the ancient past.   *from*

1. They ask many questions about the tool.
2. When was the tool used by people?
3. Was it made for a special purpose?
4. Did people use it in a particular way?
5. What does the tool tell us about them?

▶ A **preposition** relates the noun or the pronoun that follows it to another word in the sentence.

▶ The **object of the preposition** is the noun or the pronoun that follows the preposition.

Independent Practice

A. Write the preposition in each sentence.

Example: Scientists seek clues about the past. *about*

6. Sometimes they dig in the ground.
7. They have found dolls in their special searches.
8. These dolls were made from corn cobs.
9. Ancient people must have lived near these sites.
10. They may have grown corn for food.
11. The children probably played with the small dolls.
12. The scientists keep a record of their discoveries.
13. The dolls can be seen at several museums.

B. Copy each sentence. Underline the preposition once and the object of the preposition twice.

Example: Discoveries often happen in surprising ways.
Discoveries often happen <u>in</u> surprising <u>ways</u>.

14. A man found some bones on a cliff.
15. Had ancient people lived near it?
16. The man brought these bones to a scientist.
17. The bones were from a huge animal.
18. These bones had been buried for ten thousand years.
19. The scientist discovered a spear point with the bones.
20. He learned more about ancient times.
21. Ancient people had probably hunted the animal for food.
22. They may have made clothes from its fur.

Writing Application: A Story

Pretend that it is the distant future and you are a scientist. You dig up a toy from today. Write a paragraph about your discovery. Use a preposition in each sentence.

For Extra Practice, see p. 442.

6 | Prepositional Phrases

You have learned that a preposition is always followed by an object. A **prepositional phrase** is made up of a preposition, the object of the preposition, and all the words between them.

We packed the fruit <u>in our knapsacks</u>.

The object of the preposition can be a compound object.

We took enough oranges <u>for Manuel and Anita</u>.

A prepositional phrase can be at the beginning, in the middle, or at the end of a sentence.

At dawn we began our walk.

The map of the area was helpful.

The path went by a forest and a large lake .

Guided Practice The preposition is underlined in each sentence. What is the prepositional phrase?

Example: How would you travel <u>across</u> a river?   *across a river*

1. You might swim <u>to</u> the other side.
2. You might cross <u>at</u> a shallow place or a rocky spot.
3. Perhaps you would travel <u>by</u> boat.
4. Bridges are a better solution <u>to</u> the problem.
5. <u>On</u> bridges, traffic moves safely and easily.
6. Bridges have saved time <u>for</u> commuters and other travelers.
7. Travelers have also been spared many miles <u>of</u> travel.
8. The George Washington Bridge is used <u>by</u> many travelers.
9. It is an important route <u>between</u> New York and New Jersey.

across

a river

> **Summing up**

> ▶ A **prepositional phrase** is made up of a preposition, its object, and all the words between them.

Independent Practice

A. Write the prepositional phrase in each sentence. Then underline the preposition.

Example: People in every age have built bridges. *in every age*

10. The oldest bridge was found in England.
11. Piles of rock form the bridge.
12. The Romans used wood for their bridges.
13. During the Middle Ages, stone bridges were built.
14. The bridges were lined with shops and dwellings.
15. You can still walk across these bridges.
16. Bridges have changed with people's needs and new materials.
17. Some early bridges were made from rope.
18. The first iron bridge was built in the eighteenth century.
19. In the United States, covered bridges were once popular.
20. People drove wagons and rode horses through them.
21. Today's bridges are made from steel.
22. These bridges are strong enough for heavy trucks and trains.

B. Write the prepositional phrase in each sentence. Then underline the object of the preposition.

Example: There are many kinds of bridges. *of bridges*

23. Most bridges are built over water.
24. Boats and ships pass under the bridges.
25. Some bridges can be raised for tall boats and ships.
26. Large bridges are designed by engineers.
27. Traffic patterns in the area are studied.
28. The width and depth of the water are measured.
29. A tiny bridge may cross a brook in your town.
30. The bridge might be made from a log or a board.
31. Bridges across land are also common.
32. In a city, bridges sometimes connect buildings.

Writing Application: A Description

Write a paragraph about a journey that you have taken or that you dream of taking. Describe the sights and sounds of your journey. Remember to use exact words and sense words. Include a prepositional phrase in each sentence.

For Extra Practice, see p. 443. **Prepositional Phrases 423**

7 | Object Pronouns in Prepositional Phrases

You have learned that the object of a preposition is the noun or the pronoun that follows the preposition. When the object of the preposition is a pronoun, use an object pronoun. Object pronouns are *me, you, him, her, it, us,* and *them.*

People sometimes get confused when the pronoun is part of a compound object. To see whether the pronoun is correct, remove the other object and check the pronoun alone.

I gave a picture to Tom and her .   I gave a picture to her .

Guided Practice Which pronoun in parentheses correctly completes each sentence?

Example: My brothers wouldn't clean the house without my sisters and (I, me). *me*

1. I chased after Larry and (her, she).
2. Cleaning the garage was a good job for Marcy and (he, him).
3. In the garage, an old toy box was found by Marcy and (I, me).
4. The toys had belonged to Karen and (him, he).
5. With Larry and (she, her), I carried the box to the yard.
6. My little brother ran behind Karen and (us, we).
7. Meanwhile, Nate cleared the garage with Ken and (her, she).
8. The garage was swept by Marcy and (I, me).
9. In the yard, Larry looked at the toys with Ken and (she, her).
10. Mom told me to clean the porch with (she, her) and Dad.
11. The boards below Dan and (us, we) needed new paint.
12. That job would be fun for Larry and (I, me).

Summing up

▶ Use object pronouns as objects in prepositional phrases.
▶ Check the pronoun in a compound object by removing the other object.

Independent Practice

A. Write the prepositional phrase in each sentence. Then underline the object pronoun.

> Example: I went to the bike race with
> Jim and her. *with Jim and her*

13. The judge showed the starting line to us.
14. Jim sat with Sally and me.
15. Pete, Alonso, and Rita waved to Sally and us.
16. Jim focused his camera on Pete and them.
17. Three other riders waited beside them.
18. When the race started, Pete and Rita sped past Alonso and them right away.
19. Behind Pete and her, the remaining riders formed a line.
20. The crowd around us began cheering.
21. Suddenly Alonso rode past Pete and her.
22. The victory belonged to him!
23. Jim got a perfect shot of Alonso and them.

B. Choose the pronoun in parentheses that correctly completes each sentence. Write the sentences.

> Example: Dad bought a camera for Stacy and (I, me).
> *Dad bought a camera for Stacy and me.*

24. We planned a family picture for Mom and (he, him).
25. We would give it to Dad and (her, she) on their anniversary.
26. Lennie agreed to take a picture of our parents and (us, we).
27. I read the camera's instructions to Stacy and (he, him).
28. Grandma sat near Lennie and (us, we) and watched.
29. Lennie arranged chairs for Grandma and (we, us) in the den.
30. Jo arrived and sat between Mom and (me, I).
31. Stacy and Dad stood behind Mom and (her, she).
32. Rick finally took his place beside Stacy and (he, him).

Writing Application: A Paragraph

You have gathered some people and pets for a picture. Write a paragraph describing where everyone will sit or stand. Use a prepositional phrase with an object pronoun in each sentence. At least three sentences should have compound objects.

For Extra Practice, see p. 444.   Object Pronouns in Phrases   **425**

8 | Adverb or Preposition?

Sometimes the same word can be used as either an adverb or a preposition.

ADVERB: Susan ran inside .

PREPOSITION: Her hat was inside the store.

ADVERB: The shopkeeper looked up .

PREPOSITION: Susan raced up the stairs.

You can tell the difference between an adverb and a preposition if you look carefully at how the word is used in the sentence. If the word begins a prepositional phrase, it is a preposition. Otherwise, it is an adverb.

Here are some of the words that can be used as either adverbs or prepositions.

above	below	in	off	outside
along	by	inside	over	under
around	down	near	out	up

Guided Practice Is the underlined word an adverb or a preposition? If it is a preposition, what is the prepositional phrase that it introduces?

Example: Anita looked around the button shop.
          preposition   around the button shop

1. She had worn her blue coat outside.
2. A large blue button had fallen off.
3. Buttons were displayed along the counter.
4. Bright blue buttons filled a glass case near the door.
5. Anita walked over.
6. She saw the right button under the glass.
7. A salesperson came by and helped Anita.
8. She took the button from the case.
9. Anita held the button in her hand.
10. She took her wallet out and paid the salesperson.

▶ Do not confuse adverbs with prepositions. Prepositions introduce prepositional phrases. Adverbs do not.

Independent Practice If the sentence has an adverb,
write the adverb. If it has a preposition, write the prepositional
phrase and underline the preposition.

Example: Sarah stood outside the shop.   _outside_ *the shop*

11. She was curious and went inside.
12. In every corner, she saw strange, wonderful things.
13. An old fur coat and several heavy sweaters lay over a chair.
14. Ball gowns hung above a huge trunk and a small table.
15. Sarah walked around.
16. A brass horn was shining under a fancy lamp.
17. Blue and green umbrellas stood in a Chinese vase.
18. A purple fan beside the vase caught Sarah's attention.
19. Sarah looked up.
20. Colorful oil paintings hung near the ceiling.
21. Below the pictures was a brass bed.
22. Near the shiny bed was an old rocking chair.
23. Sarah sat down.
24. The rocking chair was beside a curtained window.
25. Sarah lifted the curtain and looked outside.
26. A jogger ran by.
27. A grandfather clock above the wooden desk chimed.
28. Sarah hurried out the door.
29. She ran past shops and houses.
30. Sarah raced down her aunt's street.
31. She ran inside her aunt's house.
32. Her cousins were already sitting around the large table.

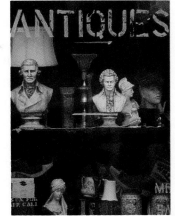

Writing Application: A Description
Imagine that you have discovered an old trunk in a basement
or a closet. Write a paragraph that describes the objects inside,
using adverbs and prepositions. Remember to use sense words
and exact words.

Grammar-Writing Connection

Placement of Prepositional Phrases

Prepositional phrases add meaning and detail to a sentence. When prepositional phrases appear in the wrong places, they can make a sentence unclear or silly. Notice that the prepositional phrases are misplaced in the sentence below.

ORIGINAL

We can talk to almost anyone   over the telephone   in the world .

In the following sentence, each prepositional phrase is placed as close as possible to the word that it describes. The sentence is easier to read and its meaning is clearer.

REVISED

We can talk over the telephone   to almost anyone   in the world .

Revising Sentences

Rewrite each sentence below. Make its meaning clearer by moving one prepositional phrase as close as possible to the word that it describes.

1. Through the sky, telephone lines run.
2. Over wires, signals are sent from one place and carried to another.
3. From storms, telephone wires under the ground are safe.
4. Some phone messages under the water are carried across the ocean by cables.
5. Calls in less than a minute can be made to foreign countries.
6. Satellites carry telephone messages of the earth to distant parts.
7. I visited for a month my cousins in Belgium last summer.
8. My mother and father on my birthday called me from the United States.
9. Without the help of an operator from their home phone, they dialed the number.
10. The connection in thirty seconds was made across the Atlantic Ocean.

Creative Writing

You can almost smell the smoke and hear the pounding hoof-beats in *Prairie Fire* by Blackbear Bosin. This Native American artist studied the history of his ancestors and painted scenes of their life.

- What parts of the painting create a sense of movement?
- How do the colors in the painting add to its mood?

Prairie Fire, Blackbear Bosin,
Philbrook Art Center, Tulsa, Oklahoma

Activities

1. **Write a news report.** Imagine that you are a reporter for the *Wild West Weekly*. You have just witnessed this scene. Write a news report describing it. Include such made-up details as how the fire got started and how long it has lasted.
2. **Make up a myth.** Myths are stories that try to explain natural events. Often in these stories, natural forces, such as wind and fire, are given human qualities. Write a myth about this painting, explaining why the Fire Spirit grew angry.

Adverbs *(p. 412)* Write each sentence. Underline the adverb and draw an arrow to the verb that it describes.

1. Some animals travel often.
2. Whole herds move together.
3. Deer live quietly in the mountains.
4. They graze calmly in the meadows.
5. Sheep often live on cliffs.
6. They go down to the valleys in the early fall.
7. They walk slowly in long lines.
8. Plants grow well in the valleys.
9. The animals find food easily.
10. In spring the snow finally melts, and grass begins to grow.
11. The animals eagerly climb.
12. They happily eat grass in the beautiful green mountains.

Comparing with Adverbs *(p. 414)* For each sentence, write the correct form of the adverb in parentheses.

13. Klaus paints ___ this year than last year.   (often)
14. He thinks of topics ___ than I do. (easily)
15. Chandra paints ___ of the three girls.   (skillfully)
16. Danielle mixes paint ___ than Elise does.   (fast)
17. Neil cleans up ___ than Warren does.   (carefully)
18. Maida finished her painting ___ of all.   (soon)

Adjective or Adverb? *(p. 416)* Write the word in parentheses that correctly completes each sentence. Then write whether it is an adjective or an adverb in the sentence.

19. Last week I had a cold, but now I am (good, well).
20. The catalog came (quick, quickly).
21. These roses will look (beautiful, beautifully) in our yard.
22. A strong wind rattles the windows (noisy, noisily).
23. Snow falls (soft, softly) onto the large field.
24. The ice thaws (slow, slowly).
25. I am (impatiently, impatient).
26. The rains are (heavily, heavy).
27. Spring will come (swift, swiftly).

Negatives *(p. 418)* Rewrite each sentence so that there is only one negative.

28. Isn't nobody in the library?
29. I don't have nowhere to go.
30. I haven't read nothing today.
31. There aren't no new books at home.
32. I didn't bring no magazines.
33. Don't you never read newspapers?
34. I can't find no poetry books.
35. You haven't read no plays lately.
36. I don't never buy paperbacks.
37. I don't have nowhere to look.
38. Won't none of you lend me a book?

Prepositions *(p. 420)* Write each sentence. Underline the preposition once and its object twice.

39. Sam will fly his kite in the park.
40. It flies over the tallest trees.
41. The kite is bright blue with a large silver moon.
42. Sam and I will go past the enormous white farmhouse.
43. We will go through the meadow.
44. My kite sails like a bird.
45. Your kite has the shape of a powerful eagle.
46. Did you buy it in town?
47. Hold the string with a tight grip.
48. Your kite may fly above that tree.
49. My dad makes kites of paper.
50. Before dark we should head home.

Prepositional Phrases *(p. 422)* Write the prepositional phrase in each sentence. Then underline the object of the preposition.

51. I went by bus and train.
52. At the museum, I saw beautiful and unusual pearls.
53. Some pearls are made in Japan.
54. A bead is placed in an oyster.
55. The oyster covers the bead with a thin coating.
56. A pearl is removed from the oyster.
57. The pearls are sorted in factories.
58. A pink color is sometimes added to these pearls.
59. I also saw a display of shells.
60. The shells glowed in rich colors.
61. They came from oceans and lakes.

Object Pronouns in Prepositional Phrases *(p. 424)* Choose the correct pronoun in parentheses.

62. I waited for Bill and (she, her).
63. I take a class with (they, them).
64. Jay was a model for Al and (me, I).
65. Mia drew a picture of (he, him).
66. Sue stood right behind Tom and (her, she).
67. I sat near Manuel and (they, them).
68. My picture looks very good to Manuel and (I, me).
69. Our teacher is happy with (we, us).
70. We have always worked hard for (he, him).
71. My teacher gives excellent advice to my classmates and (me, I).
72. I have learned a lot about art from my teacher and (they, them).

Adverb or Preposition? *(p. 426)* Write each adverb or prepositional phrase. Underline each preposition.

73. It was dark outside.
74. Tina stepped inside the door.
75. She looked around the ice rink.
76. Bright lights were shining above.
77. White ice sparkled below.
78. Tina climbed up the steps.
79. She walked along the row.
80. Tina sat down and watched.
81. She looked out and waited.
82. Skaters appeared in red costumes.
83. They twirled under the spotlights.
84. They leaped over the ice.
85. A clown skated by and fell.
86. People around Tina laughed.

Cumulative Review

Unit 1: The Sentence

Kinds of Sentences *(pp. 14, 16)* Label each fragment. For each complete sentence, write *declarative, interrogative, imperative,* or *exclamatory.*

1. What a great telephone you have!
2. Listen for the dial tone.
3. Who invented the telephone?
4. Alexander Graham Bell.
5. He also taught deaf children.

Subjects and Predicates *(pp. 20, 22, 24)* Write each simple subject and simple predicate.

6. Mr. Jackson is a scientist.
7. This scientist invented a robot.
8. The small robot does many things.
9. It talks with a low voice.
10. Get a robot soon.

Combining Sentences *(pp. 26, 28, 30, 32)* Rewrite each pair as one sentence. Use the conjunction in a compound subject, a compound predicate, or a compound sentence.

11. Jeff mowed the grass.　(and)
    Iris mowed the grass.
12. Brad will rake the leaves.　(and)
    Stan will put them in a bag.
13. Rosa will weed the garden.　(or)
    Rosa will pick some flowers.
14. It was hard work.　(but)
    They finished in one day.

Unit 3: Nouns

Common and Proper Nouns *(pp. 82, 88)* Write a list of the common and proper nouns.

15. Lian visited Sweden last June.
16. This country is in northern Europe.
17. Forests grow on its mountains.
18. The government is in Stockholm.
19. Jenny Lind, the famous singer, was born in that city.

Plural Nouns and Possessive Nouns *(pp. 84, 86, 90, 92)* Rewrite these phrases, using the plural forms of the underlined nouns. Then rewrite the new phrases, using plural possessives.

20. the toy of the baby
21. the watch belonging to the man
22. the tail of the fox
23. the radio belonging to the girl
24. the scarf belonging to the child

Unit 5: Verbs

Action Verbs and Direct Objects *(pp. 142, 144)* Write the action verb and the direct object in each.

25. Leo's class visited two factories.
26. One factory manufactures bicycles.
27. The other factory makes paper.
28. The guide answered questions.
29. Each child received a small gift.

Main Verbs and Helping Verbs
(p. 146) Write the verbs in these sentences. Underline the main verb once and the helping verb twice.

30. The Gordons have flown to China.
31. They are planning day trips.
32. The first trip will start in Peking.
33. Steve is taking his camera along.
34. He will develop the film himself.

Linking Verbs *(p. 148)* Write each sentence and underline the linking verb. Draw an arrow connecting the words that the verb links.

35. The car seems very old.
36. It is a Model T.
37. I feel excited about it.
38. My brother is the new owner.
39. The Lees were also collectors.

Verb Tenses *(pp. 150, 152, 154)* Write each underlined verb in the tense shown.

40. Jody <u>studies</u> for the test.   (past)
41. He <u>outlined</u> the topics.   (present)
42. The test <u>lasted</u> one hour.   (future)
43. Mrs. Angelo <u>graded</u> it.   (present)
44. Jody <u>has passed</u> the test.   (future)

Subject-Verb Agreement *(pp. 156, 158)* Write the correct verbs.

45. Bryce Canyon (are, is) beautiful.
46. Lin and I (take, takes) a tour.
47. I (see, sees) a fossil in the rocks!
48. We (has, have) warm jackets.
49. It (gets, get) cold at night.

Contractions *(p. 160)* Write the words that have been combined to form these contractions.

50. won't
51. didn't
52. shouldn't
53. hasn't
54. couldn't
55. aren't

Irregular Verbs *(pp. 162, 164)* Write the past form of each verb.

56. I had (make) a box kite.
57. I (run) across the field with it.
58. The kite (fly) high in the sky.
59. Suddenly a strong wind (blow).
60. My kite had (break) in two.

Confusing Verbs *(pp. 166, 168, 170)* Write the correct word or words.

61. (May, Can) you drive us?
62. We should (let, leave) now.
63. Try to (set, sit) near the stage.
64. Will the speaker (teach, learn) us about different kinds of cats?
65. Greg (should of, should've) come.

Unit 7: Adjectives

What Is an Adjective? *(p. 222)* Write each sentence, underlining the adjectives. Then draw an arrow from each adjective to the noun that it describes.

66. Oysters live in shallow water.
67. They have heavy shells.
68. Many oysters produce pearls.
69. White pearls are common.
70. Black pearls are rare and valuable.

Cumulative Review, *continued*

Articles and Demonstratives
(p. 224) Write the correct word in parentheses.

71. Every few years (a, an) unusually severe hurricane strikes.
72. (Those, These) houses over there were damaged in the last storm.
73. (The, A) winds uprooted trees.
74. (This, That) river in front of us almost overflowed.
75. We had to repair (an, a) dock.

Comparing with Adjectives
(pp. 226, 228) Write the correct form of each adjective.

76. Your shirt is (pretty) than mine.
77. Tina's shirt is (nice) of all.
78. She wears a (big) size than I do.
79. Does the wide belt look (good) than the narrow belt?
80. Of the three, the leather belt looks (good) by far.

Proper Adjectives *(p. 230)* Write the proper adjective that is made from the noun in parentheses.

81. My (Switzerland) watch always keeps good time.
82. I like to read (Japan) poetry.
83. That (Africa) monkey is playful.
84. The Prado Museum is in the (Spain) city of Madrid.
85. The (Mexico) fiesta lasted two days.

Unit 9: Capitalization and Punctuation

Correct Sentences *(pp. 282, 284, 286)* Write each sentence. Use capital letters and commas correctly, and add end punctuation as needed.

86. ann which sports do you like best
87. I like football baseball and hockey
88. do not forget lori to wear your uniform sara will bring the gloves
89. yes ted your cousin plays well
90. what a great run that was lennie

Quotations *(p. 292)* Write each sentence. Use punctuation marks and capital letters correctly.

91. what did you like best about your trip to Arizona asked Carrie
92. I saw a cactus that was over forty feet tall exclaimed Suki
93. she added it's a Giant Cactus
94. did it have flowers asked Carrie
95. in the spring replied Suki flowers blossom on its stem

Abbreviations *(p. 294)* Rewrite these groups of words, using abbreviations for the underlined words.

96. Memphis, <u>Tennessee</u> 38115
97. Sunshine Box <u>Company</u>
98. <u>Monday</u>, <u>August</u> 29, 1922
99. Philip <u>Alan</u> Burke, <u>Junior</u>
100. 129 Essex <u>Road</u>, Austin, <u>Texas</u>

Titles *(p. 296)* Write each of the titles correctly.

101. ramona the pest   (book)
102. summer rain   (poem)
103. the shaggy dog   (movie)
104. the first airplane   (book chapter)
105. los angeles times   (newspaper)

Unit 11: Pronouns

Subject Pronouns, Object Pronouns, and Possessive Pronouns *(pp. 346, 348, 350, 352)* Write each sentence correctly.

106. Holly attended the safety patrol meeting with Maria and (I, me).
107. (Us, We) elected a new president.
108. (Our, Ours) votes went to Maria.
109. The new president is (her, she).
110. Maria thanked (we, us).

Double Subjects *(p. 356)* Write each sentence correctly.

111. The Chens they own a travel agency.
112. My brother and I we work there.
113. Mrs. Chen she calls the airlines.
114. Fred he is our best customer.
115. His job it takes him overseas.

we and *us* with Nouns *(p. 358)* Write each sentence, using *we* or *us*.

116. The crowd saw ___ swimmers.
117. ___ students cheered loudly.
118. The winners were ___ friends.
119. The coach praised ___ winners.
120. ___ reporters made notes.

Unit 13: Adverbs and Prepositions

Adjective or Adverb? *(pp. 412, 414, 416)* Write the correct word.

121. Al prepared (careful, carefully).
122. He spoke quite (clear, clearly).
123. The speech went (good, well).
124. Mrs. Lee smiled (proud, proudly).
125. She said he had done (good, well).

Negatives *(p. 418)* Rewrite each sentence, using only one negative.

126. Hasn't nobody seen my sneakers?
127. You don't never clean your room.
128. I can't find no hangers.
129. There isn't no room in my closet.
130. Won't no one help me?

Prepositional Phrases *(pp. 420, 422, 424)* Write the prepositional phrase. Underline the preposition once and its object twice.

131. We learned about *Twelfth Night*.
132. It is a comedy by Shakespeare.
133. A woman plays the part of Viola.
134. She dresses in men's clothing.
135. People are fooled by her.

Adverb or Preposition? *(p. 426)* Copy the underlined word, and label it *adverb* or *preposition*.

136. People heard a noise <u>above</u> them.
137. They looked <u>up</u> curiously.
138. A glider circled <u>in</u> the sky.
139. It landed <u>near</u> the lake.
140. The pilot stepped <u>out</u> proudly.

Enrichment

DESIGN A SIGN

A new children's store is holding a contest to find the most original name for the store. The name must be interesting to children, and it must contain a prepositional phrase. Some names already entered are *Under the Lavender Elephant* and *Beside a Picnicking Rhino*. Think up a name and design a sign for it.

Robot Remarks

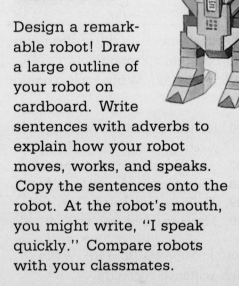

Design a remarkable robot! Draw a large outline of your robot on cardboard. Write sentences with adverbs to explain how your robot moves, works, and speaks. Copy the sentences onto the robot. At the robot's mouth, you might write, "I speak quickly." Compare robots with your classmates.

Adverb Proverbs

Proverbs are short, popular sayings that express well-known truths. An example is "There's no place like home." Try writing your own proverbs, using two adverbs in each one.

Deal honestly; sleep soundly.

Copy your proverb onto white paper and illustrate it.
Extra! Collect proverbs from classmates and make a book.

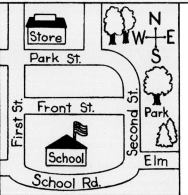

Begin <u>on</u> the corner <u>of</u> First St. and Park St. Go south <u>on</u> First St. until you come <u>to</u> Front St. . .

Treasure Mapping

Think of a good location for hidden treasure. Then draw a map. Fold a large piece of paper in half. On the left half, draw the map. Label compass directions, streets, and important places. On the right half, write directions for the treasure hunter. Use prepositional phrases in your directions. Underline the prepositions. Exchange maps with a classmate.

Hibernation Mural

With other classmates, make a mural of animals that hibernate. Select a hibernating animal that interests you. Draw and cut out the shape of that animal. On it write three sentences. Use prepositional phrases to tell how, when, and where the animal hibernates. Paste all the animals onto large paper to make a mural. Add other artwork if you wish.

Extra Practice: Unit 13

1 **Adverbs (p. 412)**

● Write the adverb that describes each underlined verb.

Example: Joy <u>waited</u> impatiently.   *impatiently*

1. Her parents carefully <u>planned</u> the trip.
2. They all <u>boarded</u> the train eagerly.
3. The train <u>arrived</u> at the station early.
4. They <u>traveled</u> far to the hotel.
5. Joy excitedly <u>looked</u> at all the sights.
6. Finally, they <u>reached</u> the hotel.
7. The tired travelers <u>would unpack</u> later.

▲ Write the adverb that describes the underlined verb in each sentence. Then write whether it tells how, when, or where.

Example: Dan recently <u>visited</u> Washington, D.C.   *recently   when*

8. His friend Russ <u>lives</u> there.
9. Russ and Dan <u>took</u> the bus downtown.
10. They immediately <u>headed</u> for the Air and Space Museum.
11. First, they <u>watched</u> the museum's film on flying.
12. The usher swiftly <u>guided</u> them to their seats.
13. Afterward, the boys <u>ate</u> lunch in the cafeteria.
14. Russ sadly <u>waved</u> good-by to Dan at the train station.

■ Write each sentence, using an adverb. The word in parentheses tells what kind of adverb to write.

Example: ＿＿ an inch of rain fell in one hour.   (when)
            Yesterday an inch of rain fell in one hour.

15. The rain hammered ＿＿ on the roof.   (how)
16. ＿＿ we were dry and warm.   (where)
17. Cars moved ＿＿ along the wet roads.   (how)
18. Sections of School Street were ＿＿ closed.   (when)
19. We hoped that Dad was not stuck ＿＿.   (where)
20. ＿＿ he told us what had happened.   (when)

2 | Comparing with Adverbs (p. 414)

● Copy the correct form of the adverb for each sentence.

Example: Jon arrived (sooner, soonest) than Neil.   *sooner*

1. Leah skates (more often, most often) than Rita does.
2. Of the four, Neil tries (harder, hardest).
3. Rita skates (more smoothly, most smoothly) of all.
4. I can lace my skates (faster, fastest) than Leah can.
5. She glides (more gracefully, most gracefully) than I.
6. Jon jumps (higher, highest) of all the boys.
7. Of everyone, Ava skates (more confidently, most confidently).

▲ Write each sentence, using the correct form of the adverb in parentheses.

Example: Joe kicks _____ of all the children.   (evenly)
    Joe kicks most evenly of all the children.

8. Lori can float _____ of all the girls.   (long)
9. Al climbed into the pool _____ than Joe did.   (slowly)
10. Henry swam the two laps _____ of all the swimmers.   (quickly)
11. Move your arms up and down _____ than I did.   (gently)
12. Of everyone, Wayne swims _____.   (straight)
13. Maria breathes _____ than Wayne.   (easily)
14. Lori held the kickboard _____ than Henry did.   (firmly)

■ Rewrite each sentence, using the kind of comparison shown.

Example: Charlie listens to the coach carefully.   (two actions)
    Charlie listens to the coach more carefully than I do.

15. After hitting the ball, Kelly runs swiftly.   (two actions)
16. Sal practices tirelessly.   (three or more actions)
17. Toby comes early to practice.   (two actions)
18. Alex stays at the field late.   (three or more actions)
19. Charlie swings a bat confidently.   (two actions)
20. Ella throws the ball smoothly.   (three or more actions)
21. At the last game, Sam hit the ball powerfully.   (two actions)
22. Louisa dives for the ball daringly and catches it often.   (three or more actions)

3 | Adjective or Adverb? (p. 416)

● Write *adjective* or *adverb* to name each underlined word.

Example: Our teacher paints landscapes <u>well</u>.   *adverb*

1. I left <u>quickly</u> for my art class this morning.
2. Last Saturday I had a cold, but today I am <u>well</u>.
3. Our teacher is giving a <u>good</u> lesson in water color.
4. He painted a landscape with <u>dark</u> thunderclouds.
5. First, he <u>lightly</u> sketched the landscape on paper.
6. Then he spread a <u>thin</u> coat of water over the sky.
7. He <u>swiftly</u> brushed paint across the wet area.

▲ Write each sentence, using the correct word. Label it *adjective* or *adverb*.

Example: Mindy had the flu, but now she is (good, well).
          Mindy had the flu, but now she is well.   adjective

8. Mindy and Sue's day at the museum was quite (good, well).
9. They looked (careful, carefully) at a Mary Cassatt painting.
10. The sunlight around the boat is (bright, brightly).
11. The mother holds the child (gentle, gently) in her arms.
12. The child watches the father (curious, curiously).
13. The family seems (happy, happily) in the boat.
14. Cassatt painted scenes of family life (good, well).

■ Write the word in parentheses that correctly completes each sentence. Then write a sentence, using the other word in parentheses correctly.

Example: Sandy draws landscapes (skillful, skillfully).
          skillfully   As an artist, Sandy is skillful.

15. She works (main, mainly) in pencil.
16. Her drawings in pen and ink are (good, well).
17. Today she works (happy, happily) in the park.
18. The scene she paints looks (pleasant, pleasantly).
19. The sun is shining (bright, brightly).
20. Ducks swim in the pond (quiet, quietly).
21. Two boats sail (swift, swiftly) across the water.
22. Sandy (quick, quickly) makes a sketch.

4 | Negatives (p. 418)

● If the sentence has a double negative, write the two negatives. If the sentence is correct, write *correct*.

Example: Al had never been to no circus before.   never   *no*

1. The circus wasn't really in a big tent.
2. I didn't see no man with the peanuts.
3. None of the clowns could skate very well.
4. The juggler didn't drop none of his props.
5. The woman had no more balloons.
6. The dog wouldn't do nothing for its trainer.
7. Nobody wanted to stay for the whole show.

▲ Write each sentence, using the correct word.

Example: Doesn't (anyone, no one) want to see the elephants?
Doesn't anyone want to see the elephants?

8. Those two elephants (have, haven't) no riders.
9. Hasn't Carol (ever, never) stayed up this late before?
10. We can't find (any, no) seats in this section.
11. I've never been (anywhere, nowhere) like the circus.
12. Isn't (anybody, nobody) holding onto the rope?
13. Wasn't there (anyone, no one) to catch her?
14. I (will, won't) never forget the excitement.

■ Write a negative statement to answer each question. Use a different negative in each sentence.

Example: Do you need to earn money this summer?
I don't need to earn money this summer.

15. Have you thought of any ways to earn money in your neighbor-hood this summer?
16. Is selling juice at a sidewalk stand a good idea?
17. Did you ever think of having a circus?
18. Is there somewhere that you could have a circus?
19. Would any of your friends help you?
20. Have your friends ever made a circus?
21. Is there anyone who can make costumes?
22. Will you have enough time to get ready?

● ▲ ■ **Three levels of practice   441**

5 | Prepositions (p. 420)

● Write the preposition in each sentence.

Example: The ship had disappeared without a trace.   *without*

1. What had happened to the crew?
2. The answers were hidden in the ship.
3. No one except the diver had seen the ship.
4. She dove skillfully into the deep water.
5. What would she discover at the bottom?
6. The diver rubbed a dirty window with her glove.
7. She looked through the glass.
8. The mystery would be solved by the diver.

▲ Copy each sentence. Underline the preposition once and the object twice.

Example: Scientists were studying the ruins of an old city.
        Scientists were studying the ruins of an old city.

9. Ashes from a volcano had buried the city.
10. The people had escaped before the disaster.
11. Now scientists were digging around the area.
12. Their discoveries explained daily life in the city.
13. They discovered different kinds of buildings.
14. People had sold pottery from one shop.
15. The houses had beautiful paintings on the walls.
16. The scientists found some paintings of blue monkeys.

■ Rewrite each sentence. Change the preposition, the object of the preposition, or both. Underline the prepositional phrases.

Example: Kim worked for the city.   *Kim worked in a store.*

17. Kim kept careful records about the city's history.
18. Once she spent a whole day looking for clues.
19. Suddenly she noticed something colorful in the soil.
20. Kim removed the dirt and looked at the object.
21. She had discovered an old piece of pottery.
22. She examined the dish and found some writing on the side.
23. The pottery was from the Chicago World's Fair.
24. This colorful dish had been made in 1892!

6 | Prepositional Phrases (p. 422)

● The preposition is underlined in each sentence. What is the prepositional phrase?

Example: Water covers a large part <u>of</u> the earth's surface.
of the earth's surface

1. The ocean floor lies <u>under</u> the water.
2. Many maps have been made <u>of</u> the ocean floor.
3. These maps are often used <u>by</u> sailors.
4. The maps guide them <u>over</u> dangerous rocks.
5. Their ships can travel safely <u>through</u> narrow places.
6. Very deep canyons have also been shown <u>on</u> these maps.
7. Underwater maps are used <u>for</u> other purposes.
8. Some scientists seek food and oil <u>on</u> the ocean floor.
9. <u>During</u> their explorations, they use maps.

▲ Write the prepositional phrase in each sentence. Then underline the preposition once and the object twice.

Example: In the past, people drew maps.   *In the past*

10. Today some maps are made by special computers.
11. Spacecraft take pictures of the earth and other planets.
12. Information from these spectacular pictures is stored.
13. On the computer screen, a detailed picture appears.
14. The map maker presses a few keys on his keyboard.
15. To the picture, he adds a new road.
16. The printer produces a copy of the map immediately.
17. The map maker checks for mistakes and corrects them.
18. Maps in beautiful colors are often produced.

■ Write each sentence, using a prepositional phrase.

Example: I found a pencil ____.
I found a pencil in my green knapsack.

19. I sketched a map ____.
20. It showed the way ____.
21. I drew a line ____.
22. I added a box ____.
23. I showed the trees ____.
24. I made a circle ____.
25. It was a mile ____.
26. X was the place ____.
27. I gave the map ____.
28. We would meet ____.

7 | Obj. Pronouns in Prep. Phrases (p. 424)

● Copy each prepositional phrase. Underline the object pronoun.

Example: Ansel Adams loved nature and took pictures of it.   *of it*

1. Yosemite National Park was special to him.
2. He photographed many parts of it often.
3. His pictures have famous scenery in them.
4. Some scenes may be familiar to Hoshi and you.
5. The huge landscapes are exciting to Linda and me.
6. Many photographers have learned from him.
7. For them, his pictures are excellent examples.

▲ Choose the pronoun in parentheses that correctly completes each sentence. Write the sentences.

Example: When Chirp landed, I took a picture of (he, him).
When Chirp landed, I took a picture of him.

8. Chirp and the other sparrows were familiar to my two brothers and (me, I).
9. We were writing an article about the robins and (they, them).
10. An editor had assigned the article to Larry and (us, we).
11. The birds were not upset by my brothers and (I, me).
12. We watched from a shed near (they, them).
13. Tom hid with Larry and (me, I) for hours.
14. The article was written by all of (we, us).

■ Rewrite each incorrect sentence correctly. For each sentence that is correct, write *correct*.

Example: Are you taking a picture of your sister and he?
Are you taking a picture of your sister and him?

15. Is there enough light to take a picture of Cal and her?
16. You should sit between Lily and I on the couch.
17. I like the background behind David and them.
18. I will develop this picture for Katie and she.
19. This picture of Frank and he at the beach is excellent.
20. Will you make a copy for Sharon and me?
21. Have you ever photographed your brother or they before?
22. Who is standing between Greta and she in the doorway?

8 | Adverb or Preposition? (p. 426)

● Write the underlined word. Label it *adverb* or *preposition*.

Example: Doug pulled a book <u>off</u> the shelf.   *off*   **preposition**

  1. Something slipped <u>over</u> the edge.
  2. It fell <u>on</u> the floor.
  3. Doug picked it <u>up</u>.
  4. He held the arrowhead <u>in</u> his hand.
  5. He had found the arrowhead <u>near</u> Black Hill.
  6. Ancient people had hunted <u>around</u> that area.
  7. Many arrowheads have been found <u>along</u> the river.
  8. Doug loved exploring <u>outside</u>.
  9. He was often lucky <u>in</u> his explorations.

▲ Write each adverb or prepositional phrase. Underline each preposition.

Example: The model train raced along the track.   *along the track*

  10. The long, metal track looped around.
  11. The electric train clattered by.
  12. Suddenly it disappeared into a dark tunnel.
  13. Inside the tunnel, the conductor blew the whistle.
  14. The train passed through the large mountain.
  15. Then it rushed out, and the engine roared.
  16. The tiny train continued its journey over a river.
  17. On the bridge, the train stopped and waited.
  18. When the light changed, the train chugged past a city.

■ Each sentence below has an adverb. Write another sentence, using that same word as a preposition.

Example: Alexander hurried inside.
        I left my bicycle inside the cluttered garage.

  19. Linda skipped along.   **24.** Ted stayed outside.
  20. Stan leaped across.   **25.** Everyone walked out.
  21. Gina marched around.   **26.** Lena raced by.
  22. Carlos jumped up.   **27.** Katya looked above.
  23. Anna climbed down.   **28.** Sam hid below.

Student's Handbook

Dictionary: Guide Words and Entry Words

Guide words At the top of each page in a dictionary are guide words. The guide word on the left tells the first entry word on the page, and the one on the right tells the last entry word. In the sample dictionary page below, *lotion* and *lower* are the guide words. Any entry words that fall alphabetically between these two words will appear on this page.

• What would be the first word on the sample dictionary page? the last word?

Entry words Each main word listed in your dictionary is called an *entry word*. It is printed in heavy, dark type.

guide words ⸺

lotion • lower

lotion *noun* A liquid that is used to heal, cleanse, or soften the skin.
lo·tion (lō′shən) ◊ *noun, plural* **lotions**

lotus *noun* A water plant with large, usually pink or white flowers.
lo·tus (lō′təs) ◊ *noun, plural* **lotuses**

entry word ⸺ **loud** *adjective* **1.** Having a high volume of sound: *We heard a loud crash.* **2.** Too bright: *That outfit is too loud to wear to school.*
◊ *adverb* In a loud manner: *Speak louder.*
loud (loud)
◊ *adjective, adverb*

other forms ⸺ **louder, loudest**

loudspeaker *noun* A device that changes an electrical signal into sound and makes the sound louder.
loud·speak·er (loud′spē′kər) ◊ *noun, plural* **loudspeakers**

▲ lotus

Other forms of words Entry words are usually listed in their simple forms, without endings such as *-ed, -ing, -s, -er,* and *-est.* Suppose you are looking for the word *louder* on the sample dictionary page. The basic form of *louder* is *loud.* Find *loud* as an entry word. The other forms of the word—*louder* and *loudest*—are listed at the end of the entry.

Practice

A. Which of these words would you find on a page with the guide words *essay/eternity?* Copy each word, and write *before this page, on this page,* or *after this page* to tell where you would find it.

1. estate	**5.** enchant	**9.** examine
2. evacuate	**6.** evaporate	**10.** eternal
3. etch	**7.** esteem	**11.** essential
4. ether	**8.** estuary	**12.** especially

B. Copy each numbered pair of guide words. Then write the words from the box that would appear on the same dictionary page with the pair of guide words.

13. dock/dogma   **16.** leisurely/less
14. drew/drive   **17.** orate/orderly
15. leaky/leave   **18.** Olympia/once

omen	leopard	Omaha
learning	orchestra	least
orbit	lean-to	doe
leap-year	on	drip-dry
drift	lengthy	order
document	drill	dodge

C. Write each of the following words. Then write the entry word under which you would find it in your dictionary.

19. focusing	**23.** scorching	**27.** invented
20. neglected	**24.** jollier	**28.** choruses
21. palest	**25.** drawn	**29.** quotients
22. clicking	**26.** injuries	**30.** easiest

Dictionary: Definitions

When you come across an unfamiliar word in your reading, try to first use the context of the sentence to figure out its meaning. If these words do not help you, look up the word in a dictionary. An example sentence or phrase also may help you to understand the word.

More than one meaning Many words have more than one meaning. Which meaning of *harbor* fits the sentence?

The wild deer found **harbor** in the canyon.

> **harbor** *noun* **1.** A sheltered place along a coast where ships can safely anchor or dock; port. **2.** A shelter; refuge.
> ◊ *verb* **1.** To give shelter to. **2.** To keep in the mind; hold: *Don't harbor grudges.*
> **har·bor** (här′bər) ◊ *noun, plural* **harbors**
> ◊ *verb* **harbored, harboring**

Parts of speech Some words, such as *harbor,* can be used as more than one part of speech. The entry above gives two meanings for *harbor* as a noun and two meanings for *harbor* as a verb. (Some dictionaries use the abbreviations *n.* and *v.*) What part of speech is *harbor* in this sentence?

I **harbor** warm memories of my early years.

Homographs Two or more different words that have the same spelling but different meanings are called *homographs*. Homographs come from different word roots. In the following entries for *mint*, each homograph is marked with a raised number.

> **mint^1** *noun* **1.** A plant with leaves that have a strong, pleasant smell and taste. **2.** A candy flavored with mint.
> **mint^1** (mĭnt) ◊ *noun, plural* **mints**

> **mint²** *noun* **1.** A place where coins are made by a government. **2.** A large amount of money: *The diamond necklace cost a mint.* ◊ *verb* To coin money.
> **mint²** (mĭnt) ◊ *noun, plural* **mints** ◊ *verb* **minted, minting**

- Which entry for *mint* is used in this sentence?

   Rebecca visited the huge Denver **mint**.

Formal and informal language Sometimes you may see the word *informal* or *slang* before a dictionary definition. This means that the word can be used in everyday conversation, but it should not be used in formal writing such as business letters. Look at the following entry for *cutup*.

> **cut·up** (kŭt′ŭp′) *n. Informal.* A mischievous person: prank-ster.

- What would be a more formal way of saying *cutup*?

Practice

A. Use the dictionary entry on page 449 to figure out the meanings of *harbor* in the following sentences. For each sentence, write the part of speech and the number of the meaning that fit the use of *harbor*.

   1. We must seek harbor from the rain.
   2. Jake doesn't harbor bad feelings about his injury.
   3. The old tugboat pulled slowly into the harbor.
   4. Our birdhouse harbors many cardinals in the winter.
   5. Your home seems like a warm harbor for all who visit it.

B. Look again at the entries for *mint*. Then write sentences, using *mint* with each of the following meanings.

   6. mint¹–meaning 1
   7. mint¹–meaning 2
   8. mint²–noun, meaning 1
   9. mint²–noun, meaning 2
   10. mint²–verb

C. Look up *card* in the dictionary. What is its informal meaning? Write a sentence using *card* in its informal sense.

Dictionary: Pronunciations

This drawing shows a flying lizard that lived during the age of dinosaurs. Can you pronounce the creature's name?

pter·o·dac·tyl |tĕr′ə dăk′təl|

If you look up *pterodactyl* in your dictionary, you will find the listing shown above. Notice that the entry word is broken into four syllables.

Phonetic respelling Following the entry word is a phonetic respelling. It tells you how to pronounce the word. In the phonetic respelling of *pterodactyl*, the consonant letters stand for the common sounds of those letters. To get the sounds for the vowels, you need to refer to the pronunciation key.

Pronunciation key On every page or every other page of a dictionary, there is a pronunciation key. One is shown below.

ă	pat	ŏ	pot	û	fur
ā	pay	ō	go	*th*	the
â	care	ô	paw, for	th	thin
ä	father	oi	oil	hw	which
ĕ	pet	o͝o	book	zh	usual
ē	be	o͞o	boot	ə	ago, item
ĭ	pit	yo͞o	cute		pencil, atom
ī	ice	ou	out		circus
î	near	ŭ	cut	ər	butter

Look again at the phonetic respelling of *pterodactyl*: tĕr′ə dăk′təl. To find the sound that ĕ stands for in the first syllable, look at the pronunciation key. The ĕ in the word *pet* is given as an example of the ĕ sound.

In the second syllable of the phonetic respelling of pterodactyl, you see this mark: ə. Find it in the key. After ə are five words: *ago*, *item*, *pencil*, *atom*, and *circus*. The dark letters in those words stand for the ə sound, called the **schwa sound**.

Look at *dăk*, the third syllable of the phonetic respelling. Which word in the pronunciation key is given as an example of the ă sound? The word *pat* has the same vowel sound as *dăk*.

Accent marks You cannot be sure of the pronunciation of *pterodactyl* until you look at the accent marks in the phonetic respelling.

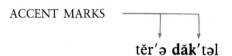

ACCENT MARKS

tĕr′ə dăk′təl

When a word has more than one syllable, one of those syllables is said with more stress, or force. The dark accent mark after the third syllable of *pterodactyl* means that *dăk* is spoken with more stress than the other word parts.

Notice the light accent mark after the first syllable of *pterodactyl*. That syllable is said with more stress than the second and fourth syllables, but it is not spoken as forcefully as the third syllable.

Practice

Look at these words and their phonetic respellings. Use them to answer the questions that follow.

foliage (fō′lē ĭj)   perforate (pûr′fə rāt′)
jovial (jō′vē əl)   ricochet (rĭk′ə shā′)
microscopic (mī′krə skŏp′ĭk)   zoology (zō ŏl′ə jē)

1. How many syllables are in *foliage*?
2. Does the first syllable of *foliage* rhyme with *go* or *doll*?
3. Which syllable of *jovial* is stressed?
4. Which syllable of *microscopic* is spoken with more stress—the first or the third?
5. Which syllable of *perforate* is spoken with no stress?
6. What is a word that rhymes with the last syllable of *ricochet*?
7. Which syllable of *ricochet* is spoken with the most stress?
8. How many syllables are in *zoology*?

Library: Fiction and Nonfiction

Libraries provide all sorts of materials. Once you know how these materials are arranged, it's easy to find them.

Fiction Books created from an author's imagination are called *fiction*. Books of fiction are arranged alphabetically by the authors' last names.

Nonfiction Books containing factual information are called *nonfiction*. These books are arranged by subject. Each subject is given a number that appears on the spine, or back, of the book. The numbers also appear in the card catalog.

FICTION SHELF

NONFICTION SHELF

Reference books Books containing particular kinds of information, such as dictionaries and encyclopedias, are called *reference books*. Read "Finding Facts" on page 388 for more information.

Practice

A. Write the word you would use to find each fiction book.

1. *Blue Moose* by Manus Pinkwater
2. *The Yearling* by Marjorie Kinnan Rawlings
3. *Call It Courage* by Armstrong Sperry

B. Write one word that tells the subject of each nonfiction book.

4. *Penguins Live Here*
5. *The Story of Folk Music*
6. *Volcanoes: Nature's Fireworks*

Library: The Card Catalog

The **card catalog** contains cards that list all the books in the library. The cards are arranged alphabetically in drawers. The letters on each drawer show which cards are inside. (See the picture below.) The card catalog contains three kinds of cards —author cards, title cards, and subject cards.

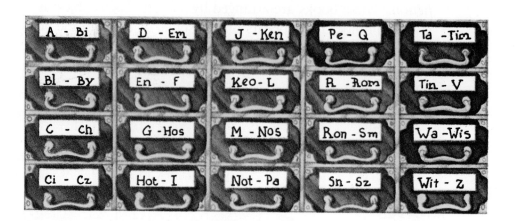

Author card If you know the author's name, you can find the titles of the author's books by using the author card. The author's name appears at the top, followed by the book title, the location and name of the publisher, the year of publication, and the number of pages. Author cards are filed alphabetically by the authors' last names. A separate card is filed for each of one author's books.

Title card If you know only the title of a book, use the title card to find the author's name. The book title appears on the top line, followed by the author's name and all the information on the author card. Title cards are filed alphabetically by the first main word in the title.

Subject card If you want to find books about the ocean, look for subject cards that are labeled OCEAN. One book title is listed on each subject card, followed by the same information as on the author and title cards.

Call number A card for a nonfiction book has a call number to the left of the author's name. This number is given to all the books on the same subject. The letter after the number is the first letter of the author's last name. The call number and letter also appear on the spine of the book.

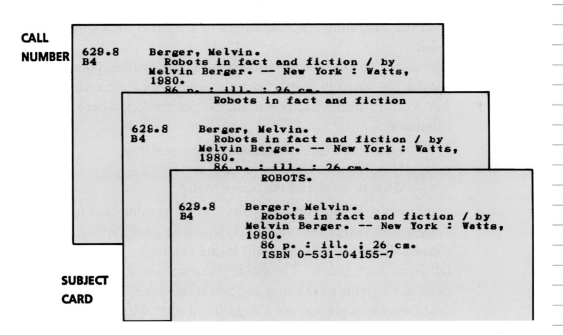

CALL
NUMBER

SUBJECT
CARD

Practice

Which drawer in the card catalog on page 454 would help you answer each question? Write the letters that appear on that drawer.

1. Does the library have any books by Rose Blue?
2. Are there any books about coin collecting in the library?
3. Is *The Borrowers* in the library?
4. Does the library have a book about the dancer Maria Tallchief?
5. Who wrote the book, *From Anna?*
6. What books on windsurfing does the library have?
7. What poetry books by Robert Frost does the library have?
8. Does the library have any almanacs?
9. Who wrote *The Adventures of Tom Sawyer?*
10. What are some books by Betsy Byars?

Using an Encyclopedia

An encyclopedia is a set of books containing articles about people, places, things, and events.

Volume The articles in an encyclopedia are arranged in alphabetical order in books, or volumes. Each volume is lettered with the beginning letter or letters of the main topics in that book.

Key word To find information in an encyclopedia, you must have a key word in mind. Sometimes you need more than one key word to find what you need. Notice the key words in these questions:

How was a cure for **smallpox** discovered?
How is a meteor different from a **comet?**
What is the size of the **planet Mars?**

Guide word When you have a key word in mind and have chosen the correct volume, guide words in dark type at the tops of the pages will help you locate the topic. Look at the left-hand page below. The guide word shown at the top of the page directs you to the first article on the page. The guide word shown at the top of a right-hand page will direct you to the last article on that page.

APRIL

APRIL is the fourth month of the year. It is named for *Aprilis*, a Latin word meaning *to open*. April was the second month in an early Roman calendar, but it became the fourth month when Julius Caesar established the Julian calendar in 46 B.C.

In the Temperate Zone of the Northern Hemisphere, the appearance of the outdoor world usually changes more in April than in any other month of the year. The last of the ice and snow disappears, grass grows green, the Southern Hemisphere, people are enjoying mild autumn days.

Activities. April is mainly a sowing time on many northern farms. In some parts of the world, April is a harvest time for grain. The professional baseball season begins in the United States. Amateurs in many other sports are lured out of doors with the first warm days. Householders begin their spring cleaning and start work on their gardens and lawns.

Special Days. On the first day of April, children and grown-ups play jokes on one another. Arbor Day is a

---

Cross-reference Sometimes when you locate a topic, you will find that there is no article—only a **cross-reference.** This tells you to look under another topic to find the information you want. For example, you may see this cross-reference after the topic CARVING: *See* SCULPTURE; WOOD CARVING. You would look up either or both topics to learn about carving.

You also may find a cross-reference at the end of an encyclopedia article. The reference tells you where to find more information. At the end of an article about milk, this cross-reference might appear: *See also* BUTTER; CHEESE; YOGURT.

Practice

A. Which volume of the pictured encyclopedia would contain the answer to each question below? Write the letters of the volume you would choose. You may find some answers in two volumes.

1. Where is New Zealand?
2. How do scientists measure calories in foods?
3. How is an artery different from a vein?
4. Who was Joseph Haydn?
5. Why is pottery baked in an oven?
6. How do dolphins breathe?
7. When was the typewriter invented, and who invented it?
8. How do bees produce honey?
9. What is the North Star?
10. What is the capital of South Dakota?
11. How long does a butterfly remain in a cocoon?
12. Where is Mount Whitney?

B. Use an encyclopedia to find answers to any five of the questions above.

Parts of a Book: The Front

The first few pages of a book contain information that may be important to you.

Title page The first page of a book is called the title page. It tells you the title of the book, the name of the author, and the name and location of the company that published the book.

- What is the title of the book below? Who are the authors?

Copyright page Every book includes a copyright page, which is usually on the back of the title page. The copyright notice tells the year in which the book was published. Check the copyright date when you write a research report. You would want to use the most up-to-date facts in your report.

TITLE PAGE

COPYRIGHT PAGE

Table of contents A nonfiction book—and some fiction books—has a table of contents, which lists the section or chapter titles and their page numbers. The table of contents helps you to locate chapters and find out what topics are discussed in a book. Look at the table of contents on the next page.

- What is the title of Chapter 4? On what page does it begin? What three topics does it include?

CONTENTS

Preface Some books contain a preface, a statement usually made by the book's author. The preface may introduce the book, explain its purpose, or give background information about how it was written.

Practice

Write answers to the following questions, using the table of contents shown above.

1. Which chapter tells about wildflowers?
2. On which page would you begin reading about the legends of the aborigines?
3. In which chapter can you read about the koala?
4. On which page would you begin reading about insect-eating plants?
5. What three natural wonders are discussed in the book?
6. On which page does Chapter 3 begin?

STUDY STRATEGIES

Parts of a Book: The Back

Sometimes special sections—such as an index, a glossary, or an appendix—are included in the back of a nonfiction book.

Index The alphabetical list of specific topics covered in a book is called an *index*. The index below is for a book about Australia.

INDEX

Aborigines, 7–30; art, 13, 18–20; ceremonies, 13–15, 19; dwellings, 12–13; hunting and fishing, 15–18; language, 18; legends, 25–30, 84

Acacias. *See* Wattle trees.

Alexandria Station, 106

Alice Springs, 86, 97

Archer fish, 64, 67

Australian Alps, 109–112; animals, 112; hydroelectric power, 110–111; skiing, 109–110

Ayers Rock, 86–89

Bald Head, 35

Baobab tree, 79

Barking lizard, 51

Barking worms. *See* Earthworms.

Bendigo, 95. *See also* Mining.

Canberra, 18

Cassowary, 45

Clams, 66

Cockatoos. *See* Parrots.

Cook, James, 10, 81, 116; discovery of New South Wales, 10; members of his crew, 81, 116

Crocodiles, 68–70

Death adder, 54

Dingo, 34–35; "Dingo Fence," 35

Dragon lizard. *See* Frilled lizard.

Dunk Island, 71

Dunstan, Jack, 94. *See also* Dunstan's Stone.

Dunstan's Stone, 103

Earthworms, 55

Elastic lizard, 51

Emu, 42–45; care of young, 44–45

The words printed farthest to the left in each column are called **main topics.** They name the people, animals, places, things, and events covered in the book. If the main topic is a person, the last name is listed first.

• On what pages is James Cook discussed?

After some main topics, you will find **subtopics** listed alphabetically. They tell what kind of information is given about the main topic.

• What subtopics follow the main topic *Australian Alps?*

Page numbers tell where to find information. If page numbers are given as 86–89, for example, the information appears on pages 86, 87, 88, and 89.

- On what pages are crocodiles discussed?

When you want specific information, think of a key word that names a topic. Then look for it in the index.

- What is the most specific key word in this question: *Why is the cassowary an unusual bird?*

In the index on page 460, find the main topic *Cockatoos.* This main topic is followed by the cross-reference, "*See* Parrots." This means that information about cockatoos is listed under the main topic *Parrots.*

The listing *Bendigo* shows another type of cross-reference. The words "*See also* Mining" tell you that more information about Bendigo appears on the pages about mining.

Glossary At the back of many books is a list of words from the book, along with their meanings. A glossary includes special words and terms that may be unfamiliar to readers.

Appendix Some books include an appendix. This special section contains additional information such as important documents, tables, charts, and maps. For example, in a book about United States history, you might find a copy of the Declaration of Independence in an appendix.

Practice

Using the sample index on page 460, write the numbers of the pages on which you might find answers to these questions.

1. What is a death adder?
2. When did James Cook discover New South Wales?
3. What are barking worms?
4. What did the early aborigines use to make paintings?
5. What is the "Dingo Fence"?

Skimming and Scanning

When you need information, you should not *always* read an article slowly and carefully. Sometimes it is better to skim or scan for information. These ways of reading help you to find quickly the facts that you need.

Skimming When you want an overview, or a general idea, of the important points in a piece of writing, skim the article.

Steps for Skimming

1. Read the title and any headings and captions.
2. Carefully read the first paragraph.
3. Read the first sentence of each of the other paragraphs. Look for key words as you read.
4. Carefully read the last paragraph of the article.

Scanning When you need specific information such as the answer to a question, scan the article.

Steps for Scanning

1. Think of key words to help you find the information you need. (If you want to know how many people live in Alaska, look for such words as *population* or *residents*.)
2. Next, look for typographic aids, such as words in dark or slanted type, numerals, and proper nouns. (For the names of cities, look for words that begin with capital letters.)
3. When you find the information that you need, read slowly and carefully to get the facts right.

Practice

A. Skim the article "A Horse's Body" on pages 380–382. Then write a complete sentence, stating the main idea.
B. Scan the article "Before Misty" on pages 374–379 to answer the following questions. Write your answers.
1. What was the name of the ship that carried the ponies?
2. How many ponies survived the storm?
3. Where is Assateague Beach?

Summarizing

When you are reading or studying, you may want to summarize to help you remember key points. A summary includes only the most important information from an article or a story.

Summarizing an article Suppose that you have read a lengthy article about how raisins are made. Writing a summary like the one shown below can help you understand and remember the steps in the process. Read the summary about raisins.

> Grapes go through several steps to become raisins. First, harvested grapes are dried in the sun for ten to fifteen days. Then the fruit is stacked, dried again, and stored to retain moisture. At a packing house, stems are removed and the raisins are washed. The fruit is then packaged for shipment to stores.

Notice that this summary begins with a clear statement of the main idea. The other sentences give details that support this main idea. The following guidelines should help you to write your own summary of an article.

Guidelines for Summarizing an Article

1. State the main idea of the article clearly and briefly.
2. Look for key words and important names, dates, and places from the article.
3. Use these facts to write sentences that support the main idea.
4. Be sure to explain events or steps in the correct order.
5. Use as few words as possible. Put the facts into your own words without changing the meaning of what you have read.

Summarizing a story When summarizing a story, briefly retell what happens, making sure to include all the important characters and events. Read the following summary of "Wol Walks on Water," which appears on pages 54–57.

> During summer holidays, three boys often rode their bikes to a secret cave. They took along their pet owls, Wol and Weeps, and their dogs, Mutt and Rex. The boys liked to play in a wonderfully muddy swimming spot near the cave. Usually, Wol would watch from a perch in the Hanging Tree and get quite excited as the boys played below. On this day, though, Wol wanted to be closer. He flew from his perch to the water's edge. Wol had never been this close to water before, except in his drinking bowl. Instead of flying across the water to the boys on the sand bar, Wol started to walk across. Of course, he splashed right in and came up wet, muddy, and embarrassed. With hurt feelings and feathers too wet for flying, Wol gallumphed home through the woods.

Notice that this summary includes the main events and characters. It also explains the characters' feelings and actions. Use these guidelines when you summarize a story.

Guidelines for Summarizing a Story

1. Decide what is the most important feature of the story. If it is a mystery, you might focus on plot. If the story is about friendship, you might focus on characters.
2. Write clear, brief sentences stating the most important details. Include important names, dates, and places from the story.
3. Be sure to give enough information so that the summary makes sense.
4. To catch the tone or mood of the story, describe a specific character's actions or give a direct quotation.

Practice

A. Reread "A Horse's Body" on pages 380–382. Write a summary of the article. Try to use no more than six sentences.
B. Reread "The Needle in the Haystack" on pages 194–200. Write a summary of the story, using no more than seven sentences.

Tables

Nonfiction articles sometimes contain facts and figures in tables or charts.

Table chart Facts can be shown on tables or charts in easy-to-read rows, columns, and boxes. The table below shows the average, or typical, temperatures of some cities in the United States.

Average Temperatures in U.S. Cities

	January	July
Chicago, Illinois	24°F (−4°C)	75°F (24°C)
Denver, Colorado	30°F (−1°C)	73°F (23°C)
Fairbanks, Alaska	−12°F (−24°C)	61°F (16°C)
Honolulu, Hawaii	72°F (22°C)	80°F (27°C)
New York, New York	32°F (0°C)	77°F (25°C)
Phoenix, Arizona	51°F (11°C)	91°F (33°C)
Portland, Oregon	38°F (3°C)	67°F (19°C)
San Diego, California	55°F (13°C)	70°F (21°C)

This table has captions across the top and along the left side. The top captions are *January* and *July*. The side captions name the eight cities.

The lines that go across are called rows. The lines that go up and down are called columns.

- What is the average January temperature in Chicago?
- What is the average July temperature in Denver?

Practice

Use the temperature table to answer these questions.

1. Which city has the coldest July temperature?
2. Which city has the warmest July temperature?
3. Which city is cooler in the summer—Denver or Portland?
4. Which cities average below 32°F in January?
5. Which cities average above 50°F in January?

Graphs

A graph is another type of drawing that shows facts and figures in an easy-to-read form.

Bar graph The bar graph below shows how long several types of zoo animals are expected to live. Like the table on page 465, this graph has captions. Notice that ages in years are shown by lines that go up the entire length of the graph. You can also use the graph to compare the number of years that the different animals are expected to live.

To figure out how long an animal lives, look where a bar meets a number line.

• How long may an elephant live?

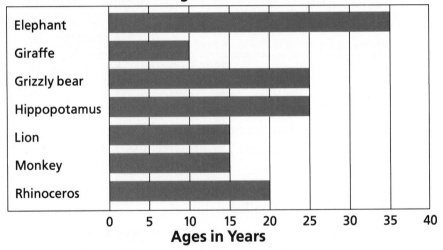

How Long Zoo Animals Live

Practice

Use the zoo animal bar graph to answer these questions.

1. Which animal has the shortest life?
2. How long does a rhinoceros live?
3. Which animals live longer than a rhinoceros?
4. Which animal has the longest life?
5. Which animals live only 15 years?
6. Which animal lives longer—a giraffe or a lion?

Maps

Some writing is easier to understand when accompanied by a graphic aid. A graphic aid is a drawing or a list that clearly shows specific information.

A map is a drawing or chart of all or part of the earth's surface including features such as mountains, rivers, boundaries, and cities. Maps show how the places mentioned in your reading relate to one another.

The map below could serve as a graphic aid for the story "Wol Walks on Water" by Farley Mowat. The map shows the province of Saskatchewan in Canada. Mowat lived in the town of Saskatoon. Find Saskatoon on the map.

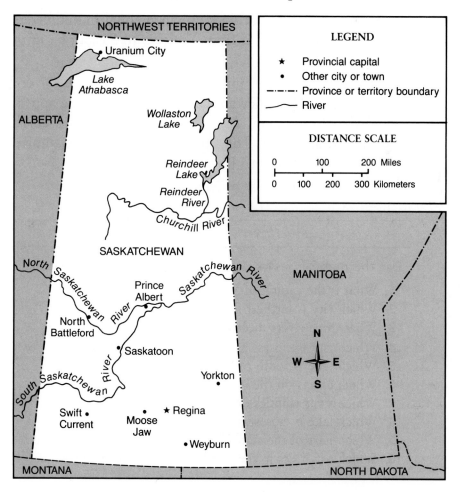

Legend Every map has a legend, which usually appears in a box near the map. The legend explains the map's *symbols,* the marks that stand for various things. For example, a star shows the provincial capital. Other symbols on this map's legend show other cities and towns, boundaries, and rivers.

• What symbol shows the boundary of Saskatchewan?

Distance scale Below the legend is a distance scale. It shows how a particular distance on the map relates to real distance in miles or kilometers. One inch on the Saskatchewan map is equal to about two hundred miles on the earth's surface.

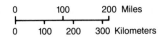

• On this map, what does one inch equal in kilometers?
• About how far is it from Yorkton to Saskatoon in miles? in kilometers?

Compass rose Another important part of a map is the compass rose. On the Saskatchewan map, the compass rose appears in the lower right section. Arrows show the directions *north, south, east,* and *west.* They help you to see, for example, that Regina is *east* of Moose Jaw.

• What town is *west* of Moose Jaw?

Practice

Use the map of Saskatchewan to answer these questions.

1. What is the capital of Saskatchewan?
2. Which city is farthest north?
3. What three rivers meet near the city of Prince Albert?
4. Which city is closest to the southern boundary?
5. Which lake is south of Wollaston Lake?
6. Which city is on the North Saskatchewan River?
7. Which river empties out of Reindeer Lake?
8. Which lake is closest to the northern boundary?
9. Which part of the state has the largest number of towns?
10. Which town lies in the southeast corner of the province?

Diagrams

A diagram shows how something is put together or how it works. To understand a diagram fully, read the captions and all the labels naming the various parts.

Crown

Ear tufts, or horns

Facial disk

Beak

Throat collar

Wing

Talons

HORNED OWL

If a diagram uses unfamiliar words, check the accompanying text for definitions. If you found this owl diagram in a book and did not understand the term *facial disk*, you would read the paragraphs near the diagram. You might discover that a facial disk is the ring of short feathers surrounding the owl's eyes.

Practice

Using the diagram of an owl, write answers to these questions.

1. What are the feathers around the eyes called?
2. Why is this creature called a horned owl?
3. What does an owl use to grasp a tree branch?
4. What is the top of the owl's head called?
5. What are the feathers around the owl's neck called?

Test-taking Tips

Follow the steps below to prepare properly for a test.

Guidelines for Preparing for a Test

As you study:

1. Look through your textbook for important headings, words, phrases, and summaries.
2. Answer the end-of-chapter questions in your textbook.
3. Reread any notes you have taken.
4. Look over past assignments and quizzes.
5. Ask questions about anything you do not understand.
6. Get plenty of rest the night before the test.
7. On the day of the test, bring pens, pencils, or other materials that you may need.

As you begin the test:

1. Listen closely to oral directions.
2. Read and reread all printed directions.
3. Ask for an explanation if you do not understand the directions.

Read the sample directions below.

> DIRECTION A: After each sentence, write *T* if the statement is true and *F* if it is false.
>
> DIRECTION B: Complete each sentence by filling in the blank with a word from the box.

Direction A tells you to write only the letter *T* or *F*.

- Where should these letters be placed?
- In Direction B, how do you complete each sentence?

Always read sample items carefully.

> In each sentence below, cross out the incorrect word. Then write the correct word in the blank.
> Example: The color of a stop light is ~~green.~~ <u>red</u>

- In this sample, where should the correct word be written?

Once you understand the directions, you are ready to start the test. Follow these guidelines.

Guidelines for Taking a Test

1. Look quickly over the whole test, noticing the number and types of questions.
2. Complete the questions you know you can answer correctly. If there are answer choices, read them all.
3. Next, answer the more difficult questions. Write the answer that makes the most sense for each item.
4. Finally, work on the hardest questions. If you do not understand a question, ask for an explanation. Then write the best answer you can. If you run out of time, you may have to skip one or two questions.
5. When you have finished, check your work. Ask yourself:
   Did I write my name on the test?
   Did I follow the directions carefully?
   Did I answer all the questions? Have I left out any?
   Did I mark or write my answers clearly?

Practice

Read the sentences below. Then write only the sentences that give helpful tips for taking a test.

1. Before the test, reread your entire textbook.
2. While studying, look over past quizzes.
3. Borrow a pen or a pencil from a classmate.
4. Read the directions as quickly as possible.
5. Ask the teacher to explain a direction or a question that is unclear.
6. Read examples only if you don't understand the directions.
7. Record your answers in the proper place.
8. If there are several answer choices, read them all before selecting one.
9. Check a watch or a clock while you are working.
10. Answer the easiest questions first.
11. If a question is difficult, do not try to answer it.
12. Check all your answers before handing in the test.

■ LISTENING AND SPEAKING STRATEGIES ■

How to Listen

To understand what a speaker is saying, you must listen actively. Listen for the speaker's purpose, main idea, supporting details, and organization. Use these guidelines.

Guidelines for Keeping TRACK

T = Think!
Think about what the speaker is saying. Do you understand it? If not, ask questions.

R = Review!
In your mind, go over what the speaker has said. What are the main points? If you do not remember them, find out what they are. Ask questions if anything is not clear.

A = Attention!
Listen carefully. Listen for the main points and important words. Do you have questions to ask?

C = Concentrate!
Keep your mind on what the speaker is saying. Do not let yourself think about other subjects and sounds.

K = Keep up!
Keep up with the speaker. Do not let yourself get lost.

Guidelines for Listening for the Speaker's Purpose

1. Ask yourself: Does the speaker want to inform? entertain? persuade? Knowing the speaker's purpose will help you understand what the speaker is saying.
2. Listen for statements beginning *My purpose is . . .* , *I want to . . .* , *I hope you will . . .* , *I intend to . . .* .
3. Pay attention to the speaker's tone. Is it serious? light? friendly? matter of fact? demanding?

Guidelines for Listening for Information

1. Why are you listening—to find out how to do an assignment? how the earth revolves? Keep in mind the kind of information you want. You will find it more easily.
2. Do not try to remember everything. Pick out key facts.
3. Listen and watch for clues to key points. The speaker may gesture, pause, or get louder or softer. Listen for word signals such as *important, furthermore, above all.*
4. You may want to take notes. Write only key information.

Guidelines for Listening for the Main Idea

1. Start listening early for a statement about the main idea.
2. Listen for signals such as *I would like to tell you about. . .*
3. In your mind, try to summarize the main idea in a sentence.

Guidelines for Listening for Details

1. Determine the main idea. Listen for details that support it.
2. Listen for signals such as *for example, second, in addition.*
3. Do not try to remember every detail.

Guidelines for Listening for Logical Organization

1. Is the purpose to instruct? Instructions usually use step-by-step order. Listen for signals such as *first, next.*
2. Is the purpose to describe? Descriptions usually use spatial order. Listen for signals such as *near, on the left.*
3. Is the purpose to persuade? Persuasion often uses order of importance. Listen for signals such as *most important.*

Practice

A. Listen to a passage. Then tell a partner what you learned.

B. Listen to another passage. Picture what you hear. Draw it.

LISTENING AND SPEAKING STRATEGIES

How to Make Introductions

If you are with a friend and your cousin comes along, how will you introduce them? You might say something like this.

> "Leo, this is my cousin Julia. Julia, this is my friend Leo. We're in the same class at school."

Suppose you and Leo meet your uncle. What will you say?

> "Uncle Harry, I'd like you to meet my friend Leo. Leo's in my class at school. Leo, this is my uncle, Mr. Chen."

• How do the two introductions differ?

When you introduce people, be polite and offer some information.

Guidelines for Making Introductions

1. Look at the people you are introducing.
2. Say each person's name clearly. Use the full name if you know it.

> "Julio, this is Lisa Berger. Lisa, this is Julio Gomez."

3. Tell something interesting about each person.

> "Lisa lives on our street, Pedro. Lisa, Pedro just moved into the neighborhood."

4. When you introduce a younger person to an adult, always speak to the adult first.

> "Mom, this is Pedro Gomez. His family just moved into the red house on the corner. Pedro, this is my mother, Mrs. Mayo."

Practice

Work with two partners. Take turns making introductions. First, use real names. Then make up names and histories for each other.

How to Explain a Process

When you explain how something works or how something is done, you are explaining a **process**. A process is made up of steps that follow a certain order. Here are some examples of processes.

how a snowflake forms
how a plant grows
how a bicycle works

how a volcano erupts
how a ship is built
how a refrigerator works

Read this explanation of the process of pottery making.

Have you ever watched potters at work? Here is what they usually do. First they press and squeeze some clay to make it soft and smooth. Then they shape it. Some potters pinch the clay into shape. Others roll it into strips, which they wind on top of one another. Most potters, however, use a *potter's wheel*. With their hands, they shape the clay as it turns on the wheel. To make decorations, they may press their fingers into the clay or scratch lines into it. They may also brush or spray on colored designs. Finally, they bake the pottery in a very hot oven, a *kiln*. Out comes a finished piece of pottery.

- What are the main steps in making pottery?

Guidelines for Explaining a Process

1. Think about your audience. What do they already know? What do they need to be told?
2. Begin by telling what process you are going to explain.
3. Explain the steps in order. Show how one leads to another.
4. Use clear, exact language.
5. Encourage your audience to ask questions.

Practice

What process do you know well? Explain it to a partner. Was your explanation clear enough so that your partner can repeat it?

How to Have a Discussion

When you and your friends talk together to decide how to spend a free afternoon, you are having a discussion. A discussion is a talk about a specific topic. Groups and committees also hold discussions to consider a particular problem.

Follow these guidelines for taking part in a discussion.

Guidelines for Discussing

1. Stick to the topic of the discussion.
2. Listen carefully to what others say.
3. Ask questions if something is not clear to you.
4. Take part in the discussion. Make comments that keep to the topic. Give reasons for your opinions.
5. Speak clearly so that everyone can hear you.
6. Be polite. Don't interrupt or try to talk at the same time as someone else. Respect the opinions of others.

Now read this example of how *not* to have a discussion. The students are talking about a story they have read.

DAVID: What do you think the theme of the story was?

ABIGAIL: Poor people make better rulers than rich ones.

MOLLY: That's silly. It was that good rulers are hard to find.

DAVID: Why do you think that's it?

MOLLY: Uh, I don't know . . . I think . . .

ABIGAIL: What? You're mumbling.

- Which guidelines were not followed?
- How would you change the discussion to follow them?

Practice

Team up with some of your classmates to discuss one of the following topics. Follow the guidelines.

1. If your class made a mural, what would it look like?
2. If you could create a park, what would it be like?
3. What activities would you plan for a beautiful spring day?

How to Give a Talk

Has something funny or unusual happened to you? Have you come across some interesting information? Is there something you would like to persuade others about? Give a talk! Be sure to keep your purpose and audience in mind. Use these guidelines to help you prepare.

Guidelines for Giving a Talk

1. Prepare your talk well. Know what you want to say about your subject and the order in which you will present your ideas. Do any necessary research.
2. You may want to make notes on cards or slips of paper. Do not write out your whole talk. Your notes should include key words to help you remember the sequence of your ideas. Glance at your notes only as needed.
3. If pictures or illustrations will help your talk, use them.
4. Speak clearly. Keep your voice at an even pace and at a level that can be heard by everyone in your audience. Speak with expression and show enthusiasm.
5. As you speak, look at the people in your audience. Try to make eye contact with several people.
6. Practice your talk before you give it. Ask a friend or family member to listen and make helpful comments. Practice using any notes or pictures. Try to relax and enjoy the experience!

Practice

A. Prepare a talk about a funny experience that you have had, information that interests you, or an opinion that is important to you. Whether your purpose is to entertain, to inform, or to persuade, remember to keep your audience in mind. Use the guidelines above.
B. Practice your talk with a partner. Then present it to a group of three or four students.

LISTENING AND SPEAKING STRATEGIES

How to Adapt Language

You change the way you speak to fit your audience. Read this passage from a letter in the story "Sarah, Plain and Tall." The letter was written by grown-up Sarah to little Caleb.

> My cat's name is Seal. . . . She is glad that Lottie and Nick send their greetings. She likes dogs most of the time. She says their footprints are much larger than hers (which she is enclosing in return).
>
> *from "Sarah, Plain and Tall" by Patricia MacLachlan*

Sarah's choice of *how* to say things fits her reader. To communicate with Caleb, she uses words that he can understand. Her choice of *what* things to say also fits her reader.

You often change how you say things to fit your purpose, even when your listener remains the same. Sometimes you want to inform, entertain, or persuade. Read these examples.

> **1.** "Mr. Williams, I am very interested in the job at your art gallery. You can be confident that I would be careful, thorough, and dependable."
>
> **2.** "Mr. Williams, the funniest thing happened in art class today! You won't believe it! I had just finished a drawing when . . ."

- What is the speaker's purpose in each example?
- How does the language in each suit the speaker's purpose?

These guidelines will help you be an effective speaker.

Guidelines for Adapting Language

1. Keep your audience and purpose in mind.
2. Choose language that suits both.

Practice

Write your side of a conversation in which you try to persuade your uncle to take you to a movie. Then persuade a friend.

How to Recognize Propaganda

"Everyone who's anyone has a ZK-750!" "Wanda Cool says, 'Stay a step ahead. Wear Bebop sneakers!'" You hear and read advertisements like these every day. Should you do what they suggest? Advertisements often use **propaganda techniques** to try to persuade you. Learn to recognize these techniques so that you can make up your own mind about what you hear and read.

1. **Overgeneralization** This technique makes a general statement about something, based on only a few facts. Read the example below.

   All the people in Maine fish for a living. In fact, ten people we asked said that they fish for a living.

   On how many "facts" is this generalization based? If only ten Maine workers were asked about their jobs, that would not be enough to back up a statement about "all" people in Maine. Before you let such a statement persuade you, be sure to carefully examine "facts" that seem to support it. Ask yourself if these facts give enough proof to make such a statement, or if it is an overgeneralization.

2. **Testimonial** This technique uses a celebrity or an expert to make a statement supporting a product. Read the example below.

   "The best fishing rod is Catch-a-Lot. I won't leave home without it!" says Alexander, the famous cat.

   Here you are led to believe that Catch-a-Lot is the best fishing rod on the market simply because a famous cat like Alexander recommends it. Are you like Alexander? Will you automatically like what he likes? Ask yourself why the product is good and whether or not it is right for *you*.

3. Bandwagon   This technique pressures you to do something because "everyone else" is doing it. Read the example below.

> *A sign says, "Vote with the people who know. Everyone in town wants Ted Logan to head the Harbor Committee."*

Is everyone in town *really* voting for Ted Logan? You cannot know because you are not given any proof. Even if the statement were true, should you vote for Ted Logan just because everyone else does?

4. Transfer   This technique associates a celebrity with a product. Its aim is to have you transfer your admiration for the celebrity onto the product. Unlike the person in the testimonial, however, the celebrity here makes no statement supporting the product. Look at the example below.

The advertiser wants you to think that Purrl, the millionaire cat, likes to fish in a Posh Canoe and that you will be like Purrl if you buy one. Judge a product for its own value, not because someone well known and successful uses it.

Practice

Divide your paper into four columns labeled *Overgeneralization*, *Testimonial*, *Bandwagon*, and *Transfer*. Listen as your teacher reads six ads, and decide which propaganda technique each one uses. Write the number of the ad in the correct column.

How to Solve Problems

How can you earn money to buy your sister a present? What should you do for the talent show? You face problems like these every day. Use these five steps to find solutions.

How to Solve a Problem

1. **Define the problem.** State the problem clearly.
2. **Consider the possible solutions.** Brainstorm different ways to solve the problem and make a list of your ideas.
3. **Examine possible solutions.** Look at all the information you have for each solution.
4. **Decide on a solution.** Choose the best solution.
5. **Carry out the solution.** Put your solution to work.

A fifth-grade student named Mario decided to buy a guinea pig and write a report on its habits for his science project, which was due in two weeks. After a few days, Mario developed an allergy to the guinea pig. By the end of the week, he was sneezing uncontrollably whenever he was near it.

Mario returned the guinea pig to the pet store. However, he still had to complete a science project. Mario and his class used the five steps to find a solution.

1. **Define the problem.** The class defined the problem: Mario needed an idea for a project that he could complete in one week and that would make use of the work he had done.
2. **Consider possible solutions.** The class discussed the problem and brainstormed these possible solutions.
   a. Mario could use the information he collected during the first week to write his report.
   b. He could find an animal that he is not allergic to and compare its habits to the guinea pig's habits.
   c. He could learn about guinea pigs from other sources, and add his findings to the information he already has.
   d. He could use his experience with the guinea pig to write a report on allergies.

3. **Examine possible solutions.** The class discussed how each solution might work.

   a. Mario could write a report from the information he has, but his report would not be thorough.

   b. Comparing two animals would use the information he has, but finding the right animal might take too long.

   c. Adding information from other sources would make use of the work he has done and might result in an even more interesting report.

   d. If Mario wrote on allergies, he would have to throw out all the work he had done and complete an entirely new project in just one week.

4. **Decide on a solution.** The class decided that the third solution was the best choice because it would make the best use of Mario's time and his past work. In addition, the new project might be better than the original one.

5. **Carry out the solution.** Mario gathered information from the library, the pet store owner, and the veterinarian on the habits of guinea pigs and on their diseases. He combined this information with his own observations and successfully completed his project.

Practice

A. You and your friends are hiking through the woods. When it is time to start home, you take a trail that looks familiar. After an hour, the trail ends abruptly in a tangle of undergrowth. You are lost. How can you get home? As a group, use the five steps to find a solution to your problem.

B. As a class or in small groups, use the five steps to solve one or more of these problems.

   1. On the same Sunday, your cousin in the next town is having a birthday party, and your class is having its final picnic. Which event will you attend?

   2. Your favorite TV show is on at the same time as some special programs that other members of your family want to see. What show will be watched?

How to Classify

Have you ever played a game called "Families"? It is known by different names, but it is played all over the world. The object is to see who can name the most things that belong in the same "family." The family, or **category**, can be almost anything, such as sports cars or green vegetables or outdoor events.

When you group together similar things or events, you **classify** them. For example, you might classify animals as shown below.

Meat Eaters	dogs, lions, bats, leopards, lizards, seals, whales, bears, spiders, snakes, anteaters, rats
Plant Eaters	chickens, elephants, giraffes, squirrels, cows, horses, goats, pandas, gorillas, bears, rats

• Which animal or animals fit in both categories?

There is usually more than one way to classify things. For example, the animals above can also be classified this way.

Solid Color	dogs, lions, bats, seals, whales, bears, goats, spiders, anteaters, rats, chickens, elephants, squirrels, cows, horses, gorillas, hippopotamuses
Patterned	dogs, leopards, lizards, spiders, snakes, chickens, giraffes, cows, horses, goats, pandas

• Which animals fit in both categories?
• What other categories could you use to classify the animals?

You can classify just about anything, including events. Look at the events below. Notice how they are grouped together.

Outdoor	soccer game, tennis match, parade, picnic, marathon
Indoor	birthday party, spelling bee, play, concert, chess tournament

• Which events could fit in both categories?

This list of events can be classified in other ways. Here is one way.

Competition	soccer game, tennis match, marathon, spelling bee, chess tournament
Amusement	parade, picnic, birthday party, play, concert

• What other categories can you think of?

Classifying is important when you want to organize things. For example, books in the library are classified, and so are groceries in the supermarket. Otherwise, the items would be very difficult to find. Here are some questions to ask yourself when you want to classify items of any kind.

Guidelines for Classifying

1. **What kinds of items are they?** For example, are they things that grow? events you celebrate? items you use in writing?
2. **What are their features?** What is their shape? their color? their size? When do they occur? Are they helpful? dangerous? Do they wiggle? Are they rare? common?
3. **What features do some items have in common?** Are any the same color? Are any found in the same place? Do any occur at the same time of year?
4. **Which items share features?** Group together these items. Remember that some items may fall into more than one category. For example, one kind of dog might be both intelligent and gentle.

Practice

A. With a partner, list as many items of clothing as you can think of. Then classify the items as *Clothing for Cold Weather* and *Clothing for Hot Weather*. Did you list any items in both categories?
B. With a partner, list as many kinds of celebrations as you can think of. Then decide how to classify them. Finally, think of another way to classify the same events.

How to Draw Conclusions

If you wake up in a bright room, do you immediately think that morning has come? Before you draw this **conclusion,** you need more information. Is the light on? Is the sun shining?

Read about Leon's conclusion and decide whether you agree.

> Leon came home from school, hungry as usual, and walked into the kitchen. To his surprise, he almost kicked over a bowl of water on the floor. Next to it stood another bowl, with some crumbs in it. He also discovered a can of dog food on the counter and a leash hanging from one of the chairs.
>
> "Wow!" he exclaimed. "Mom and Dad have finally gotten me a dog!"

- What conclusion did Leon draw? Why?
- What other conclusion could Leon draw?
- Did he need more information? If so, what?

You draw conclusions all the time. For example, you conclude that if cars are approaching, it is not safe to cross the street.

Guidelines for Drawing Conclusions

1. Look carefully at all the available information.
2. Ask yourself whether you have all the information you need.
3. Use the information to draw a conclusion.
4. Ask yourself whether your conclusion makes sense.

Practice

Read the paragraph below. What conclusion would you draw? Why? What other information would be useful?

On your birthday, your friends are too busy to see you. As you sit on your porch, several walk by. You wave, but they ignore you. Suddenly they turn around and walk smiling toward you.

THINKING STRATEGIES

Sound Words

Some of the words in the English language imitate sounds. These words are called **sound words**.

The sound words *bang* and *crash* describe the loud, sudden noise of thunder. The word *murmur* describes a low, soft noise that keeps going.

Many English words imitate noises made by animals. The word *chirp* imitates the short, high sound made by a small bird or a cricket.

Sound Words

bang	clatter	hiss	neigh	smash
beep	crack	honk	purr	splash
blast	crunch	hum	quack	squeal
buzz	gobble	meow	rip	tick
clang	growl	moo	roar	zip

Practice

Write a sound word for each description below.

1. the sound made by a turkey
2. the sound of a clock
3. the loud, deep sound of a lion
4. the sound of an angry dog
5. the sound of a large bell
6. the sound made by a bee

Words That Come from Names

Some of the words in the English language come from the names of people and places. Your dictionary gives information about the origin of such words.

Word	Meaning	Named for
tarantula	large, hairy spider	Taranto, a town in Italy where tarantulas are found
sousaphone	musical instrument	John Philip Sousa, an American composer who invented the sousaphone
rugby	game	Rugby School, England, where rugby was invented

Practice

Write the name from this list that matches each numbered item below. Then write the word that comes from that name. Use your dictionary to check the words.

a. Canary Islands   **c.** Cheddar   **e.** R. J. L. Guppy
b. Amelia Bloomer   **d.** Earl of Sandwich

1. This Englishman liked to eat meat between slices of bread.
2. Many yellow songbirds live on these Spanish islands.
3. This editor's name was given to her long, baggy trousers.
4. A firm cheese was first made in this English village.
5. This man brought to England a kind of small tropical fish.

Homographs

Some words are spelled the same but have different meanings and histories. These words are called **homographs**. Homographs usually appear as separate entries in a dictionary.

The two brothers dug a well in their yard.

They worked well together.

In the first sentence, the noun *well* comes from a word that means "spring of water." In the second sentence, the adverb *well* comes from a word that means "in a good manner."

Some homographs are also pronounced differently: |wĭnd|, |wīnd|.

The wind is strong today.

Does this path wind through the hills?

Practice

Write a meaning for each underlined homograph. You should have twelve meanings in all. You may use your dictionary to help you.

1. My last pair of shoes did not last very long.
2. Use the pen to write about the animals in the pen.
3. Does changing a tire usually tire you?
4. That was not a dove that dove into the water.
5. The nurse wound a bandage around the wound.
6. What did you mean by the mean remark?

Idioms

You have probably heard people use the expression *raining cats and dogs*. This expression is called an idiom. An **idiom** is a phrase that has a special meaning as a whole. The meaning of an idiom is different from the meanings of its separate words. The idiom *raining cats and dogs* does not mean that cats and dogs are falling from the sky. It means "raining heavily."

Sometimes the context of an idiom makes its meaning clear. Can you figure out the meaning of this idiom?

> Fred is talking through his hat when he says that he can spell every word in the English language.

Fred cannot possibly spell every word in the English language. What we really mean is that he is talking nonsense.

Practice

Write a word or a phrase from the box of words to replace each underlined idiom.

living well	is busy	make sense	from memory

1. Stan <u>has his hands full</u>. He can't take on more work.
2. We all read our speeches, but Nan knew hers <u>by heart</u>.
3. I can't <u>make heads or tails</u> of this story.
4. Ted is <u>in clover</u>. He has a new house and a new car.

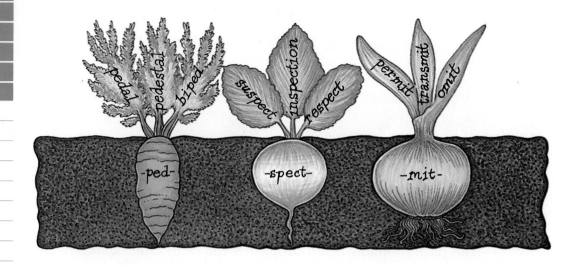

Word Roots

You can often figure out the meaning of an unfamiliar word by looking at its parts. Prefixes, suffixes, and base words are all parts of words. Sometimes the main part of a word is called a **word root.** A word root has a special meaning but usually cannot stand alone as a word.

Word Root	Meaning	Example
-port-	to carry	**port**able
-spect-	to look or see	in**spect**
-ped-	foot	**ped**al
-loc-	to place	**loc**al
-mit-	to send	trans**mit**
-ject-	to throw	re**ject**

Practice

Write the word root in each word. Then write the meaning of each word. You may use your dictionary.

1. project
2. pedestrian
3. submit
4. transport
5. admit
6. porter
7. location
8. eject
9. import
10. spectacle
11. biped
12. spectator

SENTENCE MAPPING: DIAGRAMING

A diagram of a sentence is a set of lines that show how the words of that sentence are related. You will begin by diagraming the most important words in the sentence. In beginning lessons, sentences contain words that you do not yet know how to diagram. Work only with the words that you are asked to diagram. You will learn about the others as you work through the lessons.

Simple Subjects and Simple Predicates (pp. 20–23)

The simple subject and the simple predicate are written on a horizontal line called the **base line**. The simple subject is separated from the simple predicate by a vertical line that cuts through the horizontal line.

Find the simple subject and the simple predicate in the sentence below.

Wheat has lost its Number 1 place.

Study this diagram of the simple subject and the simple predicate from the sentence above.

Wheat	has lost

Find the simple subject and the simple predicate in this sentence. Note that the subject is *you* understood.

Guess the largest crop.

Study the diagram of this sentence.

(you)	Guess

Practice Diagram only the simple subjects and the simple predicates in these sentences.

1. Rice has gained first place.
2. It must have a hot, wet climate.

3. Name some rice exporters.

4. The biggest growers are in the Rice Bowl.

5. This area stretches from Japan to Indonesia.

Compound Subjects *(pp. 28–29)*

Each part of a compound subject is written on a separate horizontal line. The word *and* is written on a vertical dotted line that joins the horizontal lines.

Find the compound subject in this sentence.

India and China grow the most rice.

Study this diagram of the compound subject.

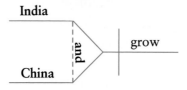

A compound subject can have more than two parts. Find the compound subject in this sentence.

Japan, Burma, and South Korea export more.

Study the diagram of this sentence. Note that the conjunction *and* is placed on the dotted line that connects the parts of the compound subject.

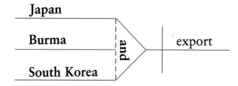

The word *or* can also join the parts of a compound subject.

Does Brazil or the United States grow more rice?

Although the sentence above is a question, it is diagramed just like a statement. Study the diagram.

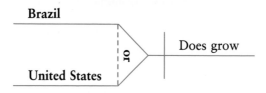

Practice Diagram the subjects and the predicate in each of these sentences.

1. Grains and potatoes have fed people for ages.
2. Rice and corn supplied Native Americans.
3. Quebec, the Midwest, and Louisiana had wild rice.
4. Europe and colonial America liked white rice better.
5. Is rice, potatoes, noodles, or tortillas your favorite food?

Compound Predicates *(pp. 30–31)*

Each part of a compound predicate is written on a separate horizontal line. The words *and, or,* and *but* are written on a vertical dotted line that joins the horizontal lines.

Find the compound predicate in this sentence.

We dressed and raced outside.

Study this diagram of the compound predicate.

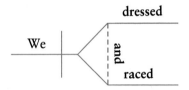

A sentence may have both a compound subject and a compound predicate.

My twin and I stumbled, slipped, and skidded along.

Study this diagram. Note where each *and* is placed.

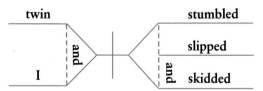

Practice Diagram only the subjects and the predicates in each sentence. Either or both may be compound.

1. Our yard sparkled and shone after the winter storm.
2. Each branch and twig had grown and had changed.
3. Pine needles looked and felt like diamond spikes.
4. Trees groaned and complained to the wind.
5. The heavy ice bent, broke, or cracked many branches.

Direct Objects *(pp. 144–145)*

A direct object is diagramed on the base line after the verb. A vertical line is placed between the verb and the direct object. Notice that it does not cut through the base line.

Find the direct object in this sentence.

Paul needed some new clothes.

A verb can have more than one direct object. Find the compound direct object in this sentence.

Yesterday he bought boots and a jacket.

Study this diagram of the compound direct object.

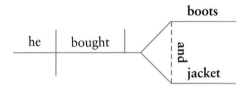

Each verb in a compound predicate can have its own direct object. Read this sentence. Find each verb and its direct object.

He liked the boots but disliked the jacket.

Study the diagram of the compound predicate and its separate direct objects.

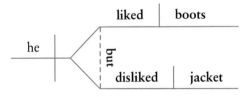

Practice Diagram only the subjects, the verbs, and the direct objects in these sentences.

1. First, Paul found boots.
2. Then he saw a red wool jacket.
3. It had a hood and yarn cuffs.
4. Paul paid half and charged the rest.
5. Later he changed his mind and returned the jacket.

Linking Verbs *(pp. 148–149)*

A linking verb is diagramed differently from an action verb. A slanting line, not a vertical one, follows a linking verb.

Remember, a linking verb joins the subject of a sentence with a word in the predicate. The word after the slanting line may name the subject or describe what it is like.

Find the linking verb in this sentence.

A cold is an insult.

Now study this diagram. Notice that the slanting line points back toward the subject but does not cut through the base line.

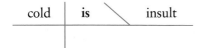

More than one word can follow a linking verb to describe the subject. Find the two words that describe the subject of this sentence.

Sally is miserable and cranky.

Study how these compound parts are diagramed.

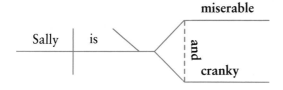

Practice Diagram each linking verb and the two parts of the sentence that it joins.

1. Meals are not fun for a cold sufferer.
2. Food was tasteless yesterday.
3. Today my nose is red.
4. I am feverish and dizzy.
5. This head cold is a real pain.

Adjectives *(pp. 222–223)*

Adjectives are diagramed on a slanting line right below the word that they describe.

Find the adjectives in this sentence.

I have brown, curly hair.

Study this diagram of the sentence.

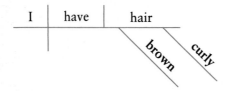

The words *a, an,* and *the* are diagramed like adjectives.

My older sister has a long ponytail.

Study this diagram of the sentence.

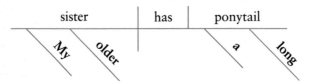

More than one adjective can describe the same word. Sometimes the word *and, or,* or *but* joins adjectives.

A long, braided, or straight hairstyle is not for me!

Note the position of the word *or* in this diagram.

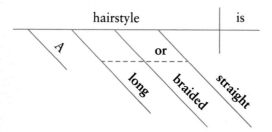

Practice Diagram all the words in these sentences.

1. This magazine has funny costumes.
2. See the blue, pink, and green wig!
3. That outfit wins the ugly prize.
4. I like that red satin cape.
5. You have unusual taste.

Adverbs *(pp. 412–413)*

Adverbs are diagramed in the same way that adjectives are. An adverb is placed on a slanting line below the word that it describes. Find the adverb and the verb that it describes in the following sentence.

We patiently watched the tadpoles.

Study this diagram of the sentence.

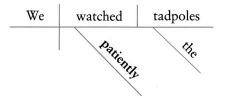

An adverb can appear anywhere in a sentence. It is not always right next to the word that it describes. Find the adverb in this sentence.

Soon the tadpoles became frogs.

Study this diagram of the sentence.

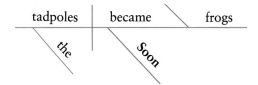

Several adverbs can describe the same word. In this sentence, find the adverbs and the words that they describe.

Then they changed swiftly and completely.

Notice the position of the word *and* in this diagram.

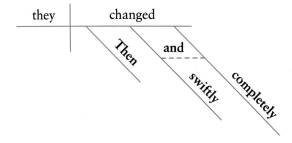

Practice Diagram all of the words in these sentences.

1. Recently a box arrived.
2. We put a heater nearby.

3. It had twelve eggs inside.
4. Monday we heard one faint peep.
5. Now all the chicks peep constantly and happily.

Prepositional Phrases (pp. 422–423)

A prepositional phrase is diagramed below the word that it describes. Prepositional phrases that tell where, when, or how often describe verbs. On the other hand, a prepositional phrase that tells what kind, how many, or which one describes a noun.

Find the prepositional phrase in this sentence. What word does it describe?

I like stories about twins.

Study this diagram of the sentence. Notice that the preposition is written on a slanting line below the word that it describes.

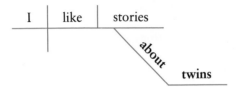

Find the prepositional phrase in this sentence. What word does it describe?

We have two sets in our family.

Study the diagram of this prepositional phrase.

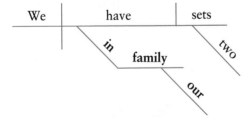

Practice Diagram all of the words in the following sentences.

1. Jamie lives near me.
2. He plays with some twins.
3. Once we wrote invitations for his party.
4. Jamie drew a funny picture on one invitation.
5. The two boys laughed about it.

Nouns in Direct Address (pp. 288–289)

Diagram a noun in direct address on a short line above and just to the left of the base line.

Find the noun in direct address in this sentence.

Students, today we are having a quiz.

Study this diagram of the sentence.

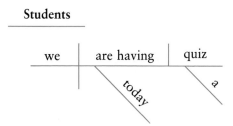

A noun in direct address is diagramed in the same way no matter where the word appears in the sentence. Find the noun in direct address in this sentence.

Share that table with Aaron, Suzie.

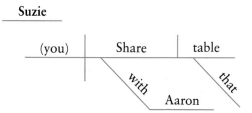

Practice Diagram all of the words in these sentences.

1. Mr. Savchick, I have a problem.
2. My only pencil, sir, just broke.
3. You may use this pen, Liz.
4. Listen carefully, class.
5. Everyone, I will read each question twice.

How to Write a Personal Narrative

A **personal narrative** is a story about yourself. It tells about something you have experienced.

Guidelines for Writing a Personal Narrative

1. Think about your purpose. Do you want your story to be exciting? sad? Think about who will read your story. Will your readers be your age? older? younger?

2. Write a beginning that makes your reader curious about what will happen. Some beginnings tell about character or setting. Others give hints about the action.

3. Use details to help your reader picture the action. Show, don't tell, what happens in each scene.

4. Include dialogue. Help your reader get to know your characters by having them tell what they think and feel. Put quotation marks around a speaker's exact words. Begin a new paragraph each time a new person is speaking.

5. Write a title for your story. Give your reader an idea of what the story is about, but don't give it away.

An Unexpected Visitor

Last Saturday started out like an ordinary Saturday. Dad was out shopping, Mom was driving my sister to the movies, and my brother and I were cleaning the house. I dumped the trash in a barrel in the garage. Just as I started back inside, I heard a noise. I turned around to see a large raccoon pushing the top off the trash barrel.

"Brian!" I screamed. "There's a gigantic raccoon out here!"

"Sure there is," called Brian. "And there's a dragon under the porch. Now quit teasing me and come inside."

Writing Prompt

Directions: In this picture, the girl is helping her brother. Think about times when you have helped someone. Why did the person need help? What did you do to help? Write a story about your experience. Write it for someone your own age.

How to Write Instructions

Instructions are sets of directions that explain how to do something. Good instructions are clearly written and easy to follow. The steps are arranged in a specific order.

Guidelines for Writing Instructions

1. Think about your purpose. Is your purpose to explain or to describe? Think about your audience. For whom are you writing your instructions?

2. Write a paragraph of instructions about one main idea. Every sentence in your paragraph should keep to the main idea.

3. State the main idea in a topic sentence. The other sentences in your paragraph should give supporting details about the main idea.

4. Give clear step-by-step directions in your paragraph. Make sure your steps are in an order that makes sense.

5. Use order words such as *first, then, next,* and *finally* to make the sequence, or order, of your instructions clear. Keep in mind that not every sentence needs an order word.

Self-portrait

To make a self-portrait, you will need one sheet of light colored construction paper and one sheet of dark colored construction paper. You will also need some tape, a flashlight or a lamp, a pencil, and scissors. First, begin by taping the dark sheet of colored paper to the wall. Then stand in front of the paper with your profile facing the paper. Next, ask a friend to shine the light on you, so that your shadow appears on the paper. Have another friend trace the outline of your head. Finally, cut out your silhouette, or shadow, and paste it in the center of the other piece of colored paper.

Writing Prompt

Directions: This is a picture of a pay telephone. Have you ever made a phone call from a public telephone? What would you do first to make a call? What would you do next? Write a paragraph telling someone your own age how to use a pay telephone.

How to Write a Story

When you write a **story**, you create a tale, using your imagination. A story can be an adventure or a true happening. It can happen in any time and in any place.

Guidelines for Writing a Story

1. Think about your purpose. Do you want your story to be scary? humorous? exciting? Think about your audience. For whom are you writing your story?

2. Think about the setting. Where and when will your story take place? Think about the plot. What events will you include in your plot?

3. Write the beginning of your story. You can describe the setting, introduce characters, or present a problem.

4. Show what your characters are like by telling what they think, do, say, and tell about other characters. Use dialogue to bring your characters to life.

5. Write the middle of your story. Keep your story moving with action events. Tell of any complications that might have arisen as a result of a problem.

6. Write the ending of your story. Solve any problems. Make sure your reader will feel the story has ended.

7. Write an interesting title for your story to get your reader's attention.

The Gold Doubloon

One Saturday morning Ned Greene was in his yard fixing his bike and watching his little sister Anna. Anna picked up something from the ground. When she started to put it in her mouth, Ned ran quickly over to her.

"No, Anna!" he shouted. "Don't put that in your mouth."

Ned took the object from Anna's hand. It looked like a very old coin. He brushed off the dirt and then dropped the coin in surprise. It was a gold doubloon!

Writing Prompt

Directions: This picture shows what Jan saw one morning when she looked in the mirror. The evening before, she mistakenly washed her hair with her dog's shampoo. How could this happen to Jan? Write a story for someone your age about what happened to Jan. Make sure your plot has a beginning, a middle, and an end.

How to Write a Description

When you write a **description**, you use words to share an observation with a reader. A good description will let your reader "see" what you are describing.

Guidelines for Writing a Description

1. Think about your purpose. What kind of impression do you want your reader to have? Think about your audience. For whom are you writing this description?

2. Think about how the thing you are describing looks, feels, tastes, sounds, and smells. What sense words can you use in your description?

3. Think about using comparison and contrast in your description. How can you show how two things are alike and how they are different?

4. Write a topic sentence that supports the main idea of your paragraph. Include details that support your purpose.

5. Organize the details in your description. One way is to use spatial order, organizing from left to right, top to bottom, near to far, or far to near.

6. Use exact, vivid words in order to create a clear mental picture for your reader.

Duncan's Place

My hamster, Duncan, loves his home. He lives in a large plastic house. It has three large rooms that lie side-by-side. A long narrow tube connects the rooms.

The room on the left is Duncan's bedroom. It smells wonderful because of the cedar shavings that cover the floor. In one corner is Duncan's fluffy tissue bed.

The middle room is the playroom. Duncan spends a lot of time running on the squeaky wheel in the center of the room. The room on the right is the dining room. Two small glass bottles are wired to a wall. One has rolled oats in it, and the other has fresh water.

Writing Prompt

Directions: Imagine that you are at this cookout. What do you see, smell, and taste? What are you doing? Write a description of the cookout so that a classmate would be able to imagine what it would feel like to be there.

How to Write a Persuasive Letter

A **persuasive** letter is a letter written to convince someone to agree with your point of view.

Guidelines for Writing a Persuasive Letter

1. Think about your purpose and audience. What do you want your reader to do? Who will read your letter?

2. State your opinion in a clear topic sentence.

3. Support your opinion with strong reasons that appeal to your audience.

4. Arrange your reasons in order of importance. List them from the most important to the least important or from the least important to the most important.

5. End your letter with a statement that restates and emphasizes your argument.

6. Use correct letter form. Include the heading, the greeting, the body, the closing, and the signature. For a business letter add an inside address.

11 Ferncroft Rd.
Atlanta, GA 30324
May 3, 1990

Dear Anika,

I just got your letter, and I still think you should trade me one of your Roberto Clemente baseball cards. I know you don't think this will help your collection, but I think it will. I have an extra Ted Williams card. I know he's your all-time favorite player, and I know you don't have his card. I think trading Roberto Clemente for Ted Williams is a great deal for both of us. Please write soon and let me know if you want to make a trade.

Your pal,

Martin

Writing Prompt

Directions: Imagine that your best friend has moved far away. You would like your friend to visit during the next school vacation. Write a letter inviting your friend to your house. Include several convincing reasons to persuade your friend to come.

How to Write a Research Report

A **research report** presents information that you have learned about a specific topic.

Guidelines for Writing a Research Report

1. Think about your purpose and audience. What do you want your readers to learn? Who will read your report?

2. Choose an interesting topic. Write questions about the topic that you would like to answer in your report.

3. Gather information. Use nonfiction books, reference books, newspapers, magazines, and interviews. Try to use two or more sources. Choose the most recent sources.

4. Write each of your questions on a separate note card. Then take notes. Write just enough to recall important facts and main ideas. Include your sources on each card.

5. Write an outline, using your note cards. Put the cards in order. Turn each of your questions into a main topic. The subtopics are facts that answer the question.

6. Turn your outline into a report. Use each main topic to write a topic sentence for each paragraph. Use the subtopics to write sentences that support the main idea.

7. Write a brief introduction to capture the reader's interest and to tell what the report is about.

8. Write a conclusion that sums up the main ideas. Then add an interesting title and list your sources.

City of Light

Paris, the capital of France, is one of the most beautiful cities in the world. It has many magnificent palaces and monuments. The use of floodlights at night has given Paris the nickname City of Light.

One of the most famous landmarks in Paris is the Eiffel Tower. This huge iron tower stands 984 feet high. It was designed by Alexandre Eiffel for the World's Fair in 1889.

Writing Prompt

Directions: A volcano overflowing with lava is a spectacular sight. What causes a volcano to erupt? Where are the most famous volcanoes located? Use a reference source to learn about volcanoes. Take notes and make an outline. Using your outline, write several paragraphs to share what you have learned with your classmates.

How to Write a Paragraph of Comparison and Contrast

A **paragraph of comparison and contrast** tells how two or more things are alike and different. When you compare, you show likenesses. When you contrast, you show differences.

Guides for Writing: Comparison and Contrast

1. Choose at least two things that are alike in some ways yet different in others. Tennis and badminton, carrots and parsnips, and walruses and elephants are good examples of things you might compare and contrast.

2. Make two lists. In one, note ways in which your two subjects are alike. In the other, note ways in which your subjects are different.

3. Begin with a topic sentence that states what you are comparing and contrasting. Look at this example:

   Tennis and badminton are similar yet different kinds of games.

4. Write several sentences that give details about how your subjects are alike. Use words such as *both, like,* and *similar* to present the likenesses.

5. Write several sentences that give details about how your subjects are different. Use words such as *unlike, different,* and *instead of* to present the differences.

Baseball and Softball

The games of baseball and softball have many similarities, but they are different too. Both games use a ball, a bat, and two opposing teams of nine players each. The object of each game is to score as many runs as possible. Like baseball, softball is played on a diamond-shaped field that contains four bases. However, a softball field is smaller than a baseball field. Also, softball players use a ball that is larger and softer than a baseball. A softball is pitched underhand, while a baseball is pitched overhand. The distance between the pitcher and the batter is closer in a softball game than in a baseball game.

Writing Prompt

Directions: Look at the pairs of items pictured below. How are the items in each pair alike? How are they different? Write a paragraph of comparison and contrast about the items in one pair. Show some of the items' likenesses and differences.

How to Write a Friendly Letter

A **friendly letter** is a letter written to someone whom you know well. It is a way of sharing news or just visiting. You use informal language in a friendly letter.

Guidelines for Writing Friendly Letters

1. Write a **heading** in the upper right corner. A heading has three lines: your street address; your city, state, and ZIP Code; and the current date. Follow the capitalization and punctuation shown in the model below.

2. Skip a line and write a **greeting** at the left margin. Include the word *Dear* and the person's name. Capitalize each word and put a comma after the greeting.

3. Write the **body** of your letter below the greeting. Here you write your news, ask questions, or tell how you are feeling. Indent each paragraph.

4. Skip a space and write a **closing** at the right, in line with your heading. Use an informal closing such as *Love, Your friend,* or *Your nephew.* End with a comma.

5. For the **signature,** write your name under the closing.

24 Newman Street
Houston, TX 77019
October 29, 1990

Dear Uncle Max,

Guess what! I won a robot last week! His name is Robbie, and he's three feet tall. He's great company, except when I'm trying to teach him a new dance. Then he makes strange noises and shakes a lot.

Are you coming for Thanksgiving? Please write soon.

Your niece,

Toni

Writing Prompt

Directions: Imagine that you are one of the children shown below. You have just taken part in one of the events pictured. Write a letter to your best friend or to a relative, describing your experience. Include the five parts of a friendly letter.

How to Write a Firsthand Biographical Sketch

A **firsthand biographical sketch** is the true story of a person's life. It is written by someone who knows or has interviewed the subject.

Guides for Writing: Firsthand Biographical Sketch

1. Choose an interesting subject. It should be someone whom you already know or could interview. Good choices might be an adult who has helped you, a favorite relative, or a person whom you admire.

2. List the important facts and interesting details of the person's life. If you can, interview your subject.

3. Write an opening that tells something interesting that the person said, thought, or did. Your opening should make the reader want to read the rest of your sketch.

4. Use the information from your list to write the rest of your biographical sketch. Most sketches cover their subjects' early lives first and then move on to later events.

5. Be sure to use exact words if you use quotations.

6. Give your biographical sketch a good title. Capitalize the first, last, and most important words.

Nicolas the Great

Nick gently placed my hand on the neck of my guitar and guided my fingers into place on the strings. Then he said, "Now! See how easy strumming these strings can be!" Before long, I was playing a simple tune and humming along. If it hadn't been for Nick, I would have given up music lessons and sold my guitar long ago.

Nick, as he is known to his friends and students, was born Nicolas Diamantes thirty-eight years ago. When he was five years old, he and his mother moved from Greece to the United States. They went first to New York City, and from there they

Writing Prompt

Directions: The twins in the picture are thinking about some of the interesting people they know. Use the people in the pictures to help you think of interesting people you know. Choose one of them to use as a subject for a biographical sketch. Interview your subject if you can.

How to Write a Limerick

A **limerick** is a nonsense poem. It has five funny or silly lines and special rhyme and rhythm schemes.

Guidelines for Writing a Limerick

1. Write five lines. Make the first, second, and fifth lines rhyme and give each one this beat: de-de-DUM, de-de-DUM, de-de-DUM. Make the third and fourth lines rhyme and give them this beat: de-de-DUM, de-de-DUM.

2. Begin your first line with the words *There once was* or *There was.* End the line by naming or describing a person, place, or thing. For example, you might write *There once was a thin man from L. A.*

3. Write a second line that rhymes with the first. To go with the line above, you might write *Who ate peas at each meal every day.*

4. Then write two shorter lines that rhyme with each other. Look at these examples:

   He turned green and grew round,
   And 'fore long he had found,

5. Write a last line that rhymes with the first two lines. A good rhyme for the example here is, *That a fourth of a ton he did weigh.*

6. Begin each line with a capital letter.

7. Give your poem a title. Capitalize each important word.

> The Man from L. A.
>
> There once was a thin man from L. A.
> Who ate peas at each meal every day.
> He turned green and grew round,
> And 'fore long he had found,
> That a fourth of a ton he did weigh.

Writing Prompt

Directions: Don't the people in this picture look silly? Each of them would make a great subject for a nonsense poem. Write a limerick about one of them. Remember, write five lines and use the special rhyme and rhythm schemes.

Words Often Misspelled

accept	busy	fourth	nickel	to
ache	buy	Friday	ninety	too
again	by	friend	ninety-nine	tried
all right	calendar	goes	ninth	tries
almost	cannot	going	often	truly
already	can't	grammar	once	two
although	careful	guard	other	tying
always	catch	guess	people	unknown
angel	caught	guide	principal	until
angle	chief	half	quiet	unusual
answer	children	haven't	quit	wasn't
argue	choose	hear	quite	wear
asked	chose	heard	really	weather
aunt	color	heavy	receive	Wednesday
author	cough	height	rhythm	weird
awful	cousin	here	right	we'll
babies	decide	hers	Saturday	we're
been	divide	hole	stretch	weren't
believe	does	hoping	surely	we've
bother	don't	hour	their	where
bought	early	its	theirs	which
break	enough	it's	there	whole
breakfast	every	January	they're	witch
breathe	exact	let's	they've	won't
broken	except	listen	those	wouldn't
brother	excite	loose	though	write
brought	expect	lose	thought	writing
bruise	February	minute	through	written
build	finally	muscle	tied	you're
business	forty	neighbor	tired	yours

Spelling Guidelines

1. A short vowel sound before a consonant is usually spelled with just one letter: **a, e, i, o,** or **u**.

staff	dwell	fond
grasp	mist	crush
slept	split	bulb

2. The |ā| sound is often spelled **ai, ay,** or **a-consonant-e**. The |ē| sound is often spelled **ee** or **ea**.

claim	stake	greet
brain	male	seal
sway	fleet	lease
stray	speech	beast

3. The |ī| sound is often spelled **i, igh,** or **i-consonant-e**. The |ō| sound is often spelled **o, o-consonant-e, oa,** or **ow**.

mild	strike	loaf
slight	stroll	boast
thigh	stole	sow
stride	hose	flow

4. The |o͞o| or the |yo͞o| sound is often spelled **ue, ew,** or **u-consonant-e**. The |o͞o| sound may also be spelled **oo** or **ui**.

hue	fume	mood
clue	duke	boom
dew	flute	cruise
brew	troop	bruise

5. The |ou| sound is often spelled **ou** or **ow**. The |ô| sound is often spelled **aw, au,** or **a** before **l**. The |oi| sound is spelled **oi** or **oy**.

ounce	hawk	bald
sour	fawn	moist
coward	haunt	joint
scowl	fault	royal
claw	stalk	loyal

6. The |ûr| sounds are often spelled **ir, ur, er, ear,** or **or**. The |îr| sounds are often spelled **eer** or **ear**.

squirm	stern	worm
chirp	germ	steer
blur	pearl	smear
hurl	earl	rear

7. The |ôr| sounds are often spelled **or, ore,** or **oar.** The |âr| sounds are often spelled **are** or **air.** The |är| sound is usually spelled **ar.**	lord torch tore sore bore	soar hare fare snare lair	flair harsh scar carve barge
8. Homophones sound alike but have different spellings and meanings.	loan lone	flea flee	berry bury
9. The final |ər| sounds in two-syllable words are often spelled **ar, or,** or **er.**	lunar pillar burglar	humor major tractor	clover banner thunder
10. The final |l| or |əl| sounds in two-syllable words are often spelled **le, el,** or **al.**	single angle whistle	jewel bushel angel	normal legal local
11. The **-ed** or **-ing** ending may simply be added to some words. A final **e** is usually dropped before adding **-ed** or **-ing.**	arrested offered attending directing	seeking awaiting borrowed squeezing	rising amusing freezing providing
12. In one-syllable words ending with a single vowel and consonant, the consonant is usually doubled when **-ed** or **-ing** is added. In two-syllable words ending with an unstressed syllable, the final consonant is usually not doubled.	winning hitting swimming bragging wrapped dropped	shipped whipped begged stunned chopped spotted	suffering gathering visiting covered wandered ordered

13. A suffix is a word part added to the end of a base word.

dread**ful**	count**less**	settle**ment**
breath**less**	active**ly**	soft**ness**

14. Final |ĭj| sounds are often spelled **age**. Final |tĭv| sounds are often spelled **tive**. Final |tĭs| sounds are often spelled **tice**.

bagg**age**	yard**age**	defec**tive**
lugg**age**	langu**age**	detec**tive**
sav**age**	cap**tive**	prac**tice**
post**age**	na**tive**	jus**tice**
voy**age**	crea**tive**	no**tice**

15. Final |n| or |ən| sounds may be spelled **ain**. Final |chər| sounds may be spelled **ture**. Final |zhər| sounds may be spelled **sure**.

capt**ain**	crea**ture**	mea**sure**
fount**ain**	adven**ture**	expo**sure**
curt**ain**	fix**ture**	trea**sure**
mount**ain**	lec**ture**	plea**sure**

16. Prefixes are added to beginnings of words or word roots.

decide	**un**known	**ex**cuse
improve	**com**fort	**pre**fix

17. The suffix **-ion** changes verbs to nouns. Sometimes the spelling changes.

correct	reduce	explode
correct**ion**	reduc**tion**	explo**sion**

18. If a word ends with a consonant + **y,** change the **y** to **i** when adding **-es, -er,** or **-est.**

hobb**ies**	cop**ied**	tin**iest**
abilit**ies**	nois**ier**	happ**iest**
sp**ied**	earl**ier**	lonel**iest**

19. The suffixes **-able, -ible, -ant,** and **-ent** are added to words or word roots.

suit**able**	poss**ible**	vac**ant**
comfort**able**	horr**ible**	stud**ent**
valu**able**	serv**ant**	differ**ent**

CAPITALIZATION, PUNCTUATION, AND USAGE GUIDE

Abbreviations

Abbreviations are shortened forms of words. Most abbreviations begin with a capital letter and end with a period. Use abbreviations only in special kinds of writing, such as addresses and lists.

Titles

Mr. *(Mister)* Mr. Juan Albino
Mrs. *(Mistress)* Mrs. Frances Wong
Ms. Leslie Clark
Dr. *(Doctor)* Dr. Janice Dodds

Sr. *(Senior)* John Helt, Sr.
Jr. *(Junior)* John Helt, Jr.
Note: *Miss* is not an abbreviation and does not end with a period.

Words used in addresses

St. *(Street)*
Rd. *(Road)*
Ave. *(Avenue)*
Dr. *(Drive)*

Blvd. *(Boulevard)*
Rte. *(Route)*
Apt. *(Apartment)*

Pkwy. *(Parkway)*
Mt. *(Mount or Mountain)*
Expy. *(Expressway)*

Words used in business

Co. *(Company)*
Corp. *(Corporation)*

Inc. *(Incorporated)*
Ltd. *(Limited)*

Other abbreviations

Some abbreviations are written in all capital letters, with a letter standing for each important word.

P.D. *(Police Department)*
J.P. *(Justice of the Peace)*

P.O. *(Post Office)*
R.N. *(Registered Nurse)*

The United States Postal Service uses two capital letters and no period in each of its state abbreviations.

AL *(Alabama)*	IL *(Illinois)*	MO *(Missouri)*
AK *(Alaska)*	IN *(Indiana)*	MT *(Montana)*
AZ *(Arizona)*	IA *(Iowa)*	NE *(Nebraska)*
AR *(Arkansas)*	KS *(Kansas)*	NV *(Nevada)*
CA *(California)*	KY *(Kentucky)*	NH *(New Hampshire)*
CO *(Colorado)*	LA *(Louisiana)*	NJ *(New Jersey)*
CT *(Connecticut)*	ME *(Maine)*	NM *(New Mexico)*
DE *(Delaware)*	MD *(Maryland)*	NY *(New York)*
FL *(Florida)*	MA *(Massachusetts)*	NC *(North Carolina)*
GA *(Georgia)*	MI *(Michigan)*	ND *(North Dakota)*
HI *(Hawaii)*	MN *(Minnesota)*	OH *(Ohio)*
ID *(Idaho)*	MS *(Mississippi)*	OK *(Oklahoma)*

OR *(Oregon)*	TN *(Tennessee)*	WA *(Washington)*
PA *(Pennsylvania)*	TX *(Texas)*	WV *(West Virginia)*
RI *(Rhode Island)*	UT *(Utah)*	WI *(Wisconsin)*
SC *(South Carolina)*	VT *(Vermont)*	WY *(Wyoming)*
SD *(South Dakota)*	VA *(Virginia)*	

Initials are abbreviations that stand for a person's first or middle name. Some names have both a first and a middle initial.

E.B. White *(Elwyn Brooks White)*

T. James Carey *(Thomas James Carey)*

Mr. John M. Gordon *(Mister John Morris Gordon)*

Titles

Underlining	**The important words and the first and last words in a title are capitalized. Titles of books, magazines, TV shows, movies, and newspapers are underlined.**

<u>Oliver Twist</u> *(book)*   <u>Treasure Island</u> *(movie)*

<u>Cricket</u> *(magazine)*   <u>The Phoenix Express</u> *(newspaper)*

<u>Nova</u> *(TV show)*

Quotation marks with titles	**Titles of short stories, songs, articles, book chapters, and most poems are set off by quotation marks.**

"The Necklace" *(short story)*

"Home on the Range" *(song)*

"Three Days in the Sahara" *(article)*

"The Human Brain" *(chapter)*

"Deer at Dusk" *(poem)*

Quotations

Quotation marks with commas and periods	**Quotation marks are used to set off a speaker's exact words. The first word of a quotation begins with a capital letter. Punctuation belongs *inside* the closing quotation marks. Commas separate a quotation from the rest of the sentence.**

"Where," asked the stranger, " is the post office?"

"Please put away your books now," said Mr. Emory.

Linda whispered, "What time is it?"

"It's late," replied Bill. "Let's go!"

Capitalization

Rules for capitalization

Capitalize the first word of every sentence.
What an unusual color the roses are!

Capitalize the pronoun I.
What should I do next?

Capitalize proper nouns. If a proper noun is made up of more than one word, capitalize each important word.
Emily G. Messe   District of Columbia   Lincoln Memorial

Capitalize titles or their abbreviations when used with a person's name.
Governor Bradford   Senator Smith   Dr. Ling

Capitalize proper adjectives.
We ate at a French restaurant.
She is French.
That is a North American custom.

Capitalize the names of days, months, and holidays.
My birthday is on the last Monday in March.
We watched the parade on the Fourth of July.

Capitalize the names of buildings and companies.
Empire State Building
Central School
Able Supply Company

Capitalize the first, last, and all important words in a title. Do not capitalize words such as _a_, _in_, _and_, _of_, and _the_ unless they begin or end a title.
From Earth to the Moon   "The Rainbow Connection"
The New York Times   "Growing Up"

Capitalize the first word of each main topic and subtopic in an outline.
I. Types of libraries
   A. Large public library
   B. Bookmobile

Capitalize the first word in the greeting and the closing of a letter.
Dear Marcia,   Yours truly,

Punctuation

End marks	**There are three end marks. A *period* (.) ends a declarative or imperative sentence. A *question mark* (?) follows an interrogative sentence. An *exclamation point* (!) follows an exclamatory sentence.** The scissors are on my desk. *(declarative)* Look up the spelling of that word. *(imperative)* How is the word spelled? *(interrogative)* This is your best poem so far! *(exclamatory)*
Apostrophe	**To form the possessive of a singular noun, add an apostrophe and *s*.** doctor's teacher's grandmother's family's
	For a plural noun that ends in *s*, add only an apostrophe. sisters' families' Smiths' hound dogs'
	For a plural noun that does not end in *s*, add an apostrophe and *s* to form the plural possessive. women's mice's children's geese's
	Use an apostrophe in contractions in place of dropped letters. Do not use contractions in formal writing. isn't *(is not)* we're *(we are)* they'll *(they will)* can't *(cannot)* it's *(it is)* could've *(could have)* won't *(will not)* I'm *(I am)* would've *(would have)* wasn't *(was not)* they've *(they have)* should've *(should have)*
Colon	**Use a colon after the greeting in a business letter.** Dear Mrs. Trimby: Dear Realty Homes:
Comma	**A comma tells your reader where to pause.** **For words in a series, put a comma after each item except the last. Do not use a comma if only two items are listed.** Clyde asked if we had any apples, peaches, or grapes.
	Use commas to separate two or more adjectives that are listed together unless one adjective tells how many. The fresh, ripe fruit was placed in a bowl. One red apple was especially shiny.
	Use a comma before the conjunction in a compound sentence. Some students were at lunch, but others were studying.

Comma (continued)	Use commas after introductory words such as *yes, no, oh,* and *well* when they begin a sentence.
	Well, it's just too cold out. No, it isn't six yet.
	Use a comma to separate a noun in direct address.
	Jean, help me fix this tire. How was your trip, Grandpa?
	Can you see, Joe, where I left my glasses?
	Use a comma between the names of a city and a state.
	Chicago, Illinois Miami, Florida
	Use a comma after the greeting in a friendly letter.
	Dear Deena, Dear Uncle Rudolph,
	Use a comma after the closing in a letter.
	Your nephew, Sincerely yours,

Problem Words

Words	Rules	Examples
a, an, the	These words are articles.	
a, an	Use *a* and *an* before singular nouns. Use *a* before a word that begins with a consonant sound. Use *an* before a word that begins with a vowel sound.	a banana an apple
the	Use *the* with both singular and plural nouns.	the apple the apples
	Use *the* to point out particular persons, places, or things.	The books that I like are long.
can	*Can* means "to be able to do something."	Nellie can read quickly.
may	*May* means "to be allowed or permitted."	May I borrow your book?

CAPITALIZATION, PUNCTUATION, USAGE

Words	Rules	Examples
good	*Good* is an adjective.	The weather looks good.
well	*Well* is usually an adverb. It is an adjective only when it refers to health.	She swims well. Do you feel well?
its	*Its* is a possessive pronoun.	The dog wagged its tail.
it's	*It's* is a contraction of *it is.*	It's cold today.
let	*Let* means "to permit or allow."	Please let me go swimming.
leave	*Leave* means "to go away from" or "to let remain in a place."	I will leave soon. Leave it on my desk.
sit	*Sit* means "to rest in one place."	Please sit in this chair.
set	*Set* means "to place or put."	Set the vase on the table.
teach	*Teach* means "to give instruction."	He teaches us how to dance.
learn	*Learn* means "to receive instruction."	I learned about history.
their	*Their* is a possessive pronoun.	Their coats are on the bed.
there	*There* is an adverb. It may also begin a sentence.	Is Carlos there? There is my book.
they're	*They're* is a contraction of *they are.*	They're going to the store.
two	*Two* is a number.	I bought two shirts.
to	*To* means "in the direction of."	A squirrel ran to the tree.
too	*Too* means "more than enough" and "also."	I ate too many cherries. Can we go too?
your	*Your* is a possessive pronoun.	Are these your glasses?
you're	*You're* is a contraction for *you are.*	You're late again!

Adjective and Adverb Usage

Adjective or Adverb?	**Use adjectives to describe nouns or pronouns. Use adverbs to describe verbs.** Lena is a quick runner. *(adjective)* Lena runs quickly. *(adverb)*
Comparing	**To compare two things or actions, add -er to adjectives and adverbs or use the word more.** This plant is taller than the other one. It grew more quickly.
	To compare three or more things or actions, add -est or use the word most. This plant is the tallest of the three. It grew most quickly.
	Use more or most with an adjective or adverb that has two or more syllables, such as careful or politely. Do not add -er or -est to long adjectives or adverbs. agreeable—more agreeable—most agreeable slowly—more slowly—most slowly
good, bad	**The adjectives good and bad have special forms for making comparisons.** good—better—best bad—worse—worst

Negatives

	A negative is a word that means "no" or "not." Do not use double negatives in a sentence. **INCORRECT:** We didn't go nowhere. **CORRECT:** We didn't go anywhere.

Pronoun Usage

Agreement	**A pronoun must agree with the noun to which it refers.** Kee bought a newspaper. Mary read it. Jeff and Cindy came to dinner. They enjoyed the meal.
Double subjects	**Do not use a double subject—a noun and a pronoun—to name the same person, place, or thing.** **INCORRECT:** The food it was delicious. **CORRECT:** The food was delicious.

I, me	**Use *I* as the subject of a sentence and after forms of *be*. Use *me* after action verbs or prepositions like *to, in,* and *for*. (See *Subject and object pronouns*.)**
	Jan and <u>I</u> are going to the show.
	She is taking <u>me</u>.
	Will you hold my ticket for <u>me</u>?
	When using *I* or *me* with nouns or other pronouns, always name yourself last.
	<u>Beth and I</u> will leave. Give the papers to <u>Ron and me</u>.
Possessive pronouns	**A possessive pronoun shows ownership. Use *my, your, his, her, its, our,* and *their* before nouns.**
	<u>My</u> report was about <u>our</u> trip to the zoo.
	Use *mine, yours, his, hers, its, ours,* and *theirs* to replace nouns in a sentence.
	<u>Hers</u> was about a visit to the museum.
Subject and object pronouns	**Use subject pronouns as subjects and after forms of the verb *be*.**
	<u>He</u> composed many works for the piano.
	I am <u>she</u>.
	The most talented singers are <u>we</u>.
	Use object pronouns after action verbs and prepositions like *to* and *for*.
	Clyde collected old coins and sold <u>them</u>. *(direct object)*
	Let's share these bananas with <u>her</u>. *(object of preposition)*
Compound subjects, compound objects	**To decide which pronoun to use in a compound subject or a compound object, leave out the other part of the compound. Say the sentence with the pronoun alone.**
	Lu and _____ ride the bus. *(we, us)*
	<u>We</u> ride the bus.
	Lu and <u>we</u> ride the bus.
	I saw Dad and _____. *(he, him)*
	I saw <u>him</u>.
	I saw Dad and <u>him</u>.
	Mom sang to Amy and _____. *(she, her)*
	Mom sang to <u>her</u>.
	Mom sang to Amy and <u>her</u>.

We and *us* with nouns	**Use *we* with a noun that is a subject or that follows a linking verb.**
	INCORRECT: Us girls are the stagehands.
	CORRECT: <u>We</u> girls are the stagehands.
	INCORRECT: The ushers are us boys.
	CORRECT: The ushers are <u>we</u> boys.
	Use *us* with a noun that follows an action verb or that follows a preposition such as *to, for, with,* or *at*.
	INCORRECT: Dr. Lin helped we players.
	CORRECT: Dr. Lin helped <u>us</u> players.
	INCORRECT: She talked to we beginners.
	CORRECT: She talked to <u>us</u> beginners.

Verb Usage

Agreement: subject-verb	**A present tense verb and its subject must agree in number. Add *s* or *es* to the verb if the subject is singular. Do not add *s* or *es* to the verb if the subject is plural or if the subject is *I*.**
	The road ben<u>ds</u> to the right.
	Mr. Langelier teach<u>es</u> fifth graders.
	These books <u>seem</u> heavy.
	I <u>like</u> camping.
	Change the forms of *be* and *have* to make them agree with their subjects.
	He <u>is</u> taking the bus today. <u>Have</u> you seen Jimmy?
	They <u>are</u> going swimming. Mary <u>has</u> a large garden.
Agreement: compound subjects	**A compound subject with *and* takes a plural verb.**
	<u>Jason</u>, <u>Kelly</u>, and <u>Wanda</u> <u>have</u> new dictionaries.
could have, should have	**Use *could have, would have, should have, might have, must have*. Avoid using *of* with *could, would, should, might,* or *must*.**
	She <u>could have</u> (*not* could of) spoken louder.
	Juan <u>would have</u> (*not* would of) liked this movie.
	We <u>should have</u> (*not* should of) turned left.
	I <u>might have</u> (*not* might of) left my wallet on my desk.
	It <u>must have</u> (*not* must of) rained last night.

Verb Usage continued

Irregular verbs   Irregular verbs do not add *-ed* or *-d* to form the past tense. Because irregular verbs do not follow a regular pattern, you must memorize their spellings. Use *has, have,* or *had* as a helping verb with the past tense.

Verb	Past	Past with helping verb
be	was	been
begin	began	begun
blow	blew	blown
break	broke	broken
bring	brought	brought
choose	chose	chosen
come	came	come
fly	flew	flown
freeze	froze	frozen
go	went	gone
grow	grew	grown
have	had	had
know	knew	known
make	made	made
ring	rang	rung
run	ran	run
say	said	said
sing	sang	sung
speak	spoke	spoken
steal	stole	stolen
swim	swam	swum
take	took	taken
tear	tore	torn
think	thought	thought
wear	wore	worn
write	wrote	written

■ THESAURUS PLUS ■

How to Use This Thesaurus

Why do you use a thesaurus? One reason is to make your writing more exact. Suppose you wrote the following sentence:

The thin ballerina twirled gracefully.

Is *thin* the most exact word you can use? To find out, use your Thesaurus Plus.

Look up your word Turn to the index on pages 537-542. You will find

thin, *adj.*

Entry words are printed in blue type. Because *thin* is blue, you can look up *thin* in the Thesaurus Plus.

Use your thesaurus The main entries in the thesaurus are listed in alphabetical order. Turn to *thin.* You will find

main entry word **thin** *adj.* having little fat on the body. *After his diet, Joe looked* **thin**.	part of speech meaning sample sentence
skinny having very little fat on the body; bony. *The sick kitten was so* **skinny** *that we could see its ribs.* subentries	
slender having little fat or width. *The* **slender** *ballerina seemed almost like a doll.*	
antonyms **antonyms:** fat, plump, stout	

Which word might better describe the ballerina in the sentence above? Perhaps you chose *slender.*

Other index entries There are two other types of entries in your Thesaurus Plus Index.

1. The slanted type means you can find other words for *splendid* if you look under *nice*.

2. The regular type tells you that *start* is the opposite of *finish*.

splendid nice, *adj.*
spotless clean, *adj.*
spring jump, *v.*
spy look, *v.*
stare look, *v.*
start finish, *v.*

Practice

A. Write each word. Look it up in the Thesaurus Index. Then write *main entry, subentry,* or *antonym* to show how it is listed.

1. required
2. calm
3. get
4. instant
5. ask
6. gloomy
7. shout
8. smash

B. Use the Thesaurus Index and the Thesaurus Plus. Replace each underlined word with a more exact or interesting word. Write the new sentence.

9. As long as it kept raining, we stayed inside.
10. It was really too cold to go out anyway.
11. Later we looked at a great rainbow.
12. We were nervous about the weather.
13. We had to start planning our museum trip.
14. Clara was worried that there was little time.
15. Jim thought she was being unreasonable.
16. Jim's thoughts angered Clara.
17. Mrs. Lee helped us to create a plan.
18. We decided to stick to her plan.
19. We were grateful for Mrs. Lee's help.
20. Everyone was now happy.

■ THESAURUS PLUS INDEX ■

A

abandon leave, *v.*
able capable, *adj.*
abnormal common, *adj.*
absurd funny, *adj.*
accept argue, *v.*
accomplish do, *v.*
achieve do, *v.*
achieve succeed, *v.*
acquire get, *v.*
act do, *v.*
active, *adj.*
actual real, *adj.*
additional further, *adj.*
admirable nice, *adj.*
agree argue, *v.*
agreeable nice, *adj.*
alarm warning, *n.*
alarming scary, *adj.*
also, *adv.*
alternative choice, *n.*
amaze surprise, *v.*
amiable nice, *adj.*
amusing funny, *adj.*
ancient new, *adj.*
angry, *adj.*
annoyed angry, *adj.*
answer ask, *v.*
antique new, *adj.*
anxious nervous, *adj.*
appealing nice, *adj.*
appealing pretty, *adj.*
appreciation, *n.*
appreciative grateful, *adj.*
approve argue, *v.*
argue, *v.*
arid wet, *adj.*
arrive leave, *v.*
artificial real, *adj.*
as long as while, *conj.*
ask, *v.*
assemble gather, *v.*
assert think, *v.*
astonish surprise, *v.*
astound surprise, *v.*

at the end last, *adv.*
attain do, *v.*
attempt try, *v.*
attractive pretty, *adj.*
audacious bold, *adj.*
avoid look, *v.*

B

be worthy of deserve, *v.*
beautiful pretty, *adj.*
begin finish, *v.*
begin start, *v.*
believe think, *v.*
besides also, *adv.*
big, *adj.*
blubber laugh, *v.*
blunt dull, *adj.*
blunt sharp, *adj.*
boast, *v.*
bold, *adj.*
bored eager, *adj.*
boring, *adj.*
brag boast, *v.*
brave, *adj.*
break, *v.*
bright dark, *adj.*
bright shiny, *adj.*
brilliant pretty, *adj.*
bring, *v.*
build make, *v.*
bulky big, *adj.*
bury hide, *v.*
buy get, *v.*

C

cackle laugh, *v.*
calm angry, *adj.*
calm nervous, *adj.*
calm upset, *adj.*
calm, *adj.*
capable, *adj.*
careful, *adj.*
careless careful, *adj.*
carry bring, *v.*

case example, *n.*
cause effect, *n.*
cause source, *n.*
cautious bold, *adj.*
cautious careful, *adj.*
change, *v.*
changeable faithful, *adj.*
charge price, *n.*
charming nice, *adj.*
charming pretty, *adj.*
cheerful happy, *adj.*
chief, *adj.*
chilly cold, *adj.*
chipper lively, *adj.*
choice, *n.*
chortle laugh, *v.*
chuckle laugh, *v.*
clash argue, *v.*
clean, *adj.*
clear, *adj.*
close finish, *v.*
close start, *v.*
cloudy clear, *adj.*
cloudy unclear, *adj.*
cold, *adj.*
cold-hearted nice, *adj.*
collect gather, *v.*
colossal big, *adj.*
come leave, *v.*
comfortable upset, *adj.*
comical funny, *adj.*
commence finish, *v.*
commence start, *v.*
common, *adj.*
companionable nice, *adj.*
competitor opponent, *n.*
complete do, *v.*
complete finish, *v.*
complex easy, *adj.*
composed upset, *adj.*
conceal hide, *v.*
conceive think, *v.*
conclude finish, *v.*
conclusion, *n.*
confuse do, *v.*
confusing unclear, *adj.*

THESAURUS PLUS INDEX

fine nice, *adj.*
finish do, *v.*
finish start, *v.*
finish, *v.*
first last, *adv.*
fit healthy, *adj.*
flawed nice, *adj.*
flawed perfect, *adj.*
flooded wet, *adj.*
foggy clear, *adj.*
forget think, *v.*
form make, *v.*
frank honest, *adj.*
frantic calm, *adj.*
fraud fake, *n.*
freezing cold, *adj.*
fresh new, *adj.*
friendly nice, *adj.*
frightened brave, *adj.*
frightening scary, *adj.*
fulfill do, *v.*
fuming angry, *adj.*
funny, *adj.*
furious angry, *adj.*
further, *adj.*
fuzzy unclear, *adj.*

G

gain succeed, *v.*
gape look, *v.*
gather, *v.*
gawk look, *v.*
gaze look, *v.*
general common, *adj.*
gentle nice, *adj.*
get, *v.*
giant big, *adj.*
gigantic big, *adj.*
giggle laugh, *v.*
give, *v.*
glad happy, *adj.*
glamorous pretty, *adj.*
glance look, *v.*
glance, *v.*
glare look, *v.*
gleaming shiny, *adj.*
glimpse glance, *v.*
glimpse look, *v.*

glistening shiny, *adj.*
gloomy funny, *adj.*
glorious pretty, *adj.*
glower look, *v.*
gorgeous pretty, *adj.*
gracious nice, *adj.*
grateful, *adj.*
gratitude appreciation, *n.*
great big, *adj.*
great, *adj.*
green, *adj.*
grow, *v.*
guard protect, *v.*
guarded careful, *adj.*
guffaw laugh, *v.*

H

handsome pretty, *adj.*
handy useful, *adj.*
happy, *adj.*
hard easy, *adj.*
hasty quick, *adj.*
haul pull, *v.*
hazard danger, *n.*
healthy, *adj.*
heedless careful, *adj.*
helpful useful, *adj.*
hide, *v.*
hilarious funny, *adj.*
holler shout, *v.*
homely pretty, *adj.*
honest, *adj.*
hot cold, *adj.*
howl laugh, *v.*
huge big, *adj.*
humorous funny, *adj.*
hunter green, *adj.*
hurdle jump, *v.*

I

icy cold, *adj.*
ideal perfect, *adj.*
identical opposite, *adj.*
identical same, *adj.*
ignorance education, *n.*
ignore see, *v.*
ignore look, *v.*

ignore think, *v.*
ill healthy, *adj.*
illogical unreasonable, *adj.*
imagine think, *v.*
immense big, *adj.*
important, *adj.*
impostor fake, *n.*
in addition also, *adv.*
inactive lively, *adj.*
incompetent capable, *adj.*
indifferent eager, *adj.*
inefficient useful, *adj.*
inferior great, *adj.*
inquire ask, *v.*
insincere honest, *adj.*
instance example, *v.*
instant moment, *n.*
insulting nice, *adj.*
interested eager, *adj.*
interesting boring, *adj.*
invent create, *v.*
investigate examine, *v.*
investigate explore, *v.*
irate angry, *adj.*
irrational unreasonable, *adj.*
irritated angry, *adj.*

J

join, *v.*
judge think, *v.*
jumbo big, *adj.*
jump, *v.*

K

keen dull, *adj.*
keen eager, *adj.*
kelly green, *adj.*
knowledge education, *n.*

L

large big, *adj.*
large little, *adj.*
last, *adv.*
laugh, *v.*
laughable funny, *adj.*
lax careful, *adj.*

raise grow, *v.*
rapid quick, *adj.*
rare common, *adj.*
ravishing pretty, *adj.*
real, *adj.*
receive give, *v.*
recognition appreciation, *n.*
reflect think, *v.*
refreshing nice, *adj.*
regular common, *adj.*
remain change, *v.*
remove put, *v.*
repair break, *v.*
repellent nice, *adj.*
reply ask, *v.*
repulsive pretty, *adj.*
required necessary, *adj.*
resolve decide, *v.*
resolve do, *v.*
result effect, *n.*
result source, *n.*
return leave, *v.*
reveal hide, *v.*
revolting pretty, *adj.*
ridiculous funny, *adj.*
risk danger, *n.*
rival opponent, *n.*
roar laugh, *v.*
rounded sharp, *adj.*
rude nice, *adj.*

S

sad funny, *adj.*
sad happy, *adj.*
safety danger, *n.*
same, *adj.*
satisfied upset, *adj.*
saturated wet, *adj.*
scan look, *v.*
scary, *adj.*
scatter gather, *v.*
scowl look, *v.*
security danger, *n.*
sedate calm, *adj.*
see, *v.*
selection choice, *n.*
sense meaning, *n.*
sensible unreasonable, *adj.*

separate gather, *v.*
separate join, *v.*
serene calm, *adj.*
serious funny, *adj.*
set put, *v.*
several many, *adj.*
several some, *adj.*
shake, *v.*
sharp unclear, *adj.*
sharp, *adj.*
shatter break, *v.*
shiny, *adj.*
shiver shake, *v.*
shout, *v.*
shove pull, *v.*
show hide, *v.*
shriek laugh, *v.*
shudder shake, *v.*
shun look, *v.*
sick healthy, *adj.*
sidesplitting funny, *adj.*
signal warning, *n.*
significance meaning, *n.*
significant important, *adj.*
similar opposite, *adj.*
simple easy, *adj.*
sizable big, *adj.*
skillful nice, *adj.*
skinny fat, *adj.*
skinny thin, *adj.*
slack careful, *adj.*
slender fat, *adj.*
slender thin, *adj.*
slim fat, *adj.*
slow quick, *adj.*
sluggish active, *adj.*
small big, *adj.*
small little, *adj.*
smash break, *v.*
snicker laugh, *v.*
snigger laugh, *v.*
snoop look, *v.*
soaked wet, *adj.*
sob laugh, *v.*
sodden wet, *adj.*
soggy wet, *adj.*
soiled clean, *adj.*
solemn funny, *adj.*
solve do, *v.*

some, *adj.*
sopping wet, *adj.*
soppy wet, *adj.*
sorrowful happy, *adj.*
sound healthy, *adj.*
source effect, *n.*
source, *n.*
speculate think, *v.*
speedy quick, *adj.*
spirited lively, *adj.*
splendid nice, *adj.*
spotless clean, *adj.*
spring jump, *v.*
spy look, *v.*
stare look, *v.*
start finish, *v.*
start, *v.*
stop finish, *v.*
stop start, *v.*
stout fat, *adj.*
stout thin, *adj.*
strange common, *adj.*
strange, *adj.*
strict careful, *adj.*
studious careful, *adj.*
study explore, *v.*
study think, *v.*
stunning pretty, *adj.*
stunt grow, *v.*
succeed, *v.*
superb nice, *adj.*
supply give, *v.*
surprise, *v.*
sweet nice, *adj.*
swift quick, *adj.*
sympathetic nice, *adj.*

T

take bring, *v.*
take give, *v.*
take away put, *v.*
teammate opponent, *n.*
teeny big, *adj.*
terrible nice, *adj.*
terrific great, *adj.*
terrifying scary, *adj.*
test try, *v.*
thankful grateful, *adj.*

A

active *adj.* full of movement. *Tennis is an active sport.*
energetic full of strength and energy. *My energetic friend Janet is always busy.*
lively full of life, alert. *The lively puppy kept tugging at his leash.*
antonyms: lazy, sluggish

also *adv.* too. *Peter likes that album, but he likes this one also.*
in addition plus, as well. *We went to the park and to the zoo in addition.*
besides together with, over and above. *Tom plays three other instruments besides the guitar.*

How **Angry** Were You?

angry *adj.* feeling or showing displeasure.

- - - - - - - - - - - - - - - -

1. slightly angry:
   displeased
   annoyed
   irritated
   peeved

2. very angry:
   upset
   cross
   mad

3. extremely angry:
   furious
   enraged
   irate
   fuming

- - - - - - - - - - - - - - - -

antonyms: calm, peaceful, delighted

appreciation *n.* knowledge and enjoyment of something's value. *Dad showed his appreciation of our gift by giving us a big hug.*
gratitude feeling of being grateful. *The stray dog showed its gratitude by licking my hand.*

recognition attention, praise, or favorable notice. *Most artists look for recognition more than money.*
antonyms: ungratefulness, disregard

argue *v.* to give reasons for or against something, especially to someone with a different opinion. *Rose was in favor of a town pool, but Jean argued against it.*
quarrel to have a fight with words. *We quarreled about who was smarter.*
clash to be against one another on an issue. *Employers and employees clashed during a recent strike.*
disagree to have a different opinion. *A few senators disagreed with the others and voted against the treaty.*
antonyms: accept, agree, consent

ask *v.* to put a question to. *Sam asked me who else was invited.*
inquire to try to find out certain information. *Jan inquired about my health.*
question to quiz. *The guards had to question every visitor.*
antonyms: reply, answer

B

Word Bank

big *adj.* of great size or importance.

- - - - - - - - - - - - - - - -

huge	mammoth
immense	enormous
large	gigantic
mighty	towering
jumbo	sizable
bulky	great
massive	
giant	
colossal	
magnificent	

- - - - - - - - - - - - - - - -

antonyms: little, tiny, miniature, small, wee, petite, microscopic

boast *v.* to praise oneself, one's belongings, or one's actions. *Sara always boasts about how fast she can run.*

brag to use words about oneself to show off. *Leroy bragged to everyone about his new bike.*

crow to utter a cry of delight or victory. *We all smiled when Pat crowed, "I won! I won!"*

bold *adj.* not timid or fearful. *Mary Read was a bold woman who joined the Royal Navy.*

daring brave enough to take on a big challenge, adventurous. *Two daring climbers decided to go to the top of a steep mountain.*

audacious not afraid of any risk. *One audacious bear came right up to our tent.*

antonym: cautious

boring *adj.* not interesting. *The TV program was so boring that I fell asleep.*

dull lacking excitement. *Not one player scored during the dull soccer match.*

dry tiresome. *It was hard to finish reading the long, dry government report.*

monotonous not interesting because of being always the same. *Monotonous songs just repeat the same words over and over.*

antonyms: exciting, lively, interesting, varied

brave *adj.* able to face danger or pain without fear. *You seemed brave when the doctor set your broken leg.*

courageous able to face difficult situations. *Only a courageous person can be an explorer.*

valiant acting with great courage. *The valiant farmers risked their lives to save their animals.*

fearless without the feeling of fright. *The fearless cat stood still as the dog ran toward it.*

antonyms: cowardly, frightened

break *v.* to separate into pieces as the result of force or strain. *A beam broke under the weight of the snow.*

shatter to come apart suddenly into many pieces. *The delicate cup shattered against the floor.*

smash to crush into pieces. *Bulldozers smashed the house into a pile of boards.*

crack to come apart with a sudden sharp sound. *Dale hit the ball hard enough to crack the bat.*

antonyms: mend, patch, repair

bring *v.* to take along or transport. *Don't forget to bring your camera with you.*

carry to take from one place to another. *Please carry these books home.*

fetch to go after and return with. *Will Brian fetch our luggage for us?*

antonym: take

C

calm *adj.* without excitement or motion. *The calm surface of the water looked like a mirror.*

peaceful without worry or trouble. *Their argument spoiled our peaceful day at the beach.*

tranquil quiet and undisturbed. *We found a tranquil picnic spot far from the main path.*

serene untroubled; composed. *The trees were reflected in the serene lake.*

sedate composed; dignified. *He remained sedate throughout the interrogation.*

antonyms: excited, frantic, raging, wild

capable *adj.* having or showing particular ability or strength. *Is Ernie capable of repairing his ten-speed bike?*

able having special power to do something. *Dawn, an able gymnast, has won several competitions.*

efficient working without wasting time, materials, or energy. *Because Leon is an efficient worker, he was promoted quickly.*

qualified suited for a particular purpose, position, or task. *Ed passed the test and became a qualified lifeguard.*

antonym: incompetent

Shades of Meaning

careful *adj.* giving serious thought and attention to what one is doing.

- - - - - - - - - - - - - - - - - - -

1. alert for danger or trouble:
   cautious
   vigilant
   watchful

2. wise and thoughtful:
   prudent, studious, mindful

3. paying attention to details:
   meticulous, conscientious, particular, thorough, strict

4. showing lack of trust:
   wary, guarded, protective

- - - - - - - - - - - - - - - - - - -

antonyms: heedless, careless, thoughtless, slack, lax

change *v.* to make or become different. *I like the way that you **changed** your hair.*

convert to put something to a new use. *The builder **converted** the barn into a two-family house.*

transform to alter completely the form of something. *The scientists tried to **transform** heat into energy.*

antonyms: continue, remain

chief *adj.* highest in rank or importance. *The **chief** product of the state is wheat.*

main most important. *The **main** library is bigger than its branches.*

principal leading all others. *The panda's **principal** food is a kind of bamboo.*

antonyms: minor, unimportant

choice *n.* the act of choosing or deciding. *Pedro had to make a **choice** between soccer and football.*

selection the act of picking one or a few out of several. *I tried on eight pairs of shoes before I made my **selection.***

preference a liking for one thing over another. *What is your **preference**—mashed or baked potatoes?*

alternative decision between two or more possibilities. *The **alternative** is between walking to school or riding your bike.*

clean *adj.* free from dirt, stains, and clutter. *Dad needs a **clean** shirt for work tomorrow.*

spotless completely free of dirt. *The operating rooms in hospitals must be **spotless.***

antonyms: dirty, filthy, soiled

clear *adj.* free from clouds, dust, or anything that would make it hard to see through. *The sky was so **clear** that we could see the Milky Way.*

transparent able to be seen through easily. *We watched the sharks through a **transparent** tank.*

antonyms: cloudy, foggy, misty

cold *adj.* at a low temperature. *Cold water is the most refreshing drink of all.*

chilly not warm enough for comfort. *If you feel **chilly,** you can sit in the sun.*

cool at a somewhat low temperature. *The **cool** breeze felt good after the heat of the day.*

icy feeling like ice. *How do birds stay alive in such **icy** winds?*

freezing producing icy conditions. *The **freezing** rain made driving difficult and dangerous.*

antonyms: hot, warm

common *adj.* often found or occurring; familiar. *A **common** response to a kind host is a thank-you note.*

ordinary not unusual in any way. *On an **ordinary** day, I dress, eat breakfast, and catch the bus.*

normal of the usual kind; natural. *The guest speaker provided a break from our **normal** school schedule.*

general widespread; prevalent. *The students had a **general** feeling of excitement before the big game.*

regular usual or standard. *Because our **regular** teacher is ill, we had a substitute today.*

antonyms: abnormal, extraordinary, rare, strange, unusual

conclusion *n.* 1. the close or finish of something. *The mystery was not solved until the* **conclusion** *of the book.* 2. a judgment made after careful thought. *The judge reached a* **conclusion** *after listening to the witness.*

end point at which something stops or finishes. *At the* **end** *of summer, we return to school.*

outcome something that happens as a result. *Because everyone was safe, the adventure had a happy* **outcome.**

decision the act of making up one's mind. *Please make a* **decision** *about whether to go or stay.*

deduction a judgment made by reasoning. *The famous detective based his* **deductions** *on clues.*

create *v.* to bring into being. *Spiders* **create** *webs to trap insects.*

establish to begin or set up. *The settlers soon* **established** *a small town.*

invent to make something that did not exist before. *No one is sure who really* **invented** *the camera.*

produce to bring forth, manufacture. *How many cars a year does Detroit* **produce?**

design to make a plan or a drawing for something. *An art student* **designed** *the school's new sign.*

antonym: destroy

D

danger *n.* the chance of great harm or loss. *There was no* **danger** *of getting lost if we stayed on the path.*

hazard something that could cause trouble. *A blocked door can be a fire* **hazard.**

risk the possibility of harm in an activity. *The* **risk** *of an accident increases on icy roads.*

peril a condition that can threaten one's life. *Anyone out in this storm will be in great* **peril.**

antonyms: safety, security, protection

dark *adj.* without light or sun. *It was so* **dark** *that we turned on the lights.*

dim not well lit. *Do not read in such* **dim** *light.*

murky very gloomy. *Evans was afraid to step into the* **murky** *cell.*

antonyms: bright, light

decide *v.* to make up one's mind. *I* **decided** *to buy the red bike instead of the blue one.*

determine to make a firm decision. *Dr. Tsao* **determined** *to do all that he could to save the cat.*

resolve to make a firm plan. *I* **resolve** *to eat a good breakfast every day.*

deserve *v.* ought to have or receive. *An animal lover like Paul* **deserves** *a pet.*

merit earn the right to something. *June's courage* **merits** *high praise.*

be worthy of be good or valuable enough to receive. *The animal shelter* **is worthy of** *your support.*

Shades of Meaning

do *v.*

1. to carry out an action:
   perform, execute, produce, make, work, act

2. to solve something:
   unscramble
   solve
   work out
   decode
   resolve

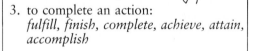

3. to complete an action:
   fulfill, finish, complete, achieve, attain, accomplish

antonyms: omit, undo, fail, quit

---

dull *adj.* not sharp. *It is difficult to cut anything with a* **dull** *knife.*

blunt having a thick end. *One end of an ax is* **blunt.**

antonyms: pointed, keen

E

eager *adj.* full of strong desire. *Eager campers arrived at dawn to set up their camp.*

keen full of enthusiasm and interest. *Ben, a **keen** sports fan, attends every game that he can.*

interested involved or concerned with. *Peg, an **interested** committee member, asks many questions.*

antonyms: bored, indifferent

easy *adj.* not difficult. *Tad solved the **easy** puzzle quickly.*

simple not complicated. *Use a **simple** drawing of a few lines.*

uncomplicated not hard to understand, deal with, or solve. *We followed Dad's **uncomplicated** directions without any problem.*

effortless easily done. *The athlete made weightlifting seem **effortless.***

antonyms: complex, difficult, hard

education *n.* schooling or instruction in a subject. *Reading is part of every student's **education.***

knowledge information on a subject. *Ida has no **knowledge** of chemistry.*

training guidance and practice in a skill. *Doctors must go through many years of **training.***

antonym: ignorance

effect *n.* something brought about by a cause. *The moon has an important **effect** on the ocean tides.*

consequence a direct outcome of something. *The musicians' fine performance was a **consequence** of their hard work.*

result something that happens because of something else. *The broken branches are the **result** of the storm.*

antonyms: cause, source

examine *v.* to look at closely. *If you **examine** this handwriting, you will notice that the tall letters curve slightly.*

investigate to look into carefully. *The fire chief **investigated** the cause of the unusual fire.*

example *n.* something that is picked out because it is like others of the same kind. *Here is an **example** of a paragraph that begins with a topic sentence.*

case a particular incident. *There were two **cases** of chicken pox in our class.*

instance one occurrence of something. *I cannot think of a single **instance** when our car has ever broken down.*

explore *v.* to look into or through closely. *Katie **explored** every inch of her closet for her missing shoe.*

study to examine closely and carefully. *Doris **studied** her math notes before the test.*

probe to search into thoroughly. *An investigator **probed** Rick's background but found nothing unusual.*

investigate to research carefully. *Who will **investigate** the jewel's disappearance?*

F

faithful *adj.* worthy of trust. *Ben knew his **faithful** friend would keep his secret.*

loyal offering constant support to a person, country, or cause. *The spy insisted that he was **loyal** to his country.*

true trustworthy and devoted. *Ariel was a **true** friend when I needed her.*

antonyms: changeable, treacherous, false

fake *n.* someone or something that is not what he, she, or it pretends to be. *The audience realized that the police officer was a **fake** soon after she came onstage.*

fraud a person who lies about himself or herself. *That **fraud** claimed that he could get us a free ticket, but he could not!*

phony an insincere person. *Pete tries to act friendly, but he is a **phony.***

impostor a person who pretends to be another person. *Was that woman really the queen or only an **impostor?***

fat *adj.* having much or too much body weight. *We put our dog on a diet because it is not healthy for an animal to be **fat.***

THESAURUS PLUS

fat (continued)

plump rounded and full in shape. *Karen's baby brother has **plump** cheeks that look like ripe peaches.*

stout large and heavy in build. *Al is slim, but his brother Ben is **stout**.*

antonyms: skinny, slender, slim, thin

finish *v.* to get done. *When you **finish** cleaning, you may go for a bike ride.*

end to bring or come to the final moments. *The first half **ended** when the whistle blew.*

complete to get to the end of something. *I **completed** the test just as the bell rang.*

stop to come to a halt. *The engine **stopped** when the car ran out of gas.*

conclude to be or cause to be over. *The crowd cheered when Ms. Wang **concluded** her speech.*

close to come to or bring to an end. *Alice **closed** her letter with greetings to the family.*

antonyms: begin, commence, start

How **Funny** Was It?

funny *adj.* causing laughter or amusement.

1. somewhat funny:
   amusing
   droll
   whimsical
   witty

2. quite funny:
   humorous
   laughable
   comical

3. extremely funny:
   ridiculous
   hilarious
   sidesplitting
   ludicrous
   absurd

antonyms: serious, sad, solemn, gloomy, depressing

---

further *adj.* added or other. *As the storm developed, the news station released **further** bulletins.*

more greater in size, quantity, extent, or degree. *We need **more** ice for the fruit juice.*

additional extra. *Take **additional** socks in case one pair gets wet.*

G

gather *v.* to bring or come together in one place. *They **gathered** around the campfire and sang songs.*

assemble to bring or come together as a group. *The band members must **assemble** in the auditorium at noon.*

collect to bring things together. *Tina has **collected** twenty different baseball hats in only one year.*

antonyms: scatter, separate

get *v.* to receive. *Did you **get** any payment for your work in the garden?*

earn to gain by working or by supplying a service. *Jay **earns** five dollars a week by baby-sitting for families in his neighborhood.*

obtain to gain by means of planning or effort. *Carol took a test to **obtain** her driver's license.*

win to receive as a prize or reward. *Did Joe **win** a prize in the school essay contest?*

acquire to gain by one's own efforts. *Ed worked many hours to **acquire** his skill in typing.*

buy to gain by paying a price for. *Ana used her allowance to **buy** a gift for her mother.*

antonym: lose

give *v.* to hand over to another. *Sara **gave** her sister a music box for her birthday.*

offer to put forward to be accepted or refused. *Jan **offered** Ina half of her sandwich and apple.*

supply to make available something that is needed. *The blood **supplies** oxygen to the brain.*

present to make a gift or award to. *Coach Hart **presented** the trophy to the captain of our basketball team.*
antonyms: receive, take

glance *v.* to look briefly. *I **glanced** at him quickly.*
glimpse to get a brief view of. *She only **glimpsed** the passing car.*
peek to look briefly. *He **peeked** around the corner.*

grateful *adj.* feeling or showing thanks. *The Smiths were **grateful** when their neighbors helped rebuild their porch and barn.*
appreciative expressing or feeling gratitude. *The **appreciative** man thanked Lori for finding his cat.*
thankful showing an understanding of how fortunate one is. *Dad was **thankful** that no one was hurt.*

great *adj.* remarkable. *Pearl took **great** pictures of the baseball game.*
terrific excellent. *A **terrific** swimmer like Natalie should make the team.*
fantastic extraordinary. *There is a **fantastic** view of the ocean from our porch.*
wonderful astonishing. *This is a **wonderful** museum.*
marvelous notably superior. *Your speech was **marvelous.***
antonyms: inferior, ordinary

Shades of **Green**

green *adj.* having the color of grass; a mix of blue and yellow.

- - - - -

olive: light yellowish-green, like green olives
lime: bright yellowish-green, like limes
kelly: bright green, like grass or clover
emerald: bright, slightly dark green, like emeralds
hunter: dark green, like pine trees and cucumbers

---

grow *v.* to become or cause to become larger. *Lots of rain helped the plants **grow** tall.*
raise to promote the development of. *Kate **raised** her puppy with love and discipline, and he grew into a wonderful dog.*
produce to bring forth; yield. *Kansas **produces** wheat that is sent all over the world.*
mature to develop fully. *Has the fruit **matured** enough to be picked?*
antonym: stunt

H

happy *adj.* showing or feeling pleasure or joy. *Tina was **happy** because she got the lead part in the play.*
cheerful being in good spirits. *It is always pleasant to be around **cheerful** people.*
glad pleased. *Sam was **glad** to be home again after his long trip to twelve countries.*
antonyms: sad, sorrowful

healthy *adj.* free from disease or injury. *The **healthy** plants grew strong and tall.*
fit being in good physical shape. *Since he began jogging, Drew has felt healthy and **fit.***
sound having no damage or disease. *Surprisingly, the shabby old house still had a **sound** frame.*
well not sick. *Even during the flu season, Molly stayed **well.***
antonyms: diseased, ill, sick

hide *v.* to keep or put out of sight. *The cat **hid** under the bed, but her long, bushy tail stuck out.*
conceal purposely to keep from being seen or known. *Allan **concealed** his sadness behind a happy face.*
bury to cover from view. *The dog **buried** another bone under the rose bush.*
antonyms: reveal, show

honest *adj.* straightforward; truthful. *The **honest** witness told the truth in court.*
direct to the point. *I will be **direct** and not waste time.*

honest (continued)

frank free and open in expressing thoughts or feelings. *In a **frank** talk, I told Lina how I felt.*

antonyms: deceitful, insincere, misleading

I

important *adj.* strongly affecting the way things happen. *Since Joe has something **important** to tell us, please listen to him carefully.*

significant notable. *The year 1776 is a **significant** one in the history of the United States.*

antonyms: minor, unnecessary, worthless

J

join *v.* to put together or attach. *We all **joined** hands to form a circle.*

connect to link things together. *A bridge **connects** the two cities.*

unite to bring together to form a whole. *The thirteen colonies **united** to form one nation.*

antonyms: part, separate

jump *v.* to rise up or move through the air. *The cow in the nursery rhyme **jumps** over the moon.*

hurdle to go over a barrier. *The horse **hurdled** the fence and galloped away.*

leap to jump or cause to jump quickly or suddenly. *Carl **leaped** away from the falling tree.*

spring to move upward or forward in one quick motion. *I **spring** out of bed when my alarm rings.*

L

last *adv.* after all the others. *Add the ice **last** so that it does not melt.*

finally after a long while. *After waiting two hours, the train **finally** arrived.*

at the end at the conclusion. *Flo delivered a good speech, but she stumbled **at the end.***

antonym: first

Shades of Meaning

laugh *v.* to make sounds in the throat to express amusement.

- - - - - - - - - - - - - - - - - - -

1. to laugh quietly:
   giggle, chuckle, titter

2. to laugh in a mean or sly way:
   snicker, snigger

3. to laugh loudly:
   cackle, chortle, guffaw, roar, shriek, howl

- - - - - - - - - - - - - - - - - - -

antonyms: whimper, weep, cry, wail, sob, blubber

---

leave *v.* to go away from. *Please **leave** this dangerous place at once!*

abandon to go away from because of trouble or danger; to desert. *The crew **abandoned** the sinking ship.*

quit to depart from. *Phil wants to **quit** Seattle and move to Tulsa.*

antonyms: arrive, come, return

little *adj.* not big in size or quantity. *Leroy is six feet tall, but he looks **little** next to that thirty-foot statue.*

tiny extremely reduced in size. *Dan could not read the **tiny** print without his glasses.*

small reduced in size. *I cannot wear this coat because it is too **small.***

miniature reduced from its usual size. *Ella built a **miniature** city with toothpicks and glue.*

antonyms: enormous, large

lively *adj.* full of energy, active. *They were out of breath after dancing a **lively** polka.*

chipper full of cheer. *Ike felt **chipper** on this lovely morning.*

energetic full of strength and action. *The **energetic** children played on the swings all morning.*

spirited full of life. *Our team played a* **spirited** *game and won.*
antonyms: inactive, lazy

Shades of Meaning

look *v.* to focus one's eyes or attention on something.

1. to look quickly:
   glimpse, glance, scan

2. to look secretively:
   spy
   peek
   peep
   snoop

3. to look long and thoughtfully:
   gaze, contemplate, view

4. to look steadily and directly:
   stare, gape, gawk

5. to look with anger or displeasure:
   glower, glare, scowl

antonyms: overlook, dismiss, ignore, avoid, shun

M

make *v.* to shape or put together out of materials or parts. *Mrs. Lewis* **made** *that rug from pieces of old clothes and curtains.*
build to put up something with materials or parts. *Dad* **built** *a tree house in our yard.*
construct to make by fitting parts together. *Will the town* **construct** *a bridge over the river?*
form to shape. *Ali* **formed** *a bird out of her piece of clay.*
manufacture to put things together with machines. *That factory* **manufactures** *many popular toys and games.*
antonyms: destroy, dismantle

many *adj.* adding up to a large number. *Jay learned to identify the* **many** *different birds on the island.*
several more than two but not a large number. *The power was out for* **several** *hours after the storm.*
numerous made up of a large number. **Numerous** *people lined up outside the factory to apply for a job.*
antonym: few

meaning *n.* the intended thought or message of something. *Ms. Clark explained the* **meaning** *of the poem to her puzzled students.*
significance the special message or intention. *What is the* **significance** *of the maple leaf on the Canadian flag?*
sense the many ideas implied by a word. *The* **sense** *of a word usually depends on its use in a sentence.*
antonyms: nonsense, pointlessness

moment *n.* a very short period of time. *Please wait just a* **moment,** *and a salesperson will help you.*
instant a second in time. *In an* **instant,** *before anyone could blink, the clown had disappeared.*

N

necessary *adj.* having to be done. *It is* **necessary** *that you complete this form in order to apply for a license.*
essential very important, basic. *Regular brushing is* **essential** *to healthy teeth.*
required called for or needed. *Frank earned the* **required** *number of stripes to become a sergeant.*

nervous *adj.* shaken and jittery because of fear or challenge. *The* **nervous** *actor was afraid that he would forget his lines.*
anxious upset or fearful about something uncertain. *Olive feels* **anxious** *about whether it will rain for the picnic.*
edgy tense. *Bill was* **edgy** *the night before the exam and could not sleep.*
antonyms: calm, placid

new *adj.* never used, worn, or thought of before. *When our old car stopped running, we finally bought a **new** one.*

fresh just made, grown, or gathered. *These are **fresh** beans, straight from grandfather's garden.*

original not copied from or based on anything else. *The brilliant inventor came up with another **original** idea.*

novel strikingly different. *The detective's **novel** method of investigation has never been duplicated.*

antonyms: old, ancient, antique

Shades of Meaning

nice *adj.*

1. pleasing:
   pleasant, agreeable, appealing, delightful, refreshing, lovely, charming, enchanting, delicious

2. good:
   fine, skillful, admirable, splendid, superb, excellent

3. kind:
   *sweet
   companionable
   gentle
   sympathetic
   friendly
   amiable
   mild*

4. polite:
   gracious, considerate, proper, well-mannered, courteous

antonyms: insulting, offensive, displeasing, repellent, terrible, flawed, vile, mean, contemptible, vicious, rude, cold-hearted, crass

---

O

opponent *n.* a person who is against another in a game or contest. *Eva tried to win the race, but she lost to Sue, her **opponent**.*

competitor a person or group that wants to win against another. *Susan and I were **competitors** for the senior class presidency.*

rival someone who tries to do as well as or better than another. *Jim was my **rival** for the top prize.*

antonym: teammate

opposite *adj.* altogether different. *Because we have such different tastes, we came to **opposite** decisions.*

contradictory disagreeing. *The two **contradictory** stories of the accident confused the officer.*

contrary extremely different. *Jane and I are friends even though we have **contrary** opinions about everything.*

antonyms: identical, similar

P

perfect *adj.* having no errors, flaws, or defects. *A **perfect** day for sailing is sunny and slightly breezy.*

ideal thought of as being the best possible. *Casey has an **ideal** job that allows her to travel and make important decisions.*

excellent of the highest quality. *The chef made our **excellent** meal from the freshest ingredients.*

delightful very pleasing. *A **delightful** breeze cooled the hot beach.*

antonyms: faulty, flawed

persuade *v.* to cause someone to do or believe something by pleading, arguing, or reasoning. *I **persuaded** Jim to clean my room for me.*

convince to cause someone to feel certain. *I **convinced** my mother that I was telling the truth.*

antonyms: dissuade, deter

Word Bank

pretty *adj.* pleasing to the eye or ear.

attractive	lovely	radiant
beautiful	charming	glamorous
stunning	handsome	ravishing
cute	gorgeous	glorious
appealing	dazzling	brilliant

antonyms: ugly, unattractive, homely, offensive, unappealing, disgusting, repulsive, revolting

price *n.* the amount of money asked or paid for something. *The price of this shirt at Ames's store is $10.95.*

charge a fee asked or paid, particularly for a service. *Is there a charge for washing the car windshield and windows, or is it a free service?*

cost amount of payment for a product or a service. *The cost of a concert ticket has risen to fifteen dollars.*

expense something paid out. *Can we afford the expense of piano lessons?*

protect *v.* to keep safe from harm or injury. *Calvin wears a helmet to protect his head when he rides his bike or goes roller skating.*

guard to defend or keep safe from danger. *The police guarded the museum against theft.*

antonym: endanger

pull *v.* to apply force to in order to draw someone or something in the direction of the force. *I pulled the door toward me as hard as I could.*

drag to draw along the ground by force. *Jim dragged the heavy trash barrel across the lawn.*

haul to draw along behind, usually with great effort. *The horse hauled the heavy wagon up the mountain.*

tow to draw along behind with a chain or a rope. *With a strong rope, the big boat towed our canoe into the harbor.*

antonyms: push, shove

put *v.* to cause to be in a particular position. *Put your bike in the shed.*

place to lay something in a certain space. *Place your hands on your hips.*

locate to establish something in a certain area. *Locate your garden in a sunny place.*

set to cause to be in a particular location. *Set your books on the table.*

antonyms: remove, take away

Q

quick *adj.* done or happening without delay. *We took a quick trip to the store just before dinner.*

fast moving or acting with speed. *Traveling by plane is faster than traveling by car.*

hasty in a hurried way. *Jim scribbled a hasty note and then ran out the door.*

rapid marked by speed. *The rapid subway train zoomed through the tunnel.*

swift able to move at great speed. *You will need a swift horse if you want to get to the farm before dinner.*

speedy able to get from one place to another in a short time. *A speedy little rabbit outran my dog.*

antonym: slow

R

real *adj.* not imaginary, made up, or artificial. *This apple looks real, but it is wax.*

actual existing or happening. *Tory's visit to the palace was an actual event, not just a dream.*

true in agreement with fact. *Whether or not you believe it, the story is true.*

antonyms: artificial, fake

S

same *adj.* being the very one. *This train is the same one that I rode last week.*

equal being alike in any measured quantity. *The two questions were worth an equal number of points.*

identical exactly alike. *The twins were identical; no one could tell them apart.*

antonym: different

scary *adj.* causing fear. *Your story was so scary that I was afraid to walk home.*

alarming causing a feeling of approaching danger. *The police siren was alarming to drivers.*

frightening causing sudden, great fear. *He told us that the frightening crash was only a thunderstorm.*

terrifying causing overpowering fright. *The terrifying noise made me freeze in my tracks.*

see *v.* to take in with the eyes. *Julie stared at the tree, but she could not see the bird.*

notice to pay attention to. *Ron entered quietly, but we noticed he was late.*

observe to watch carefully. *The cat observed the bird in the tree.*

view to look at. *On our field trip, we viewed the entire city from the top of the Washington Monument.*

antonyms: ignore, overlook

shake *v.* to move back and forth or up and down with short, quick movements. *The leaves on the oak tree shook in the wind.*

quake to move suddenly, as from shock. *The ground quaked when the herd of cattle moved by.*

shiver to move without control, as from cold or nervousness. *The child shivered in the cold rain.*

shudder to move with sudden, sharp movements, as from fear or horror. *Joe shuddered when he read about the disaster.*

tremble move back and forth gently or slightly, as from cold or fear. *My lips trembled as I began my speech.*

sharp *adj.* having a thin edge that cuts or a fine point that pierces. *I need sharp scissors to cut this heavy cloth.*

pointed having a fine tip that can puncture, as a pin or a pencil. *Be careful of the pointed ends of nails and tacks, for they can hurt you.*

antonyms: blunt, dull, rounded

shiny *adj.* reflecting light. *Craig's shiny new bike sparkled in the sun.*

bright giving off strong rays of light. *Mrs. Ruiz wore sunglasses to protect her eyes from the bright sun.*

gleaming glowing with light. *The gleaming runway lights showed the pilot where to land.*

glistening sparkling. *The sun turned the lake into a glistening pool of light.*

antonyms: dark, dim, dull

shout *v.* to call out at the top of one's voice. *The fans at the football game shouted, "Go, team, go!"*

yell to make a loud outcry, often in anger. *Helen yelled, "Your dog is eating my glove!"*

cry to utter a special sound or call. *Jeremy cried out in sudden pain.*

holler to call out to. *"Sue, come in for dinner," I hollered.*

antonym: whisper

some *adj.* being an unspecified number or amount of. *Joanne invited some friends to play volleyball next Saturday.*

few being a small number of. *Few people today get enough exercise.*

several more than two but not a large number. *Carl moved several blocks away, but we can still walk there easily.*

source *n.* the person, place, or point from which something comes. *The source of the leak was a broken pipe.*

cause someone or something that makes something happen. *Heavy rain was the cause of the flood.*

origin the beginning of something. *Both of these vocabulary words have a Middle English origin.*

antonyms: effect, end, result

start *v.* to take the first step in an action. *Joan turned to page one and **started** to read her book.*

begin to get a process underway. *I will **begin** my homework right after school.*

commence to perform the first part of an action. *The graduation ceremony **commences** at noon and should be over by one o'clock.*

antonyms: close, end, finish, stop

strange *adj.* different; unfamiliar. *I felt **strange** on my first day at the new school.*

weird odd or peculiar. *My brother has a **weird** sense of humor.*

antonyms: normal, familiar

succeed *v.* to carry out something attempted or desired. *After days of trying, Alice finally **succeeded** in fixing the radio.*

achieve to do or accomplish successfully. *Evan **achieved** his goal when he won the race.*

gain to get or obtain by effort. *Jill **gained** good experience from her summer job in an office.*

antonym: fail

surprise *v.* to cause to feel wonder because of the unexpected. *The sudden thunder **surprised** the picnickers in the park.*

amaze to fill with wonder or awe. *The skilled juggler **amazed** the crowd with his remarkable act.*

astonish to startle greatly. *The unexpected news **astonished** the world.*

astound to strike with great wonder. *People were **astounded** by the speed of the new plane.*

T

thin *adj.* having little fat on the body. *After his diet, Joe looked **thin**.*

skinny having very little fat on the body; bony. *The sick kitten was so **skinny** that we could see its ribs.*

slender having little fat or width. *The **slender** ballerina seemed almost like a doll.*

antonyms: fat, plump, stout

Shades of Meaning

think *v.*

1. to use one's mind:
   consider
   evaluate
   reflect
   study

2. to have an opinion:
   feel
   judge
   assert
   believe

3. to suppose:
   imagine
   conceive
   dream
   speculate

antonyms: forget, ignore

try *v.* to evaluate the quality or effect of. *Carl **tried** a new pasta recipe.*

attempt to make an effort. *The pole vaulter **attempted** to break a world's record.*

test to study or examine to find out the nature or value of something. *Scientists **tested** each new product to be sure that it was safe.*

U

unclear *adj.* not easy to see, hear, or understand. *Those complicated directions are **unclear**.*

fuzzy blurred. *The TV picture was so **fuzzy** that we could not see any details.*

confusing mixed up. *The recipe was so **confusing** that we could not follow the steps.*

cloudy hazy; not clear. *The powder made the water **cloudy**.*

faint not distinct or bright. *The star was only a **faint** speck in the sky.*

antonyms: distinct, obvious, sharp

THESAURUS PLUS

unreasonable *adj.* not having or showing good sense. *Ms. Jacobs is always fair and never makes unreasonable demands.*

illogical not using or showing sound reasoning. *It is illogical to think that because one dog barks too much, all dogs do.*

irrational lacking the ability to think things through. *The irrational man refused to consider the facts.*

nonsensical foolish, silly, or absurd. *The suggestion was too nonsensical to be discussed seriously.*

antonym: sensible

upset *adj.* sad or unsettled. *I was upset when I heard the bad news.*

worried uneasy because of fear. *Janet was worried about getting lost.*

nervous shaken and jittery because of fear or challenge. *Dean was nervous because he had to give a speech.*

troubled concerned because of pain, fear, or sadness. *Phil was troubled by his father's illness.*

disturbed being bothered or feeling unsettled. *They were disturbed by some noisy fire engines.*

antonyms: calm, comfortable, pleased, satisfied, composed

useful *adj.* being of service. *A rake is useful for cleaning up the yard.*

handy convenient, easy to use. *A wastebasket is a handy thing to have in each room of the house.*

helpful providing assistance. *I found this book helpful when I was looking for facts about Bill Cosby.*

antonyms: inefficient, useless, worthless

W

warning *n.* something that urges one to watch out for danger. *The sign was a warning to drivers about a dangerous curve ahead.*

alarm a bell or light that alerts one to danger. *The fire alarm clanged as smoke filled the attic.*

signal a sign or other device that gives information or urges caution. *As the traffic signal turned from green to red, the cars came to a stop.*

How **Wet** Was It?

wet *adj.* covered or moistened with liquid.

1. extremely wet:
   drenched
   saturated
   soaked
   water-logged
   sopping
   flooded

2. quite wet:
   dripping
   soppy
   soggy
   sodden

3. slightly wet:
   moist
   damp
   dank
   dewy
   wettish

antonyms: parched, arid, dry, dehydrated

while *conj.* at the same period of time as. *I was waiting at the airport for Lois while she was waiting at the train station for me.*

as long as for an entire length of time. *We vowed to remain friends as long as we lived.*

wish *v.* to want, hope for. *What sights do you wish to see in the city?*

desire to want strongly. *More than anything else, Jan desired to travel around the world.*

crave to long for intensely. *The thirsty runners craved a cool drink.*

■ L I T E R A T U R E   V O C A B U L A R Y ■

A

advertisement |ăd′ vər tīz′ mənt| *n.* A public notice, as in a newspaper, to call attention to a product or employment opportunity. *I read your advertisement about dogs for sale.*

aft |ăft| *adv.* Toward or at the rear of a ship. *The crew ran forward and aft to reach all the fire hoses.*

almighty |ôl mī′ tē| *adj.* Great; very noticeable. *Those cats make an almighty racket at night.*

aspen |ăs′ pən| *adj.* Relating to a type of poplar tree with leaves that flutter in the lightest breeze. *I saw a bird's nest in the aspen tree.*

audience |ô′ dē əns| *adj.* Relating to a formal meeting with a head of government or other official. *We waited for the prince in his audience room.*

B

ballast |băl′ əst| *n.* Any heavy material carried in a ship to add weight for steady sailing. *On this ship we use sandbags for ballast.*

banish |băn′ ĭsh| *v.* banished, banishing To force to leave a country or place; to exile. *The sheriff banished the outlaw from town.*

battered |băt′ ərd| *adj.* Damaged by heavy use. *She found that definition in an old battered dictionary.*

betray |bĭ trā| *v.* To be disloyal or unfaithful to. *He did not betray his promise to me.*

bilge |bĭlj| *adj.* Relating to the stale water that collects in the lowest part of a ship's hull. *Bilge water leaked into the ship's hull.*

C

calloused |kăl′ əsd| *adj.* Having thickened skin as a result of some activity or work. *His calloused fingertips plucked the guitar strings.*

cascade |kăs kād′| *v.* To fall in sheets like moving water over rocks. *Water cascades down hundreds of feet at Niagara Falls.*

caution |kô′ shən| *v.* cautioned, cautioning To warn against possible danger or trouble. *She cautioned me to stay away from the river.*

chief |chēf| *adj.* Highest ranking. *My cousin was appointed chief engineer.*

confidence |kŏn′ fĭ dəns| *n.* The trust that someone will keep a secret. *I am telling you this story in strict confidence.*

conquistadore |kŏn kwĭs′ tə dôr′| *n., pl.* conquistadores One of the Spanish conquerors of Mexico and Peru in the 16th century. *Cortes, one of the conquistadores, landed in Mexico in 1519.*

consult |kən sŭlt′| *v.* consulted, consulting To seek advice or information of. *I will answer after consulting my lawyer.*

counselor |koun′ sə lər| *n.* 1. A person of knowledge and experience who gives wise advice. 2. A person who gives wise advice to a leader of state. *She was counselor to the president.*

courtyard |kôrt′ yärd′| *n.* An open space next to or within a castle where a King or Queen would hold open court. *We walked through the old courtyard of the French kings.*

crow's-nest |krōz′ nĕst′| *n.* A small lookout platform near the top of a ship's mast. *From the crow's-nest, the mate spotted land.*

D

deliberately |dĭ lĭb′ ər ĭt lē| *adv.* 1. Very carefully. 2. Not in a hurried way; slowly. *He moved each foot deliberately when I began ice skating.*

destine |dĕs′ tĭn| *v.* destined, destining 1. To determine or decide in advance. 2. To train or set apart for a special use. *Rover is destined to be a good hunting dog.*

digestive |dĭ jĕs′ tĭv| *adj.* Relating to the body's breakdown of food into energy. *Food breaks down in the body's* **digestive** *system.*

duplicate |dōō′ plĭ kĭt| *adj.* Being exactly like another. *Rose had a* **duplicate** *key made.*

E

elongate |ĭ lông′ gāt′| *v.* elongated, elongating To make longer; extend; lengthen. *The ballet classes helped her form* **elongated** *muscles.*

encase |ĕn kās′| *v.* encased, encasing To close in as if in a case. *This sea shell is* **encased** *in clear plastic.*

energetic |ĕn′ ər jĕt′ ĭk| *adj.* Full of energy; very active. *Kittens are very playful and* **energetic.**

exaggerate |ĭg zăj′ ə rāt′| *v.* To describe something as being larger than it really is; to overstate. *Janet* **exaggerates** *when she says her brother is a giant.*

F

fantastic |făn tăs′ tĭk| *adj.* Very remarkable; better by far than imagined. *He wrote a* **fantastic** *report.*

fashion |făsh′ ən| *v.* fashioned, fashioning To give a form or shape to. *We* **fashioned** *figures from the wet clay.*

fawn |fôn| *v.* fawned, fawning To show friendliness or affection. *The kitten was purring and* **fawning** *over me.*

flare |flâr| *v.* flared, flaring To expand in shape; to become suddenly larger often due to emotion. *The bull's nostrils* **flared** *at the sight of another bull.*

fog-bound *or* **fogbound** |fôg′ bound′| *adj.* Completely covered by fog. *No ships will sail when the harbor is* **fog-bound.**

furl |fûrl| *v.* To roll up and fasten. *The sailor was ordered to* **furl** *the sails.*

G

galleon |găl′ ē ən| *n.* A large sailing ship of former times with three masts and several decks. *The Spanish* **galleon** *left port loaded with gold.*

generation |jĕn′ ə rā′ shən| *n.* The average length of time between the birth of parents and the birth of their children. *Only one* **generation** *of my family lives in this country.*

H

heir |âr| *n.* A person who is in line to succeed to the rank, title, and property of another. *The young princess was* **heir** *to the kingdom.*

I

immense |ĭ mĕns′| *adj.* Extremely large; huge. *A whale is an* **immense** *mammal.*

inscribe |ĭn skrīb′| *v.* inscribed, inscribing To write, print, or engrave words on a surface. *Our names were* **inscribed** *on the trophy.*

K

knothole |nŏt′ hōl′| *n.* A hole in a tree or board where a knot has been knocked out. *There is a huge* **knothole** *in this piece of lumber.*

L

latitude |lăt′ ĭ tōōd′| *n.* Distance north or south of the equator measured in degrees. *We found the* **latitude** *of Rome in the atlas.*

light |līt| *v.* To come to rest; to perch. *Joel saw a robin whirl and* **light** *on a branch.*

M

memorable |mĕm′ ər ə bəl| *adj.* Worth remembering. *Many of Abraham Lincoln's speeches contain* **memorable** *words.*

methodically |mə **thŏd′** ĭ kəl lē| *adv.* The quality of a regular or deliberate way of doing something. *She methodically looked through the card catalog.*

minister |**mĭn′** ĭ stər| *n.* A person who is head of a government department. *The minister of the treasury spoke to the king first.*

mushroom |**mŭsh′** rōōm′| *v.* mushroomed, mushrooming To grow, spread, or multiply quickly. *Houses mushroomed at the edge of the city.*

musty |**mŭs′** tē| *adj.* Having a stale or moldy smell. *The dress I found in the cellar smells musty.*

N

neigh |nā| *n.* The long, high-pitched sound made by a horse. *We heard the loud neigh of a horse.*

O

offspring |**ôf′** sprĭng′| *n., pl.* offspring The young of a person, animal, or plant. *Rabbits can have many offspring.*

P

plucked |plŭkt| *adj.* Looking as if all the feathers have been pulled out. *My very short haircut made me look like a plucked chicken.*

plummet |**plŭm′** ĭt| *v.* plummeted, plummeting To drop straight down; to plunge. *The brick came loose and plummeted to the ground.*

poop deck |pōōp dĕk| *n.* The raised deck at the rear of a sailing ship. *The first mate paced back and forth on the poop deck.*

poplar |**pŏp′** lər| *n., pl.* poplars A kind of tree with triangle shaped leaves and soft light-colored wood. *The leaves from the poplars floated to the ground.*

pouch |pouch| *n.* A small leather or cloth bag tied together at its top by a string. *Lee untied his pouch and spilled the coins on the table.*

prehistoric |prē′ hĭ **stôr′** ĭk| *adj.* Belonging to the time before people began to record events in writing. *Dinosaurs lived in prehistoric times.*

proclamation |prŏk′ lə **mā′** shən| *n.* An official written public notice of an event, holiday, or emergency. *The mayor's proclamation will make tomorrow a holiday.*

purse |pûrs| *v.* To draw together, to pucker. *The sour taste made Ana purse her lips.*

Q

quality |**kwŏl′** ĭ tē| *n., pl.* qualities A special feature of a person, usually of an excellent nature. *She has the qualities of a good leader.*

quote |kwōt| *n.* The words of another repeated exactly. When in print the words are surrounded by quotation marks (""). *I began my report with a quote from a book.*

R

range |rānj| *v.* ranged, ranging To travel or roam over an area. *Buffalo once ranged over much of this land.*

recycle |rē **sī′** kəl| *v.* recycled, recycling To treat materials that have been thrown away in order to use them again. *Our city is recycling old newspapers.*

reef |rēf| *n., pl.* reefs A strip or ridge of rocks, sand, or coral at or just below the surface of the water. *The coral reefs have torn apart many boats.*

resume |rĭ **zōōm′**| *v.* resumed, resuming To begin again; to continue. *The game resumed after a brief break.*

reveal |rĭ **vēl′**| *v.* To make known. *Please don't reveal my secret.*

ruffle |**rŭf′** əl| *v.* ruffled, ruffling To cause a bird's feathers to stand up. *The mother goose was ruffling her feathers.*

S

sand bar *or* **sandbar** |**sănd′** bär′| *n.* A mass of sand near a shore built up by the motion of waves or currents. *The girls pulled their sailboat onto the sand bar.*

LITERATURE VOCABULARY

secrecy |sē′ krĭ sē| *n.* The practice of keeping secrets. *We were sworn to **secrecy** not to reveal the formula.*

shoal |shōl| *n.* A shallow place in a body of water; a sandbar. *Many boats have hit this **shoal**.*

shuck |shŭk| *v.* shucked, shucking 1. To remove the outer covering. 2. To remove as in one's clothes. *We **shucked** off our sandals and dove into the lake.*

shuffle |shŭf′ əl| *v.* shuffled, shuffling To walk slowly while dragging the feet. *The man was **shuffling** toward the corner store.*

skylark |skī′ lärk′| *v.* skylarked, skylarking To frolic or romp in a playful way. *They were laughing and **skylarking** in the field.*

slat |slăt| *n., pl.* slats A narrow strip of metal or wood. *We burned the **slats** of wood in the fireplace.*

slimy |slī′ mē| *adj.* Like something thick, slippery, or sticky. *After rolling in the mud, our dog's fur was black and **slimy**.*

smoke |smōk| *v.* smoked, smoking To preserve meat or fish by exposing it to smoke. *She is **smoking** a turkey in the grill.*

spar |spär| *n., pl.* spars A wooden pole used as a mast on a sailing ship. *The sails are rigged from the **spars** on old sailing ships.*

squall |skwôl| *n., pl.* squalls A sudden, brief, violent windstorm, usually with rain. ***Squalls** are sudden, dangerous storms.*

stalk |stôk| *v.* stalked, stalking To move in a quiet way as to sneak up on an animal. *The tiger was **stalking** a zebra.*

stammer |stăm′ ər| *v.* stammered, stammering To falter or stumble in speaking, often because of fear. *"B-but I'm innocent," he **stammered**.*

starch |stärch| *n.* A compound found in wheat, corn, rice, and potatoes used to make paste. *You need **starch** to make some kinds of paste.*

sterilize |stĕr′ ə līz′| *v.* sterilized, sterilizing To rid of germs usually by boiling or steaming. *My father **sterilized** the baby's bottles.*

stern |stûrn| *n.* The rear part of a ship or boat. *A ship's rudder is found at the **stern**.*

sternpost |stûrn′ pōst′| *n.* A device at the rear of a ship which holds the rudder. *The old sailing ship has a carved wooden **sternpost**.*

subject |sŭb′ jĭkt| *n.* A person or thing about which something is said or done; a topic. *The **subject** of my report is Marco Polo.*

swear |swâr| *v.* swore, sworn, swearing To promise; to vow. *The witness was **sworn** to tell the truth.*

T

torment |tôr′ mĕnt′| *v.* tormented, tormenting 1. To cause great pain. 2. To tease or annoy. *The bluejay swooped down and **tormented** my cat.*

tremor |trĕm′ ər| *n.* A shaking or trembling. *The **tremor** in her hands showed that she was nervous.*

trickster |trĭk′ stər| *n.* Someone who cheats or deceives. *The **trickster** fooled the unsuspecting audience.*

V

vexation |vĕk sā′ shən| *n.* The condition of being annoyed, bothered, or puzzled. *A look of **vexation** crossed her face when she saw the broken bowl.*

vibration |vī brā′ shən| *n., pl.* vibrations The waves of sound which travel through air, water, or solids. *I can feel the engine's **vibrations** when I sit in your car.*

viceroy |vīs′ roi′| *n.* The person chosen by a king as the governor of a country, province, or colony. *The **viceroy** ruled the province wisely.*

W

wick |wĭk| *n.* A thin strip of cloth placed in oil, wax, or animal fat which burns slowly. Found in a candle or an oil lamp. *Make sure the **wick** of the kerosene lamp is soaked with oil.*

▪ LANGUAGE TERMS ▪

abbreviation a shortened form of a word.

action verb shows what the subject does or did.

adjective a word that describes a noun or a pronoun.

adverb a word that describes a verb and that tells how, when, or where.

articles the special adjectives *a*, *an*, and *the*.

common noun names any person, place, or thing.

complete predicate contains all the words in the predicate.

complete subject contains all the words in the subject.

compound predicate two or more simple predicates that have the same subject. Use a conjunction to join the simple predicates.

compound sentence two sentences with related ideas that are connected by a conjunction.

compound subject two or more simple subjects that have the same predicate. Use a conjunction to join the simple subjects.

conjunction used to connect words or groups of words (*and, but, or*).

contraction the shortened form of one or more words. An apostrophe replaces the missing letter or letters.

declarative sentence tells something and ends with a period.

demonstrative adjective tells which one (*this, that, these,* and *those*).

direct object a noun or a pronoun in the predicate that receives the action of the verb.

direct quotation gives a speaker's exact words and is set off by quotation marks.

exclamatory sentence expresses strong feeling and ends with an exclamation point.

future tense verb tells what will happen.

helping verb works with the main verb.

imperative sentence gives an order and ends with a period.

interrogative sentence asks something and ends with a question mark.

introductory words words such as *yes, no, oh,* and *well* when they begin a sentence.

irregular verbs have special forms to show the past.

linking verb joins the subject to a word in the predicate that names or describes the subject.

main verb shows action.

negative a word that means "no" or "not."

noun a word that names a person, a place, a thing, or an idea.

noun in direct address the name of a person who is spoken to.

object of the preposition the noun or the pronoun that follows a preposition.

object pronouns used after action verbs and prepositions (*me, you, him, her, it, us,* and *them*).

past tense verb shows that something already happened.

plural noun names more than one person, place, thing, or idea.

plural possessive noun shows that more than one person, place, or thing has or owns something. It is formed by adding an apostrophe or an apostrophe and *s* to a plural noun.

possessive pronoun shows ownership. Use *my, your, his, her, its, our,* and *their* before nouns. Use *mine, yours, his, hers, its, ours,* and *theirs* to replace nouns.

predicate tells what the subject is or does.

preposition relates the noun or the pronoun that follows it to another word in the sentence.

prepositional phrase made up of a preposition, its object, and all the words between them.

present tense verb shows action that happens now.

pronoun a word that replaces a noun.

proper adjective formed from a proper noun.

proper noun names a particular person, place, or thing.

regular verbs   form the past tense by adding -*d* or -*ed* to the verb.

run-on sentence   two or more sentences that run together.

sentence   a group of words that expresses a complete thought.

sentence fragment   a group of words that does not express a complete thought.

simple predicate   or verb is the main word or words in the complete predicate.

simple subject   the main word or words in the complete subject.

singular noun   names one person, place, thing, or idea.

singular possessive noun   shows that one person, place, or thing has or owns something. It is formed by adding an apostrophe and *s* to a singular noun.

subject   tells whom or what the sentence is about.

subject pronouns   used as subjects and after forms of the verb *be* (*I, you, he, she, it, we,* and *they*).

verb phrase   made up of a main verb and a helping verb.

■ INDEX ■

responding to, 59, 76, 117, 136, 201, 216, 257, 276, 321, 340, 383

types of
autobiography, 54–57
nonfiction, 115–116, 380–382
novel excerpts, 110–114, 248–253, 314–319, 374–379
poetry, 58, 80, 108, 140, 220, 246, 254, 255, 256, 280, 344, 410
short story, 194–200
writing about, 59, 76, 136, 216, 276, 320, 340, 406
See also Literary terms

Literature Vocabulary, 557–560

Logical conclusions. *See* Drawing conclusions

M

Main idea
identifying, **122**
listening for, **473**
stating, **123**
supporting with details, **123**

Main topics, in outlines, 391–392

Main verbs. *See* Verbs

Maps
creating, 383, 437
using, 467–468

Mechanics. *See* Capitalization; Punctuation

Metaphor, 256

Models. *See* Composition, models

Modes. *See* Composition, modes

Modifiers. *See* Adjectives; Adverbs; Usage

more, most, **226–228**, 234, 243, 531

Multimeaning words. *See* Homographs

N

Naming yourself last, **350–351**, 362, 367, 435, 532

Narratives. *See* Literature, types of; Personal narrative; Stories

Negatives, 418–419, 430, 435, 441, 531

Nonfiction, 379, 382, 388, **453**

Note taking
for interviews, **385–386**
for reports, **389–390,** 510
as a study skill, 470
for talks, **477**

Noun(s)
common, **88–89,** 97, 99, 105, 237, 432
in direct address, **288–289,** 300, 307, 499
exact, using, **127**
identifying, **82–83,** 96, 100, 101
plural, **84–85, 86–87,** 96, 97, 99, 101, 103, 104, 107, 237, 432
possessive, **90–91, 92–93,** 97, 99, 100, 101, 106, 107, 237, 432
proper, **88–89,** 96, 97, 99, 105, 237, **284–285,** 300, 305, 432
singular, **84–85, 90–91,** 96, 97, 103, 106, 237, 432
See also Agreement

Novel excerpts, 110–114, 248–253, 314–319, 374–379

O

Object pronouns. *See* Pronouns

Object(s)
compound, **348–349,** 532
direct, **144–145,** 178, 237, 432, 494
of preposition, **420–421,** 431, 435, 443

Observing, 121

Onomatopoeia, 259–260. *See also* Sound words

Opinion
distinguishing fact from, **323–325**
stating and supporting an, **329–330,** 508
writing an, 330–341

or (conjunction), **26–27,** 28–29, 30–31, 32–33, 38, 39, 47, 48, 49, 50, 98, 99, 236, 286–287, 492–497

Oral language activities, 13, 53, 59, 69, 79, 81, 109, 117, 139, 193, 201, 209, 219, 247, 269, 279, 281, 313, 321, 333, 343, 373, 397, 409, 411, 473, 474, 475, 476, 477, 478. *See also* Discussions; Listening; Speaking; Writing conferences

Order
chronological, **61–62, 125–126**
of importance, **267, 330–331,** 508
in paragraphs, **125–126,** 502
sequential, **61–62, 125–126,** 502
spatial, **266, 506**

Order words, 61, 125–126, 502

Organizing
oral presentations, 477

I N D E X

(Acknowledgments continued.)

"Snow Toward Evening," from *And Pastures New* by Melville Cane. Copyright 1926 by Harcourt Brace Jovanovich, Inc.; renewed 1954 by Melville Cane. Reprinted by permission of the publisher.

"The Toothpaste Millionaire," adapted from *The Toothpaste Millionaire* by Jean Merrill. Copyright © 1972 by Houghton Mifflin Company. Reprinted with permission of Houghton Mifflin Company.

"Wol Walks on Water," from *Owls in the Family* by Farley Mowat. Copyright © 1961 by Farley Mowat. By permission of Little, Brown and Company, Toby Eady Associates, and the author.

"Word Power" in LITTLE BY LITTLE: A WRITER'S EDUCATION by Jean Little. Copyright © 1987. Reprinted by permission of Penguin Books Canada Ltd.

"Writing," from *Blue Mandolin, Yellow Field* by Olivia Castellano. Copyright © 1980 by Tonatiuh International, Inc. Reprinted by permission of the author.

Brief Quotations

from "Meet Your Author" by Lucille Clifton in *Cricket Magazine,* Volume 8, #9, May 1981. Copyright © 1981 by Open Court Publishing Company. Reprinted by permission of *Cricket Magazine.* (p. 1)

from *I Have a Sister—My Sister Is Deaf* by Jeanne Whitehouse Peterson. Text copyright © 1977 by Jeanne Whitehouse Peterson. Reprinted by permission of Harper & Row, Publishers, Inc. (p. 52)

from "Landscape," in *Finding a Poem* by Eve Merriam. Copyright © 1970 by Eve Merriam. All rights reserved. Reprinted by permission of Marian Reiner for the author. (p. 80)

from "The Princess on the Glass Hill," in Peter Christen Abjornsen's *Popular Tales from the Norse,* translated by George Webbe Dasent. (1908). (p. 192)

from "The Garden of Bamboos," translated by Powys Mathers. Best efforts have been made to locate the copyright holder. (p. 312)

from "The Spanish Horse," by Otis Hays, Jr., in *Cobblestone's* March, 1981 issue: Spanish Conquest, copyright © 1981, Cobblestone Publishing, Inc., Peterborough, NH 03458. Reprinted by permission of the publisher. (p. 372)

from *Horses of America* by Dorothy Hinshaw Patent. Copyright © 1981 by Dorothy Hinshaw Patent. Reprinted by permission of Holiday House. (p. 390)

from *Collier's Encyclopedia:* Use of reference to *Collier's Encyclopedia* by permission of Macmillan Educational Company.

Dictionary entries from *Houghton Mifflin Intermediate Dictionary,* copyright © 1986 by Houghton Mifflin Company. Reprinted by permission of Houghton Mifflin Company.

Pronunciation key from *Houghton Mifflin Spelling Program,* copyright © 1985. Used by permission of the publishers.

from *The World Book Encyclopedia.* © 1987 World Book, Inc. Reprinted by permission of World Book, Inc.

from *The Pueblo* by Charlotte and David Yue. Copyright © 1986. Reprinted by permission of Houghton Mifflin Company. (p. 458)

from *The American Heritage Dictionary,* copyright © 1985 by Houghton Mifflin Company. [Definition] Reprinted with permission of Houghton Mifflin Company.

Grateful acknowledgment is given to Brad Carver, Brian Gilmore, Nadia Hamdi, Michael Laird, and Laura Malone, for permission to adapt and reprint original material as student writing models in the Writing Process lessons. Special thanks to the Gwinnett County School System, Georgia, for help in obtaining some of these models.

The publisher has made every effort to locate each owner of the copyrighted material reprinted here. Any information enabling the publisher to rectify or credit any reference is welcome.

Credits

Illustrations

Lisa Adams: 154, 350, 356, 422
Philip Argent: 191–202, 205, 216
Mary Jane Begin: 286, 288, 289, 352
Nancy Edwards Calder: 320
Dan Clifford: 2–3
Bonnie Gee: 79, 139, 219, 279, 280, 343, 346, 352, 385, 409
Marsha Goldberg: 68, 70, 71, 73, 128, 130, 131, 133, 208, 210–211, 213, 268, 270–271, 273, 332, 334–335, 337, 396, 398–401, 403
Judith Griffith: 346
Sharon Harker: 144, 150, 170, 296, 488, 489
Higgins Bond: 136
Tim Jones: 61
Meg Kelleher Aubrey: 7, 129, 135, 278
Christa Kieffer: 248–258, 276
Stella Ormai: 54–60, 76
Linda Phinney: 22, 24, 34, 84, 85, 93, 110–119, 152, 158, 166, 416, 418
Irena Roman: 222
Claudia Sargent: 14, 26, 32, 69, 90, 92, 129, 148, 209, 222, 224, 226, 231, 269, 302, 333, 397, 487, 490, 491, 494
Carol Schwartz: 40, 100, 101, 176, 240, 302, 303, 364, 436–437
Michael Smith: 18, 160, 486
Susan Spellman: 451–469, 500–519
George Ulrich: 543–556
James Watling: 384, 406

Photographs

1 Arnold J. Kaplan **13** Llewellyn **15** Dr. E.R. Degginger **17** Frank J. Staub/The Picture Cube **19, 21** Dr. E.R. Degginger **25** Menschenfreund/Taurus Photos **27** T.J. Cawley/Tom Stack & Assoc. **29** Taurus Photos **31** John Lawlor/The Stock Market **52–53** Nancy Sheehan **80–81** Phil Degginger **82** Elliot Varner Smith **83** Ellis Herwig/The Picture Cube **87** Stan Osolinsky/The Stock Market **88** Culver Pictures **89** Martha Swope **108–109** Robert Frerck/Odyssey Productions **124** Mark Sherman/Bruce Coleman Inc. **140–141** Robert McKenzie/Tom Stack & Assoc. **142** Historical Pictures Service, Chicago **143** P. Brouillet/Focus West **145** Ed Robinson/Tom Stack & Assoc. **147** Daemmrich **149** Jeff Rotman **151** Eric Carle/Stock Boston **155** Mitch Reardon/Photo Researchers Inc. **159** Earth Scenes/Zig Leszczynski **161** Alec Duncan/Taurus Photos **163** Photo Researchers Inc. **167, 169** Dr. E.R. Degginger **173** Milt and Joan Mann/Cameramann Inter. **192–193** David Muench Photography **209** R.P. Kingston Collection **217** Four X Five **220–221** C.H. Rose/Stock Boston **223** David Falconer/West Stock **225** Dr. Georg Gerster/Photo Researchers Inc. **229** Owen Franken/Stock Boston **230** Panhaj Shah/The Stock Market **246–247** Robert Frerck **276** Historical Pictures Service, Chicago **277** Plimoth Plantation Photo **280–281** Photo by Kazmori/Taurus Photos **283** P. Vandermark/Stock Boston **295** Russ Lappa **296** Charles Hogg **312–313** Ed Cooper Photographer **340** Historical Pictures Service, Chicago **341** Donald Dietz/Stock Boston **344–345** Cary Wolinsky/Stock Boston **347** Ellis Herwig/The Picture Cube **349** Frank J. Staub/The Picture Cube **351** Nancy Dudley/Stock Boston **355** Tom & Pat Leeson/Photo Researchers Inc. **357** Springer/Bettmann Film Archive **359** Charles Hogg **372–373** Stock Imagery **407** Tom Tracy/The Stock Shop **410–411** George Herben/Woodfin Camp & Assoc. **413** A. Anholt-White **415** Rick McIntyre/Tom Stack & Assoc. **421** Peter Menzel **423** Jim McNee/Tom Stack & Assoc. **425** Gabe Palmer/The Stock Market **427** Philip Jon Bailey/The Picture Cube

Fine Art

37 *The Two Majesties* Jean-Léon Gérôme, Layton Art Collection, Milwaukee Art Museum. Bequest of Louis Allis. **95** *A Boy Playing A Flute* Judith Leyster, Oil on canvas, 73 × 62 cm, Nationalmuseum, Stockholm. **233** *Wild Poppies* Claude Monet Collection of the Louvre. Photo: Service de Documentation Photographique de la Réunion des Musées Nationaux. **299** *View of the Riva degli Schiavoni* Canaletto (Giovanni Antonio Canal) 1697–1768. Late 1730's oil on canvas, 18 1/2 × 24 7/8 in. (47.1 × 63.3 cm) The Toledo Museum of Art, Toledo, Ohio; Gift of Edward Drummond Libbey. **361** *Ladder to the Moon* Georgia O'Keeffe, 1958. Photo by Malcolm Varon, New York City. c 1977. **429** *Prairie Fire* Blackbear Bosin, Philbrook Art Center, Tulsa, OK.

Cover Photographs

Cover and title page photograph: Judy Poe

The photograph shows Malcesine, a small walled city on Lake Garda in northern Italy.

Back Cover: Jon Chomitz